SIR PHILIP SIDNEY

SIR PHILIP SIDNEY

An Anthology of Modern Criticism

EDITED BY

DENNIS KAY

CLARENDON PRESS · OXFORD
1987

Oxford University Press, Walton Street, Oxford OX2 6DP
Oxford New York Toronto
Delhi Bombay Calcutta Madras Karachi
Petaling Jaya Singapore Hong Kong Tokyo
Nairobi Dar es Salaam Cape Town
Melbourne Auckland
and associated companies in
Beirut Berlin Ibadan Nicosia

Oxford is a trade mark of Oxford University Press

Published in the United States
by Oxford University Press, New York

British Library Cataloguing in Publication Data
Sir Philip Sidney: an anthology of modern criticism.
1. Sidney, Sir Philip—Criticism and
interpretation
I. Kay, Dennis
821'.3   PR2343
ISBN 0-19-811204-1

Library of Congress Cataloging-in-Publication Data
Sir Philip Sidney: an anthology of modern criticism.
Bibliography: p.
Includes index.
1. Sidney, Philip, Sir, 1554-1586—Criticism and
interpretation.   I. Kay, Dennis.
PR2343.S55 1987   821'.3   87-5745
ISBN 0-19-811204-1

Typeset by Joshua Associates Limited, Oxford
Printed and bound in Great Britain by
Biddles Ltd, Guildford and King's Lynn

PREFACE

Interest in Sidney's writings is now firmly established. Not since the Restoration has his reputation as a writer been as secure as it seems today; he appears to have regained the status as a writer of the first rank which he had lost by the eighteenth century. Since 1945 Sidney's centrality to the remarkable literary achievements of the English Renaissance has been generally acknowledged by scholars: C. S. Lewis, after all, proposed that we show the extent of our understanding of the Renaissance by what we make of Sidney. And nowadays it is rare to find *Arcadia* scorned because it is not a novel, or *Astrophil and Stella* castigated for insincerity or excess of art.

Now that most of Sidney's works are available in accessible editions, students are in a position to test the scholarly revival in his fortunes for themselves, and to read him alongside his great contemporaries. And I can vouch that students today find Sidney more than simply a passport to his age, more than a golden-tongued ambassador from an alien civilization. His writings, as his first readers saw, lend themselves to close inspection, and to analysis in terms which most modern students find both congenial and challenging. His self-consciousness, his apparent preoccupation with problems of meaning and expression, his elusiveness, his combination of intense seriousness with detached and ironic wit, his engagement with the great movements, issues, and events of his age—whether political, intellectual, or artistic—are all qualities which excite his new generation of readers.

This volume is primarily designed to meet the practical needs of such readers, to guide them around the products of the expanding Sidney 'industry', and to introduce them to some of the more representative and stimulating articles published in recent years. Of course no book of this size could hope adequately to represent all the ways in which Sidney is read today. But the essays collected here have been chosen both for their individual qualities and because, taken together, they cover a wide range of Sidney's art and illustrate a variety of approaches to it. I have quite deliberately eschewed the temptation of seeking, or attempting to impose, an artificial homogeneity of view: my hope is that these essays will, like the works of which they treat, stimulate in their readers debate, argument, and controversy.

The Sidney revival began with an excellent and still influential essay by Theodore Spencer, 'The Poetry of Sir Philip Sidney', *ELH* 12 (1945), 251–78; it continued with Hallett Smith's *Elizabethan Poetry* (Cambridge, Mass., 1952) and C. S. Lewis's *English Literature in the Sixteenth Century (Excluding Drama)* (Oxford, 1954), which included a characteristically vigorous account of Sidney's art. Since then studies have proliferated, as the numerous bibliographies indicate, and greater attention has been paid to individual texts.

For many years after its first publication—which was not until 1926—the *Old Arcadia* was conventionally viewed as an essentially minor work, clearly inferior (because less like epic) to the *New*. Two writers in the 1960s attempted—in markedly contrasting ways—to argue for the text's importance in its own right. Richard Lanham (1965) wittily and vigorously proposed *OA* as a comic, satiric work whose 'whole purport . . . is to show how ridiculous . . . characters are' (p. 250). Franco Marenco, on the other hand, inaugurated a tradition of reading *OA* in terms of Calvinist thought. His *Arcadia Puritana* (1968) shows the princes declining into a morass of sinfulness: Marenco's vision of a sombre Arcadia, of a world in which human heroism is undermined, was epitomized for English-speaking readers in his 'Double Plot in Sidney's *Old Arcadia*' (1969). There are still disagreements about the tone of the work; but nowadays it is more a question of the balance between serious and comic elements than the exclusive consideration of one or the other. There are exceptions, such as Andrew Weiner's sternly Calvinist reading (1978). Studies of rhetoric in *OA*, starting with Lorna Challis (1956), have inevitably come to consider gesture and drama as well as words, and students should see J. B. Altman's important account in his *The Tudor Play of Mind* (1978). Robert Stillman's recent book (1986) grows, like *Arcadia* itself, from consideration of the issues raised in the Eclogues. Three other areas of interest represented in the select bibliography are the work's sources, its political dimension, and the relation of its literary elements, its fiction, to its meaning. I hope that the essays reprinted here will promote the close engagement with the text that *OA* both invites and requires, not least because, in Margaret Dana's words, in Sidney's work 'The act of reading becomes a metaphor for the difficulty of reading life itself', of experiencing what Davis calls 'the growth of an unlikely design'.

The *Defence* is perhaps Sidney's most finished, most polished performance. But it does not follow that critics have found it any less problematic than his other works. Even its title is unstable and uncertain. Many valuable studies have explored its models and sources (Plato, Aristotle, Cicero, Quintilian) and considered its Renaissance contexts (Gosson, Languet, Ramus). Others have examined the ways in which Sidney, in Elizabeth Story Donno's words, 'made the *Apology* itself a demonstration of his proposition that a "fiction" . . . has the power to move, to instruct, and, above all, to delight'. Robinson's (1972) is still the only book-length study of recent times, but Ferguson's *Trials of Desire* (1983) discusses the *Defence*, as does Levao's *Renaissance Minds and Their Fictions* (1985), which develops material included here.

It would be rash to attempt to sum up in a few sentences the highly various and numerous critical responses to *Astrophil and Stella* in modern times. But some areas of interest may be identified. The sequence's structure and meaning (whether it is idealistic, optimistic, satiric) can hardly be treated separately, and the relation between the reader's perception of Sidney's design and the dramatic voice of Astrophil has been extensively explored. Roche's article, even in an abbreviated form, engages with most of his predecessors, and his footnotes are themselves a helpful guide to earlier criticism. Another focus has been the sense in which *Astrophil and Stella* is a poem about poems, writing about writing. Williamson's essay inspects a small detail of Sidney's art in the sestets and shows how a feature of poetic technique embodies a fundamental characteristic of the poet's mind and art. From a rather different perspective, Germaine Warkentin examines Sidney's creative use of rhetorical procedures as a principle of composition, and investigates the ways in which Sidney can be seen, as he was by Ralegh and Harington, as the 'English Petrarke'.

The *New Arcadia* is now the focus of critical attention. An increasingly sophisticated understanding of Renaissance genre-theory has enabled critics to discern art, purpose, and subtle variety in Sidney's masterpiece as much as in *Orlando Furioso* or *The Faerie Queene*. Greenblatt's influential 'Sidney's *Arcadia* and the Mixed Mode' (1973) argued for the essential seriousness of *Arcadia*'s generic variety:

when Sidney is at his best, his art raises disturbing questions about men's fictions and actions. Heroic, pastoral, comic, tragic, romantic—each of the conventions is embraced and then discarded, each tells only part of the truth. And in playing off one genre against another, Sidney . . . pushes beyond aesthetics into the realm of ethics, for he treats the genres, not only as literary categories, but as 'strategies for living'. (p. 272.)

A further model for Sidney's narrative procedure is the *Ethiopian History* of Heliodorus (see Skretcowicz (1976)). The pictorial elements in the text have been investigated most recently by Duncan-Jones (1980), Skretcowicz (1982), and Farmer (1984). To the present age *Arcadia* has come to seem a disturbing, gloomy text; to many readers it appears sombre, problematic, far from unequivocally heroic. John Carey's re-examination of Sidney's rhetoric leads him to propose that the alert reader encounters in Sidney's fiction 'a lived experience of tentativeness'. Other critics have seen this troubling *Arcadia* as the reverse of escapist fiction, as an urgent engagement with the political and religious crises of its day. Annabel Patterson's study (part of her important book *Censorship and Interpretation* (1984)) exemplifies the best qualities of this increasingly active area of investigation.

A word about the organization of this volume. The introductory essay, 'Sidney—A Critical Heritage', was written specifically for this book, and traces the history of Sidney's reputation as writer up to the middle of the present century. The other contributions have all been published previously. Two general essays are followed by studies of each of the major works in turn. Considerations of space have made it impossible to include studies of other texts, such as the *Psalms* and *The Lady of May*. The final piece is a revision of Bent Juel-Jensen's bibliography of Sidney editions, which has been the authoritative work on the subject since 1962. After these studies comes a select bibliography, which offers a guide to Sidney scholarship (and where readers will find full references to books and articles mentioned in this preface). There is also a brief chronological table at the beginning of the volume.

Apart from minor alterations and corrections, most of the essays appear as they were originally published. John Carey has, like Dr Juel-Jensen, taken the opportunity offered by republication to revise his essay extensively. I have, with the author's generous permission, and with some nervousness, made substantial cuts (which I hope do not distort the argument) to Thomas Roche's lengthy and controversial study of *Astrophil and Stella*.

As is inevitable in a collection of essays which were not originally written as a single volume, there have been problems for an editor seeking to achieve consistency. A variety of titles and spellings are used for Sidney's works in the different editions, and contributors have not always referred to the same edition. Even references to Feuillerat's *The Complete Works of Sir Philip Sidney* cause problems, as this was reprinted (minus most of the verse) as *The Prose Works of Sir Philip Sidney*. Where possible, the works have been referred to by the titles used in the Oxford editions. In the case of the *Arcadia*, textual references are to the *Old Arcadia*, or to the *New Arcadia*, or the revised *Arcadia*, to avoid ambiguity. The *Defence* offers rather more of a problem as it was published with two different titles in 1595: the Oxford edition uses the title *A Defence of Poetry*, but the two articles in this volume both refer to Geoffrey Shepherd's edition, *An Apology for Poetry or The Defence of Poesy*, while another contributor refers to Gregory Smith's 1904 edition, *The Defence of Poesy*. Contributors who refer to W. A. Ringler's edition of Sidney's *Poems* follow his spelling of *Astrophil and Stella*, but references specifically to the earliest edition use the spelling 'Astrophel'. Where possible, Ringler's numbering of the *Poems* has been used, with references, for example, to *OA* 9, *OP* 4, *AS* 1, and Song x.

I am especially grateful to the contributors and to their publishers for their support and encouragement, to Lincoln College, Oxford, for help of various kinds, and to all those of my students, graduate and undergraduate, from both sides of the Atlantic, for their enthusiastic co-operation in the planning and design of this collection. Katherine Duncan-Jones has assisted the project most helpfully from its inception. My own essay owes much to the wisdom and scholarship of the late Bill Ringler, to whose memory I should like to dedicate it.

D. K.

CONTENTS

THE *NEW ARCADIA*

EARLY EDITIONS

CHRONOLOGICAL TABLE OF
SIDNEY'S LIFE

1554   Born at Penshurst, Kent (30 November). Named after Philip II of Spain.

1559   Sir Henry Sidney Lord President of the Marches of Wales.

1564   Enters Shrewsbury School (on the same day as Fulke Greville). Robert Dudley, Earl of Leicester (Sidney's uncle) Chancellor of Oxford University.

1565   Sir Henry Sidney Lord Deputy of Ireland.

1566   Sidney present at ceremonies to welcome Queen Elizabeth to Oxford.

1568   Matriculates (?February) at Christ Church, Oxford (?leaves 1571). Perhaps spends some time at Cambridge.

1572   Embarks (May) on continental expedition in train of the Earl of Lincoln. In Paris, witnesses the Massacre of St Bartholomew's Day (24 August). Travels to Rhine (September): spends winter in Frankfurt. Meets Hubert Languet.

1573   Leaves Frankfurt in spring for journey through Heidelberg, Strasbourg, Basle to Vienna. Visits Bratislava briefly. Travels from Vienna to Venice (October).

1574   Studying in Padua. Several visits to Venice (sits for Veronese in February), also travels to Genoa and Florence. To Vienna (August): with Edward Wotton, studies horsemanship with Giovanni Pietro Pugliano. Brief trip to Poland; winter in Vienna.

1575   Returns to England via Brno, Prague, Dresden, Frankfurt, Heidelberg, Antwerp, arriving in May. Brief stay at court, then with Royal Party to Kenilworth (July), Lichfield, Chartley, Stafford, Chillington, Dudley, Worcester (August). To Shrewsbury with Sir Henry Sidney, who prepares to leave for Ireland. Returns to London.

1576   In Ireland with Sir Henry Sidney (July–September).

1577   Sent as ambassador to Emperor Rudolph in Prague (February–June). Discusses formation of Protestant League. Meets Don John of Austria, William of Orange, Edmund Campion. On return, defends (October) his father's Irish policies, writing 'Discourse on Irish Affairs' (*Miscellaneous Prose*, 8–12).

1578   *The Lady of May* at Wanstead (May, perhaps). Accompanies the Queen to Cambridge (July). Begins the *Old Arcadia* at Wilton, while staying with his sister, the Countess of Pembroke. Sir Henry Sidney recalled from Ireland.

1579   Tennis-court quarrel with Earl of Oxford. Receives dedication of Spenser's *The Shepheardes Calender*. Writes (?November/December) 'A Letter to Queen Elizabeth' (*Miscellaneous Prose*, 46–57) advising against Alençon match.

1580   Probably completes *Old Arcadia*. Perhaps begins *Defence of Poetry*.

1581   Gives the Queen a New Year's present of 'a whip garnished with small diamonds'. Takes seat in Parliament. Participates in tournaments. Perhaps begins *Astrophil and Stella*. Languet dies. Penelope Devereux marries Lord Rich (1 November).

1582   Escorts Alençon to Netherlands (February).

1583   Knighted as proxy for Count Palatine John Casimir who was installed as Knight of the Garter (January). Marries Frances, daughter of Sir Francis Walsingham (21 September).

1584   Increasingly active in public affairs. Working at Ordnance Office. Begins revision of *Arcadia*. Writes *Defence of the Earl of Leicester*.

1585   Possibly begins translation of Duplessis-Mornay's *De la verité de la religion chrestienne*, perhaps starts a version of the *Psalms* (later completed by his sister), and perhaps translates Du Bartas's *La Semaine*. Joint Master of the Ordnance Office (July). Plans to accompany Drake on voyage to West Indies. Appointed Governor of Flushing: arrives in Netherlands in November.

1586   Sir Henry Sidney dies (May). Sidney involved in action: surprise of Axel (July). Lady Sidney dies (August). Wounded during skirmish at Zutphen (22 September): dies at Arnhem (17 October).

1587   Buried at St Paul's (16 February). Golding's completed translation of *The Trewnesse of the Christian Religion* published (dedication to Leicester dated 13 May).

1590   Publication of the new or revised *Arcadia*.

1591   Publication of *Astrophel and Stella* (2 editions, a third, undated, before 1598).

1593   Publication of the composite *Arcadia* (Books I–III of the *New*, III–V of the *Old*).

1595   Publication of *An apologie for poetrie* by Olney and *The defence of poesie* by Ponsonby.

1598   Publication of *Arcadia, Certain Sonnets, Defence of Poesie, Astrophel and Stella, The Lady of May* (i.e. the first 'Collected Works' of Sidney).

Sidney's Reputation, 1580–1945

INTRODUCTION
SIDNEY—A CRITICAL HERITAGE

DENNIS KAY

Sidney's continually fluctuating reputation mirrors English cultural history. His works, considered for almost a century the masterpieces of the age, were forgotten as their author was reinterpreted consecutively as Royalist virtuoso, Republican hero, and Imperialist paragon. Now, having been liberated—initially by the New Critics—from a Whiggish view of literary history, they are held in higher esteem than at any time since the Restoration.

Sidney has always tended to attract extreme opinions. Perhaps it says something about his art, with its evident relish for competing modes, languages, styles, and arguments, that there are few assertions that have been made about his work whose reverse has not also been stated. From the beginning, the unprecedented personal cult of Sidney spawned a parallel and competing counter-legend. Where Greville praised an ideal Christian courtier, Ben Jonson confronted William Drummond (an admirer and imitator of Sidney) with: 'Sir P. Sidney was no pleasant man in countenance, his face being spoiled with pimples.'[1] Accounts of Sidney's death similarly vary between extremes of eulogy and scurrility. To those anxious to canonize him, Sidney died in accordance with the traditions of 'holy dying'. Greville and Gifford depict a saintly passing with Sidney surrounded by ministers and comporting himself piously: 'he lifted both his hands, and set them together at his breast, and held them upwards, after the manner of those which make humble petition.'[2] But John Aubrey's view resembled Jonson's demythologizing: Sidney's final crisis was precipitated by the intensity of his desire for his wife ('whom he loved very well'). Aubrey recorded that Sidney, 'having received some shott or wound in the Warres in the Lowe-countreys ... would not (contrary to the injunctions of his Physitians and chirurgions)

---

[1] 'Conversations with Drummond of Hawthornden', in *Ben Jonson*, ed. C. H. Herford, P. and E. Simpson (Oxford, 1925–51), i (1925), pp. 138–9.
[2] ?George Gifford, *The Manner of Sir Philip Sidney's Death*, in *Miscellaneous Prose of Sir Philip Sidney*, ed. K. Duncan-Jones and J. van Dorsten (Oxford, 1973), p. 172.

forbeare his carnall knowledge of her, which cost him his life; upon
which occasion there were some roguish verses made'.[3]

While literary distinction habitually secures an author's posthumous social elevation, in Sidney's case the process was almost
the opposite. Chaucer, for instance, had become 'Sir' Geoffrey by
the time of Puttenham's *Arte of English Poesie* (1589). More recently,
in Professor Lodge's *Small World*, Persse MacGarrigle asks for a
copy of *The Faerie Queene* by 'Sir' Edmund Spenser.[4] But Sidney's
reputation as a public man was so generally established, and his
posthumous social status was so secure, that he effectively dignified the very profession of letters he seems when alive to have been
concerned to avoid. The massively elaborate state mourning which
followed Sidney's death was doubtless motivated more by ex-
pedient political considerations than by simple esteem for the
deceased, but nevertheless a major incidental consequence was to
establish in the English mind the potential and actual coincidence
of personal and artistic greatness. In Greville's words, while he
'purposed no monument of bookes to the world . . . yet doe not his
Arcadian Romances live after him, . . .?'[5]

And many of the earliest comments on Sidney's art see the
works as the memorial of the man, as reflections of his status and
qualities. As early as 1592 Samuel Daniel observed that 'Astrophel
. . . hath registered his owne name in the Annals of eternitie', and
referred to Sidney's 'eternal songs'.[6] Nathaniel Baxter (Sidney's
former tutor) and the epigrammatists Owen, Stradling, and
Harington all took the permanence of Sidney's fame as an author
for granted.[7] Emilia Lanyer and John Donne praised the translation of the Psalms in similar terms.[8] The comparative novelty of

---

[3] *Aubrey's Brief Lives*, ed. O. L. Dick (1949), p. 280.

[4] George Puttenham, *The arte of English poesie* (1589), I. xxxi. 74; D. Lodge, *Small
World: An Academic Romance*, pt. IV, ch. 2. (Penguin edn, Harmondsworth, 1985),
pp. 256–7. (Volumes recorded in the *STC* are generally cited in the style of that
catalogue.)

[5] *The Life of the Renowned Sir Philip Sidney, by Fulke Greville*, ed. N. Smith (Oxford,
1907), p. 72.

[6] Daniel, *Delia. Contayning certayne sonnets* (1592), Sig. A2; *Delia and Rosamond augmented* (1594), Sig. H5ᵛ, H6.

[7] Sidney appears in Baxter's *Sir Philip Sydneys Ouránia, that is Endimions song and
tragedie* (1606); John Owen, *Epigrammatum libri tres* (2nd edn, 1607), II. 67, Sig. C6; Stradling, *Joannis Stradlingi epigrammatum libri quattuor* (1607), pp. 22–3; Harington, *The most
elegant and wittie epigrams of Sir J. Harington. Digested into four bookes* (1618), III. 12, Sig. H7.

[8] Aemilia Lanyer, *Salve deus rex Judaeorum* (1611), Sig. d1v–d2; Donne, *The Divine
Poems*, ed. H. Gardner (2nd edn, Oxford, 1978), pp. 33–5.

the phenomenon is illustrated by an exchange in Jonson's *Epicoene* (1611):

CLERIMONT. A knight live by his verses? He did not make 'em to that end, I hope.

DAUPHINE. And yet the noble Sidney lives by his, and the noble family not asham'd.[9]

The status Sidney's writings had acquired by the second decade of the seventeenth century was most tangibly celebrated in the painted frieze decorating what is now the Upper Reading Room of the Bodleian Library in Oxford.[10] In the section devoted largely to men of letters, the armoured figure of Sidney occupies a place of honour, flanked on his right by Pico della Mirandola, Salluste Du Bartas, and Julius Caesar Scaliger, on his left by Joseph Scaliger, Petrus Ramus, and Justus Lipsius. The only other English writer on the frieze, and thereby the only fellow-countryman deemed worthy to participate in a tradition that began with Homer and included Aesop, Dante, Petrarch, and the rest, is Chaucer. In much the same vein, George Hakewill adduced the example of Sidney to refute the idea that the world was in decline: to compare Sidney and Homer, he argued, was to perceive that nature was not decaying.[11]

During his lifetime Sidney was rarely referred to as a poet. His writing was largely private, and apparently known only to a few intimate acquaintances. Sidney was typically praised in the common terms of dedications: for example, as 'a blossome of true Nobilitie', and as such fitted to perform the role of Maecenas.[12] There are occasional particularities—when a dedication will be said to reflect Sidney's tastes and interests. Thus Lichfield's translation of Luis Gutierrez de la Vega's *De re militari* was addressed to Sidney because he was 'most ready & aduenterous in

---

[9] Jonson, *Epicoene*, II. iii. 115–18, ed. Herford and Simpson, v. 186.

[10] See J. N. L. Myres and E. Clive Rouse, 'Further Notes on the Painted Frieze', *Bodleian Library Record* 5 (1956), 294–5; W. A. Ringler Jr., ed., *The Poems of Sir Philip Sidney* (Oxford, 1962), p. xv.

[11] George Hakewill, *An apologie of the power and providence of God* (Oxford, 1627), III. viii. 3 (pp. 236–40). Hakewill wrote: 'Touching *Poetrie* for the inventive part thereof, Sir *Phillip Sydneyes Arcadia* is in my judgement nothing inferior to the choisest peece among the Ancients . . .' (p. 236).

[12] Philips van Marnix van Sant Aldegonde, *The bee hiue of the Romishe church*, tr. G. Gylpen (1579), Sig.*5. For two instances of the commonplace identification of Sidney with Maecenas, see Fraunce in Bodley MS Rawl. D. 345, fos. 1, 56ᵛ.

all exercises of feats of warre and chivalry'.[13] The celebrated legal
theorist Alberico Gentili referred to Sidney as a compendium of
excellences.[14]

Sidney's elegists were likewise swayed by the power of the
personal cult, and said little about his literary activities. Some
augmented their praise with detail. Angel Day could note in the
margin that Sidney had written 'Arcadia, containing poems in
sundry metres'.[15] George Whetstone referred to 'Archadia, a booke
most excellently written', and speculated that Sidney may have
written the *Shepheardes Calender* as well as translating the Psalms.[16]
The University miscellanies compiled on Sidney's death are
scarcely more informative.[17] Holinshed, in his *Chronicles* (1587),
noted that Sidney had acted as an ambassador in his early twenties,
and that 'Not long after his returne from that iorneie, . . . he made
his booke which is named *Arcadia*'. A late 'additament' to the
volume records Sidney's death, and praises his 'readie penne'.[18] A
manuscript lament by Sir Edward Dymoke is slightly more
specific:

> Blist in his Byrthe by happy Influence
> In Childehood w^t y^e *Muses* milk sustayned
> In each good Grace the *Graces* all hym wayned.
> His yewthe by the eternall *Godis* dispence

[13] Luis Gutierrez de la Vega, *A compendious treatise de re militari*, tr. N. Lichfield (1581), Sig. A2.

[14] *De legationibus libri tres* (1585), Sig. T^v. Sometimes remarks made in these contexts look—with a healthy dose of hindsight—like literary comments. For instance, Giordano Bruno's *Di gli eroici furori* (Paris, 1585), a work dedicated to Sidney, contains criticism of Petrarchists for their worship of women. But Bruno makes an exception of English women, who are nymphs, goddesses, and stars: 'E siete in terra quel ch'in ciel le stelle' (Sig. *8^v). Yet it is most unlikely that Bruno is referring to *Astrophil and Stella*, even though John Florio did cite Bruno's sonnet in dedicating the second volume of his translation of Montaigne's *Essays* (1603) to Sidney's daughter the Countess of Rutland and to his 'Stella', Lady Rich (Sig. R2^v).

[15] Angel Day, *Vpon the life and death of Sir Philip Sidney* (1587), Sig. A3^v.

[16] George Whetstone, *Sir Philip Sidney, his honorable life, his valiant death, and his true vertues* (1587), Sig. B2^v-3.

[17] In William Gager's *Exequiae* (Oxford, 1587), Matthew Gwyn refers obliquely to the *Arcadia* (Sig. D2^v-3^v), as do Edward Saunders (D4) and Charles Sonibank (I3^v). Richard Latewar refers to Sidney's appearance as Philisides in *Arcadia* and perhaps to *Astrophil and Stella* (E1^v-F2). John Lloyd's *Peplus* (Oxford, 1587) is silent about Sidney's writing. In the Cambridge volume, *Academiae Cantabrigiensis lachrymae . . . etc.* (Cambridge, 1587), William Temple (M1), Alexander Neville (I1^{r-v}) and King James (K1) make brief reference to the subject.

[18] Raphael Holinshed (and others), *The chronicles of England . . . until . . . 1585* (1587, uncensored issue), pp. 1548–56.

Deck't wᵗ the myndes and Bodyes Excellence
Of *Ioue* sadd witt, and mylde Speech he obtayned
Knighthood of *Mars*, of *Phoebus* Lawrell gayned
Of *Mercury* knowledge passing vulgar Sence.
  But *Venus* Queen this noble harte addresseth, . . .
Vertues no vertues are wᶜʰ Love not blesseth
Well then, he Lov'd to perfect all the rest
  Cupid a Quill out of his wing, him tooke
And *Stella* fayre gave hym the paper-Book.[19]

Dymoke gives no indication of Stella's identity and seems to imply some ideal or abstract mistress: and such a reading sorts well with the Sidney legend. But others clearly knew more. Matthew Roydon, for instance, publicly identified Stella with her 'model', Penelope Rich, when he followed Astrophil's example in punning on her married name, calling her 'a Nymph . . . Most rare and rich of heauenly bliss'.[20] Yet the most typical poetic response in commemorative works was closer to Dymoke. Spenser's mythologizing lament *Astrophel*, and works such as *The Lamentation of Troy for the death of Hector* (1594), have much more to do with the developing cult of Sidney as a national hero than with appreciation of his writings. At this stage Stella was primarily a component in the machinery surrounding a hero in apotheosis: the implications of her heavenly name perhaps explain the display of star-covered banners at Sidney's funeral procession.[21] It would be an over-simplification to suggest that Sidney's contemporaries read his works solely as the by-products of greatness, as the trivial productions of a national hero. But much early literary judgement was clearly shaped by the personal legend.

A notable exception, the first printed comments on Sidney's work, is *Howell his deuices for his owne exercise, and his friends pleasure* (1581).[22] Howell addresses verses to a 'most excellent Booke, full of rare invention'—clearly the *Arcadia*—and urges the book to have itself published. The text runs:

---

[19] University of Edinburgh MS De. 5. 96, fo. 2ᵛ–3.
[20] Matthew Roydon, 'An Elegie, or friends passion, for his Astrophill', in *The phoenix nest* (1593), p. 5. The poem also appears in Spenser's *Colin Clouts come home againe* (1595).
[21] For a visual record of the event, see Thomas Lant, *Sequitur celebritas & pompa funeris* (1587).
[22] Sig. E4ᵛ–F1. The book was the first to be dedicated to Sidney's sister, the Countess of Pembroke.

Goe learned booke, and unto *Pallas* sing,
Thy pleasant tunes that sweetely sownde to hie
For *Pan* to reache, though *Zoylvs* thee doth sting,
And lowre at thy lawde, set nought thereby.
   Thy makers Muse in spight of enuies chinne,
   For wise deuise, deserued praise shall winne.

Who views thee well, and notes thy course aright,
And syftes eche sence that couched is in thee:
Must needes extoll the mind that did thee dight.
And wishe the Muse may neuer weary bee.
   From whence doth flowe such pithe in filed phrase,
   As worthiest witte may ioy on thee to gase.

How much they erre, thy rare euent bewrayes,
That stretch their skill the Fates to ouerthrow:
And how mans wisedome here in vaine seeks wayes,
To shun high powers that sway our states below,
   Against whose rule, although we striue to runne,
   What Ioue foresets, no humaine force may shunne

But all to long, thou hidste so perfite worke,
Seest not desyre, how faine she seekes to finde:
Thy light but lost, if thou in darknesse lurke?
Then shewe they selfe and seeme no more vnkinde.
   Vnfolde thy fruite, and spread thy maysters praise,
   Whose prime of youth, graue deeds of age displaies.

Go choyce conceits, *Minervas* Mirrour bright,
With Rubies ritch yfret, wrought by the wise:
Parfled with Pearle, and decked with delight,
Where pleasure with profite, both in their guise.
   Discourse of Louers, and such as folde sheepe,
   Whose sawes well mixed, shrowds misteries deepe.

Goe yet I say with speede thy charge delyuar,
Thou needst not blushe, nor feare the foyle of blame:
The worthy Countesse see thou follow euer,
Tyll Fates doe fayle, maintaine her Noble name.
   Attend her wyll, if she vouchsafe to call,
   Stoope to her state, downe flat before her fall.

And euer thanke thou him, that fyrst such fruite did frame,
By whome thy prayse shall liue, to thy immortall fame.

Howell confirms the existence of the *Old Arcadia*, suggests the
centrality of the Eclogues to its structure, and reinforces the text's

private status as well as implying parallels with Chaucer and Spenser. In addition, he makes two significant comments on the *Arcadia* itself, both frequently reiterated in modern readings of the text. First, Howell indicates a recognition of the didactic, perhaps satiric, qualities of the work: he argues that the *Arcadia*'s 'rare event' (its tragicomic conclusion) instructs readers 'How much they erre' and 'how mans wisedome . . . in vaine seekes wayes, / To shun high powers that sway our states below'. Secondly, Howell posits an ideal reader: one who, while delighted by the comprehensiveness and accomplishment of Sidney's fiction, is not beguiled from a duty to be vigilant; who 'views thee well, and notes thy course aright, / And syftes eche sence that couched is in thee'. Howell anticipates many later readings of the *Old Arcadia* by indicating that Sidney's urbane tragicomedy contains a didactic sense and also requires active moral participation on the reader's part.

Also from Sidney's lifetime is William Temple's *Analysis* of the *Defence*, composed probably when Temple was Sidney's private secretary (1584–6).[23] The *Analysis* affords a salutary insight into the nature of Elizabethan interpretation: it demonstrates that readers of the period actually did what they were trained to do, namely to read with close attention and intellectual engagement. Temple's closely argued commentary and analysis has been praised justly as 'an outstanding example of Tudor practical criticism', and it is almost as revealing for the modern student for exemplifying the operation of a trained Elizabethan mind, and illustrating the capacities and qualities of an educated reader, as for its specific response to Sidney.[24]

Geoffrey Whitney, in *A choice of emblemes* (1586), refers to Sidney primarily as a poet, and implies a distinction between juvenile writings and a more mature achievement, whose lasting fame, he claims, is now assured:

> . . . the pen, was by MERCVRIVS sente,
> Wherewith, hee also gaue to him, the gifte for to inuente.
> That, when hee first began, his vayne in verse to showe.
> More sweet then honie, was the stile, that from his penne did flowe.

---

[23] There is a modern edition and translation, *William Temple's 'Analysis' of Sir Philip Sidney's 'Apology for Poetry'* ed. and trans. J. Webster (Medieval and Renaissance Texts and Studies, 32; New York, 1984).

[24] *Temple's 'Analysis'*, ed. Webster, p. 11.

Wherewith, in youthe he vs'd to bannishe idle fittes;
That nowe, his workes of endlesse fame, delight the worthie wittes.[25]

Although he asserts the immortality of Sidney's art, Whitney
nevertheless bases his praise on Sidney's public achievements, and
accepts Sidney's valuation of his writing as a recreation under-
taken in the intervals between state employment.

It was not long before more straightforwardly literary appraisals
began to be made. Gabriel Harvey, for example, declared the
Arcadia and *The Faerie Queene* to be in the same category as other
modern classics (Petrarch, Ariosto, Tasso, and Du Bartas), and
praised *Astrophil and Stella* (with Watson's *Amyntas*) as 'none of the
idlest pastimes of sum fine humanists'.[26] An intellectual who read
Sidney closely and creatively was Sir John Harington, and
exceptionally close engagement with Sidney's text may be revealed
by a copy of the *Old Arcadia*, transcribed by Harington and his
scribes. Peter Croft's study of the manuscript led him to conclude
that Harington constantly 'embroiders' and consistently modifies
Sidney's text with the effects of 'lowering the tone' and, especially,
of heightening the erotic and comic elements.[27] But private jokes
with his scribes and exercises in deflation are only one side of the
coin. They need to be placed in the wider context of Harington's
published response to Sidney.[28] The matters touched on range
from the narrowly technical to general praise of Sidney as the
English Petrarch (echoing Ralegh's epitaph).[29] Throughout the
preface to Harington's translation of *Orlando Furioso* (1591), Sidney
is acknowledged as the master, as the authority for most practices
in English writing—indeed for the very act of writing itself. For
Harington, Sidney guaranteed the moral, intellectual, and aesthetic distinction of modern literary practices, however they might
appear to conflict with the precepts of the preceding generation

[25] Geoffrey Whitney, *A choice of emblemes and other deuises* (Leyden, 1586), Sig. b2ᵛ–3.
[26] *Gabriel Harvey's Marginalia*, ed. G. C. Moore Smith (Stratford-upon-Avon, 1913),
p. 232.
[27] P. J. Croft, 'Sir John Harington's Manuscript of Sir Philip Sidney's *Old Arcadia*', in
S. Parks and P. J. Croft, *Literary Autographs* (Los Angeles, 1983), pp. 37–75.
[28] T. G. A. Nelson, 'Sir John Harington as a Critic of Sir Philip Sidney', *SP* 17 (1970),
41–56.
[29] Harington defends his use of feminine rhyme by stating that 'Sir *Philip Sidney*, not
only vseth them, but affecteth them'; see *Elizabethan Critical Essays*, ed. G. G. Smith
(Oxford, 1904), i, 221. The reference to Sidney as the English Petrarch (following
Ralegh's epitaph in *The phoenix nest*, p. 8) occurs in the note to Book XVI of Harington's
translation.

and however much Harington may have enjoyed occasional private gestures of irreverence. Harington's preface begins with a summary of the *Defence*, as if both author and translator were invoking the protection of Sidney's theoretical pronouncements, which articulate the shared wisdom of 'the learneder sort'.[30]

Thomas Nashe ranks with Harington as Sidney's most notable early critic. He refers to Sidney on numerous occasions, and like Harington combines general deference with occasional irreverence (the latter exemplified by the celebrated parody tournament in *The Unfortunate Traveller*), but his most extended and significant comment is his preface to the unauthorized first edition of *Astrophil and Stella*.[31]

Long hath *Astrophel* (England's Sunne) witheld the beames of his spirite, from the common view of our dark sence, and night hath houered ouer the gardens of the nine Sisters, while *Ignis fatuus* and grosse fatty flames ... haue tooke occasion in the middest eclipse of his shining perfections, to wander abroad with a wipe of paper at their tales like Hobgoblins, and leade men vp and downe in a circle of absurditie a whole weeke, and neuer knowe where they are.

And Nashe stresses the national importance of Sidney's work, as a revolutionary new model that renders all predecessors obsolete. In a startling reversal of earlier eulogies, Nashe proclaims Sidney a national hero because of his distinction as a poet:

Put out your rush candles, you Poets and Rimers, and bequeath your crazed quaterzayns to the Chaundlers, for loe, here he cōmeth that hath broĕk your legs. *Apollo* hath resigned his Iuory Harp vnto *Astrophel*, & he like *Mercury*, must lull you a sleep with his musicke. Sleep *Argus*, sleep Ignorance, sleep Impudence, for *Mercury* hath Io & onely *Io Paean* belongth to *Astrophel*. Deare *Astrophel*, that in the ashes of thy Loue, liuest againe like the *Phoenix*; ô might thy bodie (as thy name) liue againe likewise, here amongst vs: but the earth, the mother of mortalitie, hath snacht thee too soone into her chilled colde armes, and will not let thee by any meanes, be drawne from her deadly imbrace; and thy diuine Soule, carried on an Angels wings to heauen, is installed in *Hermes* place, sole *prolocutor* to the Gods. Therefore mayest thou neuer returne from the

---

[30] *Elizabethan Critical Essays*, i, 197. Sidney is invoked to justify the mingling of amatory and heroic matter (p. 209) and breaking off stories abruptly: 'If *S. Philip Sidney* had counted this a fault, he would not have done so himselfe in his Arcadia.' (p. 217.)

[31] *Syr P. S. his Astrophel and Stella* (1591), Sig. A3^r-v. There is a facsimile published by the Scolar Press (Menston, 1970), and a text is provided in *Elizabethan Critical Essays*, i. 223–8.

Elisian fieldes like *Orpheus*, therefore must we euer mourne for our *Orpheus*.

These observations are telling in themselves, and vividly express a conviction that Sidney had at a stroke redefined the nature and scope of English letters. But it is the opening section of Nashe's preface (which he teasingly calls 'Somewhat to reade for them *that list*') that concerns the sonnet sequence most directly; and Nashe's words (as Professor Roche's article reprinted here will demonstrate) raise issues that are still alive.

Tempus adest plausus aurea pompa venit, so endes the Sceane of Idiots, and enter *Astrophel* in pompe. Gentlemen that haue seene a thousand lines of folly, drawn forth *ex vno puncto impudentiae*, & two famous Mountains to goe to the conception of one Mouse, that haue had your eares deafned with the eccho of Fames brasen towres, when only they haue been toucht with a leaden pen, that haue seene *Pan* sitting in his bower of delights, & a number of *Midasses* to admire his miserable hornepipes, let not your surfeted sight, new come fro such puppet play, think scorne to turn aside into this Theatre of pleasure, for here you shal find a paper stage strued with pearle, an artificial heau'n to ouershadow the faire frame, & christal wals to encounter your curious eyes, whiles the tragicommody of loue is performed by starlight. The chief Actor here is Melpomene, whose dusky robes dipt in the ynke of teares, as yet seeme to drop when I view them neere. The argument cruell chastitie, the Prologue hope, the Epilogue dispaire, *videte queso et linguis animisque fauete*.

Nashe proclaims and celebrates Sidney's radical use of language, and his status as a model of style was rapidly attested by rhetorical treatises and handbooks, of which the earliest and most important are by Abraham Fraunce and John Hoskins. In the first book of *The lawyers logike* (1588), Fraunce instructs his readers:

Whereas indeede the true vse of Logike is as well apparant in simple playne, and easie explication, as in subtile, strict, and concised probation. Reade *Homer*, reade *Demosthenes*, reade *Virgill*, reade *Cicero*, reade *Bartas*, reade *Torquato Tasso*, reade that most worthie ornament of our English tongue, the *Countesse of Penbrookes Arcadia*, and therein see the true effectes of naturall Logike which is the ground of artificiall, farre different from this rude and barbarous kind of outworne sophistrie; which if it had anie vse at all, yet this was all, to feede the vaine humors of some curious heades in obscure schooles, whereas the Art of reasoning hath somewhat to doe in euerie thing, and nothyng is any thing without this one thing.[32]

[32] *The lawyers logike, exemplifying the praecepts of logike by the common law* (1588), Sig. B3ᵛ.

Likewise with John Hoskins's *Directions for Speech and Style*, containing 'all the Figures of Rhetorick and the Art of the best English, exemplyfyed ... out of *Arcadia*'.[33] This is a staggering claim by Hoskins, but in his handbook the standing of the *Arcadia* as both a pinnacle of literary achievement and a treasure-house of examples is assumed. To a literary culture whose ideal of style was abundance or *copia*, Sidney had become a repository of ways of enriching vernacular discourse, of putting Erasmian ideals into practice.

Let me give some examples. Hoskins tells his student reader to look in the margins of his copy of *Arcadia*, where he will find that his tutor has marked metaphors with an *M*, so that instances may be collected. This is because 'a metaphor ... enricheth our knowledge with two things at once, with the truth and with similitude; as this: *heads disinherited of their natural seignories*, whereby we understand both beheading and the government of the head over the body as the heir hath over the lordship which he inheriteth'.[34] Sidney's texts exemplify methods of varying, amplifying, and illustrating. Thus, discussing poetic diction, Hoskins notes that Sidney 'shunned usual phrases ... to keep his style from baseness: as, being to name *a thresher*, he called him *one of Ceres' servants*'.[35] In places Hoskins lists examples. Thus *antimetabole* or *commutatio* ('a sentence inversed or turned back') is illustrated by six instances, five from *Arcadia*, including:

If any for love of honor, or honor of love.

That as you are child to a mother, so may you be mother to a child.

Hoskins observes that

Our learned knight skipped often into this figure [and gives another seven] yet he concealed the particularity of his affection ... sometimes not turning the words wholly back as they lay:
To account it not a purse for a treasure, but as a treasure itself worthy to be pursed up, etc.

And he proceeds to furnish his student with an inventory of Sidney's variations on a favoured structure.[36] Hoskins throughout

---

[33] John Hoskins, *Directions for Speech and Style*, ed. H. H. Hudson (Princeton, 1935), p. 1.
[34] *Directions*, ed. Hudson, p. 8.
[35] *Directions*, ed. Hudson, p. 47.
[36] *Directions*, ed. Hudson, pp. 14–15.

is essentially practical, urging very close inspection of the text, and recommending modes of cultivating copiousness through detailed imitation of Sidney. Like Temple's *Analysis*, Hoskins's book shows us an educated Elizabethan mind at work; it also suggests that Sidney, like T. S. Eliot, and like Spenser (with E. K.'s glosses to *The Shepheardes Calender*—dedicated to Sidney—in 1579), appears to have created the taste by which he was enjoyed, and that his works were taken to exemplify æsthetic excellence much as the greatest foreign or ancient texts had traditionally been held to do.

This very point had been made aggressively by Fraunce in his *Arcadian Rhetorike* (1588). The first trope discussed, *metonymia*, is illustrated by a line from the *Iliad*, lines from the *Aeneid* and the *Georgics*, and then, in the same company and without any preliminary apology, Fraunce continues:

Syr Philip Sydney in the 2. Act of Arcadia, speaking of the furious multitude.

> *Bacchus* they say was begotten of thunder; I thinke that euer since made him so full of stirre and debate; *Bacchus* indeed it was, which sounded the first trumpet for this rude alarum.

He gives a further three instances before moving on to Tasso and Du Bartas.[37] Even before its publication, then, *Arcadia* was placed in the first rank of texts, and Sidney comes third after Homer and Virgil whenever Fraunce lists instances. The cumulative effect of this positioning is, it seems, as central to Fraunce's purpose as the instruction in rhetoric.

As a repository of rhetorical accomplishment, Sidney's writings were an implicit criticism of, or at least an alternative procedure to, the euphuistic mode derived from Lyly. Indeed, Drayton praised Sidney as the liberator of English. After lauding 'grave morall Spencer', he wrote:

> The noble Sidney, with this last arose,
> That heroe for numbers, and for prose.
> That throughly pac'd our language as to show,
> The plenteous English hand in hand might goe
> With Greeke and Latine, and did first reduce
> Our tongue from Lillies writing then in use;
> Talking of stones, stars, plants, of fishes, flyes,

---

[37] Abraham Fraunce, *The Arcadian Rhetorike*, ed. E. Seaton (Luttrell Society Reprints, 9; Oxford, 1950), pp. 4–6.

Playing with words, and idle similies,
As th'English, apes and very zanies be
Of evry thing, that they doe heare and see,
So imitating his ridiculous tricks,
They spake and write, all like meere lunatiques.[38]

Several stylistic features apparently championed by Sidney were followed on his authority. The appearance of feminine rhyme in the later books of *The Faerie Queene*, for example, reflects Spenser's following of Harington's *Orlando*, but the practice in both writers had been authorized by Sidney's. As with any fashion, imitation could be carried too far, and alongside exhortation to follow Sidney are satirical jibes at excess. Joseph Hall, in *Virgidemiarum* (1598), paints a picture of Labeo, a typical fashionable versifier of the 1590s:

> He knows the grace of that new elegance,
> Which sweet *Philisides* fetch't late from *France*,
> That well beseem'd his high-stil'd *Arcady*,
> Tho others marre it with much liberty;
> In Epithets to ioyne two wordes in one,
> Forsooth for Adiectiues cannot stand alone;[39]

Lyly himself may have been influenced, if a passage in Hoskins means what it seems to mean. Hoskins notes that the Lylian mode had become old-fashioned and that, apparently in response to Sidney, 'Lyly himself hath outlived this style and breaks well from it'.[40] A writer who certainly did attempt to reform his writing after reading Sidney was Thomas Churchyard, whose collections *A feast full of sad cheare* (1592) and *A reuyuing of the deade* (1591) show some stumbling efforts to bring himself up to date. In 1593 he included in *Churchyards challenge* a revision of his *Legend of Shore's Wife* to show the younger generation what he was made of: 'not in any kind of emulation, but to make the world knowe my device in age is as ripe & reddie as my disposition and knowledge was in youth'.[41] That Churchyard was 'too old to change his style' is demonstrated by his 'translation' of Sidney's *Defence*, published in *A musicall consort of*

---

[38] Michael Drayton, 'Epistle to Henery Reynolds', *The battaile of Agincourt, . . . etc.* (1627), p. 206 (Drayton, *Works*, ed. Hebel, iii. 228).
[39] Joseph Hall, *Virgidemiarum* (1598), VI. i. 2, pp. 255–60; *The Poems of Joseph Hall*, ed. A. Davenport (Liverpool, 1949), p. 95.
[40] *Directions*, ed. Hudson, p. 16.
[41] *Churchyards challenge* (1593), Sig. S4^v.

heauenly harmonie (1595).[42] Churchyard's verses contain a general praise of poetry, asserting its antiquity, seriousness, and Biblical origin: he is close to Sidney only spasmodically, and even then reduces Sidney's subtleties to doggerel:

> Sir Philip Sidney praiseth those
> Whose waking wits doth see
> The depth and ground of verse or prose
> And speakes with judgement free.
>
> To rime and roue in retchles sort
> He counted reuell rash
> As whip doth make a horse to snort
> When carter giues a lash.[43]

Within a short period after his works appeared, Sidney was read widely and attentively. He was perceived not merely as an inspiration but also as a storehouse of models for imitation and emulation. Given the literary culture that received him, it was inevitable that his influence should have been widespread and profound, and that it should range from large-scale imitations to mimicry of particular effects. Before considering the reaction of a few major writers to Sidney it will perhaps be useful first to consider what we can reconstruct of the practice of reading in the period—a practice to which Sidney's works were especially well fitted.

Erasmus had taught by precept as well as example. In addition to furnishing students with compilations of adages and similes, he advocated the practice of collecting *sententiae* or axioms as being 'conducive not only to criticism but also to imitation'.[44] Hoskins, by placing marks denoting metaphors in the margin of *Arcadia*, was responding to an Erasmian injunction:

you will carefully observe when reading writers whether any striking word occurs, if diction is archaic or novel, if some argument shows brilliant invention or has been skilfully adapted from elsewhere, if there is any brilliance in the style, if there is any adage, historical parallel, or maxim worth committing to memory. Such a passage should be indicated by some appropriate mark.[45]

---

[42] John Buxton, *Sir Philip Sidney and the English Renaissance* (2nd edn, 1964), p. 193.

[43] Sig. F4ᵛ, G1.

[44] From *De ratione studii*. My text is from the Toronto edition of *The Collected Works of Erasmus*, 24, *Literary and Educational Works*, ed. C. R. Thompson (Toronto, 1978), p. 670; see also Erasmus' remarks in *De copia*, ibid., pp. 627 ff.

[45] *Literary and Educational Works*, p. 670.

Erasmus' method informs countless English texts of the period; the practice was universally acknowledged as one of the foundations of an abundant style. Schoolboys were encouraged to keep commonplace-books, and to acquire habits of reading and memory intended to facilitate cultivation of powers of imitation and invention. Francis Meres recommended students to follow the example of bees, who 'out of diuers flowers draw diuers iuices, but they temper and digest them by their owne vertue, otherwise they would make no honny: so all authors are to be turned ouer, and what thou readest is to be transposed to thine own vse'.[46] Hoskins and Fraunce demonstrate that Sidney was instantly recognized as a writer whose works were susceptible to the close scrutiny of the Erasmian method. Nicholas Ling's *Politeuphia*, *Wits Commonwealth* (1598) includes numerous passages and phrases from the *Arcadia* in its list of *sententiae*, some shared with other collections. From the same period the commonplace-book of Brian Twyne (?1579–1644) has survived, containing notes on the contents of *Astrophil and Stella*.[47]

John Webster illustrates the application of the Erasmian method to composition. He depended, like Hamlet, on his 'tables', and his art can often seem like the rearrangement of other men's flowers. Sidney was one of his major sources and actually appears in the pageant *Monuments of Honor* (1624), where the figure Troynovant, representing London, is attended by

five famous Schollers and Poets of this our Kingdome, as Sir *Jeffery Chaucer*, the learned *Gower*, the excellent *John Lidgate*, the sharpe-witted Sr. *Thomas Moore*, and last as worthy both Souldier and Scholler, Sir *Phillip Sidney*, these being Celebraters of honor, and the preservers both of the names of men, and memories of Cities . . . to posterity.

And Sidney acknowledges that honouring worthy men '*Flowes as a duty from a judging pen*'.[48]

Webster most commonly quoted Sidney directly or with little alteration. Thus, the Duchess of Malfi asks her brother:

> Must I, like to a slave-born Russian,
> Account it praise to suffer tyranny?

[46] Francis Meres, *Palladis Tamia. Wits treasury . . . etc.* (1598), Sig. Mm4ᵛ.
[47] Corpus Christi College Oxford MS 263: see J. J. Yoch, 'Brian Twyne's Commentary on *Astrophel and Stella*', *Allegorica*, 2 (1977), 114–6. In J. Stephens's *Satirical essays* (1615) is a lawyer's clerk who woos 'with bawdery in text; and with Iests, or speeches stolne from Playes, or from the common-helping *Arcadia*' (II. xi. 276).
[48] *The Complete Works of John Webster*, ed. F. L. Lucas (1927), iii. 139.

from *AS* 2: 'now like slave-borne *Muscovite*, / I call it praise to suffer Tyrannie' (lines 10–11). The narrator's intervention towards the end of the fifth book of *Arcadia*: 'in such a shadow or rather pit of darkness the wormish mankind lives that neither they know how to forsee nor what to fear, and are but like tennis balls tossed by the racket of the higher powers,' anticipates both Bosola's final speech:

> O, this gloomy world!
> In what a shadow, or deep pit of darkness
> Doth womanish and fearful mankind live!

(v. v. 100–2.)

and his earlier observation to Antonio:

> We are merely the stars' tennis-balls, struck and banded
> Which way please them.[49]

(v. iv. 63–4.)

Sidney represented a treasury of memorable phrases, although it is tempting on occasions to imagine that Webster employs allusion to suggest correspondences, as that implied above between the Duchess and Astrophil.

More substantial Arcadian borrowings in the play include the trick with the wax hand and bodies (iv. i, drawing on *NA* Book III, Chapter 21 ff.), and the echoes of the evil Cecropia in Julia's speech (v. ii. 181–2, 202–5, recalling *NA* Book III, Chapter 17). There is a further important parallel between the discussion between the Duchess and Cariola in prison—'Dost think we shall know one another, In th'other world?' (iv. ii. 21)—and the debate on the immortality of the soul between Pyrocles and Musidorus in the fifth book of *Arcadia*.[50] Not only are the predicaments similar; in each case the exchanges serve to address questions of judgement, fame, and reputation, of the relation of absolute to relative values. In other words, Webster with a deft stroke—a single question in a significant setting—creates an allusive frame of reference for the conclusion of his tragedy.

---

[49] *The Countess of Pembroke's Arcadia (The Old Arcadia)*, ed. J. Robertson (Oxford, 1973), pp. 385–6; ed. K. Duncan-Jones (Oxford, 1985), p. 333.
[50] See R. W. Dent, *John Webster's Borrowing* (Berkeley, 1960), J. R. Brown's Revels edition of *The Duchess of Malfi* (1964) (cited here), and M. C. Bradbrook, *John Webster, Citizen and Dramatist* (1980), pp. 47–55.

Shakespeare's use of Sidney was a good deal more various than Webster's. It is well known that the story of the blind Paphlagonian King (*NA* Book II, Chapter 10) is a source of *King Lear*, and that there are numerous affinities between *Astrophil and Stella* and *Romeo and Juliet*.[51] Parallels are readily drawn between characters—Sidney's doomed Amphialus and Shakespeare's Othello—and plot devices—the way clownish figures resolve plot elements in both *Much Ado* (Dogberry) and in the fourth book of *Arcadia* (Dametas). Falstaff, when he pounces upon Mistress Ford in *The Merry Wives of Windsor* (III. iii. 43), sings, 'Have I caught thee, my heavenly jewel?', echoing the fourth song of *Astrophil and Stella*, and establishing thereby a deliciously incongruous connection between himself and Astrophil. And new suggestions are constantly made—as in a recent article connecting *Love's Labour's Lost* and Sidney's *Defence*.[52] A convenient way of indicating aspects of Shakespeare's response to Sidney is to consider a single play, *As You Like It*.

There are plenty of verbal parallels between Shakespeare's play and Sidney, although few are so close as to be borrowings in Webster's vein.[53] Perceiving nature, and especially trees, as a library (II. i. 15–17), rhyming to death in Ireland (II. ii. 177) and calling deer citizens (II. i. 23, 55) are all fairly commonplace. But Touchstone's argument that 'the truest poetry is the most feigning' (III. iii. 19) is indebted to the *Defence*; and *AS* 92 has been suggested as a source for Rosalind's questions to Celia (III. ii. 180 ff).[54] One might add to the latter that Celia's exclamation, 'O wonderful, wonderful, and most wonderful wonderful, and yet again wonderful!' (line 191), seems to echo the narrator's defence of his fulsome account of the upbringing of Pyrocles and Musidorus, which 'may well seeme wonderfull: but wonders are no wonders in a wonderfull subject' (*NA* Book II, Chapter 7 (Feuillerat, i. 190; ed. Evans, 259)). The solitary melancholics Jaques and Philisides

---

[51] See the New Arden editions of *King Lear* by K. Muir (corr. edn, 1972), pp. xxxiv–xxxviii, and of *Romeo and Juliet* by B. Gibbons (1980), pp. 43–7. A recent study of Shakespeare's *Sonnets* in the light of Sidney is A. Ferry, *The 'Inward' Language: Sonnets of Wyatt, Sidney, Shakespeare, Donne* (Chicago, 1983), pp. 170–214, 251–5.

[52] R. Proudfoot, '*Love's Labour's Lost*: Sweet Understanding and the Five Worthies', *E&S* (1984), 16–30.

[53] See the New Variorum edition of *As You Like It*, by Richard Knowles, with a Survey of Criticism by Evelyn Mattern (New York, 1977), p. 498.

[54] M. S. Jamieson, *Shakespeare: As You Like It* (Sussex Studies in English Literature; 1965), p. 50; S. Lanier, *Shakespeare and his Forerunners* (New York, 1902), i. 248–9.

are linked, too: Jaques is first encountered under an oak, Philisides under a cypress; both moralize the animal world. Debates and eclogues in Shakespeare—'how like you this shepherd's life, master Touchstone?'—repeat the procedures of Sidney's pastoral world (especially the debate between Dorcas and Rixus ['I was saying the shepherd's life had some goodness in it'] in *The Lady of May* [*Miscellaneous Prose*, 26–30]), as do gestures like hanging verses on trees (derived from Ariosto), and minor figures like Audrey and William, who recall those in *The Lady of May*. The marriages at the end may echo the *Arcadia's* hymeneal *Third Eclogues*; and the wild beasts may also have Arcadian predecessors. Shakespeare's use of the rhetorical figure *gradatio* or *climax* further adds to the Sidneian flavour—for while the device was common, its associations with Sidney were powerful, and it occurs at crucial stages—including the beginning—in both *Astrophil and Stella* and the *Arcadia*. Its appearance in *As You Like It* seems designed to locate the persons of the play in the realm of Sidneian romance, and to place their affection on the same elevated plane as, for example, the love of Strephon and Klaius for the absent Urania.[55]

But let me end with a more striking parallel. The moment of *anagnorisis* in Act IV, Scene iii, where Oliver, describing the encounter with the lion, lapses into the first person and thereby reveals his true identity to Celia, is based on an Arcadian episode where Musidorus (in disguise) describes the perilous career of Pyrocles and Musidorus (*NA* Book II, Chapter 8). The supposed shepherd likewise shifts to the first person as he delivers his account to Pamela.[56] Surely the effect of this echo is to reinforce the audience's belief in the conversion by providing a literary context in which such occurrences are habitual and by associating

[55] Shakespeare puns on the name of the figure *climax* or *gradatio* when Rosalind says to Orlando: 'your brother and my sister no sooner looked, but they loved; no sooner loved, but they sighed; no sooner sighed, but they asked one another the reason; no sooner knew the reason, but they sought the remedy. And in these degrees have they made a pair of stairs to marriage.' (v. ii. 31–7; New Arden edn by Agnes Latham (1975), p. 116.) In the first chapter of *NA* Book I Klaius says to Strephon: 'let us thinke with consideration, and consider with acknowledging, and acknowledge with admiration, and admire with love, and love with joy in the midst of all woes.' (Feuillerat, i. 7; ed. Evans, p. 263.)

[56] Thus Sidney: 'never man betweene joy before knowledge what to be glad of, and feare after considering his case, had such confusion of thoughts, as I had, when I saw *Pyrocles* so neare me. But with that *Dorus* blushed, and *Pamela* smiled . . . because he had . . . forgotten in speaking of himselfe to use the third person.' (Feuillerat, i. 199; ed. Evans, p. 268.)

it with a noble and virtuous love. Perhaps Shakespeare labours the point in the following line, where Oliver ("'Twas I; but 'tis not I, . . .' etc.) appears to allude to Astrophil ('I am not I, pity the tale of me').

Even women readers, although excluded from formal education, were drawn to Sidney. The *Arcadia* had both a specific (the Countess of Pembroke) and a general (the 'dear ladies' whom the narrator regularly addresses) female audience. From its beginnings, the novel or prose romance in England addressed women readers.[57] These readers were not brought up formally by the Erasmian method, but there is plenty of evidence to indicate what they were expected to admire, how they were meant to read, and how some proceeded from study to creation.

Lyly, in the dedication to *Euphues and his England* (1580), observed that: 'Ladies had rather be sprinckled with sweete water, then washed . . . you take more delyght, to gather flowers one by one in a garden, then to snatche them by hand fulles from a Garland.' He saw women as his natural, and best, audience: '*Euphues* had rather lye shut in a Ladyes casket, then open in a Schollers studie.'[58] And we know that Ladies enjoyed readings: Lady Anne Clifford records listening to *The Faerie Queene* and to Montaigne, and on 12 and 13 August 1617 she 'spent most of the time playing at Glecko and Hearing *Moll Neville* read the Arcadia'.[59] Court ladies, like Ben Jonson's Saviolina, derived skill in speech from Sidney: the courtier Fastidius Briske comments that her wit 'flowes from her like *nectar*, and shee doth guie it, that sweet, quick grace, and exornation in the composure, that . . . she doth obserue as pure a phrase, and vse as choise figures in her ordinary conferences, as ay be i' the *Arcadia*'. [60] Later appears the suggestion that, for another class of reader, the *Arcadia* was seen as

---

[57] For later examples (from 1711) see Addison, *The Spectator*, ed. D. Bond (1965), where *Arcadia* is listed among the contents of a typical lady's library (i. 155): Addison remarks:

> People dress themselves in what they have a Mind to be, and not what they are fit for. There is not a Girl in the Town, but let her have her Will in going to a Masque, and she shall dress as a Shepherdess. But let me beg of them to read the *Arcadia*, or some other good Romance, before they appear in any such character in my house. (i. 63.)

[58] *The Complete Works of John Lyly*, ed. R. W. Bond (Oxford, 1902), ii. 8–9.
[59] *The Diary of the Lady Anne Clifford*, ed. V. Sackville-West (1923), p. 76.
[60] *The comicall satyre of Every man out of his humor* (1600), ii. iii. 221–8 and iii. v. 27–9; *Ben Jonson*, ed. Herford and Simpson, iii. 476–7, 507.

purely recreational. Fungoso remarks, 'I'le sit i'my old sute, or else lie a bed, and reade the *Arcadia*, till you [taylor] haue done' (III. v. 27–9). Such phrases parallel the puritan attack on Sidney's work as idle, frivolous, and time-wasting.

But one of the *Arcadia*'s most important qualities was that it was unfinished, literally so in the case of the *New Arcadia*, and the *Old* had concluded with a prospect of a future which 'may awake some other spirit to exercise his pen in that wherewith mine is already dulled'.[61] Inevitably others sought to complete Sidney's task for him. Gervase Markham's *The English Arcadia, alluding his beginning from Sir P. Sydney's ending* (1607) and its sequel (1613) are the most substantial and impressive continuations, with a dark and at times menacing Arcadia, intelligent working out of plot elements in a universe toyed with by uncertain Fortune, and an ironic attitude to the conventions it follows. Richard Beling's little *Sixt book* (1624) is primarily a brief exercise in tying up loose ends, and with Anne Weamys's *Continuation* (1651) we encounter a text even further removed from its origins, despite the author's attempts to imitate the style of its model.[62]

But particular incidents, situations, characters, and stories from the *Arcadia*, as well as general suggestions of Sidneian romance, continued to be collected and reproduced in the literature of the generations after Sidney's death—even as far as works like McNamara Morgan's tragedy *Philoclea* (Dublin, 1754). Popular prose romances, like Emmanuel Ford's *Parismus* (1590), plays like the anonymous but frequently revived *Mucedorus* (1598), and burlesques like *The heroicall adventures of the knight of the sea* (1600) and John Day's *Ile of guls* (1606) illustrate some varieties of early responses to the stimulus of *Arcadia*. The confusion of man and myth was assisted by Sidney's editors; Alexander gave Philisides, whom he identified as the Knight of the Sheep, a moving death after enduring a wound in the thigh (1638). And versions of Sidney appeared in many texts, such as Nathaniel Baxter's *Sir Philip Sidney's Ourania* (1606); and he provided matter for more oblique treatment, as in Ford's play *The Broken Heart*.

The final books of *Arcadia* are inherently dramatic, and there are

---

[61] *The Countess of Pembroke's Arcadia*, ed. Robertson, p. 417; ed. Duncan-Jones, p. 361.
[62] P. Salzman, *English Prose Fiction, 1558–1700: A Critical History* (Oxford, 1985), pp. 123–33; A. Patterson, *Censorship and Interpretation* (Madison, Wisconsin, 1984), pp. 170–1, 249–51, etc.

many Sidneian dramas. In addition to James Shirley's play *A Pastoral Called the Arcadia* (1640), and two manuscript plays, 'Loves Changelings Change' and 'Arcadian Loves or Metamorphosis of Princes', perhaps the most notable instances are *Cupid's Revenge* and *Philaster* by Beaumont and Fletcher.[63] Sir William Alexander's sentiments were clearly shared: 'The *Arcadia* of S. P. *Sidney* (either being considered in the whole or in several Lineaments) is the most excellent Work that, in my Judgement, hath been written in any Language . . ., affording many exquisite Types of Perfection for both the Sexes.'[64] And of all Arcadian stories, of all 'exquisite Types of Perfection', none appealed more enduringly than that of Argalus and Parthenia, which was celebrated in John Quarles's admired poem *Argalus and Parthenia* (1629) and in Henry Glapthorne's dramatization of the subject (published in 1639, although produced several years earlier). Chap-book versions of Quarles's poem appeared in the early 1670s and again in 1683, 1691, 1692, and 1700. Then in 1703 appeared *The Unfortunate Lovers: Or, The Famous and Renowned History of Argalus and Parthenia*. These cheap and crude retellings of *Arcadia* forcefully demonstrate the degree to which Sidney's stories were still read into the eighteenth century.[65] Sidney exerted influence on writers of all kinds, and of vastly different ambitions and temperaments. Wherever one turns in the period, whether to the high art of William Browne or the Fletchers—even Milton in *Arcades* ('The Arcadians'), or to more 'popular' authors like Robert Baron or the authors of the chap-books aimed at the

---

[63] There is an edition of *Loves Changelings Change* by J. P. Cutts (Fennimore, Wisconsin, 1974); also in F. Rota, *L'Arcadia di Sidney e il teatro* (Bari, 1966). See A. W. Osborn, *Sir Philip Sidney en France* (Paris, 1932). William Prynne attacked the Stuart taste for 'Arcadiaes, and fained Histories that are now so much in admiration', in *Histriomastix* (1633), p. 913.

[64] Sir William Alexander, *Anacrisis* (?1634); my text is from *Critical Essays of the Seventeenth Century*, ed. J. E. Spingarn (Oxford, 1957), i. 187.

[65] See the words of Lettice in Steele's play *The Lying Lover* (1703):

one dare not light a large Candle, except Company's coming in,—and I scarce can see to read this pitious Story.—*Well, in all these Distresses, and Misfortunes, the faithful Argalus, was renown'd all over the plains of* Arca- Arca- Arcadia—*for his loyal and true Affection to his charming Paramour,* Parthenia—Blessings on his Heart for it,—there are no such Suiterers now a Days.—But I hope they'll come together at the end of the Book.—And marry, and have several Children.' (IV. ii; *The Plays of Richard Steele*, ed. S. S. Kenny (Oxford, 1971), p. 162.)

See also *The Tender Husband*, IV. ii *passim* for echoes of Sidney, and B. S. Field Jr., 'Sidney's Influence: the Evidence of the Publication of the History of Argalus and Parthenia', *ELN* 17 (1979), 98–102.

unlearned, the image of Sidney and of his writings is, whether explicitly or not, to be found.

So profound was his entrenchment in some minds that his world became a medium through which to view the everyday. On a political level, this phenomenon is illustrated by a royalist poem describing the events of the Civil War in terms of *Arcadia*.[66] On a more personal plane, Sir Kenelm Digby composed a fictionalized autobiographical romance in which he (Theagenes) woos his wife Lady Venetia Stanley (Stelliana).[67] The romance is prefaced by a 'key' in which the correspondences are listed (so that Cyprus, for example, is shown to equal Holland). Digby's pose as author is Sidneian: he calls his writings 'trifles' (p. 170), and wishes them destroyed by fire (p. 173; see Greville, *Life*, p. 17): throughout the text parallels with Sidney occur.

Lady Mary Wroth's romance *The Countesse of Montgomeries Urania* (1621) proclaims its literary and familial ties with *Arcadia* at every step; but it is also a *roman à clef* somewhat like Digby's.[68] By concentrating on the less reputable elements in the courtly code, by directing attention to scandal and intrigue, and above all by drawing much of her matter from the real events in the world of the Jacobean aristocracy, Sidney's niece provided a version of Arcadianism that was as distinctive as it was controversial. While not as explicitly hostile to chivalric values as Charlotte Lennox's *The Female Quixote* (1752) was to be, Wroth concentrated on instances of the fate of women, condemned to perform an essentially passive role in a universe structured by masculine values. Small wonder that her romance, the first work of English fiction by a woman to be published, should have been rescued from oblivion in this generation.[69] The *Urania* is a remarkable work in many ways, and time has eroded little of its power to disturb and question; as such it may come to seem to this age one of the versions of *Arcadia* closest in spirit to the original.

Wroth deploys the machinery of chivalry to subvert it. A related

[66] John Buxton, 'A Draught of Sir Philip Sidney's Arcadia', in *Historical Essays 1600– 1750 Presented to David Ogg*, ed. H. E. Bell and R. L. Ollard (1963), pp. 60–77.

[67] BL MS Harley 6758. There is a modernized edition in Kenelm Digby, *Loose Fantasies*, ed. V. Gabrieli (Rome, 1968); references in parentheses are to this edition.

[68] See Salzman, *English Prose Fiction*, pp. 136–44.

[69] For recent studies, see C. R. Swift, 'Feminine Identity in Lady Mary Wroth's Romance *Urania*', *ELR* 14 (1984), 328–46, and D. Spender, *Mothers of the Novel* (1986), pp. 11–22.

process underlies another work from the early 1620s. Using as a model Drayton's immensely popular *England's Heroical Epistles* (1597, often reprinted), in which pairs of celebrated historical lovers exchange verse letters, an anonymous poet composed an exchange supposedly between Sidney and Penelope Rich.[70] Unlike Drayton, the poet's general attitude is scurrilous and in a sense satirical—resembling several of the mock epitaphs commemorating the death of Lady Rich, which implicitly contrasted the perceived idealism of *Astrophil and Stella* with 'Stella's' colourful later career.[71] Further, a highly cynical essay, proposing valour and honour as particularly effective strategies in seducing women, was ascribed to Sidney in *Cottoni Posthuma* (1651) and elsewhere, rather than to its more likely author, John Donne.[72] In their different ways, these texts exemplify a counter-myth spawned by the Sidney legend, by suggesting a dark, possibly disreputable reality underneath Arcadian ideals.

While Sidney's texts begot satire, they also attracted criticism. Even in 1592 Gabriel Harvey, decrying the rapidity with which literary fashions were changing, and the way the great achievements of the previous decade (not excluding his own) were less esteemed than the scribblings of Greene and Tarleton, complained that 'the Countesse of Pembrookes Arcadia is not greene inough for queasie stomackes'.[73] But with the publication of the hybrid 1593 Arcadia, which added the tragicomic conclusion of the *Old Arcadia* to the epic, heroic *Arcadia* of 1590, a new vein of criticism appeared. In 1597, for example, John King, Bishop of London, issued a blanket attack upon '*Arcadia*, and *The Faerie Queene*, and *Orlando Furioso*, with such like frivolous stories'.[74]

[70] Bodley MS Eng. Poet. f. 9, fos. 221 ff.; see J. A. Roberts, 'The Imaginary Epistles of Sir Philip Sidney and Lady Penelope Rich', *ELR* 15 (1985), 59–77.
[71] See Henry Parrot, *Epigrams* (1608), Sig. B3; for satirical epigrams and epitaphs see BL MS Add. 25303 fo. 98ᵛ; Bodley MS Douce f. 5, fo. 9. The latter reads:

> Here lies Penelope or the Lady rich
> Or the Countesse of Deuonshire choose you which.
> One stone sufficeth soe, what death can doe
> Who in here life was not content with two.
> Here is one dead under this marble stone
> Which when shee liud lay vnder moe than one.

[72] John Donne, *Paradoxes and Problems*, ed. H. Peters (Oxford, 1980), pp. xlviii, 62–7, 136–7.
[73] *Elizabethan Critical Essays*, ii. 231.
[74] John King, *Lectures upon Jonas . . . etc.* (1597), Sig. Z2.

And, however incongruously in view of Sidney's Puritan inclina-
tions, Puritan attacks upon his art continued from this time on: the
Arcadia was argued to be at best frivolous and at worst downright
vicious. Everard Guilpin in *Skialetheia* noted that Sidney was 'not
exempt from prophanation, / But censur'd for affectation'.[75] A
book of meditations by James Caldwell, entitled *The Countess of
Marres Arcadia* (1625), is proposed in its dedication by M. P.
Anderson as a corrective to Sidney, with the implication that the
earlier Arcadia had been superficial, lacking moral seriousness:
'The *Countess of Pembroke's Arcadia* is for the body; but the *Countess
of Mar's Arcadia* is for the soul.'[76] This is the tradition that leads to
Milton's censure and beyond.

There was still plenty of eulogy. Gervase Markham wrote of
Sidney that 'his contemplatiue labour ... brought him to actiue
worthinesse'; Richard Carew called him 'all in all for prose and
verse'; to the author of *Mythomystes* he was 'the generous and
ingenious Sidney, for his smooth and artfull *Arcadia*'; Henry
Peacham referred to 'the Arcadia of the Noble Sir Philip Sidney,
whom Du Bartas makes one of the foure columns of our
language'; Richard Crashaw wrote of

> *Sydnaean* showers
> Of sweet discourse, whose powers
> Can Crowne old Winters head with flowers,
>
> Soft silken Houers,
> Open sunnes; shady Bowers,
> Bove all; Nothing within that lowres.[77]

Furthermore, the Erasmian method, and the habit of reading
Arcadia for *sententiae*, did continue in spite of the various criticisms

[75] E. Guilpin, *Skialetheia; or, a shadow of truth; in certaine epigrams a. satyres* (1598),
Sig. E1ᵛ.

[76] James Caldwell, *The Countess of Marres Arcadia, or Sanctuarie. Containing meditations,
etc.* (Edinburgh, 1625), Sig. *4. On the other hand, as David Norbrook has pointed out
in his *Poetry and Politics in the English Renaissance*, 'interest in representations of female
beauty was ... far from unknown amongst Puritans' (p. 303), and he cites as evidence
the passages from *Arcadia* transcribed by the American Puritan Seaborn Cotton (see
S. E. Morrison, 'The Reverend Seaborn Cotton's Commonplace Book', *Publications of
the Colonial Society of Massachussetts* 32 (1937), 323).

[77] Markham, *The second and last part of the first booke of the English Arcadia* (1613), Sig. A4;
Richard Carew, *The excellencie of the English Tongue* (1595/6) pr. in 2nd edn of Camden's
Remaines (1614), p. 43; Henry Reynolds, *Mythomystes wherein a short suruay is taken of true
poesy* (1632), p. 8; Henry Peacham, *The compleat gentleman* (1622), p. 53; Richard
Crashaw, *Steps to the Temple* (1646), p. 137.

(moral, religious, political) that were being levelled at Sidney.[78] Peter Heylyn wrote of *Arcadia* that it was

a book which beside its excellent language, rare contrivances, and delectable stories, hath in it all the strains of *Poesie*, comprehendeth the vniversall art of speaking; and to them which can discern and will observe, affordeth notable rules for demeanour, both private and publick.[79]

Works including Alexander Gil's *Logonomia Anglica* (1619), Thomas Blount's *Academy of Eloquence* (1654) and John Smith's *Mystery of Rhetoric Unveil'd* (1657), as well as Ling's *Politeuphia* (twelve editions between 1597 and 1640) indicate the firmness with which Sidney was established as an exemplar of English style.[80]

But alongside these praises, whose dominant motif is inclusiveness, the capacity to embrace variety and stretch the limits of art, a progressive marginalization may be detected. Sidney shrank from being a 'liuely image of our Worldes perfection' to an altogether less impressive stature.[81] There is a suggestion of the genteel in some quite early comments. Anthony Scoloker, in *Diaphantus* (1604), speaks of 'the Neuer-too-well read Arcadia, where the Prose and Verse (matter and words) are like his Mistresses eyes, one still excelling another and without coriuall: or to come home to the vulgar Element, like Friendly Shakespeare's Tragedies'.[82] The peculiar suitability of Sidney for the sensibilities of women became a commonplace. In the anonymous *The returne of the knight of the post from hell* (1606), the author insists that his readers are safe with him—'yet shall they no more blush . . . than at the reporting of a tale out of *Orlando* or a Sonet out of *Portes* or *Stella*'.[83] More critical is the character of a maid in Wye Saltonstall's book of characters *Picturae loquentes* (1631): the girl 'reades now loves historyes, as *Amadis de Gaule* and the *Arcadia*, & in them courts the shadow of

---

[78] For a late example, see Jane Porter, *Aphorisms of Sir Philip Sidney* (1807): also note 80 below.

[79] Heylyn, *Cosmographie* (1652), ii. 222

[80] For two particular cases, one English, the other American, see E. E. Duncan-Jones, 'Henry Oxinden and Sidney's *Arcadia*', *N&Q* 198 (1953), 322–3 and J. A. Coffee, '*Arcadia* to America: Sir Philip Sidney and John Saffin', *American Literature*, 45 (1973), 100–4.

[81] John Davies of Hereford, *Microcosmos; the discovery of the little world* (Oxford, 1603), Sig. E1.

[82] Anthony Scoloker, *Diaphantus, or the passions of love* (1604), Sig. E4ᵛ.

[83] *The returne of the knight of the post from hell, with the divels aunswere* (1606), Sig. E2ᵛ.

love, till she know the substance'.[84] Anthony Stafford deplored the tendency to dismiss *Arcadia* as mere recreation for women: in *The guide of honour* (1634) he wrote: 'Some of them lately have not spared even Apollo's first-born, incomparable and inimitable Sir Philip Sidney, whose *Arcadia* they confine only to the reading of Chambermaids—a censure that can proceed from none but the sons of kitchenmaids.'[85] But others took the situation for granted. In the preface to Hodges's translation of Achilles Tatius' romance, *The loves of Clitophon and Leucippe* (Oxford, 1638), the women readers are enjoined: 'Faire ones, breathe: a while lay by / Blessed *Sidney's Arcady*: / Here's a Story that will make / You not repent *Him* for to forsake.'[86] In the same category is a passage in John Johnson's *The Anatomy of Love* (1641), where Cupid asserts that courtly Dames 'command . . . *Shirley* to make him acquainted with Sir *Philip*, and so they flirt him into *Arcadia* to sing a lamentation of his lost Mistresse'.[87] This is the context that explains the famous advice of Thomas Powell in his *Tom of all trades* (1631): of the management of women he writes: 'instead of reading Sir *Philip Sidney's Arcadia*, let them read the ground of good huswifery. I like not a female Poetresse at any hand'.[88] Milton, attacking censorship in *Areopagitica* (1644), paints a picture of the kind of supervisory machinery a state would require in order to exercise full control over all literary matters: 'The villages also must have their visitors to inquire what lectures the bagpipe and the rebeck reads even to the balladry, and the gamut of every municipal fiddler, for these are the countrymen's Arcadias, and his Monte Mayors.'[89]

Citing Sidney could be distinctly controversial. Milton's *Eikonoklastes* was written in response to *Eikon Basilike*, a work in which King Charles was depicted as a martyr fit to be ranked with Christ. Milton's intemperate attack deplored 'the whole rosary of . . . prayers' put into the mouth of the imprisoned King.[90] And at the core of these prayers was the 'Pamela prayer' (from *NA* Book III,

[84] Wye Saltonstall, *Picturae loquentes* (1631), Sig. E6ᵛ.
[85] Anthony Stafford, *The guide of honour, or the ballance wherein she may weigh her actions* (1634), Sig. A6ᵛ.
[86] Achilles Tatius, *The loves of Clitophon and Leucippe*, tr. A. Hodges (Oxford, 1638), Sig. A5ᵛ. The poem is by Richard Lovelace.
[87] John Johnson, *The Anatomy of Love* (1641), pp. 98–9.
[88] Thomas Powell, *Tom of all trades* (1631), p. 41.
[89] Milton, *Complete Prose Works*, ed. D. Bush *et al.* (New Haven, 1953–), ii. 524–5.
[90] Milton refers to 'the polluted orts and refuse of *Arcadia's* and Romances' (*Complete Prose Works*, iii. 364).

Chapter 6). While it is reasonable to suppose that Milton read and admired Sidney—after all, Milton had been taught by Alexander Gil, praised Sidney in the *Art of Logic*, and is often close to him in his works—it is his assault on the royal use of the 'vain amatorious poem' that has been best remembered. But Milton's purpose was primarily polemical and had little to do with literary evaluation. As Christopher Hill observed, 'It was a good debating point to stress that the church's martyr had used for intimate devotions the prayer of a pagan girl in a bawdy romance.'[91]

Eikon Basilike reminds us of the tradition of political and ethical readings of *Arcadia*. The procedure was authorized in the *Defence*, where Sidney argued that 'the whole considerations of wrong-doing and patience' could be expressed, or included, 'under the pretty tales of wolves and sheep'.[92] And there is no doubt that the Sidneian romance was an important vehicle for expressing political views—whether general or particular—throughout the first half of the seventeenth century. Dorothy Osborne suggests that writing a romance was an acceptable course of action for those removed from active participation in politics:

My Lord Saye I am tolde has writ a Romance Since his retirement in the Isle of Lundee, and Mr Waller they say is makeing one of Our Warr's, wch if hee do's not mingle with a great deal of pleasing fiction cannot bee very diverting sure, the Subject is soe sad.[93]

And the greatest of these texts of retirement, with its pastoral pattern of exile, testing, and return, its clear allusion to a Sidneian model, and its stress on the value of patience in adversity, was not from a Royalist pen at all. *Samson Agonistes* shows just how central Sidney was to the literary consciousness of the age.[94] As England was torn by division and war, most factions could find in his writings some means of articulating the 'wrongdoing and patience' of their lives.

With the Restoration came a change of taste that was to lead to a marked decline in Sidney's literary reputation. As a man, as a

[91] Christopher Hill, *Milton and the English Revolution* (1977), p. 176
[92] *A Defence of Poetry*, in *Miscellaneous Prose*, p. 95.
[93] *The Letters of Dorothy Osborne to William Temple*, ed. G. C. Moore Smith (Oxford, 1928), p. 91 (Letter 40): see also Salzman, *English Prose Fiction*, pp. 148–76 and Patterson, *Censorship and Interpretation*, pp. 159–202.
[94] See E. G. Fogel, 'Milton and Sir Philip Sidney's *Arcadia*', *N&Q* 196 (1951), 115–7.

pattern of national heroism, on the other hand, he was revered: he was refashioned in the image of a Restoration ideal. Winstanley's biography of 1660 helped to canonize the pattern of an ideal Christian knight. John Howell, dedicating to Lord Lisle Sir John Finett's *Finetti Philoxenis* (1656), had referred to 'a true *Sidneyan* soule, . . . extraordinarily inclined to the *Theory*, and *Speculative* part of Vertue, as well as to the *Practicall*'.[95] But observations about his writings became less numerous and less specific, and most seem to recognize that criticisms exist, and that, however revised to suit modern tastes, the Elizabethan masterpieces had come to seem somewhat old-fashioned. A good example of muted enthusiasm is Thomas Fuller, who calls Sidney 'a compleat Master of Matter and Language, as his *Arcadia* doth evidence': but he continues:

I confesse I have heard some of modern pretended Wits cavil thereat, meerly because they made it not themselves; such who say, that his Book, is the *occasion* that many *pretious hours* are otherwise spent no *better*, must acknowledge it also the cause, that many *idle hours* are otherwise spent no *worse*, than in reading thereof.[96]

These temperate words record Sidney's diminished status. He has shrivelled to a virtuoso from being an example. His mastery is somehow remote from the immediate concerns of his readers: there is no suggestion that they can either learn from him or be moved by him. Edward Phillips similarly implied that Sidney was no longer fashionable:

He was the great English *Mecaenas* of Vertue, Learning and Ingenuity, though in his own Writings chiefly if not wholy Poetical; his *Arcadia* being a Poem in design, though for the most part in solute Oration, and his *Astrophil* and *Stella*, with other things in Verse, having, if I mistake not, a greater Spirit of Poetry, than to be altogether disesteem'd.[97]

Dryden's response to Sidney was a good deal simpler—and cooler—than Milton's. He knew the *Arcadia* well, alluding to it in the Preface to his *Aeneis* (1697). He criticized Cowley for losing contact with English language and culture by taking too much from other literatures—'like the painter in the Arcadia, who, going to see a skirmish, had his arms lopped off, and returned, says Sir

---

[95] Winstanley, *England's Worthies* (1684 edn), pp. 217–23; Sir John Finett, *Finetti Philoxenis* (1656), Sig. A5.
[96] Fuller, *The history of the worthies of England* (1662), Sig. Ll2.
[97] Edward Phillips, *Theatrum Poetarum Anglicanorum* (1675), p. 152.

Philip Sidney, well instructed how to draw a battle, but without a hand to perform his work'.[98] But there is no vital thread linking the two writers. Dryden could find nothing to emulate, nothing to fire his imagination or stimulate his invention, in an author whom he saw primarily as a clever stylist whose day was over. In *Dramatic Poetry of the Last Age* (1672) he referred to 'that admirable wit, Sir Philip Sidney, perpetually playing with his words . . . the vice of his age'.[99] More specifically, in the *Apology for Heroic Poetry* (1677), Dryden remarked that 'Connexion of epithets, or the conjuction of two words in one, are frequent and elegant in the Greek, which yet Sir Philip Sidney, and the translator of Du Bartas, have unluckily attempted in English'.[100]

These compromising judgements signpost Sidney's decline as a major writer. By the end of the century, the era of his predominance was apparently over, although editions of Sidney—and, for that matter, of Lyly—continued to appear. But some indication of the way taste was changing is provided by the final edition of Lyly's *Euphues* before modern times. The work (published in 1718) was essentially a translation, whose title page declared that it was 'Written Originally by John Lyly, M. A. in / the Reign of Queen Elizabeth; and now revis'd / and render'd into Modern English, to make it of / more general Use to the Publick'.[101] In 1724 the first illustrated edition of Sidney's works was published in three volumes. Samuel Richardson was the printer.[102] In 1725 *Arcadia*, like *Euphues* eight years before, appeared in a modern guise. The translator, Mrs Stanley, revised Sidney's prose extensively, reducing its metaphoric component in an ultimately somewhat depressing fashion, producing a text that is as bland as it is literal.[103] Whatever its failings, Mrs Stanley's modernization

---

[98] *Essays of John Dryden*, selected and edited by W. P. Ker (New York, 1961), ii. 229–30.

[99] *Essays*, ed. Ker, i. 173.

[100] *Essays*, ed. Ker, i. 189.

[101] *Lyly*, ed. Bond, i. 113.

[102] W. M. Sale Jr., *Samuel Richardson: Master Printer* (Cornell Studies in English, 37; Ithaca, 1950), p. 204. See below, pp. 305–6.

[103] *Sir Philip Sidney's Arcadia, Moderniz'd by Mrs. Stanley* (1725). Sidney's lengthy and densely conceited passage describing the 'sight full of piteous strangenes' seen by Strephon and Klaius (*NA* Book I, Chapter 1, Feuillerat, i. 9–10; ed. Evans, p. 66) is simplified to:

a Sight of as much Horror as ever filled their Eyes: The Ship, which he had just escaped from, or rather the Carkass of it, lay encompassed with its late Stores: the Men, destroy'd by various kinds of Deaths, were floating in the Water, and seemed

attests to the vigorous and creative response Sidney's writings evidently continued to evoke in women. And her version of Sidney's disclaimer of his 'trifle' is of interest:

let it be approved or not, my chief End is answer'd which was the employing a Waste of Time I had upon my Hands, and which I knew not how better to dispose of: That continual Round of Gallantry, Play and Dress, which engrosses the Time of most of our Ladies, has no Charms for me:

She attributes the omission of the Eclogues to 'the Opinion of most of my Subscribers'—a sign of the total neglect which Sidney's verses were set to enjoy, in an age whose received wisdom was that the hexameters were quite appallingly unnatural and unmusical.[104]

The last edition of Sidney appeared in 1739. It was quoted by a troubled heroine in a work published in the following year: 'So, Mr. *Robert*, said I, here I am again! a pure Sporting-piece for the Great! a mere Tennis-ball of Fortune!'[105] Thus Pamela Andrews. Her name, her predicament, and her general relation to Sidney's tormented heroine were obvious enough to readers at the time. Richardson has Sir Simon Damford labour the point in his continuation—'Methinks I like her *Arcadian* name.'[106] The transition of genres could hardly be neater. Richardson and the novel took over from Sidney and romance, and many of the characteristics of responses to Sidney in the preceding generation were smoothly transferred to Richardson. So complete was the dominance of the new form that the former status of its predecessor perplexed and irritated some readers. As early as 1746, for example, Horace Walpole reported coolly on his investigation into Sidney's work: 'there is a little pamphlet of Sir Philip Sidney's in defence of his uncle of Leicester, that gives me a much better opinion of his parts, than his dolorous *Arcadia*, though it almost

not only to have proved the Cruelty of both Elements, but also to have suffer'd from their own Species, their Bodies being covered with grisly Wounds, which gaped as if they meant to clear the Seas of causing the Destruction . . . (p. 4).

Shortly afterwards the full account in the original of Kalendar's house (*NA* Book I, Chapter 2, Feuillerat, i. 15; ed. Evans, p. 71) is expressed briefly:

the Appearance of it spoke the Judgement of the Master: the Situation seem'd form'd for Health, Convenience, and Delight: the Building Magnificent and Great: and every Thing about it bore an Air of Hospitality. (p. 8.)

[104] From the Preface, Sig. b1^v.
[105] Samuel Richardson, *Pamela* (2nd edn, 1742), ii. 36.
[106] Richardson, *Pamela* (10th edn, 1741), iii. 136 (letter xxiv).

recommended him to the crown of Poland.'[107] Sidney's apparent advocacy of neo-classical correctness earned some approving nods during the eighteenth century, but appreciation of his art, as of many Renaissance writers, could be distinctly lukewarm. John Upton asserted that Sidney 'wanted Shakespeare's ear', and that he had 'dragged into our language verses that are enough to set one's ear on edge'.[108]

An important development of the period was initiated by Charlotte Lennox, in *Shakespeare Illustrated* (1753–4): she identified the blind Paphlagonian King as the source of Gloucester in *King Lear*.[109] Editors of Shakespeare, starting with Johnson (1765) and Capell (1768), took up the point, and inaugurated Sidney's role as a quarry for Shakespearian source-hunters. Johnson had a higher estimation of Sidney, for whom he made a serious claim as a writer whose linguistic and rhetorical achievements were of major importance. In the Preface to his *Dictionary* (1755) he listed Sidney as one of the 'pure sources of genuine diction' in English:

I have fixed Sidney's work for the boundary beyond which I make few excursions. From the authors which rose in the time of Elizabeth, a speech might be formed adequate to all the purposes of use and elegance. If the language of theology were extracted from Hooker and the trans- lation of the Bible; the terms of natural knowledge from Bacon; the phrases of policy, war, and navigation from Raleigh; the dialect of poetry and fiction from Spenser and Sidney; and the diction of common life from Shakespeare, few ideas would be lost to mankind for want of English words in which they might be expressed.[110]

But to many, the act of reading Sidney had come to seem an indulgence. He suffered from the same neglect as many of his lesser contemporaries. Smart, for example, has mowers who speak like this:

> On a bank of fragrant thyme,
> Beneath yon stately, shadowy pine,
> We'll with the well-disguised hook
> Cheat the tenants of the brook;
> Or where coy Daphne's thickest shade

[107] *The Yale Edition of Horace Walpole's Correspondence*, ed. W. S. Lewis *et al.* (New Haven, 1937–), ix. 25–6.
[108] J. Upton, *Critical Observations upon Shakespeare* (2nd edn, 1748), p. 384.
[109] iii. 268 ff.
[110] *Samuel Johnson*, ed. D. Greene (The Oxford Authors; Oxford, 1984), pp. 319–20.

Drives amorous Phoebus from the glade,
There read Sidney's high-wrought stories
Of ladies charms, and heroes glories:
Thence fir'd, the sweet narration act,
And kiss the fiction into fact.[111]

A comparably patronizing attitude is a feature of Walpole's writings. Mockingly he wrote, 'by that time Sir H. Erskine has written a long pedantic pastoral romance and some English hexameters he might be the Sir Philip of our times'. Sidney does not even warrant a separate entry in Walpole's *Catalogue of the Royal and Noble Authors of England* (1758).[112] Walpole digresses in his account of Fulke Greville to declare Sidney's hexameters 'injudicious', and to complain:

we have a tedious, lamentable, pedantic, pastoral romance, which the patience of a young virgin in love cannot now wade through; and some absurd attempts to fetter English verse in Roman chains; a proof that this applauded author understood little of the genius of his own language.[113]

No less a personage than David Hume expostulated with Walpole, and drew from him a more temperate, though still unfavourable, response, in which Sidney was accorded admiration for 'having so much merit and learning for a man of his rank', and declared to be 'not a great man in proportion to his fame'.[114]

Even Johnson, by the time of the Preface to his Shakespeare (1765), had grown more restrained: 'Sidney, who wanted not the advantages of learning, . . . in his *Arcadia*, confounded the pastoral with the feudal times, the days of innocence, quiet and security, with those of turbulence, violence and adventure.'[115] But he knew his Sidney well, and included in his edition a new 'source', when he claimed Rombus (in *The Lady of May*) as the model for Holofernes in *Love's Labour's Lost*. He also recalled (slightly inaccurately) the *Arcadian* poem 'Who doth desire that chaste his wife shall be', from the Third Eclogues (*OA* 65), in a letter to Boswell in 1777.[116]

---

[111] Smart, *Poems* (1791), i. 28.
[112] Walpole, *Correspondence*, xxxvii. 524; *A Catalogue of the Royal and Noble Authors of England, With Lists of Their Works* (Strawberry Hill, 1758), i. 168.
[113] Walpole, *Catalogue*, i. 168, 164.
[114] Walpole, *Correspondence*, xl. 136–7.
[115] *Samuel Johnson*, ed. Greene, pp. 427–8.
[116] *Boswell's Life of Johnson, ed. G. B. Hill*, rev. L. F. Powell (1924–50), iii. 131.

Sidney could no longer be unequivocally praised, even by those who championed him. Clara Reeve responded to Walpole's scorn by announcing that Sidney's writings at least display 'qualities enough, to justify the respect paid to Sir *Philip* by his contemporaries'.[117] In addition, she resented a specifically masculine element in Walpole's disdain, asking, 'has a woman nothing to say in defence of a work that has always been a favourite with her sex?'[118] But her defence is hardly passionate: 'This Romance is of a mixed kind, partaking of the heroic manners of the old Romance, and the simplicity of pastoral life.'[119] Her account of *Arcadia* concludes with a reference to Mrs Stanley's version and with a suggestion that, whatever its virtues, it was now time for the work to be quietly forgotten: 'In 1725, it underwent a kind of Translation by Mrs *Stanley*, by which it was thought to lose more beauties than it gained.—It is now time for us to leave his works to their repose, upon the shelves of the learned, and the curious in old writings.'[120] These words mark the end of the *Arcadia's* active participation in the developing tradition of English fiction. A century—and more— of neglect was to follow.

That is not to say that the ranks of 'the learned, and the curious in old writings' did not include some eminent figures. Coleridge, for example, was clearly both, and took an interest in Sidney as defender of liberty in the Netherlands as well as author of *Arcadia*.[121] Indeed, a notable feature of the age is that Sidney was reinterpreted as a republican hero. While the only people who actually read his works were intellectuals and scholars, his name in contrast was added to the republican pantheon. The ideal knight had become the model democrat. Wordsworth owned a copy of the 1598 Folio (later part of the collection of Professor Ringler), and many of the major writers of the age had at least investigated his works.[122] Among them was Hazlitt, whose reaction was hostile,

[117] Clara Reeve, *The Progress of Romance* (1785), i. 77, 118.
[118] Reeve, i. 78.
[119] Reeve, i. 75.
[120] Reeve, i. 79.
[121] See, for example, *The Friend*, I. iii, where Coleridge claims that Sidney was 'deeply convinced that the principles diffused through the majority of a nation are the true oracles from whence statesmen are to learn wisdom', in *Collected Works*, IV. i (1969), p. 182.
[122] For Keats, see *The Letters of John Keats*, ed. H. E. Rollins (Cambridge, Mass., 1958), i. 327, 397.

querulous, and profoundly influential: 'Sir Philip Sidney is a writer for whom I cannot acquire a taste . . . I cannot love the Countess of Pembroke's Arcadia, with all my good-will to it.'[123]

Hazlitt begins by observing that Sidney has fallen into neglect, and that, since the days of Addison, 'We have lost the art of reading, or the privilege of writing, voluminously', so that the decline in Sidney's fortunes is partly a question of changing fashion and taste. But the *Arcadia*, he continued, 'has . . . other defects of a more intrinsic and insuperable nature' (pp. 319–20).

The initial target of Hazlitt's attack is what he sees as the unnecessary elaboration of the style, with almost nothing stated 'simply and directly' in the creation of 'a huge cobweb over the face of nature', an authorial fraud designed by Sidney 'to aggrandize our idea of himself'. The whole exercise is characterized by Hazlitt as 'one of the greatest monuments of the abuse of intellectual power upon record' (p. 320), and he coins a number of resounding denigratory phrases in its condemnation:

It is not romantic, but scholastic; not poetry, but casuistry; not nature, but art, and the worst sort of art, which thinks it can do better than nature . . . All his thoughts are forced and painful births, and may be said to be delivered by the Caesarean operation . . . The moving spring of his mind is not sensibility or imagination, but dry, literal, unceasing craving after intellectual excitement . . . The quaint and pedantic style . . . was not . . . the natural growth of untutored fancy, but an artificial excrescence transferred from logic and rhetoric to poetry . . . He loads his prose Pegasus, like a pack-horse, with all that comes and with a number of little trifling circumstances, that fall off, and you are obliged to stop to pick them up by the way . . . In a word . . ., the Arcadia is a riddle, a rebus, an acrostic in folio: it contains about 4,000 far-fetched similes, and 6,000 impracticable dilemmas, about 10,000 reasons for doing nothing at all, and as many more against it . . . (pp. 320–5).

The account of *Arcadia* ends with a close verbal recollection of Clara Reeve, and with a more explicitly political dig at the self-advertising 'intellectual coxcomb' who wrote it:

It no longer adorns the toilette or lies upon the pillow of Maids of Honour and Peeresses in their own right (the Pamelas and Philocleas of a later age), but remains upon the shelves of the libraries of the curious in long

---

[123] Hazlitt, *Lectures on the Age of Elizabeth: The Complete Works of William Hazlitt*, ed. P. P. Howe (1930–4), vi (1931), p. 318. All parenthetical references are to Howe's edition.

works and great names, a monument to shew that the author was one of the ablest men and worst writers of the age of Elizabeth (p. 325).

Exempted from this dismissive judgement were some of the sonnets and the *Defence*; but the damage had been done, and Hazlitt's condemnation may be detected as the source of most of the hostile criticism Sidney has attracted since. He added sharpness to the Puritan dislike of *Arcadia*, and presented Sidney, not as a champion of the people, but as an aristocratic and frivolously irresponsible writer, as a kind of sport or abortion fundamentally at odds with the English tradition and native temper.

That was the aspect of Hazlitt's attack which seems initially to have stung Charles Lamb. It was one thing for standard Puritan objections to fiction to be warmed up; quite another to equate Sidney with forces of repression and tyranny. Lamb declined to accept Hazlitt's implicit distinction between Milton's lofty republican seriousness and Sidney's foppish triviality:

Milton was a courtier when he wrote the Masque at Ludlow Castle, and still more courtier when he composed the Arcades. When the national struggle was to begin, he becomingly cast these vanities behind him; and if the order of time had thrown Sir Philip Sydney upon the crisis which preceded the Revolution, there is no reason why he should not have acted the same part in that emergency, which has glorified the name of a later Sydney. He did not want for plainness or boldness of spirit... The times did not call him to the scaffold.[124]

And, addressing himself directly to Hazlitt's lecture, Lamb finds a simple explanation for the 'wantonness' of the 'prejudice' he encountered there: 'Milton wrote sonnets, and was a king-hater; and it was congenial perhaps to sacrifice a courtier to a patriot.'[125]

What Lamb offered, however, was not Sidney's prose but his verse. He left *Arcadia* to sink under the weight of Hazlitt's barrage. Instead he tried to revive interest in *Astrophil and Stella*. He argues that (unlike Milton's) Sidney's sonnets are juvenile work, and should be seen as expressing youthful exuberance and vitality. Indeed, he proposes, 'We must be Lovers ... before we can duly appreciate the glorious vanities and graceful hyperboles of the

[124] Charles Lamb, 'Defence of the Sonnets of Sir Philip Sidney', *The London Magazine* (1823), repr. as 'Some Sonnets of Sir Philip Sidney's' in *Last Essays of Elia* (1833). Text from *The Works of Charles and Mary Lamb*, ed. E. V. Lucas (1912), ii. 242 (the essay occupies pp. 242–9).
[125] Lamb, *Works*, ii. 248.

passion'.[126] Where poets of his own age might be accused of writing in a 'vague and unlocalised' way, Lamb claims that Sidney's art is 'full, material, and circumstantiated', and that in the sonnets 'Time and place appropriates every one of them. It is not a fever of passion wasting itself upon a thin diet of dainty words, but a transcendent passion pervading and illuminating action, pursuits, studies, feats of arms, the opinions of contemporaries and his judgement of them'.[127] Lamb seems to have been reading about Sidney at the time of his death: a copy of Phillip's *Theatrum Poetarum Anglicanorum* was returned to its owner, after Lamb died, with the leaf turned down at the account of Sidney.[128] But his advocacy of the sonnets was as unsuccessful as his rejection of Hazlitt's political attack. Indeed, Hazlitt effectively removed Sidney from the republican pantheon for more than a century. Only since 1945 has he been restored.

As Clara Reeve proposed, Sidney's art became the exclusive preserve of the learned and those curious in old writings. His legend survived, however, and biographical sketches—some little more than rhapsodic celebrations of chivalric perfection—continued to appear, by Fox Bourne, Symonds, and Gosse among others; Oscar Wilde's dictum about Sidney, that 'the most perfect of his poems was his own life', typifies their generally adulatory tone.[129]

The first generations of academic literary studies continued the source-hunting of the mid-eighteenth century: in these writings Sidney was found to be influential to writers other than Shakespeare, Webster, and Milton. Scott's *Ivanhoe*, and the novels of

---

[126] Lamb, *Works*, ii. 242–3.
[127] Lamb, *Works*, ii. 247–8.
[128] The book's owner, H. F. Carey, composed an elegy on Lamb on receipt of the book, beginning

> So should it be, my gentle friend;
> Thy leaf last closed at Sydney's end.
> Thou too, like Sydney, wouldst have given
> The water, thirsting and near heaven.

The elegy is printed in *The Letters of Charles Lamb*, ed. E. V. Lucas (1935), iii. 422.

[129] See Wilde's review, 'Two Biographies of Sir Philip Sidney', *Pall Mall Gazette*, 44 (1886), 5; repr. in *The Artist as Critic: Critical Writings of Oscar Wilde*, ed. R. Ellmann (New York, 1968), pp. 38–42. Wilde observed, 'What a subject Sidney is to write on!' (p. 42.) It is the image cultivated by these eulogistic biographies that is invoked by Yeats in his lament for Robert Gregory. J. A. Symonds suggested that Gosse was drawn to write on Sidney by the homosexual friendship supposedly revealed by the Sidney–Languet correspondence: see P. Grosskurth, *John Addington Symonds* (1964), p. 225.

Trollope, for example, were shown to be influenced by *Arcadia*; and Scott clearly knew the *Defence*.[130] Among the important studies from the years before the First World War were those of Greg, Wolff, and Greenlaw, and into this increasingly productive industry came, in 1907, a major discovery, when Dobell announced the survival of the *Old Arcadia* in manuscript.[131] At the same time the first volume of Feuillerat's edition and Greville's *Life* appeared. In 1915 M. W. Wallace published his excellent—and still not superseded—biography.

From outside the academy, two notable essays from the 1930s constituted a remarkable leap backwards in time, not so much to the *fin-de-siècle* essayists but to Hazlitt. There can be little doubt, for instance, that Hazlitt was in T. S. Eliot's mind when he pronounced: 'The works of Sir Philip Sidney, excepting a few sonnets, are not among those to which one can return for perpetual refreshment; the *Arcadia* is a monument of dulness.'[132] It is, perhaps, worth observing that Howe's majestic edition of the complete works of Hazlitt began to appear in 1930, and would have been an obvious source for Eliot as he prepared his lecture on Elizabethan literature.

With Virginia Woolf we can be even more certain. We know from her letters that she was reading Howe's Hazlitt for a review (published in the *New York Herald Tribune* on 7 September 1930) at the same time as she was reading, or resolving to read, Sidney, for an essay in the *Second Common Reader*.[133] Like Hazlitt, she also brings into the foreground library shelves—the very shelves, perhaps, first introduced into Sidney criticism by Clara Reeve in 1758 and reproduced almost verbatim by Hazlitt. Woolf's shelves

[130] See R. T. Kerlin, 'Scott's *Ivanhoe* and Sydney's *Arcadia*', *MLN* 22 (1907), 144–6; H. N. MacCracken, 'The Sources of *Ivanhoe*', *Nation* 92 (1911), 60; S. L. Wolff, 'The Sources of *Ivanhoe*', *Nation* 92 (1911), 11. On Trollope, see G. Green, 'Trollope on Sidney's *Arcadia* and Lytton's *The Wanderer*', *Trollopian* 3 (1946), 45–54. For Scott and the *Defence*, see his *Letters*, ed. Grierson (1932–7), i. 146, ii. 264.

[131] W. W. Greg, *Pastoral Poetry and Pastoral Drama* (1906); S. L. Wolff, *The Greek Romances in Elizabethan Prose Fiction* (New York, 1912); E. Greenlaw, 'Sidney's Arcadia as an Example of Elizabethan Allegory', *Kittredge Anniversary Papers* (New York, 1913), pp. 327–37. The discovery of the *OA* in manuscript was announced by Dobell in *The Athenaeum* (1907), p. 272. See Greg's reaction in the same volume (pp. 303, 368), and further remarks by Dobell (p. 336).

[132] T. S. Eliot, 'Apology for the Countess of Pembroke', in *The Use of Poetry and the Use of Criticism* (1933), p. 51.

[133] *A Recollection of the Other Person, The Letters Of Virginia Woolf*, iv (1929–31), ed. N. Nicolson (1978), pp. 168, 183, 185, 204, 210, 367, 410, 420.

open and close the essay: 'there is a charm even in the look of the great volumes that have sunk, like 'The Countess of Pembroke's Arcadia', as if by their own weight down to the very bottom of the shelf. . . . we pause for a moment before we return the folio to its place on the bottom shelf.'[134] The first passage also echoes Hazlitt's initial comments on the unfashionable length, the very physical magnitude, of *Arcadia*.

But Woolf took up Hazlitt, and the terms of his argument, in order to suggest a different, though related view. While conceding the remoteness of *Arcadia* from naturalism, she claimed that, 'by wilfully flouting all contact with the fact', it 'gains another reality' (p. 20), as 'Sidney leads us without any end in view but sheer delight in wandering' (p. 21). Like Lamb, Woolf found Sidney's literary personality zestful and vigorous, and identified, alongside the remote and removed register, passages of urgent intensity, where 'eager human voices' articulate 'anger and pain' (pp. 22–3). In these moments Sidney performs as a modern novelist might, although he habitually turns back from such flashes of anguish or humanity to the conventions of his day. Woolf, who knew Sidney's verse well, located energy and surprise in the Eclogues, and sensed a doubleness in his art, whose effect was to render *Arcadia* unfinishable: 'as if Sidney knew that he had breached a task too large for his youth to execute, [and] had bequeathed a legacy for other ages to inherit' (p. 27). She saw *Arcadia* as an essential part of an English literary tradition, and argued that, while it was in one sense an escapist fiction, 'one of those half-forgotten and deserted places where the grasses grow over fallen statues . . . a beautiful garden to wander in now and then' (p. 26), it also prefigured the tradition of the novel—'In the *Arcadia*, as in some luminous globe, all the seeds of English fiction lie latent' (p. 27).

Meanwhile the scholars continued, and several works of the period before the Second World War are still read with profit. Siebeck's study of Sidney's reputation, Zandvoort's comparison of the two versions of *Arcadia*, and Myrick's pioneering critical study are the three most significant.[135] Further, the completion of

---

[134] 'The Countess of Pembroke's Arcadia', in *The Second Common Reader* (1932), repr. in her *Collected Essays*, ed. L. Woolf, i (1966), pp. 19–27. References are to this edition. The shelves appear on pages 19 and 26. See also E. Pomeroy, 'Gardens and Wilderness: Virginia Woolf Reads the Elizabethans', *MFS* 24 (1978–9), 497–508.

[135] B. Siebeck, *Das Bild Sidneys* (Weimar, 1939); R. W. Zandvoort, *Sidney's Arcadia: a*

Feuillerat's edition in 1926 meant that Sidney's works were now available, at least in major libraries.

Yet he remained a minority taste, still apparently appealing only to the learned and the curious in old books. An exception was the *Defence*, which was soon established as a canonical text for the study of the history of criticism. If his sonnets were examined by Shakespearians, it was in order to demonstrate Shakespeare's superiority; if his prose was set against that of Nashe, it was frigid and artificial, if against that of the even less fashionable Lyly, it was intellectual and taut (Lyly being frigid and artificial). While scholars made their slow but occasionally substantial advances, critics (especially in England) found the prospect of reading and interpreting Sidney a much less congenial occupation than striking postures based on prejudice and ignorance derived distantly from Hazlitt.

Since 1945 Sidney has been rehabilitated. He seems now to be more widely and carefully read than at any time since the Restoration. It was the rediscovery of rhetoric by the New Critics that inaugurated the revolution in critical taste from which Sidney continues to benefit. His writings are as congenial to post-1945 critical theory and practice as they were to the culture of Erasmian humanism. Of course (as this volume demonstrates) interpretations are as varied as they were in the days of Jonson and Greville: some recent accounts of the *Old Arcadia*, for example, present it as a Calvinist tract, others as an urbane comedy; to some *Astrophil and Stella* idealizes love, while others read it as satire; and politically, Sidney has been claimed by both left and right. The vigour of such studies indicates that, for our age, Sidney's centrality to the literary achievement of the Elizabethan epoch appears to be established. More than that it would be rash to say. We do well to recall the narrator's words at the end of the *Old Arcadia*, as he looks forward to the spotless reputations his flawed and compromised creations seem set to enjoy: 'So uncertain are mortal judgements, the same person most infamous and most famous, and neither justly.'[136]

comparison between the two versions (Amsterdam, 1929); K. O. Myrick, *Sir Philip Sidney as a Literary Craftsman* (Cambridge, Mass., 1935).

[136] *The Countess of Pembroke's Arcadia*, ed. Robertson, p. 416; ed. Duncan-Jones, p. 360.

The Man and his Works

1. THE EXEMPLARY MIRAGE: FABRICATION OF SIR PHILIP SIDNEY'S BIOGRAPHICAL IMAGE AND THE SIDNEY READER

Alan Hager

The limitations of Sir Philip Sidney's biographical image may well have proceeded to limit our critical appreciation of him. His own concept of the fallacious process of making history in the *Defence of Poetry* would serve a prophetic function in relationship to his reputation as an author. When Sidney complains of the 'historian ... authorizing himself (for the most part) upon other histories',[1] we may be reminded that the image of Sidney as 'Calvinistic', 'idealistic', 'heroic', and 'serious' that found a recent form in a BBC comedy series, where he plays a feisty censor of pornographic literature,[2] is, on the whole, a file copy that has been dusted off periodically since his death. Attitudes towards him change as many times as attitudes towards serious, heroic, idealistic Calvinists change, but his posture as the 'ornament of his age', in and out of favour, seems constant in a way that fulfils Sidney's own worst apprehensions about historical enquiry. When, with a sarcasm, he goes on to complain that historical authority is based on the 'notable foundation of hearsay' and to rue the necessity of picking 'truth out of their partiality',[3] he could as well be speaking of some of the origins of his historical image in legendary anecdote and biased treatise. Since the 'mirage' of Sidney has sometimes cluttered our reading of his works, an elementary goal of criticism of his poetry and fiction, which seem on the whole ironic, comic and 'amatory', must be a reconstruction of an accurate historical reading of those works. In some criticism, this activity need not be as conscious as it is in the case of this Elizabethan courtier, who

Reprinted by permission of the John Hopkins University Press from *ELH* 48 (1981), 1–16.

[1] *Miscellaneous Prose of Sir Philip Sidney*, ed. K. Duncan-Jones and J. van Dorsten (Oxford, 1973), p. 83.
[2] *The Monty Python Show*.
[3] *Miscellaneous Prose*, p. 83.

was made to play a popular 'role' central to our understanding of Elizabethan culture.

In this article I will argue not only that Sidney's exemplary image is the product of Elizabethan propagandistic design, but that Sidney is aware, and attempts in his own life (and works) to make us aware, of the ironies of being identified with such a role: indeed he sets out to expose the dangers of the very idealism with which he has been traditionally identified. Our final image of Sidney is that of a critic of human aspiration, a didactic poet working by indirection and irony even in his own behaviour, a master of the overview that his exemplary image would deny him. Of course, only a few friends knew this Sidney who must provide a key to understanding his works.

Although Sidney's ideal in the *Defence of Poetry* was the popular poet, his real audience was limited. We may recall that he, in the only wholly unfacetious moment of the close of the *Defence of Poetry*, warns us 'to believe, with me, that there are many mysteries contained in poetry, which of purpose were written darkly, lest by profane wits it should be abused'.[4] Sidney is suggesting, with strenuous self-avowal, that even a contemporary, if he fall into the category of 'profane wit', will suffer the puzzlement of a benighted reader with some particular poetic work. No matter how many editions the *Arcadia* went through, beginning three years after his death, he indicates a select audience for his work: his sister, the Countess of Pembroke, and certain 'friends'[5] who would be likely to know his personality, life, and some of his ideas intimately. The first step in approaching an accurate historical reading of his works, then, is to apply our best analytic tools to what we know of Sidney's life, in order to reconstruct an understanding of what his friends, his first readers, already knew, to wipe clear a historical lens that has become dusty over the ages.

It is impossible to ignore the numerous facts about Sidney. Not only do we have contemporary sketches of his life, but also a mass of letters and official documents that were written either by him, to him, or about him. His portraiture alone has been the subject of a reasonable but incomplete book[6] (the Veronese portrait remaining

[4] *Miscellaneous Prose*, p. 121.
[5] Sir Philip Sidney, *The Countess of Pembroke's Arcadia (The Old Arcadia)*, ed. J. Robertson (Oxford, 1973), p. 3.
[6] A. C. Judson, *Sidney's Appearance: A Study in Elizabethan Portraiture* (Indiana Univ. Publications in the Humanities Series, 51; Bloomington, 1958).

lost). What we still need is a consistently plausible interpretation of the hard facts of his life, and we must overcome, in the process, a rather imposing deductive construct. Frances A. Yates, John Buxton, and Jan van Dorsten, in taking a close look at the thought of Sidney's English and Continental acquaintance, and Richard Lanham and Richard McCoy, in testing historically a notion of Sidney as anti-hero or 'conscious failure',[7] have already raised enough questions about traditional concepts of Sidney's idealism to make critics wary of the assumptions that lie behind Tillyard's early comment that 'platonizing created an enthusiastic idealism ... that impelled Sidney to seek education through his love for Stella and honour in sordid battles in the Low Countries'.[8] Such assumptions about Sidney the man, rarely stated in such bold terms, but often implied by Sidney critics, would make the sceptical thinker and comic poet of *The Lady of May*, *Astrophil and Stella*, the *Defence of Poetry* and the *Old* and *New Arcadias* an impossibility.

The biographical concept of Sidney as the epitome of Tudor leadership is first the product of the enshrinement of Sidney as the 'hero of Zutphen' following his early death at the age of thirty-one. As Richard Lanham writes of Sidney's standard biographer, 'here Wallace, and indeed all of Sidney's biographers, have been the heirs of a legend which was created not by Sidney's life so much as by his heroic death'.[9] Elizabethan and Jacobean memorial literature is unequivocal praise, but the genres themselves are panegyrical. Of the more famous examples, Edmund Spenser, in *Astrophel*, characteristically mixes genres in order to create a pastoral elegy for a hero of action. Thomas Moffet's *Nobilis or A View of the Life and Death of a Sidney*,[10] is largely a treatise on university learning, where the dead Sidney serves, as best he can, the function of exemplum for his own apparently rakish nephew, William Herbert. Fulke

---

[7] F. A. Yates, *Giordano Bruno and the Hermetic Tradition* (Chicago, 1964), esp. Ch. 13, 'Giordano Bruno in England'; J. Buxton, *Sir Philip Sidney and the English Renaissance* (1954, 2nd edn. 1964, reprinted 1965); J. van Dorsten, *Poets, Patrons and Professors: Sir Philip Sidney, Daniel Rogers and the Leiden Humanists* (Leiden 1962), and R. Lanham, 'Sidney: The Ornament of his Age', *Southern Review: Australian Review of Literary Studies*, 2 (1967), 319–40. R. McCoy, *Sir Philip Sidney: Rebellion in Arcadia* (New Brunswick, 1979), p. 9, says, 'His death capped a career of noble failure'.

[8] E. M. W. Tillyard, *The Elizabethan World Picture* (New York, 1966), p. 45.

[9] R. Lanham, p. 335.

[10] T. Moffet, *Nobilis or A view of the Life and Death of a Sidney* and *Lessus Lugubris*, ed. V. B. Heltzel and H. H. Hudson (San Marino, 1940).

Greville's later named *Life of Sidney* is a version of a genre conventionalized by Foxe's *Acts and Monuments*, the Protestant saint's life. Sir Walter Ralegh's epitaph builds to a stanza of self-denigration and hyperbolic comparison of Sidney with Scipio, Cicero, and Petrarch. It would require a largish monument to reflect this range, though no monument to Sidney was erected at the time of his death.[11] In accepting the body of Sidneian memorial literature as sincerely biographical, historians overlook factual distortion caused not only by convention of genre but also by specific rhetorical purposes.

The abundant memorial literature of the period on Sidney is compromised by two propagandistic motives. For one, the Leicester faction and Greville in particular used the occasion to promote their 'hawkish' position, that of hoping for a combined Protestant military offensive against Spain on the European continent, waving, so to speak, the bloody shirt of their lieutenant. Lanham writes, I think fairly, of Greville's treatise: 'It is an elaborate justification of the bellicose foreign policy which Walsingham and his party were trying to persuade the Queen to pursue on the continent.'[12] Here, Sidney becomes a martyr to the cause of the Protestant League. Perhaps it is in this capacity that John Philip has Sidney return from the grave, in a dream vision, to warn the 'noble Brutes'[13] to beware popish espionage in their midst. Yet Wallace has carefully documented Sidney's comparatively lenient attitude towards Catholics and towards the Jesuit Edmund Campion in particular.[14]

The second transformation of Sidney is the product of Elizabeth's own aims in upholding the notion of her court as the late flowering of chivalry in fealty to the virgin queen. Here, Sidney is metamorphosed from a complicated, often-neglected courtier into the ideal of chivalric heroism and courtesy, an ideal that would serve to control the impetuosity of some of her courtiers. In her articles for the *Journal of the Warburg and Courtauld Institutes*, 'Queen Elizabeth as Astraea', and 'Elizabethan Chivalry: The Romance of

---

[11] M. W. Wallace, *The Life of Sir Philip Sidney* (Cambridge, 1915), pp. 396–7. William Craft informs me that a statue exists at Shrewsbury School, but Sidney's armoured figure stands on the pedestal of a First World War monument.

[12] Lanham, p. 323

[13] J. Philip (Phillips), *Life and Death of Sir Philip Sidney* (1587), no pagination.

[14] Wallace, pp. 177–9, 287.

the Accession Day Tilts',[15] now collected in *Astraea*, Frances Yates implies that Elizabeth's tilts were a means of building up a body of quasi-religious imagery around her person in a festive chivalric setting. Her goal was political consolidation on the largest possible plane. The images connected with Elizabeth on these occasions, such as Astraea, Cynthia, Diana, vestal virgin, and even, apparently, the immaculate Mary herself, had profound effect not only on poets, but also on the aristocrats and the populace. In part, the outdoor masques and tilts, such as Woodstock 1573, were designed to replace former saint's day celebrations. Sir Henry Lee is seen as the master-mind of what Yates calls 'an imaginative re-feudalisation of culture'[16] in the English court. But she also hints at an imperial propagandistic intention behind these tilts when she points out that 'for the expense of a few pence . . . the rude country people may now instead behold the worship of Elizabeth by her knights'.[17] Clearly adulation of the commoners would follow hard upon apparent adulation by the leading figures in the realm. To effect this, she would have to reduce her leading courtiers, at least symbolically, into worshippers of a queen with the 'rank' of idol.[18]

Contemporary accounts of Elizabeth in court emphasize her very special regard for rank. In the *Apophthegms*, Francis Bacon recounts the anecdote of Elizabeth intentionally bypassing Burleigh's row of men to be knighted more or less in order of importance of service, and knighting them in reverse order, more or less by rank.[19] If the tale were not true, it would certainly be symbolic truth. When the Queen found herself in the central role of Sidney's masque, *The Lady of May*, she seems at first to have made a simple error in choosing the rich but ineffectual shepherd, Espilus, over the poor but spirited forester, Therion, to wed the lady in question. As Stephen Orgel has shown,[20] the drama was

[15] F. A. Yates, 'Elizabethan Chivalry: The Romance of the Accession Day Tilts', *Journal of the Warburg and Courtauld Institutes*, 20 (1957), 4–25; and 'Queen Elizabeth as Astraea', *Journal of the Warburg and Courtauld Institutes*, 10 (1947), 27–82. Now edited and collected in *Astraea: The Imperial Theme in the Sixteenth Century* (1975).

[16] Yates, 'Elizabethan Chivalry', p. 22; *Astraea*, p. 108.

[17] Yates, p. 15; *Astraea*, p. 101.

[18] See Norman Council's discussion of the progress of Elizabeth's image from earthly to unearthly beauty in '"*O Dea Certe*": The Allegory of *The Fortress of Perfect Beauty*', *Huntington Library Quarterly*, 39 (1976), 329–42.

[19] Francis Bacon, *The Works of Francis Bacon*, ed. James Spedding (1878), vii. 157.

[20] S. K. Orgel, 'Sidney's Experiment in Pastoral: *The Lady of May*', *Journal of the Warburg and Courtauld Institutes*, 26 (1963), 198–203.

designed to favour Therion in the debates and resolve his victory in the final songs which open with the lines 'Silvanus long in love, and long in vaine, / At length obtained the point of his desire . . .'.[21] On the other hand, we should consider the possibility that Elizabeth intentionally chose the rich, unerratic shepherd to remind Sidney and the public of the importance of economic and social hierarchical relationships. If she did so, as with Burleigh's prepared ceremony, she must have intentionally left Sidney's 'entertainment' in a state of considerable disarray, with a victorious shepherd singing a song in praise of the god of the woods, Silvanus, and a forester ruing the defeat in love of Pan, the god of shepherds. We should remember that Elizabeth's main cause for anger with Sidney in the tennis court incident with Oxford was not its near-violence but Sidney's insufficient regard for his inferiority of rank.[22] Recognition of social hierarchy was, naturally, of special importance to Elizabeth. Her own claims to the highest rank in the kingdom were questioned on several scores and periodically challenged by plot and rebellion. And she was a woman, surrounded by impulsive gallants of the new and old aristocracy, Drake and Leicester, Ralegh and Essex. These men were not easy to rule.

Bacon, in his Plutarchan version of her life, *In Happy Memory of Elizabeth, Queen of England* (1608), hints at her solution to the problem of imposing obedience on major peers and favourites alike. Having mentioned that Elizabeth surrounded herself with would-be lovers 'beyond the lot of that time of life', he adds that these activities 'certainly were in no way detrimental to her majesty'.[23] Is not Bacon suggesting that these activities were designed specifically to increase her majesty? And if obedience to the virgin queen was absolute for the courtier–lover, the commoners would follow suit. Joseph Levine has made the following comment about the Queen's problem and solution: 'If Elizabeth could become their lady and they the love-sick knights of chivalric tradition, awkwardness could be made to disappear and the problem of obedience might be resolved. What a grand perform-

[21] *The Poems of Sir Philip Sidney*, ed. W. A. Ringler Jr. (Oxford, 1962), p. 4.

[22] The incident is found in Wallace, pp. 213–16, but its 'best account', as McCoy points out, p. 2, is found in Sir Fulke Greville's *The Life of the Renowned Sir Philip Sidney*, ed. N. Smith (Oxford, 1907), pp. 67–8.

[23] Bacon, vii. 302; *In Felicem Memoriam Elizabethae Regina Angliae*, 1608, 'ultra sortem aetatis', 'nil prorsus majestati ejus officerent'.

ance this required.'[24] Largely in death, it seems, Sidney became a part of this performance and gained the rank in overplus that he never had as Leicester's heir.

Alive, Sidney was rarely an apparent favourite, though he made an appearance in several tilts. He himself complains, I think undramatically, in a letter to Walsingham, in the year of his death, 'how apt the Queen is to interpret everything to my disadvantage'.[25] But if his youthful death were to be seen as the sudden and irreparable loss of perfection, Elizabeth could set up a competition in her court to try to fill the ensuing vacuum. At least on one occasion, four years after Sidney's death, the 1590 Accession Day Tilt, the Earl of Essex took Sidney's part. George Peele, in the most extensive description in his commemoration of the event, *Polyhymnia* (1590), calls our attention to the Earl, with company, lances, horses, armour, and staves 'in funerall blacke, / As if he mourn'd to thinke of him he mist, / Sweete Sydney, fairest shepherd of our greene'.[26] Because of rather unusual circumstances, Essex had, by a special clause in Sidney's will, inherited his 'best sword'.[27] But he had also married Sidney's widow, Frances Walsingham, the year of this tilt. Peele refers to this twofold identification with Sidney in the lines that follow the above: 'Well lettered Warriour [i.e. Sidney], whose successor he [i.e. Essex] / In love and Armes had ever vowed to be.' This extraordinary reference to the sword as well as to the widow of Sidney, as somehow honours to be reaped, could not have been lost on the courtiers if on the populace.

Essex, having replaced Leicester as Master of the Horse, was already the Queen's favourite, and destined to be, away from the court, her most unruly courtier–lover. The kind of restraints she imposed on him as the inheritor of the mantle of the perfect Shepherd Knight, Sidney, served the specific political purpose of keeping him in check. As Bacon later advised the Queen when she was angry with the proceedings of Essex in Ireland, 'If you had my Lord of Essex here with a white staff in his hand, as my Lord of Leicester had, and continued him still about you for society to

[24] J. M. Levine, ed., *Great Lives Observed: Elizabeth I* (Englewood, NJ, 1969), p. 5.
[25] *The Complete Works of Sir Philip Sidney*, ed. A. Feuillerat (4 vols., Cambridge, 1912–26, reprinted, with much of the verse omitted, as *The Prose Works of Sir Philip Sidney* (Cambridge, 1962, etc.)), iii. 167.
[26] G. Peele, *Polyhymnia* (1590), no pagination, leaf 6.
[27] See the discussion of Sidney's will in *Miscellaneous Prose*, pp. 143–6. His bequest of the sword is found on p. 152.

yourself, and for an honour and ornament to your attendance and Court in the eyes of your people, and in the eyes of foreign Embassadors, then were he in his right element'.[28] Here we have an extraordinary glimpse of the immediate purpose of the cult of Elizabeth. The extreme amount of ceremony and ornament in Elizabeth's court, from the nicknaming, sonnet production, and oral euphuism, to the masques, tilts, and processions, served not only to impress the public and, through report, foreign rulers of 'a woman's rule', but also tied the hands of an aristocracy now used to thinking of the royal succession, perhaps, as the prize of military conquest, a very male activity. Bacon blames this attitude, in part, on Henry VII who decided to claim the throne on the basis of the House of Lancaster's 'ancient and long disputed title (both by plea and arms)'[29] rather than the House of York's more sound hereditary claim. Ironically, Elizabeth had to suffer for her grandfather's refusal to allow her grandmother, Lady Elizabeth (for whom she was named), a share in the royal title.

Bacon seems to have had the fullest understanding of the Machiavellianism that lay behind the artifice of Elizabeth's court, and it is clear, here, that he could discuss it openly with the Queen. Danger was created by the fact that Essex had gone out of his 'role', a role that was deliberately tied to that of the Shepherd Knight, Sidney. That the Master of the Horse should hold a shepherd's staff was part of her design, a design that in Essex's case failed. It seems probable, then, that the Queen, through her chief propagandist, Sir Henry Lee, created the cult of Sidney that modern biographers, as well as critics, have inherited. The cult of a Shepherd Knight, Sidney, who is metamorphosed so often in literature of the period into Calidore, Philisides, Astrophel, etc., served as a damper on the impetuous knights Elizabeth had some difficulty controlling. That her personal feelings about Sidney were more complex can be shown by her reaction to his death. She was moved for a period of time apparently, and then seems to have bitterly complained to Sir Charles Blount that he had thrown away a noble life with an ordinary soldier's death, as if he had never fully understood rank.

Sidney's death, however, may have contained deeper irony than

---

[28] Bacon, x. 147.
[29] Bacon, vi. 29. In *The History of Henry VII*.

the distortion, *post mortem*, of a complex career into one of simple heroism and virtue. A chronology of the period brings into focus what is, at least initially, a coincidental juxtaposition between the arrangements surrounding Sidney's death and the trial and beheading of Mary, Queen of Scots. Sidney died, after nearly a month of medical care, on 18 October 1586, two days after the recess of the original tribunal assembled for the trial of the eloquent Mary on attempted regicide and treason. The trial was then taken up by the Star Chamber, a week later, on 25 October. Sidney's body arrived at port in England on 2 November, when elaborate mourning began. Until Sidney's funeral, for instance, courtiers wore only black. But when Mary was finally beheaded, three months later, on 8 February 1587, Sidney's funeral was still a week and a day off. The initial delay of the interment was caused by Walsingham's slow liquidation of his son-in-law's debts. Perhaps by a legal oversight, Sidney had attempted, through his will, to pay off debts by the sale of mortgaged lands. At any rate, the law stated that only fee-simple land could be sold, *post mortem*, to pay off creditors, and Walsingham had to find other means to raise approximately £6,000. It seems reasonable, on the other hand, to assume that Elizabeth was party to the decision for the exact date of Sidney's extravagant funeral at St Paul's in London, the last on its scale before Admiral Nelson's.[30] The ceremonial parade through the capital, lavish and well attended, would have helped to turn the minds of the populace from the beheading of Mary. Two Continental biographers have noted this possibility. Berta Siebeck merely notes the proximity of the two dates and suggests that Elizabeth may have had such a propagandistic scheme: 'Perhaps Elizabeth was not sorry to see the people's attention diverted from the painful memory and the execution by a harmless spectacle.'[31] Michel Poirier, however, considers the possibility of a Machiavellian subterfuge on the state's part a strong theory for explaining the date and extravagance of the funeral parade: 'It was perhaps in order to distract the attention of the people from a regicide that risked shaking its own loyalty that the English government decided to surround this burial with such

[30] Neville Williams notes this fact in *Elizabeth, Queen of England* (1967), p. 293. He goes on to suggest that the extravagant funeral arrangements had another propagandistic aim, to draw attention away from military failures on the Continent.

[31] B. Siebeck, *Das Bild Sir Philip Sidneys in der englishen Renaissance* (Weimar, 1939), p. 72, 'Vielleicht sah Elizabeth das Interesse des Volkes nicht ungern von der peinlichen Erinnerung und die Hinrichtung abgelenkt auf ein unverfanglicheres Schauspiel'.

glamorous occasion.'[32] Like so many modern historians, Poirier prefers assigning subtle policy decisions to a vague political force, 'the government', rather than to Elizabeth herself. Bacon was always less reticent. If the irony of the 'smokescreen' funeral exists, Secretary of State Walsingham must have been deeply exasperated, since he went into debt for the lavish funeral parade when Elizabeth and Leicester refused to defray the costs.

No contemporary commentary on the juxtaposition of events at this time survives, nor are we likely to discover any, since such manœuvring would most likely remain a state secret. But, however we interpret the timing and extravagance of Sidney's funeral, we are left with a widespread, intentional use of Sidney's death for propagandistic purposes. Sidney's role, for instance, as the 'hero of Zutphen' is largely the product of Greville's second-hand account of his part in the battle and the decay and collapse of his medical condition:[33] that is to say, the heroic image we have of him now is not a product of his own 'self-fashioning', but of the image-making of a second party, unlike, for example, what Stephen Greenblatt has shown,[34] in the case of Ralegh at the time of his execution. Self-fashioning or assumption of roles for the purposes of advancement or self-justification, or, on a higher level, for the sheer artistry of it all, was a conscious activity perhaps of a whole generation of Elizabeth's younger courtiers. But the circumstances of Sidney's death, if we can be certain of them, seem too severe to allow for the artifice that such self-dramatization would require. One of Greville's 'facts' about Sidney before the battle, that he threw away his cuisses because the Marshall of the Camp was lightly armed, furthermore, was contradicted by Moffet, who may have been present at the battle and who claimed Sidney was not fully armed because he was in haste. And whatever we do with the image of Sidney offering water to a dying soldier, furthermore, when he is in great thirst from loss of blood, saying 'thy necessity is yet greater than mine', we know that Sidney could not have designed the act for effect, whereas Ralegh, when he imitated Sidney's supposed

[32] M. Poirier, *Sir Philip Sidney: Le Chevalier Poète Elizabethain* (Lille, 1948), p. 269, 'C'est peut-être pour détourner l'attention du peuple d'un régicide qui risquait d'ébranler son propre loyalisme que le gouvernement anglais décida d'entourer cette inhumation d'un tel éclat'.

[33] Greville, pp. 127–45.

[34] S. J. Greenblatt, *Sir Walter Ralegh: The Renaissance Man and His Roles* (New Haven, 1973), pp. 1–121.

action on his way to the scaffold, was probably exclusively concerned with effect.[35] We cannot hold Sidney responsible for the perpetuation of his heroic image, and his friends would have known this.

Evidence that Sidney took a modest view of his own achievements as a minor diplomat, courtier, and author appears so often that we are forced to accept, I believe, the image of a man who saw his own life as a kind of irony. It would be too easy to see his deprecatory references to his own writings, for example, calling the *Defence of Poetry* an 'ink-wasting toy'[36] or the *Arcadia* 'a trifle, and that triflingly handled',[37] as manifestations of rhetorical humility, or *sprezzatura*,[38] if he did not treat things supposed more important for a gentleman with similar, often self-disparaging, humour. In regard to his religion, when he was three years old, during Mary's reign, when, incidentally, the Sidneys were all ostensibly Roman Catholic, 'with clean hands and head covered' he prayed to the moon.[39] Here he forces his friends to take the reign of Mary with a kind of humour. To joke about religion at all, of course, is a surprise, and we are forced to interpret in our own way what praying to the moon signifies.

As for his career, he appeared in the tilt following the news that Leicester had produced another heir with his *impresa* altered from 'SPERO' ('I hope') to 'SPERAVI' dashed through ('I hoped' with a bar)[40] to indicate that his hope was past and to draw a laugh on that score. Here the solemn allegorical circumstances of the tilt are surprised by a personal joke on what was, in the context of Sidney's life, an important reversal. Finally on his deathbed, his shoulderblades having already broken through his skin,[41] he insisted that a poem, 'La cuisse rompue' ('the broken thigh')[42] be

---

[35] Greenblatt, p. 16.
[36] *Miscellaneous Prose*, p. 121.
[37] *The Countess of Pembroke's Arcadia*, p. 3.
[38] See K. Myrick, *Sir Philip Sidney as a Literary Craftsman* (2nd edn., Lincoln, 1965), pp. 3-45.
[39] Moffet, pp. 6, 70.
[40] William Camden, *Remaines Concerning Britaine, Fift Impression* (1636), p. 357. Katherine Duncan-Jones makes this connection in 'Sidney's Personal Imprese', *Journal of the Warburg and Courtauld Institutes*, 33 (1970), 123. The reference to the device 'SPERO' is found in G. Whetstone, *Sir Philip Sidney* (1587), Sig. B3, as Duncan-Jones points out.
[41] Greville, p. 133.
[42] Greville, p. 138.

put to music of his own choice and sung to him. Greville, somewhat puzzled, attributes this act 'partly' to a show 'that the glory of mortal flesh was shaken in him',[43] but it seems to this reader to be another manifestation of a special kind of humour, a kind of constructive irony, a dissembling, a pretending that he is less than he is, or that circumstances are less grave than they are, something far more 'humorous' in all senses of the word than *sprezzatura*, which is a more voluntary posture than Sidney's reflexive irony. What Sidney has performed in these cases is a corrective irony. He creates the special effect of surprising us into going back and re-evaluating aspects of what are conventionally understood to be solemn affairs. His characteristic mode of thought in his own life as well as in his art seems to be a criticism of weakness in our conventional understandings or constructions of experience. Of course, I have given here only a few examples of a kind of humour that found its most permanent form not in 'hearsay' but in those other 'facts', his literary works.

Based perhaps on the emphasis on love-crises in his works, there have been traces of an anti-tradition of Sidney throughout the centuries. At one moment in Book II of the 1590 *Arcadia*, Sidney makes a brief appearance as the Shepherd Knight, Philisides (which is a play on his name[44] as well as on his function as Astrophil, and 'lover' of *stella*, *sidus*, *astrum*: star). When we discover that 'his *Impresa* was a sheepe marked with pitch, with this word, Spotted to be knowne',[45] we are reminded that a 'spot' always existed in the development of the heroic image of Sidney, and it is perhaps the exception to his systematic idealization that proves the rule. It concerns Sidney's complex of sexual manœuvres with Essex's younger sister, Penelope Devereux, which apparently continued after she became Lady Rich and perhaps even after he was married to Frances Walsingham. Observing little of the secrecy recommended in the manuals of courtly love,[46] he

---

[43] Greville, p. 138.

[44] Some of Sidney's name-changing may be a reflection of the irony of having been named for a man, in this period of international strife, who was emerging as England's chief enemy, his godfather, Philip II of Spain. Elizabeth emphasized the identity of the two names by calling Sidney '"*her*" Philip, in opposition to Philip II, of Spain'. (Sir Robert Naunton *Fragmenta Regalia* (1641) in *The Harleian Miscellany* (1809), p. 93 n.)

[45] See Appendix, p. 59.

[46] Ringler (quoted in McCoy, p. 69) points out that 'Sidney went out of his way to identify himself as Astrophil and Stella as Lady Rich' (*Poems* p. xliv).

unfolded aspects of the affair in his sonnet sequence which travelled around enough in manuscript so that many at least knew it existed if they had not read it. In fact, Gifford's account of Sidney's death seems to have been doctored to remove Sidney's last words on the subject, although 'Lady Rich' is at least mentioned by name. And Moffet is probably referring to this matter when he spices his otherwise unrelieved praise in *Nobilis* and *Lessus Lugubris*[47] with disparaging references to Sidney's youthful exuberance, especially in matter of love.[48]

While Moffet and others seem to be directly contradicting the idea of the 'spotted' knight by referring to Sidney as a 'spotless' knight, there has been maintained in Sidneiana an undertone of disapproval and uneasiness with the difficulty of holding Sidney up as a perfect exemplar of social virtue when he was apparently a man of considerable sexual appetite. It will be noted that, for all his supposed political acumen, the *Arcadia* unfolds a series of sexual intrigues only occasionally relieved by 'heroic' or 'political' matter. It may take the form of somewhat veiled remarks from Dobell and Wallace[49] that Sidney was too preoccupied with sex.

The most intriguing example of the preservation of the image of Sidney's sexual 'spot' is contained in Aubrey's *Brief Lives* where Sidney's death is laid not at the door of his wound but at the door of his refusal, over the best medical advice, 'to forbeare his carnall knowledge of' his wife Frances when his wound needed healing 'upon which occasion there were some roguish verses made'.[50] Whether or not the story is true, it is an interesting tale because it is another manifestation of the image of Sidney's flaw or 'spot' that has lived a subterranean life, even in ballads perhaps, alongside the exemplary image of Sidney through the centuries. It is hardly a surprise to find that a modern edition of Aubrey, which in general shows little sign of bowdlerization has '[acted]' for 'would not . . . forebeare his carnall knowledge of her',[51] obfuscating Aubrey's sense. If the positive tradition were not so strong, it could not have contained the anti-tradition so easily.

[47] Moffet, p. 135, note to p. 92.   [48] Moffet, p. 91.
[49] Wallace, pp. 237, 245; and B. Dobell, 'New Light Upon Sir Philip Sidney's "Arcadia"', *Quarterly Review*, 420 (1909), 100.
[50] John Aubrey, *Aubrey's Brief Lives*, ed. O. L. Dick (Ann Arbor, Michigan, 1962), p. 280.
[51] *Brief Lives and Other Selected Writings by John Aubrey*, ed. A. Powell (New York, 1949), p. 36.

The permanence of the cult of Sidney results, I think, from the fact that its image of Sidney is so appealing. If no 'ideal courtier', if no 'Renaissance man' ever existed, we would have to invent one. If one was developed for specific political purpose, we still want to preserve it. But somewhere buried in eulogy and panegyric and negative reactions to that rhetoric exists the other Sidney semi-defined by his known literary works. Often, however, the works themselves, that best evidence of the 'other Sidney', are to be read allegorically to suit that all too attractive image of what C. S. Lewis called 'that rare thing, the aristocrat in whom the aristocratic ideal is really embodied'.[52] In fact, that the bright light of that image might distort our reading his works is suggested metaphorically by many of his most sensitive readers. William Hazlitt, for example compared its splendour to something 'Like a gate of steel, / Fronting the sun that renders back / His figure and his heat'.[53] And Lewis says that 'even at this distance, Sidney is dazzling'.[54] The image is blinding, in part, because it is a fictive achievement of the Renaissance mode, yoking the opposites of shepherd and knight, contemplative and active, love and friendship, nature and art, nature and grace, fulfilling a synthetic ideal of varied accomplishment. This is an ideal we would or should not part with easily, even in the search for truth through 'partiality', but in discovering it in Sidney's works we may be practising circular logic; we may be proving our assumptions about history.

The development we are led to expect of criticism of Sidney's works has not been fully realized. Since an unsound legendary image is often both our critical point of departure and our point of return, theses and antitheses about Sidney's works have accumulated somewhat unprogressively. Something of worth has accumulated, of course. The many analysers of moments in certain traditionally chosen passages of his works have located problems in the text the way, perhaps, the Babylonian priests charted problems in the location of heavenly bodies, if only on the assumption that the gods were exerting their immortal free will to move around. My proposed Ptolemaic or Copernican demythologized reading of

[52] C. S. Lewis, *English Literature in the Sixteenth Century Excluding Drama* (Oxford, 1954), p. 324.

[53] William Hazlitt, *The Collected Works of William Hazlitt*, ed. A. R. Waller and A. Glover (1902), vi. 318. The footnote corrects the citation from *Troilus and Cressida*, III, iii., to 'receives and renders'.

[54] Lewis, p. 324.

Sidney's works would owe a debt to those charts, but it would begin, I hope, with an aproach to a historically accurate 'reading' of his works. What I have proposed in this article is the first step in search of that experience: the deconstruction of a biographical image that Sidney's 'friends' could not have shared.

APPENDIX: SIDNEY'S SPOT AS LOVE-MELANCHOLY

D. Coulman and Katherine Duncan-Jones have already noted the similarity of Philisides' device 'a sheep marked with pitch, with this word Spotted to be knowne',[55] and a description of one of Sidney's devices by Abraham Fraunce in a manuscript at Penshurst: 'A sheep marked with the planet Saturn, with the motto *Macular modo noscar*.'[56] Since the motto (meaning 'to be stained merely to be known') is a Latin version of Philisides' English motto, how do we then explain the fact of the spot and also the variation of 'marking' from pitch to Saturn? Duncan-Jones suggests that the device is 'an intimate and esoteric image which succeeds all too well in concealing the author's intention from an uninformed spectator'.[57] But in the *Arcadia*, Sidney makes clear the connection of the spot with his love for Stella. When the description of Philisides' *impresa* is completed, a lady is described at the window: 'the *Star*, whereby his course was only directed' for whom his eclogue goes on to rue thwarted longing: '*For where he most would hit, he ever yet did misse.*' Like Moffet, Fraunce (among other interpretations) insists that 'spotted' really means 'spotless': 'No blemish is found on the peerless body.'[58] But he also notes that Saturn is a symbol of melancholy (in his explanation, melancholy over mutability). In his connection of Saturn with melancholy, however, we have, I believe, another Sidneian reference to his own love-melancholy in his longing for Penelope (what he called, in Gifford's account of his death, 'a vanity wherein I had taken delight, whereof I had not rid myself',[59]) suggested by all the references to loving stars in his devices and pseudonyms and sonnets. Note, for example, that the first appearance of a melancholic Sidney *persona* in the *Arcadia* is 'upon the ground at the foot of a cypresse tree'[60] a classical symbol of death and melancholy. The blackness of pitch is the colour of the bile or humour, and gloomy Saturn is the god of melancholy. In each case, Sidney is providing us with an ironic self-portrait of the gloomy young lover; he is

[55] Feuillerat, i. 285.

[56] 'Sidney's Personal Imprese', p. 323.

[57] 'Sidney's Personal Imprese', p. 324.

[58] 'Nullus in egregio reperitur corpore naevus', in D. Coulman, 'Spotted To Be Known', *Journal of the Warburg and Courtauld Institutes*, 20 (1957), 179–80.

[59] *Miscellaneous Prose*, p. 169, discussed on p. 164.

[60] Feuillerat, i. 132.

gently mocking this passion as he mocks his own choleric tendency to sudden rage at supposed slights in the Philisides passage mentioned above.[61] Rather than being truly esoteric as Duncan-Jones suggests, then, I believe that Sidney is employing *esoterica* for the purpose of self-irony. In general a spot may suggest all the aspects of mortality such as 'infected will', desire and passion, but this spot specifically symbolized the love-melancholy brought on by his longing for his star. When C. S. Lewis suggests that Sidney's complaints about melancholy were a product of 'yielding somewhat to the fashion',[62] he is interpreting Sidney's tone according to that 'dazzling image' of a serious young man who lacks the overview to be self-critical.

[61] 'But *Philisides* was much moved with it, while he thought that *Lelius* would show contempt for his youth'. (Feuillerat, i. 285.)
[62] Lewis, p. 325.

2. PHILIP SIDNEY'S TOYS

KATHERINE DUNCAN-JONES

The word 'toy' in my title needs explanation. I shall not claim to
have discovered corals, hobby horses, or spinning tops played with
by the infant hero, and for my purposes it is purely coincidental
that the stable wing at Penshurst now houses a Toy Museum. My
use of the word 'toy' is the one the OED classes as sense I. 3: 'A
fantastic or trifling speech or piece of writing ... a light or
facetious composition.' The word was more widely used in this
sense in the Elizabethan period than the OED's four examples
might suggest. Sir Arthur Gorges entitled his love-poems his
'vannetyes and toyes of yowth', presumably contrasting them with
his later, more weighty, achievement in translating Lucan's
Pharsalia. The foolish Matheo in Jonson's *Every Man in his Humour*
(the 1601 version) presses his friends to listen to a 'toy' of his—a
poem cobbled up from well-known lines of poetry from the 1580s.
Sidney referred to his *Arcadia* to his brother as his 'toyfull book',
and to his sister, the Countess of Pembroke, he called it an 'ink-
wasting toy'. It is striking that his younger brother Robert, whom
we now know to have been a poet too, was held back from prefer-
ment by the Queen apparently because of some 'youthful toy'
lodged in his brain. My concern here is to suggest that Philip
Sidney's use of the word 'toy' of his own poetry may have been
more than a studied pose of modesty. I would like to emphasize the
obvious point that all Sidney's poetry is *early* poetry. He did not
know, as we do, that he was to die before the age of thirty-two.
Sidney, I suspect, saw all the poetry we have as a kind of tuning in
or voice practice for the greater work on which he would one day
embark, following the classical prototype of Virgil. Most of the
serious poets of the age made this transition, Spenser moving from
The Shepheardes Calender to *The Faerie Queene*, Daniel from *Delia*
and *Rosamond* to the *Civil Wars*, using the epigraph *Aetas prima
canat veneres, postrema tumultus*. *A Defence of Poetry* lays out the
ground for a grandly uplifting heroic poem, directly inspiring men
to virtuous action. Sidney never wrote that work—he scarcely came

The Annual Chatterton Lecture, 1980. Reprinted by permission of the British Academy
from the *Proceedings of the British Academy*, 66 (1980), 161–78.

near to writing it, even in his revised *Arcadia*. But I think it is
reasonable to deduce from the *Defence* that he believed that only
such a work, calculated to have an immediate didactic effect on its
readers, could really be justified. Had he lived to write such a
work, he would, I think, like Gorges, have put all the poems we
possess into the charming but unpretending basket labelled 'toys'.

Another oddity in my title is my omission of my subject's
knighthood. This too is intended to underline his youth. Sidney
was not a nobleman born. He derived from 'always well esteemed
and well matched gentry', and his father, though holding in turn
the two highest offices in Wales and Ireland, was only a knight.
Philip Sidney was knighted in January 1583, purely for reasons of
court protocol, not as reward for active service, when he stood
proxy for Count Casimir's installation as a knight of the Garter at
Windsor Castle. By this date he had written virtually all his poetry.
When he wrote the last line of *AS* 83 addressing Stella's sparrow:

Leave that, sir *Phip*, lest off your neck be wrung

he was probably not identifying 'Sir' Philip Sparrow with 'Sir'
Philip Sidney, but was using the word as well defined by the OED
(sense II. 6. b) 'With contemptuous, ironic, or irate force', much as
Shakespeare's angry old men are apt to say 'Sirrah'. 'Sir' Philip
Sidney no more wrote the *Old Arcadia* than 'Dr' Johnson wrote the
Dictionary or 'Cardinal' Bembo *Gli Asolani*. Sidney the poet was
a well-connected courtier, nephew and heir to the Queen's old
favourite the Earl of Leicester. But at the period of his life when
the *Old Arcadia* was written he was referred to merely as 'Master
Philip': he was not, like Surrey or Sackville, born into the
aristocracy. I think this point worth underlining, as his supposed
rank has often been thrown in his teeth by hostile critics, from
Horace Walpole onwards.

To return to Sidney and his 'toys'. In the *Defence of Poetry* Sidney
makes high claims for an immediate connection between literature
and life, poetry and action: 'So far substantially it worketh, not only
to make a Cyrus, which had been but a particular excellency, but to
bestow a Cyrus upon the world to make many Cyruses.'[1] Or, more
forcefully: 'Truly, I have known men that even with reading *Amadis
de Gaule* (which God knoweth wanteth much of a perfect poesy)

[1] *Miscellaneous Prose of Sir Philip Sidney*, ed. K. Duncan-Jones and J. van Dorsten
(Oxford, 1973), p. 79.

have found their hearts moved to the exercise of courtesy, liberality, and especially courage. Who readeth Aeneas carrying old Anchises on his back, that wisheth not it were his fortune to perform so excellent an act?"[2]

But how far do we find this stress on active public virtue exemplified in the poetry Sidney wrote? Far from presenting us with inspiring pictures of supermen whom we long to emulate, like Cyrus or Aeneas, his poetry, as I hope to show, takes us deep into a world of internalized brooding. He was himself no superman, though it suited many writers after his death to build him up as one, nor did he write of supermen. Sidney has often been seen as Yeats's 'Sidney and our perfect man':

> Soldier, scholar, horseman he
> And all he did done perfectly
> As though he had but that one trade alone

—the man who could wield a lance or a pen with equal ease, and perhaps did both at once. The most appropriate encapsulation of this view for the present purposes is Shelley's stanza in *Adonais* linking Chatterton and Sidney as 'Inheritors of unfulfilled renown':

> Chatterton
> Rose pale,—his solemn agony had not
> Yet faded from him; Sidney, as he fought
> And as he fell, and as he lived and loved,
> Sublimely mild, a spirit without spot.

This view of Sidney as more or less living permanently on the battlefield is given a certain amount of reinforcement in his own *Defence of Poetry*. His opening praise of horses and horsemanship is not wholly ironical, and he sees soldiers as an important audience for poetry: 'I dare undertake, *Orlando Furioso* or honest King *Arthur* will never displease a soldier: but the quiddity of *Ens* and *Prima materia* will hardly agree with a corselet'.[3] Poetry is the companion of camps, and Sidney asserts an immediate connection between heroic poetry and heroic action when he cites the powerful example of Alexander the Great, whose dearest wish was

---

[2] *Miscellaneous Prose*, p. 92. One young man who takes up this challenge is Shakespeare's Orlando, who carries old Adam to dinner in the Forest of Arden (*As You Like It*, II. vii. 167).
[3] *Miscellaneous Prose*, pp. 105–6.

that Homer had been still living. 'This *Alexander* left his school-master, living Aristotle, behind him but took dead Homer with him ... He well found he received more bravery of mind by the pattern of Achilles than by hearing the definition of fortitude'.[4] Sidney has often been seen as such a figure: the soldier–poet, whose courage and leadership were directly nourished by the reading and writing of poetry. The Romantic image of him approximates to the prototype so marvellously ridiculed by Dickens in *The Pickwick Papers*, when Mr Jingle recalls his past life:

'Epic poem—ten thousand lines—revolution of July—composed it on the spot—Mars by day, Apollo by night—bang the fieldpiece, twang the lyre.'
    'You were present at the glorious scene, sir?' said Mr. Snodgrass.
    'Present! think I was; fired a musket—fired with an idea—rushed into wineshop—wrote it down—back again—whiz, bang—another idea—wine shop again—pen and ink—back again—cut and slash—noble time, sir.'[5]

Such a picture of Sidney, as simultaneous man of action and heroic poet, can be fashioned only by telescoping the fourteen years of his adult life into a few months, and by looking with the utmost myopia at what he actually wrote. In examining his poetry, it is important to keep a firm distinction between Sidney the Governor of Flushing and war hero, and Sidney the supreme poet of the Elizabethan 'Golden' age.

Sidney's life falls into three distinct phases of unequal length. He was born in 1554, and the years from then until his return from the Continent in the autumn of 1575 can be described as the period of his education, at Shrewsbury School, at Oxford and perhaps Cambridge, and in some of the great cities of Europe—Paris, Frankfurt, Vienna, Venice, Padua. The following nine years, from 1575 to 1584, seem to have been those in which all the literary works that we have were written. In 1577 he was sent as Ambassador to Prague to condole with the Emperor Rudolf on his father's death. In terms of court office, this was to be his finest hour. Something went wrong with his career in the next five years, for, in spite of vigorous bids for further court or military employ-ment, he achieved no single office that matched his aspirations. Perhaps he tried too hard. In 1580, for instance, his father, Sir Henry Sidney, indicated to Lord Grey, who succeeded him as

---

Lord Deputy Governor of Ireland, that Philip would have dearly loved to hold this post.[6] Such clear thrusts on his behalf may actually have damaged his prospects. It seems also that his uncle, the Earl of Leicester, did not really esteem him very highly until the last months of his life in the Netherlands. Sidney's gradual progress towards more responsible duties, especially in the Ordnance Office, of which he became joint Master in July 1585, culminated in his appointment in November 1585 as Governor of the cautionary town of Flushing. In this last phase of his life, ending abruptly with his death in October 1586 after less than a year of soldiering, there is no reason to believe that he wrote any poetry. Indeed, Geoffrey Whitney, in a poem published six months before Sidney's death, suggested that his career as a poet was definitely over:

> More sweete then honie, was the stile, that from his penne did flowe
> Wherewith, in youthe hee us'd to bannish idle fittes;
> That nowe, his workes of endlesse fame, delighte the worthie wittes.[7]

As an associate of Leicester's, Whitney may have been in a position to know whether his nephew had put poetry behind him. The fact that Sidney entrusted his revised *Arcadia* manuscript to Greville when he left England suggests that he did not envisage doing any more work on it in the Netherlands.

It appears, then, that all Sidney's surviving poetry (with the possible exception of the *Psalms*) was written before 1585, and much of it before 1582. During this middle period of his life Sidney was one

> . . .that never set a squadron in the field,
> Nor the devision of a battle knows,
> More than a spinster.

—though he had, like Cassio, mastered much of the 'bookish theoric' as is evident from his letters of advice to his brother Robert and to Edward Denny. Until he left for the Netherlands at the end of 1585, the only active service Sidney may have seen—and even that is far from certain—was a skirmish in the West of Ireland, when he accompanied his father, the Lord Deputy Governor, to Galway in September 1576. He is said to have met there the virago

---

[6] HMC, *De L'Isle and Dudley*, ii. 93–4.
[7] Geffrey Whitney, *A choice of emblemes* (Leiden, 1586), p. 197.

woman sea-captain, Granny O'Malley. But no echo reaches us of his taking any active part in suppressing the Earl of Clanricard's rebellion. Had he done so, a memory of such an exploit would surely have percolated into the early biographies, such as those of Whetstone, Moffet, or Greville or, even earlier, into John Derricke's *Image of Ireland*, dedicated to Sidney in 1578 (printed 1581), which eulogizes Sir Henry Sidney's reign as Governor. I think we must conclude that, though Sidney throughout his twenties longed to be actively employed, as when he attempted to leave for the West Indies with Drake in August 1585, he was in fact but a carpet knight. While seeing military valour as possibly the highest form of virtue, he had, during his short but extremely productive life as a poet, no opportunity to test his own capacities as a soldier, except in the tiltyard.

The pictures Sidney offers us of the circumstances of writing poetry scarcely suggest the breathless alternation between action and poetic effusion that Mr Jingle boasts of. Much of the *Arcadia*, Sidney reminds his sister, was written in her presence, or dispatched to her as soon as it was written—no doubt from some secluded chamber at Wilton, or, if we are to believe Aubrey, dashed off in the intervals of hunting on the pleasant Wiltshire plains. Aubrey's suggestion that Sidney, like the Canterbury Pilgrims, composed poetry on horseback, is given some confirmation in *AS* 84:

> ... my Muse, to some ears not unsweet,
> Tempers her words to trampling horses feet
> More oft than to a chamber melody.

His reading and writing on the hoof, as it were, is also implied by Moffet's remark (in *Nobilis*, 1592) that Sidney would scarcely leave his room without a book in his hand.[8] These references, along with some in the Languet letters to his excessive studying,[9] conjure up the dreamy schoolboy, unable to put his book down for one moment, rather than the compulsive man of action. Could it have been sheer absent-mindedness that led to his leaving off those vital thigh-pieces before the battle of Zutphen? In *Astrophil and Stella*

---

[8] Thomas Moffet, *Nobilis or A View of the Life and Death of a Sidney*, ed. V. B. Heltzel and H. H. Hudson (San Marino, 1940), pp. 6, 71.

[9] J. M. Osborn, *Young Philip Sidney, 1572–1577* (New Haven and London, 1972), pp. 131, 137, and *passim*.

most of the glimpses of the poet's condition while writing show
him as profoundly inactive:

> As good to write, as for to lie and groan.
>
> (*AS* 18.)

Astrophel is apathetic, time-wasting, and unsociable:

> . . . my wealth I have most idly spent,
> My youth doth waste, my knowledge brings forth toys.
> My wit doth strive those passions to defend
> Which for reward spoil it with vain annoys.
>
> (*AS* 40.)

In the *Defence of Poetry* Sidney describes himself as 'in these my not
old years and idlest times having slipped into the title of a poet'.
We might note also that he hints, with the true insensitivity of
youth in money matters, that he and Wotton were dilatory in
paying Pugliano's bill for riding lessons. Pastoral and love-poetry,
which were the kinds Sidney in practice wrote, are naturally
associated with youth and idleness.

In his earliest literary work, *The Lady of May*, Sidney gave high
praise to the quiet enjoyments of pastoral life: 'where it is lawful for
a man to be good if he list, and hath no outward cause to withdraw
him from it; where the eye may be busied in considering the works
of nature, and the heart quietly rejoiced in the honest using
them'.[10] This sounds almost like Wordsworth's 'wise passiveness',
a falling asleep in body to become a living soul. Though a counter-
claim is made, in *The Lady of May*, for the more strenuous and
dangerous life of the forester, it is striking that the Queen, who was
invited to choose between the two, opted for pastoral contemplation rather than sylvan activity. In both versions of the *Arcadia*
the country of Arcadia is praised for its quietness. Its neighbours,
like those of Elizabethan England, are torn by civil strife and
rebellion, but Arcadia has 'ease, the nurse of poetry'. Its peaceful
rural society is an essentially creative environment, as is shown at
length in the versatile poetic outpourings of the shepherds in the
Eclogues. These conform closely to Huizinga's definition of lyric
poetry as at its best hyperbolic, competitive, and close to its roots

---

[10] *Miscellaneous Prose*, p. 28.

in music and dance.[11] Unfortunately Sidney did not have the benefit of being able to read *Homo Ludens*. Instinct and tradition taught him to write playful, hyperbolic verse with little intellectual content, but the critical theory available to him, which he so brilliantly synthesized in the *Defence of Poetry*, demanded that poetry should be earnestly directed towards moral edification. We can see this split in many of the best Renaissance poets—for instance Ariosto, who felt obliged to impose a heavy didactic framework on his delightfully free-ranging, flippant, and absurd poem, or Ben Jonson, who would have been a less good dramatist if his works had really been as remorselessly disciplined as his theory would seem to claim. The split in Sidney's case is particularly clear because he wrote so lucidly both as poet and theorist.

Looking in more detail at the Eclogues, we find that Ovid's advice, 'Shun idleness, and Cupid's bow will break',[12] is disregarded by all Sidney's young men, who slip into idle ways and immediately fall passionately in love. Philisides refuses even to listen to Geron's helpful (and Ovidian) list of remedies against love-in-idleness. But the good thing about idleness, as we have seen, is that it is the nurse of poetry. A nation at peace and a man at ease are the ingredients for a rich and inventive versification. No doubt, according to theory, that eloquence should in turn be used for heroic or political purposes; but in the bulk of Sidney's poetry it is not. Even his most apparently serious poem, the beast-fable 'As I my little flock on Ister bank', is curiously muffled and inconclusive. It is a warning, possibly topical, against man's natural tendency to tyranny: a serious theme, but handled by Sidney with none of the detailed mastery of patterns of intrigue and power which is so striking in his friend Greville's *Treatise of Monarchy*. The effect of Sidney's poem is whimsical, even puerile. The language is archaic, in spite of his later assertion that he 'durst not allow' Spenser's use of an old and rustic language. In the

---

[11] Johan Huizinga, *Homo Ludens: A Study of the Play Element in Culture* ([1949], with an introduction by George Steiner, 1970), pp. 165–6. Sir John Harington, in his 'Treatise on Playe' *c.* 1597, was to commend divine 'play' in such works as the Sidney–Herbert *Psalms*, but condemned such mirth and poetic games as spring purely from idleness (*Nugae antiquae*, ed. T. Park [1804], i. 186 ff.).

[12] Ovid, *Remedia amoris*, i. 139. Sidney's *OA* 9, lines 115–34, in which Geron tries to persuade Philisides to reject love as a 'Toy', is closely based on this passage in the *Remedia amoris*.

tradition of animal stories with serious import which stretches from Aristophanes to *Animal Farm*, this poem is only a tiny backwater. Its chief charm lies in the evocation of the animals themselves:

> The fox gave craft; the dog gave flattery;
> Ass, patience; the mole, a working thought;
> Eagle, high look; wolf, secret cruelty;
> Monkey, sweet breath; the cow her fair eyes brought;
> The ermion, whitest skin, spotted with naught . . .
>
> The hare, her sleights, the cat, his melancholy;
> Ant, industry; and coney, skill to build;
> Cranes, order; storks, to be appearing holy;
> Chamelion, ease to change; duck, ease to yield;
> Crocodile, tears, which might be falsely spilled;
>   Ape great thing gave, though he did mowing stand,
>   The instrument of instruments, the hand.[13]

As in most of Sidney's poems, the speaker here is young, and sees himself as raw: such political wisdom as the fable contains derives wholly from old Languet and the 'old true tales' he learned from him. Perhaps Sidney's lack of real experience helps to explain the rather feeble conclusion, which on the literal level resembles an anti-vivisectionist pamphlet:

> But yet O man rage not beyond thy need:
> Deem it no glory to swell in tyranny.
> Thou art of blood; joy not to make things bleed:
> Thou fearest death; think they are loath to die.

Most often in other poems Sidney's speaker sees his youthful potential being frittered away either in pointless games (such as poetry itself) or, more damagingly, in introverted emotional dilemmas. Many poems in the *Arcadia* Eclogues show young shepherds engaged in futile and trivial pursuits—not the kind of play with which, as Greville tells us, Sidney used to enrich his mind, but the Elizabethan equivalents of tiddly-winks or hopscotch:

> As for the rest, how shepherds spend their days,
> At blow-point, hot cockles, or else at keels,

[13] *The Poems of Sir Philip Sidney*, ed. W. A. Ringler (Jr.), (Oxford, 1962), *OA* 66, p. 101. All quotations here from Sidney's poems are based on this edition, but have been modernized following the practice of Jean Robertson in her edition of *The Countess of Pembroke's Arcadia* (*The Old Arcadia*) (Oxford, 1973).

While, 'Let us pass our time', each shepherd feels,
And doth not feel, that life is nought but time,
And when that time is passed, death holds his heels.[14]

Sidney's real fear of time-wasting is confirmed by the parallel phrasing in his letter of advice to Edward Denny: 'When so ever you may justly say to yourself you lose your time, you do indeed lose so much of your life.'[15]

Yet the longest poem Sidney ever wrote concerns just such a time-wasting game. The poem appeared in the First Eclogues in the 1593 edition of the *Arcadia*: Ringler classed it as Other Poems 4, thinking it too overtly English to be intended by Sidney to appear in his revised romance, although it seems to have been written later than the *Old Arcadia*, probably close in time to *Astrophil and Stella*. The poem describes an extended game of 'barleybreak', a highly elaborate form of 'catch' or 'tag', between six players. A versatile reciter, Lamon, well able to 'do the police in different voices', tells how Strephon and Klaius lead an innocent and cultivated life as shepherds until both fall in love with the shepherdess Urania. Lines 225–416 describe the barley-break game, in which Strephon and Urania participate, watched by Klaius. The next hundred lines are given to Strephon's complaints of love, and a speech of equivalent length by Klaius was no doubt intended to follow, but the poem is unfinished. We are told, in the 1593 text, that the hearers enjoy and admire Lamon's recitation, but are overcome by weariness—scarcely surprising, given the poem's pace and length. As a whole, it is a very strange mixture of profound resonances and trivial surfaces. Perhaps Greville, if it was he who selected poems for the Eclogues in the 1590 edition, rejected this one because its hints at deeper meaning seem to be in the end unfulfilled. The characters' names point towards Neoplatonic allegory, yet the narrative surface is painstakingly physical in its documentation. These lines, for instance, at the end of the barley-break game, show the shepherdess Urania, whose name is that of the Muse of divine poetry, as red-faced, sweating, and breathless:

Her race did not her beauty's beams augment,
For they were ever in the best degree,

[14] *Poems*, *OA* 10, p. 28.
[15] Osborn, pp. 537–8.

But yet a setting forth it some way lent:
As rubies' lustre, when they rubbed be:
The dainty dew on face and body went
As on sweet flowers when morning drops we see:
  Her breath, then short, seemed loath from her to pass,
  Which more it moved, the more it sweeter was.

(OP 4.)

A shepherdess who sweats and pants, however flatteringly described, seems more like the outrageously physical Venus of
Shakespeare's *Venus and Adonis* than the Muse whom Milton was
to invoke. As a whole, this 550-line poem seems to be a piece of
glorious fooling, playing lightly with Platonic images, and yet
chiefly delighting in authentic details of rustic life, such as the
simile of hunted hares on the Wiltshire downs. Increasingly as it
proceeds it is dominated by wildly hyperbolical enunciations of
passionate love, reminiscent of the better-known double sestina of
Strephon and Klaius. Strephon's hundred-line lament paints a
vivid picture of the kind of miserable inactivity which I have
described as characteristic of Sidney's lovers:

  Alas! What weights are these that load my heart!
  I am as dull as winter-starved sheep,
  Tired as a jade in overloaded cart,
  Yet thoughts do fly, though I can scarcely creep.
  All visions seem, at every bush I start:
  Drowsy I am, and yet can rarely sleep.

Strephon moves finally towards a passionate incoherence verging
on nonsense and preparing for silence, as 'his pipe he burst':

  Alas! A cloud hath overcast mine eyes,
  And yet I see her shine amid the cloud;
  Alas! Of ghosts I hear the ghastly cries,
  Yet there, me seems, I hear her singing loud:
  This song she sings in most commanding wise:
  'Come shepherd's boy, let now thy heart be bowed
    To make itself to my least look a slave:
    Leave sheep, leave all, I will no piecing have.'
  I will, I will, alas, alas, I will . . .

No hints of irony or self-awareness invite us to view this as a
deliberately satirical or critical portrait of a love-madness, as in
some of Astrophil's more breathless and disjointed utterances.

Poetic display seems inseparable from an obsessive state verging on madness. The author of a seventeenth-century manuscript poem describing the love of Sidney for Penelope Devereux tells us in the notes that his grief on hearing of her marriage to Lord Rich was such that 'at that time it was doubted whether he would have fallen into a Lunacy or not'.[16] Though we can scarcely attach much authority to this late account of the legend of Sidney as a lover, the painful frenzy of the Strephon and Klaius poems makes one wonder whether Sidney may not really have passed through some such phase. Thomas Moffet associates Sidney's writings with phases of illness brought on by too much study.[17] Although Moffet's chronology is extremely confused, he may, as a distinguished medical man attending on the Sidneys and Herberts, have observed accurately that there was some link between phases of nervous collapse and poetic activity.

Strephon and Klaius, the most dignified but also the most miserable of Sidney's shepherds, are remarkable for the number of lines allotted to them: 734, even though the barley-break poem tails off before Klaius has had his say. Those who have written on Sidney's poetry have not generally found Strephon and Klaius very interesting characters—certainly they are not dramatically realized in the way that Astrophil is—but I think we should notice how much mileage he gives them. The double sestina 'Ye goatherd gods' has been admired by a wide range of critics, including Empson:[18] it too describes, with rather more concentration and control than the barley-break poem, the collapse of the two lovers into a hopelessly irrational, inward-looking despair, so overstated as almost to provoke ridicule:

> Me seems I see a filthy cloudy evening
> As soon as sun begins to climb the mountains:
> Me seems I feel a noisome scent, the morning
> When I do smell the flowers of these valleys:
> Me seems I hear, when I do hear sweet music,
> The dreadful cries of murdered men in forests.

What the Strephon and Klaius poems are in large, many of Sidney's other poems are in little: pictures of the pastoral dream

---

[16] Bodleian MS Eng. poet. f. 9, fo. 234.
[17] Moffet, pp. 10, 73.
[18] W. Empson, *Seven Types of Ambiguity* (1930), pp. 34–8.

turning into nightmare under the influence of passionate love. No doubt improving lessons could be drawn from this theme—mainly perhaps the Ovidian remedy again, 'Shun idleness, and Cupid's bow will break'. But the speakers are for the most part far too deeply enmeshed in their own subjectivity to be capable of inspiring such reflection. Like the grieving Tennyson, they write simply because they must, composing patterned verse to relieve pent-up emotions which would otherwise be intolerable:

> for the unquiet heart and brain
> A use in measured language lies,
> The sad mechanic exercise,
> Like dull narcotics, numbing pain.[19]

Astrophil claims to write only to 'paint his hell', and Sidney in his own person, addressing his sister, gives a very similar picture of the pressures which caused him to compose the *Arcadia*: writing from 'a young head, not so well stayed as I would it were . . . having many many fancies begotten in it, if it had not been in some way delivered, would have grown a monster.'[20] This modest claim may have been more than a mere pose. Though Sidney was very careful, in the *Defence of Poetry*, to avoid any claim that poetry was divinely inspired, his best poems do read as if they burst from a brain 'over-mastered by some thoughts', rather than forming part of a carefully planned programme of writing.

Sidney's longest *Arcadia* poems—his beast-fable, his Strephon and Klaius poems, and some I have not mentioned, such as the Ovidian blason of Philoclea's beauties, the rather tedious fabliau, and even the long dialogue between Plangus and Boulon on human misery and divine injustice—are all in different ways disappointing as the work of a man who set a high value on action and was a determined 'intellectual'. The Boulon–Plangus dialogue, for instance, shows that melancholy, like love, draws a man away from useful action into a condition of mental stagnation:

> Woe to poor man; each outward thing annoys him
> In diverse kinds; yet as he were not filled,
> He heaps in inward grief, that most destroys him.

---

[19] Tennyson, *In Memoriam*, stanza v.
[20] *The Complete Works of Sir Philip Sidney*, ed. A. Feuillerat (4 vols., Cambridge, 1912–26, reprinted, with much of the verse omitted, as *The Prose Works of Sir Philip Sidney* (Cambridge, 1962, etc.)), i. 3.

Thus is our thought with pain for thistles tilled;
Thus be our noblest parts dried up with sorrow;
Thus is our mind with too much minding spilled.

(*OA* 30.)

Most of the *Old Arcadia* poems have outstanding technical merit, using and stretching the language with a complex fluency un-surpassed by any poet of the period. Yet all are, by his own most exacting standards, *empty*. None offers us a picture of heroism equivalent to Aeneas carrying old Anchises from the flames of Troy, or Cyrus taking counsel in peace and war. The 'notable images' Sidney gives us, whether in Pyrocles, Philisides, Strephon and Klaius, or Plangus, are repeatedly of talents wasted and will-power sapped. And if we turn from Sidney's longest poems to his shortest, their predominant triviality is even more noticeable. For instance, the only poem which survives in Sidney's own hand is the charming and deliberately whimsical lyric 'Sleep baby mine Desire':

Sleep baby mine desire, nurse beauty singeth,
Thy cryes o Baby sett my hedd on akinge
The Baby cryes way, thy love doth keep me waking.

Lully lully my babe hope cradle bringeth
unto my babies allway good rest takinge
The babe cryes way Thy love doth keepe me wakinge

Since Baby myne frome me thy watching springeth
Sleep then a little pap content is makinge
The Babe cries nay for it abyde I wakinge[21]

This is lovely, and perfectly worked out: Beauty which tries to damp down desire serves only to stimulate it. But what does it offer besides charm? The satisfaction Sidney felt in songs such as this is suggested by his injunction to Edward Denny, second only to serious advice about Denny's historical reading: 'that you remem-ber with your good voice, to sing my songs, for they will well become another.'[22] That is, Denny's excellent voice will suit Sidney's excellent lyrics. Though Sidney is commonly thought to adopt a consistent pose of modesty about his works, several hints

---

[21] P. J. Croft, *Autograph Poetry in the English Language* (1973), i. 14. Since this poem is autograph, I have retained the original spelling.
[22] Osborn, p. 540.

such as this indicate that he knew perfectly well that his lyric gift was outstanding. But unfortunately the literary theory available to him offered little justification of lyric poetry unless it celebrated virtuous acts or the excellence of God.

What of *Astrophil and Stella*, probably Sidney's latest, and certainly his most sustained, poetic achievement? Greville does not mention it, perhaps finding it impossible to reconcile with his view of Sidney's fundamental seriousness and concern with affairs of state. Other writers in the years immediately after Sidney's death, while making play with his love for 'Stella', seem to conflate her either with the Arcadian Philoclea, or, as Spenser does, with Sidney's wife. Until Lamb's brilliant essay in 1823, it seems to have been as the author of the *Arcadia*, rather than of *Astrophil and Stella*, that Sidney was chiefly remembered.[23] Certainly *Astrophil and Stella*, though written close in time to the *Defence of Poetry*, offers surprisingly few links with the ideals on which the *Defence* is based. True, Sidney's sonnets do at their best have that 'forcibleness' which he complains that many English poets lack. But Astrophil, like the Arcadian shepherds, is shown as wasting his heroic potential. In *AS* 21, for instance, he is rebuked by a friend for having betrayed 'Great expectation', so that

> ... mine own writings, like bad servants, show
> My wits, quick in vain thoughts, in virtue lame.

Astrophil's dazzlingly ingenious attempts to convince himself that love for Stella is actually a form of virtue or heroic activity are less and less successful as the sequence proceeds, and the unsparingly physical nature of his love becomes apparent. His role, it seems, is neither that of courtier or poet, though he knows that his poetry is admired, but purely that of the happily blinded lover:

> I never drank of Aganippe well,
> Nor ever did in shade of Tempe sit:
> And Muses scorn with vulgar brains to dwell,
> Poor layman I, for sacred rites unfit.
> Some do I hear of poet's fury tell,
> But (God wot) wot not what they mean by it;
> And this I swear, by blackest brook of hell,
> I am no pick-purse of another's wit.

[23] Charles Lamb, 'Some of the Sonnets of Sir Philip Sidney', *The London Magazine* (1823), reprinted in *Last Essays of Elia* (1833).

How falls it then, that with so smooth an ease
My thoughts I speak, and what I speak doth flow
In verse, and that my verse best wits doth please?
Guess we the cause: 'What, is it thus?' Fie, no:
'Or so?' Much less. 'How then?' Sure, thus it is,
My lips are sweet, inspired with Stella's kiss.

(*AS* 74.)

By the later stages of the 'affair' Astrophil is glorying unashamedly
in his lost ambition:

Let clouds bedim my face, break in mine eye;
Let me no steps, but of lost labour trace:
Let all the earth with scorn recount my case,
But do not will me from my love to fly.
I do not envy Aristotle's wit,
Nor do aspire to Caesar's bleeding fame,
Nor ought do care, though some above me sit . . .

(*AS* 64.)

Philip Sidney, as distinct from Astrophil, cared passionately that
some above him sat, delighting to designate himself son of the
'Prorex' of Ireland—by implication, a sort of prince. Like Shakespeare's Hotspur or Henry V, he was passionately greedy for
honour. His extreme and arrogant touchiness on the subject of his
own social position, as a courtier of great talent and promise who
was scarcely even a member of the aristocracy, is manifested all too
clearly in the unpleasing *Defence of Leicester*. But his poet–lover
Astrophil collapses totally into a world of private and self-
destructive emotion, neglecting his career at court and even
ordinary forms of politeness. Lewd innuendo takes the place of the
Petrarchan love of Stella's virtue by which initially he claimed to
be moved. Philip Sidney has all too much in common with Philip
Sparrow as he comes to

Pray that my sun go down with meeker beams to bed.

(*AS* 76.)

Or, almost as in Porphyro's melting embrace of the dreaming
Madeline, he gives himself up to unrestrained erotic fantasy:

Think, think, of those dallyings
when with dove-like murmurings,

with glad moaning passed anguish
We change eyes, and heart to heart
Each to other do depart,
Joying, till joy makes us languish.

(Song X)

Hardly the stuff to give the troops. Even Sidney's supple wit could scarcely maintain that poetry like this would help to fashion a brave soldier or a just magistrate. As the sequence proceeds to its painful end, in which nothing is concluded, a very unheroic reason for the failure of the love-affair emerges. The ultimate barrier to fruition is not Stella's chastity—not Astrophil's conscience, nor his ambition—not even the disintegration of the passion itself, though there is certainly a sense of this in the last thirty or so sonnets. The bar is simply that of social embarrassment—the fear of being discovered, the fear of loss of dignity. Stella in the Eighth Song tells him:

Therefore, dear, this no more move,
Lest, though I leave not thy love,
Which too deep in me is framed,
I should blush when thou art named.

In later sonnets Astrophil has frequently to justify, with Donne-like ingenuity, what are clearly strong temptations to unfaithfulness; he hints that he wants to get on with writing something else; and in the penultimate sonnet he makes loss of dignity his final reason for ending the affair:

O let not fools in me thy works reprove,
And scorning say; 'See what it is to love'.

Like Browning's lovers in *The Statue and the Bust*, Astrophil and Stella stand apart, finally, not because they are chaste or star-crossed, but because they are social cowards. Seldom has the cul-de-sac of unfulfilled love been more mercilessly explored. Astrophil does not end, like Chaucer's Troilus, as a tragically unhappy lover who has at least learned habits of patience and single-mindedness which will stand him in good stead in the afterlife. He has marred his young mind with a passion which was in the end utterly pointless.

Most writers on Sidney use the word '*sprezzatura*' at some point, and suggest that his disparaging view of his own poetic vocation

was no more than a courtly pose. While no one in their senses
would deny that Sidney's self-image was indeed very deliberate
and self-conscious, I think he may, in his mid-twenties, have felt
such modesty to be a fitting framework for what were in the last
analysis only splendid trifles. Many Renaissance writers enacted
a ritual of rejecting their 'looser lays' (or 'toys'), as they strove
towards something more edifying. Spenser, for instance, claimed
to reject his first two *Hymnes* on Love and Beauty, written in
greener youth, in favour of the second two, on Heavenly Love and
Heavenly Beauty. But most readers feel that even the first two are
fairly rarefied, and there was not really very much to reject. More
than this routine and ritual rejection of juvenile and secular work
was entailed when Sidney, at the end of *Certain Sonnets*, bade a long
farewell to splendid trifles, striving manfully towards eternal love.
Like Keats, Sidney intended to engage himself seriously with what
he believed to be important in life: but he must have known quite
well that the poetry he actually wrote came nowhere near doing
this. Sidney's rejection of his works on his deathbed may not, I
think, have been purely the invention of writers after his death
eager to accommodate him to a Virgilian prototype. A chaplain
claiming to have been present at his death describes Sidney's
remorse for his unredeemed life in rather convincing terms. The
dying Sidney, being told that 'godly men, in time of extreme
afflictions, did comfort and support themselves with the remembrance of their former life, in which they had glorified God: "It is
not so", said he, "in me. I have no comfort that way. All things in my
former life have been vain, vain, vain." '[24] Whether or not he was
really troubled by memories of Lady Rich, as one version of this
account claims, we are given a powerful picture of a young man in
pain and despair who looked back on no part of his life with
satisfaction. Thomas Moffet, writing only six years after Sidney's
death, and addressing his account to Sidney's young nephew
William Herbert, gives a more circumstantial account of Sidney's
rejection of his poetry (here translated from Latin into American):

enraged at the eyes which had at one time admired *Stellas* so very
different from those given them by God, he not so much washed them as
corroded them away with salt tears, and exhausted them in weeping . . .
He blushed at even the most casual mention of his Anacreontics, and

[24] *Miscellaneous Prose*, p. 171.

once again begged his brother, by their tie of common birth, by his right hand, by his faith in Christ, that not any of this sort of poems should come forth into the light.[25]

The yet more fanciful and poetic speech attributed to the dying hero by Greville is at one with the earlier accounts in making Sidney identify his life with 'vanity': 'Above all, govern your Will, and Affections, by the Will and Word of your Creator; in me, beholding the end of this World, with all her Vanities.'[26] Greville, too, shows him as bequeathing the *Arcadia*, as an 'unpolished Embrio', to the fire.

Even allowing for strong elements of convention, both in Sidney's actual behaviour and in later accounts of it, I think there may be a kernel of truth in all this. Sidney's desperate last letter to Dr Weier shows him as a young man in agony and terrified of death. We should remember that until a day or two before his death everyone assumed that he would recover from what was, after all, only an infected leg wound, not an injury to a vital organ. Very little time was left him for repentance and preparation, and his remorse may have been all the more violent. An element in Sidney's terror, when it became apparent that he really was going to die, may have been the realization that he would never now be able to move on to the more serious forms of writing on which he had so eloquently based his *Defence of Poetry*. He may have felt, like Keats, that his name was writ in water: all that he had managed to create were glass and feathers, fit, according to his own criteria, to be swept away.

When Sidney referred to his poems as ink-wasting toys, he was to some extent being modest, since he must have known that even the slightest of his lyrics were technically superior to most of the English poetry written since Chaucer. But he knew also that virtually everything he had written was secular, much of it lascivious or trifling. No doubt he hoped to go on to write his *Aeneid* or his *Lusiads*, his *Franciade* or his *Faerie Queene*. Clear if unfocused impulses towards heroic writing are apparent in the *New Arcadia* before it founders amid an over-intricate plot and a growing obsession with fine details of swordsmanship and strategy, perhaps reflecting his work in the Ordnance Office.

[25] Moffet, pp. 41, 91.
[26] Sir Fulke Greville, *The Life of the Renowned Sir Philip Sidney*, ed. N. Smith (Oxford, 1907), pp. 139–40.

Sidney's unfinished works of translation, the *Psalms*, Aristotle's *Rhetoric*, Du Bartas's *La Sepmaine* and Duplessis-Mornay's *De la verité*, are all much more serious in tone than the surviving works. I suspect that he never really got very far with any of these projects. The forty-two *Psalms*, which do survive, are not particularly promising. What Sidney had finished by the time of his death were, for the most part, poetic toys, to be enjoyed as such.

The *Old Arcadia*

3. THE PROVIDENTIAL PLOT OF THE *OLD ARCADIA*

MARGARET DANA

The ending of Philip Sidney's *Old Arcadia* has proved perplexing to modern readers. In 1947 Kenneth Rowe observed that 'the *Arcadia* is distinguished by an equal and balanced presentation of the claims of romantic love and parental authority, embodied respectively in the youthful heroes Pyrocles and Musidorus, and in the person of Euarchus' and concluded that 'the *Arcadia* ends with an effect of ethical confusion'.[1] In 1965 Richard Lanham argued that Sidney had deliberately set up a 'dialectic' between the morals sanctioned by the narrator and celebrated by the rhetoric, and the action itself, which, he believed, contradicted them.[2] More recently, in 1970, Elizabeth Dipple has suggested that 'Sidney forces his reader into a dual realization—that the two princes are both virtuous and guilty, to be rewarded and punished'.[3]

Both Lanham and Dipple have been concerned with the relationship between the plot itself and the narrator's tone towards it. Noting that the narrator 'accepts Euarchus as the all-wise king ... yet also seems to be in full sympathy with the heroic seductions

Reprinted by permission of Rice University from *SEL* 17 (1977), 39–57.

[1] K. Rowe, *Romantic Love and Parental Authority in Sidney's 'Arcadia'* (Univ. of Michigan Contributions in Modern Philology No. IV; Michigan, 1947), p. 3. This has been an influential notion. It is echoed by D. Kalstone in *Sidney's Poetry* (New York, 1965), Ch. 3 and by C. Davidson in 'Nature and Judgment in the *Old Arcadia*', *PLL* 6 (1970), 348–65.

[2] R. A. Lanham, *The Old Arcadia*, in R. A. Lanham and W. R. Davis, *Sidney's Arcadia* (New Haven, 1965), Ch. 4.

[3] E. Dipple, '"Unjust Justice" in the *Old Arcadia*', *SEL* 10 (1970), 93. For a more negative view of the heroes as reduced to 'plotting, frustrated young princes whose lives are demanded by a just judge', see Miss Dipple's 'Harmony and Pastoral in the *Old Arcadia*', *ELH* 35 (1968), 320. See also W. R. Davis, *A Map of Arcadia: Sidney's Romance in its Tradition*, in Lanham and Davis; Davis's insistence on reading the *Arcadia* as an allegory of re-education predisposes him to find the princes guilty of degrading lust, and hence in deep need of regeneration, with the trial becoming a purgation. For a less blemished view of the princes within an interpretation of an order–disorder sequence similar to Miss Dipple's, see A. Isler, 'Moral Philosophy and the Family in Sidney's *Arcadia*', *HLQ* 31 (1968), 359–71. A. C. Hamilton presents a balanced discussion in 'Sidney's *Arcadia* as Prose Fiction: its Relation to its Sources', *ELR* 2 (1972), 29–60, although he, too, finds 'ethical ambiguity' in the ending. A fair and sensible examination of the princes' role may be found in J. Lawry, *Sidney's Two Arcadias* (Ithaca, 1972), Ch. 1.

carried out by the princes', Lanham resolves the difficulty by
accepting the plot as the true norm and dismissing the narrator as
untrustworthy.[4] But when he writes that 'the plot is plain,
unobtrusive, moving slowly from sin to retribution', he is actually
referring to only one part of the plot.[5] For after the sin and retribution, Basilius awakes from his death-like sleep and the mood
changes from grief to joy as the princes are cleared of the charge of
murder and reunited with the princesses in fairytale fashion.
Lanham, who sees the princes as guilty, cannot swallow this happy
ending and is forced to invent the rather odd theory that Sidney
was not only being ironic, but actually intended the conclusion as a
covert criticism of marriage.[6]

Elizabeth Dipple also finds a disparity between the plot and
narrative tone, but resolves it oppositely from Lanham, by
believing the 'cynical narrator' rather than the action. Agreeing
with Lanham that justice is not reached in the ending, she argues
more plausibly than he that Basilius over-reacts in rewarding the
princes just as he had earlier over-reacted to the oracle, and that
'the amused reader can see in his award of the princesses to the
princes and his restitution of Gynecia to high honour, a contrary
injustice to that perpetrated by the trial'. This view of the situation
'is recognized by the cynical voice of the narrator who understands
that under the comedy . . . the basic irony of unfairness exists'.[7]
Her support for this interpretation is the narrator's final comment
about Gynecia: 'the same person most infamous and most famous,
and neither justly'.[8] But while the narrator is explicitly referring to
Gynecia, to whom the statement is appropriate, Miss Dipple
would extend it to include the princes as well, an application
which is less obviously appropriate, and which stretches the
remark uncomfortably far. Moreover, Miss Dipple's reading of the
sequence virtually ignores the oracle which began all the trouble
and has now been fulfilled.

---

[4] Lanham, p. 324.

[5] Lanham, p. 373.

[6] For another argument that the ethical thrust of the work is gloomy and that the
happy ending does not fit, see F. Marenco, 'Double Plot in Sidney's *Old Arcadia*', *MLR*
64 (1969), 248–63. For the more widely accepted and plausible view that Sidney, along
with Spenser, celebrates the value of marriage, see M. Rose, *Heroic Love: Studies in Sidney
and Spenser* (Cambridge, Mass., 1968).

[7] '"Unjust Justice"' p. 101.

[8] This and subsequent references are to Sir Philip Sidney, *The Countess of Pembroke's
Arcadia* (*The Old Arcadia*), ed. J. Robertson (Oxford, 1973).

The *Old Arcadia*'s plot is based upon the workings of providence, as mediated through the ambiguous voice of the oracle,
whose message, though unhelpful to the human beings involved, is
ultimately fulfilled. Since every piece of fiction is, as both Sidney
and Tasso suggested, a little world, operating according to the
laws its maker has decreed for it, plot always in some sense pre-
supposes a concept of providence (however submerged) in relation
to human action. Sidney has given this relationship special
emphasis by hinging his plot upon the working-out of an oracular
prophecy—an ancient device, going back to Sophocles and
extending forward in time through Virgil, Heliodorus, and
Ariosto.

The question of Sidney's attitude towards this providential plot
is bound up with that of how far his narrator may be trusted to
reflect Sidney's own values in this and other matters. Richard
Lanham has accused the narrator of duplicity; Elizabeth Dipple
has called him 'cynical'. I should prefer, instead, to describe him as
ironic, sympathetic, and just.

Sidney's narrator has much in common with the ironic narrators
of *Troilus and Criseyde* and *Orlando Furioso*.[9] Like them, he is
intrusive, moralizing, urbane, and both sympathetic and amused in
his attitude towards human folly and passion. Self-deprecatory,
aware of his own—and his readers'—inclusion in the human
condition, and stressing the sympathetic interest in the characters
which this makes inevitable, he nevertheless, in his ironic remarks
to his readers, preserves enough detachment from the characters
to see them clearly and judge them accurately.

The central focus for the paradoxes of the human predicament
in the *Old Arcadia* is love, and the narrator makes it amusingly clear
that he is not only acquainted with that passion himself, but
expects the 'fair ladies' of his audience to have encountered it also.
Thus, modestly pleading, like a Chaucerian narrator, his inability
to do full justice to the effects of love upon his characters, he relies
upon his auditors to supply the deficiency from their own
experience:

But so wonderful and in effect incredible was the passion which reigned
as well in Gynecia as Basilius (and all for the poor Cleophila, dedicated

---

[9] See R. Durling's excellent discussion of Ariosto's narrator in *The Figure of the Poet in
Renaissance Epic* (Cambridge, Mass., 1965), Ch. 5. Both the *Furioso* and *Troilus* are
mentioned in the *Defence*.

another way) that it seems to myself I use not words enough to make you
see how they could in one moment be so overtaken. But you worthy
ladies, that have at any time feelingly known what it means, will easily
believe the possibility of it. Let the ignorant sort of people give credit to
them that have passed the doleful passage, and daily find that quickly is
the infection gotten which in long time is hardly cured (p. 49).

Love is an 'infection' because, among other symptoms, it produces
delusions:

The force of love, to those poor folk that feel it, is many ways very strange,
but no way stranger than that it doth so enchain the lover's judgement
upon her that holds the reins of his mind that whatsoever she doth is ever
in his eyes best. And that best, being by the continual motion of our
changing life turned by her to any other thing, that thing again becometh
best . . . (p. 230).

From this kind of self-deception, neither the narrator nor the 'fair
ladies' are presumed immune. A basic assumption of the *Old
Arcadia* is that the reader, like the narrator, will find it impossible
not to sympathize with the lovers in their human plight. This
sympathy with love in all its variability accounts for much of that
seeming vacillation on the narrator's part which Lanham has
noticed.

It is not that the narrator fails to provide a moral norm, but
rather that it is a very humanly sympathetic norm which he
exemplifies. Nevertheless, this sympathy, while making his moral
judgements more palatable, does not make them less penetrating.
His irony, cutting several ways at once, encompasses the total
situation. There could be no more crucial test of this than his
treatment of Pyrocles' bedding of Philoclea. It has been clear
throughout the *Old Arcadia* that these two characters are his
special favourites and, in describing the consummation of their
love, he is so sympathetic that we may wonder whether he has not
lost sight altogether of the impropriety of the circumstances. But
two passages which follow should reassure us as to his fundamental clear-sightedness. The first is the opening of Book IV, in
which he declares soberly enough:

The everlasting justice (using ourselves to be the punishers of our faults,
and making our own actions the beginning of our chastisement, that our
shame may be the more manifest, and our repentance follow the sooner)
took Dametas at this present (by whose folly the others' wisdom might

receive the greater overthrow) to be the instrument of revealing the secretest cunning . . . (p. 265).

Now, the action directly preceding this passage is the bedchamber scene, and the connection between that incident and this judgement is clear. The pastoral Eclogues have, however, intervened, thus enabling Sidney to modulate without abruptness from the sympathy of his tone in that scene to the severity of his present moral stance.

The second passage, taking up the idea of Dametas as the unwitting agent of an ironic providence, tells how he bumbles upon the lovers in his search for his missing charge, Pamela:

But lastly, guided by a far greater constellation than his own, he remembered to search the other lodge, where it might be Pamela that night had retired herself. So thither with trembling hams he carried himself; but employing his double key (which the duke for special credit had unworthily bestowed upon him), he found all the gates so barred that his key could not prevail, saving only one trap-door (which went down into a vault by the cellar) which, as it was unknown of Pyrocles, so had he left it unguarded. But Dametas (that ever knew the buttery better than any place) got in that way, and pacing softly to Philoclea's chamber (where he thought most likely to find Pamela), the door being left open, he entered in, and by the light of the lamp he might discern one abed with her, which he, although he took to be Pamela, yet thinking no surety enough in a matter touching his neck, he went hard to the bedside of these unfortunate lovers . . . (pp. 272–3).

Dametas, with his 'trembling hams' and great familiarity with the buttery, is here, as always, a fine figure of fun. His search is occasioned by no real concern for either of the princesses, but by fear for 'his neck', which will be imperilled when it is discovered that he has allowed his charge, Pamela, to disappear while he was off on the wild-goose chase Musidorus had set him. The narrator's irony also includes Basilius, who has been so foolish as to provide Dametas with the key with which he now opens the door and discovers the lovers in bed together.

That it should be the loutish Dametas who finds the virtuous Philoclea in the embrace of the noble Pyrocles is fully of a piece with the ironically reversed, upside-down world Basilius has created by his retreat from kingship. His entrusting of Dametas with the keys is part of this picture. But at this point we see that providence has its own irony, an irony which can turn disordered circumstances to its own uses. 'Using ourselves to be the punishers of our faults' is a principle Musidorus has already followed in relation to the whole Dametas family, whose vices he has made the instruments of their undoing; Pyrocles has played a similar trick on Basilius and Gynecia. But here we see the tables turned by providence. The princes, carried away by the force of love, have gone too far in their wooing. It is now their turn for 'chastisement', and the 'eternal justice' has provided a particularly nice ironic touch in making Dametas the 'instrument'. Pyrocles' humiliation is made all the fuller by the silliness of Dametas, 'by whose folly', as the narrator puts it, 'the others' wisdom might receive the greater overthrow'.

The lovers themselves are described as 'unfortunate'. Nevertheless, it is evident from the previous passage and its connection with this one that the narrator's sympathy does not blind him to their error.[10] Through a kind of narrative tact, Sidney has arranged matters so that his narrator can preserve his stance of sympathy with the princes, while events nonetheless reveal their culpability and punish them for it. It is as though it would be a breach of human sympathy and courtesy for the narrator to blame them. But there is really no split between his view and the plot, for, polite though he is, he never argues with events; he merely allows them to speak for themselves. This sympathetic and just narrator seems to enact, in his relationship to the 'eternal justice' which dictates the plot, the way in which a wise human being may manage to live in harmony with divine providence in the great world which the little world of the *Old Arcadia* is meant, ultimately, to reflect. Thus the narrator himself becomes a moral example to the reader.

There is a special mode in which providence operates in the *Old Arcadia*—the oracle—and this requires further comment. The oracle is really the foundation of the plot. The king's consulting of the oracle begins the action; his reaction to the oracle prepares the way for the very tying of the knot which the oracle predicts; and the knot is untied precisely when the oracle is seen to have been fulfilled. Moreover, Basilius' decision to consult the oracle has in

---

[10] By a parallel irony of providence, Musidorus is punished for his impulse to take sexual advantage of the sleeping Pamela by a band of loutish Phagonian rebels who interrupt him before he can carry out his impulse, and capture him and the princess ignominiously.

itself important moral implications which create the atmosphere within which the plot develops. The question of Sidney's concept of providence is, therefore, connected with the question of his view of the oracle.

The narrator's attitude towards the oracle is interestingly ambiguous. The world of the *Old Arcadia* is pagan, and the narrator's distaste for pagan superstition is always evident. However, though he describes the Delphic priestess as 'the woman appointed to that impiety', he notes parenthetically that she was 'furiously inspired' to give the king his answer (p. 5). The same ambiguity is reflected in the answer itself, which is 'obscure' enough to darken rather than enlighten Basilius' understanding, and threatening enough to throw him into a panic—yet is borne out by subsequent events in an unexpectedly happy way. Clearly, behind the seemingly blind shiftings of fortune, a Christian providence is at work in this world, just as in that of *Lear*,[11] and also clearly the oracle somehow taps into this providence, even though the message that comes through is too garbled to help mankind. As Plutarch, a source for much Renaissance thinking about oracles, had said, there is only one providence, no matter what name men may call it.[12]

There is no ambiguity, however, in the narrator's attitude towards the king's having consulted the oracle. He explicitly disapproves of the behaviour of Basilius, whom he describes as 'not so much stirred with the care for his country and children as with the vanity which possesseth many who, making a perpetual mansion of this poor baiting place of man's life, are desirous to know the certainty of things to come, wherein there is nothing so certain as our continual uncertainty . . .'. No crisis has impelled Basilius to consult the Delphic oracle; he has merely wished 'to inform himself, whether the rest of his life should be continued in like tenor of happiness as thitherunto it had been, accompanied with the wellbeing of his wife and children . . .'. The priestess gives the king this riddling answer:

> Thy elder care shall from thy careful face
> By princely mean be stolen and yet not lost;

---

[11] For a contrary view of *Lear*, however, see W. Elton, *King Lear and the Gods* (San Marino, 1966).

[12] Plutarch, 'De Iside et Osiride', in *Moralia*, trans. F. Babbitt (Cambridge, Mass., 1927), v. 157.

Thy younger shall with nature's bliss embrace
An uncouth love, which nature hateth most.
Thou with thy wife adult'ry shalt commit,
And in thy throne a foreign state shall sit.
All this on thee this fatal year shall hit.

His alarm now exceeds his former curiosity, 'both passions', as the narrator observes, 'proceeding out of one weakness: in vain to desire to know that of which in vain thou shalt be sorry after thou has known it' (p. 5).

Calvin had devoted a chapter of his *Institutes of the Christian Religion* (1536) to censure of superstition. In a statement relevant to Basilius' recourse to the oracle, he warned that 'out of curiosity' superstitious men 'fly off into empty speculations', continuing: 'They do not therefore apprehend God as he offers himself, but imagine him as they have fashioned him in their own presumption. When this gulf opens, in whatever direction they move their feet, they cannot but plunge headlong into ruin'.[13] I do not mean to suggest that the *Old Arcadia* is a Calvinist treatise, but readers have long recognized that a firm moral structure underlies it, even when they have disagreed about the exact nature of that structure, and it is not surprising that this moral basis should reflect Sidney's Protestant belief.

The issue comes to a head in Basilius' conference with his trusted adviser, Philanax, whom unfortunately he consults after the event. Echoing the ambiguity of the narrator, but in a more negative tone, Philanax denounces the oracle as 'nothing but fancies wherein there must either be vanity or infallibleness, and so either not to be respected, or not to be prevented'. Probably he errs in the opposite direction from superstition (Philanax has a tendency to go too far) in his Stoic assertions that 'the heavens have left us in ourselves sufficient guides' and that 'wisdom and virtue be the only destinies appointed to man to follow . . .'.[14] He

[13] John Calvin, *Institutes of the Christian Religion*, ed. John McNeil, trans. Ford Battles (Philadelphia, 1960), 47–8.

[14] In his revision, the *New Arcadia*, Sidney has Basilius request that Philanax consult the Delphic oracle a second time when Anaxius demands the hand of his daughter in marriage. This time the oracle, 'as if it would argue him of incredulitie', answers 'not in darke wonted speeches', but in plain language, and commands Philanax 'from thence forward to give tribute, but no oblation, to humane wisdome'. See *The Complete Works of Sir Philip Sidney*, ed. A. Feuillerat (4 vols., Cambridge, 1912–26, reprinted with much of the verse omitted, as *The Prose Works of Sir Philip Sidney* (Cambridge, 1962, etc.)), i. 510.

sounds very much like a Calvinist preacher, however, when he warns against curiosity: 'the heavenly powers are to be reverenced and not searched into, and their mercy is rather by prayers to be sought than their hidden counsels by curiosity . . .' (p. 7).

The 'plunge headlong into ruin' predicted by Calvin begins in Basilius' next series of acts. First, although, according to time-honoured convention, the oracle is enigmatic, Basilius presumes to interpret it and leaps to the conclusion that disaster lies ahead. This error leads naturally to his next mistake, his decision to try to avoid the blows of fortune (an attempt to go against the will of the gods, and doomed to failure, as *Oedipus* teaches us). Finally, for this purpose, he retires to the countryside for a year, putting the government into the hands of Philanax—an action shockingly at odds with Elizabethan notions of kingship. Though fortunate in his choice of a proxy ruler who is trustworthy, Basilius is nonetheless dooming his country to anarchy in the Renaissance view, because he is violating the hierarchy of political order upon which its well-being depends.

These acts occur in progression, but are from one point of view all one and the same mistake. In an existential sense Basilius not only abdicates his responsibility as king, but his personal identity as well; he declines to be who he really is—a negation already inherent in his decision to try to evade the will of the gods and escape his own fate.

The Elizabethan frame of reference for discussing this situation was that of a natural order of things which Basilius has violated. Ulysses' famous speech on 'degree' from *Troilus and Cressida* might serve as an epigram for Basilius' retirement: 'Take but degree away, untune that string, / And hark, what discord follows'. The king's abdication, disrupting the rightful order of the commonwealth at the very top of the hierarchy, is bound to lead to chaos in Arcadia just as surely as the abdication of reason will lead to madness in the individual. Sixteenth-century England would have sympathized with Philanax' advice to Basilius: 'Let your subjects have you in their eyes, let them see the benefits of your justice daily more and more; and so must they needs rather like of present sureties, than uncertain changes' (pp. 7–8).

Like *Gorboduc*, an earlier play which Sidney praised in the *Defence*, and *Lear*, which was to come twenty years later, the *Old Arcadia* reflects Renaissance concern lest the king, unmindful of his proper role, plunge the kingdom into anarchy. In all three works we find the *topos* of 'the world upside-down'.[15] Imagery of inversion reflects the disorder of affairs at every level—political, familial, and personal—stemming from the king's flawed leadership. It is the same imagery which occurs in Neville's translation of Seneca's *Oedipus*, where the chorus laments the city, disrupted by Oedipus' guilt: 'Nothing alas! remains at all in wonted old estate, / But all are turned topside-down, quite void and desolate'.[16] Lear, having given his kingdom into his daughters' hands, finds himself in a world in which parents are ruled by children, fools speak wisdom, kings can find no shelter, and reason gives way to madness.[17] Similarly, Basilius' retirement untunes the harmony of Arcadia, generating a world where shepherds are given charge of princesses, princes must disguise themselves as Amazons, and kings and queens make fools of themselves. In a series of ever-widening circles, his temporary abdication affects first his family, then the court, and finally the entire nation.[18]

Because the oracle seems to refer specifically to his two marriageable daughters, Pamela and Philoclea, Basilius takes particular care to guard them from the threatened 'princely mean' and 'uncouth love', by sequestering them in the countryside away from suitors and kinsmen. The daughters, who are not privy to their father's motive (he keeps the oracle secret from everyone but Philanax), naturally resent this disruption of all their normal activities, although they try to resign themselves to the situation. The intelligent older daughter, Pamela, is in a particularly galling position because she is put in the care of Dametas, a subservience emblematic of the topsy-turvy state of affairs Basilius has created.

Thus, when the two young princes, Pyrocles and Musidorus, arrive in Arcadia, having been thrown off course by a storm in their

---

[15] For a discussion of this *topos*, see E. Curtius, *European Literature and the Latin Middle Ages*, trans. W. Trask (New York, 1953), pp. 94–8.

[16] In *Seneca's Tragedies*, ed. E. Baade (New York, 1969), p. 12.

[17] See for instance Gloucester's speech, I. ii. 100ff. For studies of the relationship between the *Arcadia* and *Lear*, see D. M. McKeithan, '*King Lear* and Sidney's *Arcadia*', *Studies in English*, Univ. of Texas Bull. No. 14 (1934), pp. 45–9; F. Pyle, '"Twelfth Night", "King Lear" and "Arcadia"', *MLR* 43 (1948), 449–55: J. F. Danby, *Poets on Fortune's Hill* (London, 1952), Chs. 2, 3, and 4; and W. Elton, *King Lear and the Gods*, Ch. 3.

[18] The relation of the familial level to the individual and political levels has been studied by Isler. The private-folly–public-disorder theme has been studied by Davis, Chs. 5 and 6.

journey towards Byzantium to visit Pyrocles' father, Euarchus,[19] they are unable to meet the princesses at court in the customary way, but encounter, instead, a mysterious and tantalizing taboo against seeing the royal family. Having fallen in love with a picture of Philoclea—'it was Pyrocles' either evil or good fortune', says the narrator (p. 11), in the first of a series of ironic and ambiguous statements about love—Pyrocles can discover no means except disguise and subterfuge to court her, and Musidorus soon finds himself in the same dilemma with regard to Pamela.

Disguising themselves as an Amazon and a shepherd, respectively, the two young men are drawn into Basilius' upside-down world, where their disguises soon create new problems. Paradoxically, in order to follow his own natural bent, Pyrocles must go against nature by taking a woman's form. Sexual confusion compounds the muddle: Basilius further disgraces himself by falling in love with the Amazon visitor, while his queen, Gynecia, seeing through the disguise, becomes enamoured of the young man behind it, and Philoclea, responding to Cleophila's ardour, falls in love but thinks herself unnaturally attracted to a woman. Meanwhile, in parallel fashion, Musidorus' shepherd's apparel confuses the class distinctions upon which Arcadian society is built, for Pamela is attracted to the handsome stranger although her social conscience warns her that he is beneath her. Both princes are driven, paradoxically, to further deception in their very efforts to contrive occasions for revealing their real identities to their princesses.

The narrator's ironic comments on the princes in love range through all the negative Petrarchan metaphors of love as disease, wound, poison, slavery, and imprisonment. Their disguises enact literally the Ovidian–Petrarchan idea of love as metamorphosis.[20] Amused at the 'triumph of love' in the entire company, the narrator declares at the end of Book I that 'it seemed that love had purposed to make in those solitary woods a perfect demonstration of his unresistable force . . .' (p. 49). Though the princes are brave when opportunity arises, the narrator enjoys pointing out that Pyrocles is

<hr/>

[19] Here we find the first reference to providence regarding the princes, when the narrator says: 'But so pleased it God, who reserved them to greater traverses, both of good and evil fortune, that the sea . . . stirred with terrible tempest, forced them to fall far from their course' (pp. 10–11).

[20] For an interesting discussion of this motif, see E. Dipple, 'Metamorphosis in Sidney's *Arcadia*s', *PQ* 50 (1971), 47–62.

little better than the lion he slays in his attitude towards Philoclea as 'prey'.[21]

The young heroes are now seen to share in the human condition which also includes the narrator and his audience. Continuing through Book II to reinforce our sympathetic amusement with the young men in their human dilemma, the narrator shows them as admirable in the inventiveness with which they meet their burgeoning difficulties. In Book III, where they develop and carry out elaborate plots to elope with Pamela and Philoclea, he portrays them as bold and charming masqueraders able to keep their poise in a messy situation.[22] There is a *sprezzatura* in the manœuvres in which, with Chaucerian irony, they draw the impeding characters out of their way by playing to their vices.

But both plans go ironically awry. Musidorus and Pamela are first beset and captured by ruffians and then rescued by Arcadian soldiers, who arrest Musidorus for abducting the princess and return him to Basilius' lodge for trial. Pyrocles and Philoclea are discovered sleeping together by Dametas, who locks them into the chamber and then turns them over to Philanax to be tried for adultery. Despite our sympathy for them, we cannot escape the narrator's judgement that both princes deserve their dilemmas, for Pyrocles has put Philoclea in jeopardy by flouting the Arcadian law prescribing death for pre-marital intercourse, while Musidorus had been on the verge of sexually assaulting the sleeping Pamela when the ruffians attacked. Like Gawain in his encounter with the Green Knight, the heroes have discovered their human weakness and, like him, they will pay a price.

Meanwhile, events have also gone ironically awry in the dark cave where, hoping to meet Cleophila, Basilius has unwittingly fulfilled the oracle's prophecy that he would commit adultery with his wife. Also hoping to meet Cleophila (unveiled as the man she knows he is), Gynecia brings along a love potion given her by her mother. When her lover turns out to be her husband, she sets the potion aside although discreetly allowing him to go on thinking her the Amazon. Later, thirsty after his 'long disaccustomed pains', Basilius sees the potion and drinks it, thereupon collapsing like

[21] For a detailed discussion of this equivalence, and of the whole incident, see Marenco. See also Durling's discussion of Ariosto's similar treatment of love, Ch. 5.

[22] See my essay, 'Pastoral and Heroic: Sidney's *Arcadia* as Masquerade', *CL* 25 (1973), 308–20.

one dead. This unexpected outcome triggers Gynecia's guilt over her lust for Pyrocles, and, believing her husband's death a punishment of her own misdeeds, she surrenders herself to Philanax, declaring she has killed him.

Thus Sidney has tied the knot. Instead of bringing honour to their ladies by marrying them and restoring them to their proper courtly setting, as they had intended, the princes find their ladies disgraced and themselves imprisoned and accused of conspiracy, kidnapping, rape, and murder. Basilius is apparently dead, the queen a confessed murderess, and the kingdom in a state of chaos. As the narrator says at the beginning of Book V, 'the dangerous division of men's minds, the ruinous renting of all estates, had now brought Arcadia to feel the pangs of uttermost peril ...'. The responsibility for setting it all right rests on the shoulders of Philanax, who, though 'honest and wise', is 'equally distracted betwixt desire of his master's revenge and care of the state's establishment ...' (p. 351).

At this point Sidney sets a trap for the reader. Into the scene of disorder he introduces a traveller who has come to Arcadia on a friendly mission—none other than Euarchus, father of Pyrocles, uncle of Musidorus, and King of Macedonia. To Philanax, 'remembering withal the excellent trials of his equity which made him more famous than his victories', comes the welcome thought that 'he might be the fittest instrument to redress the ruins they were in ...' (p. 351). But we should beware of accepting Philanax' point of view too uncritically, for the plot does not bear out his providential expectations. Sidney is setting us up to be surprised, and manages this so skilfully that some readers, completely taken in, have refused to relinquish Philanax' providential theory even when events prove him wrong.[23] This may be partly because Philanax' theory is based upon the desire for order, and the belief that this can be achieved through human justice. I suppose many of us share his desire and would like to share his belief. Sidney's plot, however, has been constructed so as to frustrate it. Human

---

[23] In addition to the essays already cited by Lanham and Dipple, see also W. R. Davis's harsh view of the princes in 'Actaeon in Arcadia', *SEL* 2 (1962), 95–110. An example of his distortion of the plot is seen in this misleading quote: 'Pyrocles is ... condemned to death by the judgement of his own father as a monster, a shape-shifter "from all humanitie ... transformed", who "from a man grew a woman, for a woman a ravisher of women, thence a prisoner, and now a Prince. ..."' Here he conflates Philanax' railing with Euarchus' judgement.

reason—even the wisdom of Euarchus—proves unable to untie the knot. Only divine providence can bring release.

Philanax' providential theory is, in fact, only one of several hypotheses developed by the various characters as they struggle to read the meaning of events in order to try to extricate themselves from the knot in which they are entangled. None of these theories proves correct, and all illustrate, rather, the point made originally about Basilius' consulting the oracle—that it is futile and foolish to try to anticipate the workings of providence. All show, moreover, how the emotional needs of each character colour his logic and predispose him towards a biased interpretation of the will of the gods, just as they have influenced his behaviour all along. A look at the other theories is helpful in providing an appropriate context within which Philanax' view may be placed.

First, there is Basilius' notion. Wrestling alone with the oracle, he tries to convince himself that it is about to be fulfilled at the end of Book II (pp. 133–4). His obsession with Cleophila has taught him to misconstrue the adultery passage as a prediction that he will succeed in seducing her, and afterwards make her his wife. He manages to persuade himself that the other parts of the riddle may be explained so as to conform with this pleasing pattern. Basilius' theory of the workings of providence—originally based upon superstitious fear and a fond hope of avoiding fate—comes to be grounded no less fatuously upon wishful thinking.

Gynecia, who knows nothing of the oracle, has developed a providential theory based on guilt. Intelligent and clear-sighted from the first, she has always known it was wrong to love Cleophila, deceive her husband, and compete with her daughter. But her knowledge had no effect upon her 'infected will'; she did these things all the same.[24] Thus, convinced of her guilt already, she is completely unnerved by the unexpected and seemingly fatal outcome of her attempted assignation with Cleophila in the cave. When Basilius collapses after drinking the potion, she remembers a dream in which, hearing Cleophila's voice and trying to find her way to Cleophila over difficult terrain, she came instead upon the dead body of Basilius, who spoke to her and told her that here was her only 'rest'. Misinterpreting the dream in the same way Basilius has mistaken the oracle, she reads it as 'a direct vision of her fore-

---

[24] She is already constructing her melancholy view of providence as far back as Book II, p. 92: 'For nothing else did my husband take this strange resolution', etc.

appointed end' (p. 280), sees Basilius' unintended death as a judgement upon her, and believes that only death will free her from the torment of guilt. Accordingly, though innocent, she confesses to the murder of her husband.

It is interesting to note that the princes themselves have no theory of providence. During their meditations in prison on the night before the trial, their concern for each other leads each one to complain of the other's ill fortune, but they soon cease. 'O blame not the heavens, sweet Pyrocles', says Musidorus, 'as their course never alters, so is there nothing done by the unreachable ruler of them, but hath an everlasting reason for it. And to say the truth of these things, we should deal ungratefully with nature if we should be forgetful receivers of her good gifts, and so diligent auditors of the chances we like not' (p. 37). There is no indication that either of the princes sees the present calamity as a possible sign of the gods' disapproval of his behaviour. Their Stoic resignation is a step removed from the Christian view of a divine providence working through seemingly chance events, but it takes them farther than the attempts of Basilius, Gynecia, and Philanax to interpret the will of the gods.

Far from fulfilling Philanax' hopes for him as a providential instrument of moral redress, Euarchus ties the knot tighter. As the trial proceeds, he sentences Philoclea to spend the rest of her life in a nunnery, Gynecia to be buried alive with her husband, Pyrocles to be flung to his death from a tower, and Musidorus to be beheaded. Though all have erred in some degree, they certainly merit nothing like this. Just when things are at their blackest, a messenger arrives with news of the real identities of Pyrocles and Musidorus, who have hitherto concealed their true names. Ah, a recognition scene. Again our hopes rise, as they did at the initial appearance of Euarchus. But for the second time Sidney arouses our expectations and foils them. In an amazing display of absolute justice, Euarchus refuses to reverse his decision even though he now sees that it is his own son and nephew he has condemned to death.

The pattern should be clear. Sidney's intent in the trial sequence is to create a situation as astonishing and ironic as possible. Reversal is piled upon reversal, each growing plausibly out of the previous circumstances, and building just that chain of terrible inevitability which Aristotle had recommended for epic and tragedy.[25] Unlike Ariosto, Tasso, and Spenser, who achieve the marvellous through flying horses, magic rings, and other supernatural devices, Sidney manages the effect through natural means, thus consistently holding to the anti-superstition stance which the narrator has maintained throughout.

During the trial, the narrator pauses again and again to point out the ironies and marvels. Sidney has constructed the sequence in such a way that all the characters have a limited knowledge of the full situation and of each other's identities, while the reader knows everything except one crucial fact—that Basilius is not really dead. The reader is thus in suspense as to the outcome, yet in a position to see the irony of the characters' actions. He sympathizes with their reasons while knowing them to be based upon incomplete information.

Gynecia's special irony is that, in her remorse for her guilty love of Cleophila, she confesses to a far greater crime she did not commit—the murder of Basilius. It is true that she provided the potion, but she neither meant it for him nor had any idea of its effect. She confesses as the quickest way to death, believing God to have condemned her. At the trial she cuts off Philanax' eager accusations by becoming her own accuser. Her words stir the spectators, who had always liked her, to compassion. To us they reveal the suffering and despair of a woman over-reacting to her folly. But Euarchus deliberately steels himself against the emotional effect of her speech: 'Having well considered the abomination of the fact, attending more the manifest proof of so horrible a trespass, confessed by herself, and proved by others, than anything relenting to those tragical phrases of hers (apter to stir a vulgar pity than his mind, which hated evil in what colours soever he found it) . . . he definitively gave . . . sentence' (pp. 382–3). She is to be buried alive in Basilius' tomb. The narrator stresses the wonderful irony of the situation.

Thus the excellent lady Gynecia, having passed five and thirty years of her age even to admiration of her beautiful mind and body, and having not in her own knowledge ever spotted her soul with any wilful vice but her inordinate love of Cleophila, was brought, first by the violence of that ill-answered passion, and then by the despairing conceit she took of the judgement of God in her husband's death and her own fortune, purposely to overthrow herself, and confirm by a wrong confession that abominable

[25] *Poetics*, Chs. IX and XVI. Italian critics such as Minturno, Giraldi Cinthio, Pigna, and Tasso had stressed the importance of *meraviglia* in epic.

shame which, with her wisdom, joined to the truth, perhaps she might have refelled (p. 384).

The irony of Philanax' behaviour is that, out of the best of motives, he jumps to all the wrong conclusions. His devotion to Basilius, his king, turns to desire for revenge when he discovers his death. This passion causes him to accept Gynecia's confession at face value, turn a deaf ear to Philoclea's plea of love for Pyrocles, suppress the letters Philoclea and Pamela wrote which were meant for the judge, and bring to bear against Gynecia and the princes at the trial every sophisticated argument, every appeal to emotion, every distortion of the facts which he can muster. Out of love for the king he seeks to dishonour his daughters, condemn his wife to death, and bring death to the princes who had earlier served him. The narrator frequently refers to Philanax' 'zeal' during the trial. His behaviour illustrates that terrible self-righteous and mis-directed zeal through which a well-intentioned and basically good man, convinced that he has read God's signs rightly, can do a great deal of harm.

Of the multiple ironies surrounding Pyrocles and Musidorus, the most striking one comes from their desire to protect the honour of their ladies. Musidorus' first concern is for Pamela, and his first speech is on her behalf. Similarly, Pyrocles' first speech is a plea for Philoclea's innocence, based on the false contention that she never consented to his act. When Euarchus responds by announcing that Philoclea's life is spared, Pyrocles is delighted, even though this involves a 'great prejudicating' of his own case, since it means that he stands accused of rape. To the reader, the young men reveal their virtue by protecting their ladies. But Euarchus, who has no way of knowing what really happened, judges them on their given word. Later, when the messenger reveals the identity of the princes, and Euarchus refuses to change his judgement, the young men again reveal their nobility, each pleading to die in the other's stead. In their indifference to death and their love of the good, all three men at this point—Pyrocles, Musidorus, and Euarchus—demonstrate their Stoic virtue and claim our admiration, at the same time that they stand opposed to each other through a tragic and ironic misunderstanding.

Perhaps the most ironic figure of all is Euarchus. Since the misinterpretation of his role is at the centre of several recent readings of the *Old Arcadia*,[26] he must be considered in some detail. Philanax had first proposed the Arcadian trial to Euarchus as a kind of test of his renowned equity: 'a fair field to prove whether the goodly tree of your [Euarchus'] virtue will live in all soils'. 'Here it will be seen,' he had said, 'whether either fear can make you short or the lickerousness of dominion make you beyond justice' (p. 361). Sidney handles the trial scene in such a way that it becomes a test of Euarchus' justice as much as—perhaps more than—a trial of the guilt of the princes. Throughout the whole sequence, the narrator presents him as a paradigm of constancy, a man unmoved by appeals to the senses or the passions. He is 'neither beguiled with the painted gloss of pleasure nor dazzled with the false light of ambition. This made the line of his actions straight and always like itself, no worldly thing being able to shake the constancy of it ...' (pp. 357–8). During the trial his calm is played off against the violently emotional speeches of Philanax, Gynecia, and the two princes. His unemotional, measured response to these speeches is contrasted with the passionate outbursts of the crowd of Arcadians, who move from one extreme to another, responsive to whatever rhetorical appeal is being made to them. The supreme test of his integrity comes when the messenger brings word of the princes' identity. The people, 'amazed at the strange event of these matters' (p. 410), now switch their sympathy to the two young men. Even Philanax, their zealous accuser, relents. But Euarchus stands unmoved. He has passed the test.

Yet, paradoxically enough, at the same time that we admire his justice, we recognize it as unjust.[27] We respect Euarchus' justice because it represents his own incorruptibly honest evaluation of the situation, but we also see that even he, the exemplary Just Man, cannot judge rightly in this case because of his human limitations. With commendable humility, he himself has warned the Arcadians when they eagerly besought him to judge their troubled affairs: 'Remember I am a man; that is to say, a creature whose reason is often darkened with error' (p. 365). Among the factors which limit

---

[26] In general, scholars have accepted Euarchus as totally admirable. See, for instance, both Lanham and Davis in *Sidney's Arcadia*. A rare exception is Rose, who notes that Euarchus' judgement makes 'no allowance whatever for human imperfection' (p. 70).

[27] See Dipple, ' "Unjust Justice" ', for a discussion of this situation from a slightly different angle.

him, one of the most ironic is that the situation is 'so entangled a matter' (p. 375) that the real facts never come to light.[28] But perhaps the ultimate irony is that Euarchus' very imperviousness to emotion works against his discovering the truth. As it happens, the emotions expressed by the speakers are frequently a better clue to the reality of the situation than what they actually say, but Euarchus shuts his mind to everything but the circumstantial evidence and the substance of the testimony. Thus, ironically, the characters convince Euarchus of their guilt in the very same words with which they reveal to us their noble *ethos*.

Euarchus cannot untie this knot. The narrator points out the moral in another context: 'In such a shadow or rather pit of darkness the wormish mankind lives that neither they know how to forsee nor what to fear, and are but like tennis balls tossed by the racket of the higher powers' (pp. 385–6). If the point is not made explicitly by the narrator in relation to Euarchus, this is consistent with his earlier behaviour. As reluctant to spell out Euarchus' limitations as he was to scold the princes for going too far, he, rather, again allows the circumstances to speak for themselves. Once more Sidney's narrative tact spares his narrator the unpleasantness of having to comment adversely on a character who is fundamentally noble.

Sidney's ending is not meant to give 'an effect of ethical confusion', in Rowe's words, but, rather, a sense of life's paradoxes. A key to one of the major preoccupations of the *Old Arcadia* is the recurrent word 'strange'. Both the style, with its antitheses (in which the Petrarchan contraries fit so naturally) and frequent oxymorons, and the plot, with its ironic reversals, demonstrate this concern. The narrator, who can admire both Euarchus' justice and the princes' nobility, is neither untrustworthy nor cynical, but a faithful reflector of Arcadian complexity. The paradoxes of the human condition do not ultimately yield to human effort. Only providence can resolve them.

It is fitting that the happy ending should be achieved through Basilius, since it was he who, by consulting the oracle and trying to

---

[28] For instance, Gynecia has confessed to murdering Basilius out of her own generalized sense of guilt, although she actually did no such thing. Pyrocles has confessed to using force against Philoclea, although he did not actually do so. Philanax has suppressed important evidence, including the letters of the princesses which make it clear that they love the young men and regard them as their husbands.

evade its prediction, set the plot in motion in the first place. Basilius has been 'chastised' for his follies through his misadventure in the cave and his semi-death—merely an extreme extension, in one sense, of his original abdication. Just as it was ironically appropriate that Dametas should have been the 'instrument' of Pyrocles' humiliation, so it is fitting that Gynecia and Basilius have become the agents of each other's embarrassment and that Basilius, through his seeming death, has put all the characters into a jeopardy from which only his awakening can release them.

The *Old Arcadia* is a warning against superstition and the abdication of a king, and it is also an assertion of the power of providence to bring order out of human disorder, but it is more than these. By pitting human hopes and fears against a providential plot which inevitably works itself out, Sidney shows us the variety of inadequate responses of which well-intentioned human beings are capable when faced with life's paradoxes. The surprise ending is a means through which the inability of Basilius, Gynecia, and Philanax to anticipate providence is not only reinforced by Euarchus' failure, but dramatized by the reader's discovery of his own fallibility. The act of reading becomes a metaphor for the difficulty of reading life itself. The reader, motivated by his human desire for a happy ending, is adroitly led to identify with Philanax' hopes and then, when they miscarry, to expect resolution through the literary convention of the recognition scene. Suspense, thwarting of expectation, and surprise ending function thematically to show the reader that he, too, is caught in the same human dilemma in which the characters are enmeshed. The most convincing example Sidney offers for our emulation is not Euarchus, with his rigid literalistic interpretation of the law and Calvinistic condemnation of the individuals trapped in it, but the flexible narrator himself, whose mellow tact and ironic compassion for all the characters finally seem the most humane response to life's riddling text.

4. NARRATIVE METHODS IN SIDNEY'S
OLD ARCADIA

Walter Davis

The five 'Books' or 'Acts' into which Sidney's *Old Arcadia* was cast
are extremely important for an understanding of the romance, for
by such a division Sidney highlighted many facets of its theme, its
form, and its narrative method. Each of the four 'Eclogues' or verse
interludes between 'Books' sets up a theme that makes clear the
unity among diverse actions in the book preceding; the romance
therefore progresses book-by-book from the beginnings of passion,
through suffering under love, hope for success, and failure, to
reason's final judgement of the affair.[1] The word 'Act' furthermore
defines the structure of the romance as that of five-act drama
according to Donatus and other theorists;[2] each 'Book' or 'Act'
therefore, has not only its own thematic integrity but makes diverse
actions into measured parts of a continuous action. Moreover, each
of the five books is analogous in form, each proceeding from a static
ideal to its collapse in action.[3]

My thesis in this essay is that each of the books within the five-
act structure of the *Old Arcadia* has a distinct and different kind of
narrative method, and that the changes in narrative method book-
by-book are significant for the romance's meaning.

What immediately strikes one about Book I is its web of ironic
parallels. For example, when Pyrocles discovers Musidorus in
love, he (disguised as Cleophila) mocks him thus:

The perfect friendship Cleophila bare him, and the great pity she (by
good experience) had of his case could not keep her from smiling at him,
remembering how vehemently he had cried out against the folly of lovers;
so that she thought good a little to punish him, playing with him in this

Reprinted by permission of Rice University from *SEL* 18 (1978), 13–33.

[1] See W. R. Davis, 'Thematic Unity in the *New Arcadia*', *SP* 57 (1960), 126–7 and 135–
6; W. A. Ringler Jr., ed. *The Poems of Sir Philip Sidney* (Oxford, 1962), pp. xxxviii–xxxix;
and E. Dipple, 'The "Fore-Conceit" of Sidney's Eclogues', *Literary Monographs*, i, ed.
E. Rothstein and T. K. Dunseath (Madison, 1967), pp. 3–47.
[2] R. W. Parker, 'Terentian Structure and Sidney's Original *Arcadia*', *ELR* 2 (1972),
65–9, and C. L. Chalifour, 'Sir Philip Sidney's *Old Arcadia* as Terentian Comedy',
SEL 16 (1976), 51–63.
[3] E. Dipple, 'Harmony and Pastoral in the *Old Arcadia*', *ELH* 35 (1968), 322ff.

manner: 'Why, how now, dear cousin,' said she, 'you that were even now so high in the pulpit against love, are you now become so mean an auditor? Remember that love is a passion, and that a worthy man's reason must ever have the masterhood.' (p. 42.)[4]

Pyrocles is alluding to Musidorus' objection to him in an earlier scene: 'And let us see what power is the author of all these troubles: forsooth, love; love, a passion, and the basest and fruitlessest of all passions.' (p. 19.) That earlier scene had been filled with comic irony directed at Pyrocles: his wandering mind had caused a deliberative speech on contemplation to turn into a set piece in praise of Arcadia, thus forcing Musidorus to abandon his own counter-speech; and when Musidorus had entered into an examination of love, we found that Pyrocles was not listening, his mind 'all this while so fixed upon another devotion' (p. 20). That scene had led directly into a second in which Pyrocles, in fulfilment of his cousin's fear that 'love doth . . . womanize a man' (p. 20), appears disguised as an Amazon singing:

> Transformed in show, but more transformed in mind,
> I cease to strive, with double conquest foiled;
> For (woe is me) my powers all I find
> With outward force and inward treason spoiled. (p. 28.)

The scene centring on Musidorus is a studied answer to Pyrocles' scenes; Musidorus enters in disguise singing a counter-song to his:

> Come shepherd's weeds, become your master's mind:
> Yield outward show, what inward change he tries:
> Nor be abashed, since such a guest you find,
> Whose strongest hope in your weak comfort lies. (p. 40.)

The debate that follows is a parody of the earlier one, drawing Musidorus hence into its comic ambit; and Musidorus' account of falling in love matches Pyrocles'. It in turn leads to the climactic scene of the first book wherein a lion and a bear erupt into the landscape, the lion killed by Pyrocles in defence of his mistress Philoclea, the bear by Musidorus in defence of his mistress Pamela.

---

[4] Quotations are from *The Countess of Pembroke's Arcadia* (*The Old Arcadia*), ed. J. Robertson (Oxford, 1973), and page references are to that edition.

Book I is scenic, and the scenes revolve around deliberative oratory determining what is to be done (as Book V will be taken up with forensic oratory judging what has been done). The opening scene of the book is a debate between the Arcadian duke Basilius and the statesman Philanax about the advisability of retirement; Richard Lanham relates it to the amatory debates thus: 'This debate between the two friends, more elaborate than that between Philanax and Basilius, still turns on the same opposition of forces: the demands of duty and the active life on the one hand, and the pursuit of one's desires and hopes into a life of retirement on the other. Each of the "serious" double plots begins with a formal debate on the same subject.'[5] Thus Book I proceeds by paired scenes: the debate between Basilius and Philanax and the parallel debate between Pyrocles and Musidorus, the amorous disguise of Pyrocles and that of Musidorus, and the eruption of lion and bear with resulting rising action for both lovers.

The narrative method is discontinuous, closed, that of 'segmentation' wherein each episode is brought to a satisfactory conclusion before the next episode takes place; it stresses series, sequence.[6] Each scene is closed (the debate form helps the sense of closure by its pattern of speech–counter-speech) and is then juxtaposed to a succeeding analogous scene, usually with an effect of comic irony resulting from the reader's perception of likeness within distinctness. It is a method frequently used to give the reader a sense of overriding design that is not at all apparent to the characters involved, as in the case of Malory's tale of Balin where a series of analogous episodes roughs out the fate of the hero.[7]

After Book I, analogy between separate narrative segments will yield to more complex interrelations, and in fact the differing cases of the heroes establish a set of contrasts that subsequent books will pursue.[8] Musidorus clothed as a shepherd sings 'Come shepherd's weeds, become your master's mind', and most of his problems until the end of Book III will be concerned with his accommodation to his chosen position, forcing him into unusual postures of

[5] R. A. Lanham, *The Old Arcadia*, in R. A. Lanham and W. R. Davis, *Sidney's Arcadia* (New Haven, 1965), p. 204.

[6] See E. Vinaver, *The Rise of Romance* (New York and Oxford, 1971), pp. 95–6, and P. Johnson, *Form and Transformation in Music and Poetry of the English Renaissance* (New Haven, 1972), pp. 70–1.

[7] See W. R. Davis, *Idea and Act in Elizabethan Fiction* (Princeton, 1969), pp. 19–23.

[8] See further Davis, *Idea and Act*, p. 64.

humility or humiliation. Pyrocles, more radically altered by passion, is clothed as a woman and sings 'Transformed in show, but more transformed in mind';[9] his/her mode for much of the romance will consist of radical complications (Basilius loving her as a woman, Gynecia as a man) and will issue in several scenes of Ovidian metamorphosis visited both on himself and on those around him.

Book II continues the basic method of segmentation; however, now episodes are not held in parallel, but rather branch out into contrasts in action and in method. One contrast in method that figures large here is that of scene against summary: while we as readers receive the action in Pyrocles' plot directly in dramatized scenes, we receive Musidorus' in summary, often by means of his own narrations. The second book opens with a series of three scenes illustrating the statement at the beginning and end of the segment that 'in this one lodge was lodged each sort of grievous passions':[10] the complications to Pyrocles' affairs revealed in the soliloquies and scenes of Gynecia, Basilius, and Pyrocles himself, all of whom find radical changes in their souls. The narrator then draws our attention to Musidorus, centring on his mind, purposes, and point of view: 'he found that a shepherd's either service or affection was but considered of as from a shepherd, and the liking limited to that proportion.' (p. 98.) His solution to the problem of his lowly estate—and it is one that distances the reader from his affairs even further than the method of summary would normally do by itself—is to become a maker of fictions:

He resolved to take this mean for the manifesting of his mind—although it should have seemed to have been a way the more to have darkened it: he began to counterfeit the extremest love towards Mopsa that might be; and as for the love, so lively indeed it was in him (although to another subject) that little he needed to counterfeit any notable demonstration of it. He would busily employ himself about her, giving her daily some country tokens, and making store of love songs unto her. (pp. 98–9.)

He must create an allegorical fiction of his life in Arcadia, wherein Pamela must read 'Prince Musidorus' for 'the shepherd Dorus', 'Pamela' for 'Mopsa',[11] and so on. The distance between the literal

---

[9] See also p. 43, 'this captiving of us within ourselves which hath transformed the one in sex, and the other in state'.

[10] pp. 91 and 98.

[11] See further p. 99 and his allegorical song 'My sheep are thoughts', p. 107.

and allegorical levels is so great that the result is comic. For example, Musidorus praises 'Mopsa' in high Neoplatonic terms and in high style involving the appeals of anaphora:

O Mopsa, Mopsa, if my heart could be as manifest to you as it is uncomfortable to me, I doubt not the height of my thoughts should well countervail the lowness of my quality. Who hath not heard of the greatness of your estate? Who sees not that your estate is much excelled with that sweet uniting of all beauties which remaineth and dwelleth with you? Who knows not that all these are but ornaments of that divine spark within you which, being descended from heaven, could not elsewhere pick out so sweet a mansion? (p. 100.)

And the response from the literal level (and a low level it is) is this:

Mopsa (who already had had a certain smackering towards Dorus) stood all this while with her hand sometimes before her face, but most commonly with a certain special grace of her own, wagging her lips and grinning instead of smiling. But all the words he could get of her was (wrying her waist): 'In faith, you jest with me; you are a merry man indeed!' (p. 100.)

Many times over in the course of this account, we see Musidorus' and Pamela's high resolves and words thus undercut by Mopsa's low style.[12]

Musidorus has made his life a fiction. Throughout all his complicated gambits, he has sought to solve the problem of accommodating his desires to his position by creating a world that mediates between his actual position and his real higher nature. Life once cast into fiction, actions become distanced into summary and adventures pulled into the comic mode by exploiting diverse responses. Narrative methods and tones are now diverging, for Pyrocles' actions are dramatically presented, and are tragic and pathetic.

The remainder of the second book is devoted to three highly wrought metaphorical scenes of suffering, reversal, metamorphosis. The first of them is the remarkable scene of Philoclea's fall (the religious terms are insistent)[13] from innocence into experience by love's means. Full of the turbulence of her newly felt passion, she enters by moonlight a grove where she finds an ancient altar that she

[12] For example, Pamela's summary of Dorus' love and Mopsa's reply, pp. 101–2, or Musidorus' account of his real-life adventures and Mopsa's response, pp. 105–6.

[13] See, for example, p. 108 on the knowledge of good and evil.

had previously made the emblem of her mind, its white marble standing for her virginity. The altar of chastity and the moonlight of the virgin goddess Diana, however, now stand only to accuse her (p. 110), and, still keeping the altar an emblem, she writes a recantation proclaiming her change; as she does so the skies too change as if in response to her:[14] 'In this depth of her muses there passed a cloud betwixt her sight and the moon which took away the present beholding of it. "O Diana," said Philoclea, "I would . . . the cloud that now hides the light of my virtue would as easily pass away as you will quickly overcome this let"'. (pp. 111–12.) A remarkable scene this, the whole of it governed by the metamorphic moon, the altar passing in change from a projection of the mind to its accuser, in keeping with the action recorded.

The second scene contrasts the first in its emblematic imagery, for in it Philoclea discovers Pyrocles lamenting beside a river whose sands (in contrast to the altar stone) he makes an emblem of the mutability and flux he has subjected himself to (p. 118). The two lovers then use the sands as symbols of their shifting identities, his in his disguise, hers in the new womanhood she has discovered in herself; they sense this mutability as tragic and psychically disorienting (p. 120). But now, in complement to the altar scene, the process they undergo is from shapelessness to form. As Pyrocles reveals his true estate and love, Philoclea her full-hearted response to his love, they come alive to each other:

The joy which wrought into Pygmalion's mind while he found his beloved image wax little and little both softer and warmer in his folded arms, till at length it accomplished his gladness with a perfect woman's shape, still beautified with the former perfections, was even such as, by each degree of Cleophila's words, stealingly entered into Philoclea's soul, till her pleasure was fully made up with the manifesting of his being. . . . (p. 120.)

Philoclea becomes joyful like Pygmalion at seeing her hopes become formed into a real being; the growth of warmth and softness in itself images the materialization both of hope and of her own state, as love softens her; and as her lover's words steal into her soul *she* is likewise transformed, by his words, and she feels like both the lover and the beloved, sculptor and statue.

This beautiful scene is broken by inroads of emotions both

[14] The use of moonlight as a symbol here is rather like Dickens's poetic use of sunset and moonrise on the Dedlocks in Ch. 40 of *Bleak House*.

strong and corrupt, as Gynecia enters enraged; this third scene
culminates a process of enchainment whereby to loss of innocence
and the full tide of love succeeds the decay of love into jealousy.
The state of Gynecia's mind divided by 'two strange fires' of love
and jealousy is presented by the narrator in terms of warfare: 'she
began to denounce war to all the works of earth and powers of
heaven. But the envenomed heat which lay within her gave her not
scope for many words, but (with as much rageful haste as the
Trojan women went to burn Aeneas's ships) she ran headlongly
towards the place ...' (p. 122.) Her private passion, imaged as
warfare, almost seems to erupt literally into what had been
metaphor, for as she begins to reveal her state she is in turn
interrupted by another sort of tumult, a public one: 'Then began
she to display to Cleophila the storehouse of her deadly desires,
when suddenly the confused rumour of a mutinous multitude gave
just occasion to Cleophila to break off any such conference.'
(p. 123.) Gynecia's mind has projected itself on to the peasants'
rebellion and the scene, like one large metaphor spread over all the
tumultuous events of the second book, becomes its fitting climax.

Segmentation has continued as the method of Book II, but it is
used quite differently from Book I. The two plots are not now
juxtaposed in parallel, but have become broad contrasts in many
ways—scenic versus summary, tragic versus comic. And the plots
have developed a symmetrical rhythm: three brief scenes from one
plot, one large summary from the other, three highly developed
scenes from the first plot.

Book III intensifies the contrasts between the plots of Pyrocles
and Musidorus, but complicates the tone of the romance by
bringing the plots into close relation, not by juxtaposition but by
interlace, which replaces segmentation as the characteristic
narrative method. The book opens with narratorial insistence on
the interaction of contraries, in a scene wherein the two lovers
compare their respective progresses in love. Musidorus' fortunes
have been happy, and his talk is spiced with courtly wit,[15] while
Pyrocles' tone is unwaveringly grim. Their contrasting postures
are gathered into two contrasting songs: Musidorus says 'I will
now sauce those sorrows with some more pleasant exercises', and
sings a happy song (p. 170); Pyrocles defines their contrast as a

---

[15] See the comment on Musidorus' customary eloquence, p. 173.

literary one—'I will mingle your comical tunes with my long used tragical notes'—and sings a point-by-point parody of his cousin's song (p. 171).

The plot comes to focus on Pyrocles even more fully than before in this book; the narrator's summary of Musidorus' happy progress raises in Pyrocles' mind and from his point of view 'the images of her own fortune; her tedious longings; her causes to despair . . . loathsomely loved, and dangerously loving' (p. 174), pathetic emotions that come to rest in a scene of parting. The approach of Basilius modulates the tone to satiric irony: '"Alas", said Cleophila, "behold an evil foretoken of our sorrowful departure. Yonder see I one of my furies" . . . Cleophila [went] towards Basilius, saying to herself with a scornful smiling, "yet hath not my friendly fortune wholly deprived me of a pleasant companion."' (p. 176.) And when Pyrocles escapes from his elderly lover into a nearby cave, the irony becomes tragic.[16]

Escaping into the cave to give vent to his passions, Pyrocles finds it a fit emblem for his mind, and so his songs there re-echo with its darkness ('passions dark', 'dungeon dark'). But he also finds that it has become an emblem for another, for the mind of Gynecia, whom he will find there: certain lines of her verse he either finds or hears there echo his,[17] and their separate songs are linked by rhyme, his entrance song a sonnet rhyming on 'dark' and 'light' (pp. 179–80), her first song rhyming on 'dark' sounds in the octave and her second song rhyming entirely on 'light' and its rhymes (pp. 180–1). Their songs present two minds engulfed in the common imagery of 'passions dark' having obscured 'reason's light' in the cave, and of course Pyrocles must face the discovery that his enemy Gynecia, a self-confessed villainess, feels very much the same emotions towards him as he does toward her daughter. His penetration of the cave forces on him a growing consciousness of the reality of Gynecia and her lust, and an exploration of his own mind and the potential depths of his passion as well. The scene, with its emphasis on a place expressive of the mind and its changes, is Pyrocles' parallel to Philoclea's moonlight scene at the altar, and the transformation it records is similarly one from innocence to a very radical kind of experience:

[16] I have treated this cave scene more fully in 'Actaeon in Arcadia', *SEL* 2 (1962), 95–110.

[17] See Davis, 'Actaeon in Arcadia', p. 108.

Pyrocles had assumed that his love had nothing in common with his persecutor's, but he is now forced to admit that the membrane dividing his own carefully practised continence from Gynecia's outrageous lust is very thin indeed. A reversal of position, a change of mind, and the tragic note emerges fully: Gynecia, in discovering him as he had her, cries, 'I will not be the only actor of this tragedy'. (p. 184.) Shortly after this cry the narrator breaks off the action.

Jean Robertson is the latest critic to have called our attention to the intrusive narrator of the *Old Arcadia*, and she does so by citing Sir John Harington's notice of him in 1591:

One [objection is] that he [Ariosto] breaks off narrations verie abruptly, so as indeed a loose unattentive reader will hardly carrie away any part of the storie: but this doubtlesse is a point of great art, to draw a man with a continuall thirst to reade out the whole worke, and toward the end of the booke to close up the diverse matters briefly and clenly. If S. *Philip Sidney* had counted this a fault, he would not have done so himselfe in his Arcadia.[18]

Actually, the narrator advances and retreats in the *Old Arcadia*. In Book I he is intrusive, always at hand in moments of transition, his function being to keep the theme of love uppermost in the reader's mind.[19] He is almost totally absent in Book II, on the other hand, so that the reader can perceive close up the interplay between the characters' own diverse points of view. He is most to the fore here in Book III,[20] and his chosen function here is not as presenter of theme but rather, as Harington put it, 'to draw a man with a continuall thirst to reade out the whole worke,' to create suspense, and to draw attention to the interlace that carries suspense.

Interlace is continuous or open-ended, in distinction from segmentation; in this method of plot management, one episode is brought near its climax and then dropped while another episode is introduced, and so forth. Unlike segmentation, interlace involves a violation of time; as Eugene Vinaver writes, 'since it is always possible, and often even necessary, for several themes to be presented simultaneously, they have to alternate like threads in a

---

[18] Harington, Preface to the translation of *Orlando Furioso* in *Elizabethan Critical Essays*, ed. G. G. Smith (2 vols., Oxford, 1904), ii, 216–17; quoted in Robertson, *The Countess of Pembroke's Arcadia*, pp. xxii–xxiii.

[19] For example, pp. 27, 38, 39–40, 49, 54–5.

[20] For example in the early part of Book III, pp. 172, 176, 178.

woven fabric, one theme interrupting another and again another, and yet all remaining constantly present in the author's and the reader's mind.'[21] Interlace is characteristic of Greek romance, and Paula Johnson finds it the typical method of the revised *New Arcadia*,[22] so often described as the *Old* rewoven on the loom of Heliodorus,[23] where its effect is to give the reader a constant sense of suspenseful motion in the relatively static context of all the new inserted material.

As we return to our plot, it is interesting to notice that, as the interview between Pyrocles and Gynecia draws us on towards its tragic crisis, the narrator intervenes to announce contrast as a means of working up suspense: 'But me thinks I hear the shepherd Dorus calling me to tell you something of his hopeful adventures.' (p. 185.) These adventures form a comic interlude, in fact, a series of three jests playing on three diverse passions, of covetousness, jealousy, and curiosity. Still operating as fiction-maker, Musidorus contrives significant reversal scenes whereby each of his clogs will be removed by his master passion so that he can elope; and he has broadened the tone of his fictions into jests. For Dametas he invents buried treasure; for Miso he creates an intricate allegorical fiction of Dametas' love-affair with one Charita ('Love' to counter Miso or 'hate'). Here the focus falls on Musidorus' delight in his jest by stressing his facial contortions: he 'framed towards her such a smiling countenance as might seem to be mixed between a tickled mirth and a forced pity', 'then with a formal countenance' (p. 189), and so on. With Mopsa he plays the part of yokel:

So that Dorus was compelled to take her in the manner he first thought of, and accordingly, Pamela sitting musing at the strange attempt she had condescended unto, and Mopsa hard by her (looking in a glass with very partial eyes), Dorus put himself between them, and casting up his face to the top of the house, shrugging all over his body, and stamping sometimes upon the ground, gave Mopsa occasion (who was as busy as a bee to know anything) to ask her lover Dorus what ailed him that made him use so strange a behaviour?

He (as if his spirits had been ravished at some supernatural contemplation) stood still mute, sometimes rubbing his forehead,

---

[21] Vinaver, p. 76; see also p. 81 on the effect of interlace on the reader's experience.
[22] Johnson, pp. 82–90.
[23] See S. Lee Wolff, *The Greek Romances in Elizabethan Prose Fiction* (New York, 1912), pp. 353 and 350.

sometimes starting in himself; that he set Mopsa in such an itch of inquiry that she would have offered her maidenhead rather than be long kept from it. (pp. 193–4.)

And he comes out with 'a far fet tale' (derived from the myth of Admetus) about a magic wishing tree. Musidorus operates in this interlude as jester; he is enjoying a set of roles ('to play his last part', p. 193), entering into the fun, and constantly exhibiting in his pliable face that enjoyment ('I must needs a little accord my countenance with others' sport', p. 189).[24]

When he enters on his own action in abducting Pamela, the tone modulates towards the tragic. To give up his role as jesting manipulator, always in control of expectations and their subsequent reversals, and act out his own desires instead, endangers control. And the narrator emphasizes difficult balance, between fear and desire, reason and passion, in the enterprise (p. 196 for example). Fragile control of this sort collapses when Musidorus, idly gazing on his sleeping mistress, anatomizes her body in a battle metaphor that expresses the inroads of passion on his mind, and that then becomes literal as the rebels enter and start a real battle (pp. 201–2). The shift from metaphorical battle of the senses to actual battle (as in the end of Book II), completing rebellion in the soul by rebellion in the state, expresses fully the confusions one faces when turning from the comic world of control to the tragedies of real unstructured existence.

Again the narrator intervenes to leave us in suspense, and when he returns us to the cave it is an exchange from uncontrolled tragic reversal to the regaining of some control in Pyrocles, whose skill in manipulating people calls attention to the narrator's skill in interlacing plots: 'But Cleophila (whom I left in the cave hardly bested, having both great wits and stirring passions to deal with) makes me lend her my pen awhile to see with what dexterity she could put by her dangers.' (p. 202.) Appropriately, Pyrocles' action here typifies control, for it is a deliberative oration in the plain style ('resolved now with plainness to win trust', p. 203); with the establishment of some moderate verbal control and the uniting of minds in Gynecia's belief that Pyrocles does actually love her, the tone of this plot-strand evens out. Hence the exit from the cave marks a point of symmetry: they meet Basilius (from whom

[24] See also p. 186.

Pyrocles had fled into the cave in the first place), and he is singing
a madrigal, rhyming on sounds derived from 'dark' and 'light',
addressing the setting sun and rejecting it for 'Cleophila' as
metaphorical sun (p. 207). The song echoes the one he had sung
before the cave episode (p. 177) and it is in these songs that
Basilius completes his foolish reversal of values (as if the cave
scene were a pivot for him too), preferring a woman to the sun-god
Apollo that he, as king, serves.[25] And so, in addition to symmetry
by character and light imagery, there is a symmetry of tone here,
for we have returned to the irony and satire with which Pyrocles'
adventures in Book III began.

Pyrocles' next enterprise brings his activities into parallel with
his cousin's: feigning love to both Basilius and Gynecia in manner
like 'a prologue to the play' (p. 215), he arranges a tryst with each of
them at the cave a few nights hence, at which time he plans to
consummate his love for Philoclea. This is not quite the jest-book
material we have seen earlier, but rather sophisticated comedy of
cross-purposes, in which the effect grows from discordant points
of view as the lovers bustle about 'to deceive each other' (p. 223).
Gynecia lies waiting full of ironic expectation in Pyrocles' bed in
the cave. And Basilius sneaks out of the marital bed where he
thinks his wife lies, little realizing that it is in fact occupied by
Pyrocles, the 'woman' he desires.

Pyrocles has set up ironic parallel plots of consummation all
centring significantly on bed-scenes, and the narrator is present
both to underscore the irony to the characters and to create
suspense in his readers. At this point in Book III interlacing plots
are pushed to completion by Pyrocles' attempt to consummate his
own love with Philoclea, in a similar manner to that used by
Musidorus with Pamela, and at the very same time, as the narrator
insists (p. 217). As the grove scene modulated from comedy to
tragedy, so the bedroom scene modulates from the pathetic to high
comedy.

Of the bedchamber scene Richard Lanham writes, 'One cannot
belittle the style of this scene. It is subtle, amusing, and touching'.[26] Its tone arises in part from the speeches, each exhibiting a

---

[25] Thus it is that the whole motive for the Arcadian adventures comes from the oracle
of Apollo (p. 5), its assumed fulfilment at the end of Book II (pp. 133–4), and its actual
fulfilment at the end of Book V.

[26] Lanham, p. 283.

new set of cross-purposes, he seeking relief, she seeking satisfaction for her hurt (for she has believed in his feigned love for her
mother); in part it arises from the alternation of narrative comment
and action centring on the characters' own inner views (for
example, pp. 227–8 and 230). The action that ends the scene is
comically indirect, for in Pyrocles' swoon is combined erotic excitement and idealistic grief; and when Philoclea brings him out of
his swoon he awakens only to greater sexual excitement, and deals
with it by fantasizing in a long anatomy of his mistress he had heard
before this. Upon this song, and the state of mind it shows, the narrator intervenes to undercut all in concluding:

But do not think, fair ladies, his thoughts had such leisure as to run over
so long a ditty; the only general fancy of it came into his mind, fixed upon
the sense of that sweet subject. Where, using the benefit of the time, and
fortifying himself with the confessing her late fault (to make her now the
sooner yield to penance), turning the passed griefs and unkindness to the
excess of all kind joys (as passion is apt to slide into his contrary),
beginning now to envy Argus's thousand eyes, and Briareus's hundred
hands, fighting against a weak resistance, which did strive to be
overcome, he gives me occasion to leave him in so happy a plight, lest my
pen might seem to grudge at the due bliss of these poor lovers whose
loyalty had but small respite of their fiery agonies. (pp. 242–3.)

In this scene pathos constantly modulates towards comedy by the
rich and deliberate erotic detail and by the intrusive narrator
whose detachment is always distancing us from the action.

   Book II had separated the actions of the two heroes, making one
pathetic and the other comic, and had held them side by side for
purposes of contrast in action, form, and style, as well as tone.
Book III, in drawing the action together at the moment of its
turning, made the two actions distant parallels in form and
interlaced them so that a point of suspense in one action became a
lead-in to the other. In so doing, Sidney not only made the hitherto
separate plots interdependent, but he also gradually blended their
tones.

   With Book IV their interdependence becomes complete,
because it is the backfiring of Musidorus' plans that brings about
the discovery and failure of Pyrocles. Interlace yields to almost
logical cause–effect linkage between one action and another, and
in the process the heroes lapse from motivators of intrigue to its
victims, to elements in a large half-understood design. 'The

Fourth Book or Act' opens with what will become an insistent assertion of design among diverse events, and with a new tone of stern moral judgement on events, replete with appeals to divine providence:

The everlasting justice (using ourselves to be the punishers of our faults, and making our own actions the beginning of our chastisement, that our shame may be the more manifest, and our repentance follow the sooner) took Dametas at this present (by whose folly the others' wisdom might receive the greater overthrow) to be the instrument of revealing the secretest cunning—so evil a ground doth evil stand upon, and so manifest it is that nothing remains strongly but that which hath the good foundation of goodness. For so it fell out . . . (p. 265.)

This note is the ironic introduction to a series of comic un-windings whereby each of the three clowns' disappointments and reversals spirals upwards towards disaster. Dametas' disappointment is presented in mock-heroic terms, as he knocks his head, howls, grunts like a she-goat in labour 'with such grudging lamentations as a nobler mind would (but more nobly) make for the loss of his mistress' (p. 266). When he discovers Mopsa in the tree, her very physical fall is made to suggest the pride to which they have all fallen prey:

for Dametas, rubbing his elbow, stamping and whining, seeing neither of these take place, began to throw stones at her, and withal to conjure her by the name of hellish Mopsa. But when he had named her the third time, no chime can more suddenly follow the striking of a clock than she, verily thinking it was the god that used her father's voice, throwing her arms abroad, and not considering she was muffled upon so high a tree, came fluttering down like a hooded hawk, like enough to have broken her neck, but that the tree, full of boughs, tossed her from one bough to another, and lastly well bruised her to receive an unfriendly salutation of the earth. (p. 267.)

The whole scene is done over with dogged physicality—gesture, the hard intractability of objects, the central importance of the sense of touch as the main conveyor of knowledge. After the fall, pain:

'O where is Pamela?' said Dametas.
'O a lusty husband!' said Mopsa.
Dametas (that now verily assured himself his daughter was mad) began utterly to despair of his life; and therefore amazedly catching her in his

arms, to see whether he could bring her to herself, he might feel the weight of a great cudgel light upon his shoulders, and for the first greeting he knew his wife Miso's voice by the calling him 'ribald villain', and asking him whether she could not serve his turn as well as Charita. (pp. 268–9.)

The scene descends to a Punch and Judy show, as Miso continues to pursue 'the wooden salutation you heard of' (p. 270) and all three cry out in 'rude discord', ' "O Pamela", "O my dun cow", "O wife Miso", "O hands" ' (pp. 271–2).[27]

This low comedy is what leads, in the most unlikely fashion, to the discovery of Pyrocles and Philoclea in bed together, as Dametas rushes at random from chamber to chamber of the lodge:

But Dametas, looking with the lamp in his hand, but neither with such a face nor mind, upon these excellent creatures, as Psyche did upon her unknown lover, and giving every way freedom to his fearful eyes, did not only perceive it was Cleophila (and therefore much different from the lady he sought), but that this same Cleophila did more differ from the Cleophila he and others had ever taken her for. (p. 273.)

The discovery itself, as the discordant allusion to Cupid and Psyche indicates, is still within the mock-heroic mode. But it changes as soon as Dametas goes out; and his strictly limited point of view (of whose limits the narrator's mock-heroic style makes us aware), which allows our sense of unwitting human co-operation with providence to come through clearly, is exchanged for that of others.

As Book III was the book of the cave and darkness, so Book IV is the book of dawn and light, for all of the main characters awaken from sleep to find a clear light, both literal and figurative, cast on their deeds. Basilius awakens and, looking on Gynecia for Cleophila, 'did now (being helped by the peeping light wherewith the morning did overcome the night's darkness) know her face and his error' (p. 276); to Gynecia's accusations of guilt he replies with sincere repentance, but then accidentally drinks poison, at which point it is Gynecia who erupts with guilt in a speech responding to the dark suggestiveness of the episode as if it were stage tragedy (pp. 280, 281).

---

[27] On some comic word-play in this episode, see Robertson's notes, p. 467; on the comic subplot in general, see R. N. Reeves III, *The Ridiculous to the Delightful: Comic Characters in Sidney's New 'Arcadia'* (Cambridge, Mass., 1974).

So far in Book IV, the point of view has shifted from Dametas' shallow view coloured by the narrator to the deep point of view (into which we enter fully) in Gynecia's own words, and the tone has shifted from comic to tragic. That tragic tone is generally fixed, in this book, in the choric voice of the Arcadian populace, whose concern catapults events into their broadest field of importance. Such was the case at the news of Basilius' death (p. 274), and so it is now that it has been confirmed; the shepherds cast the tragic into formal ritual by their mourning and their ceremonial sestina 'Since wailing is a bud of causeful sorrow', making the case universal: 'Lastly, having one after the other cryingly sung the duke's praise and his own lamentation, they did all desire Agelastus, one notably noted among them as well for his skill in poetry as for an austerely maintained sorrowfulness ... to make an universal complaint for them in this universal mischief ...' (p. 284.) Twice now we have observed the growth of design in a strange co-operation of human purposes and 'natural' accidents as first Musidorus' and then Pyrocles' plans backfire and cause reversal. The book of discoveries is governed by growing light: to Basilius' dawn (p. 276) succeeds, two hours later (p. 285), the advent of Philanax, who becomes the central intelligence for most of the rest of Book IV.[28] It was he who 'saw the body of his dearly beloved Prince and heard Gynecia's waymenting' (p. 286), and he responded by putting the state into some provisional strict military order and by acting as the agent of a rather severely conceived divine justice, 'seeking just revenge' while being 'transported with an unjust justice' (p. 287). His accidental arrival with troops both illustrates the assertion of providence which the opening promised and helps to carry it out into action. He underlines design. And until the end of this fourth book all actions will undergo a rhythmic return to Philanax, who will view each anew and redirect each to the end of strict justice, as he has done here. As that happens, accident becomes redefined as design, as part of an obscure causal chain. Philanax it is who redefines for us, who seeks to make random events causative, and who by judging them draws out their effects.

The second occurrence of such a rhythm begins when dawn comes to Pyrocles (p. 289); when he, like Gynecia, realizes the

[28] On his character and point of view, see W. R. Davis, *A Map of Arcadia: Sidney's Romance in its Tradition*, in Lanham and Davis, pp. 160–1; also E. Dipple, '"Unjust Justice" in the *Old Arcadia*', *SEL* 10 (1970), 83–101.

terrible consequences of his deeds, he utters an impassioned tragic speech and attempts suicide so as to exonerate his beloved. But— once more the intrusion of accident into design—his attempt fails and only succeeds in awakening Philoclea. To accidental action succeeds formal oratory on the very nature of a universe in which accident and design become problematic; the two lovers debate the lawfulness of suicide, and into their debate enters a full range of ideas about the nature and value of life as conceived by pagan and by Christian.[29] Action has produced questions of value obviously central to the dominating theme of Book IV, and after those questions have been pursued the episode ends with a narrative assertion of the rightness of Philoclea's view as Philanax casts the cold eye of judgement on the whole affair after it has fallen into his hands.

Musidorus goes through the same sort of rhythm. A guilty awakening (p. 306), a serio-comic battle with the rebels who, like Dametas, are said to be 'guided by the everlasting justice to be chastisers of Musidorus's broken vow' (p. 307), resulting in capture, a debate between the lovers on patience, a formal oration by Musidorus at dawn, ending with their deliverance to the governing figure Philanax.[30]

The final movement of this 'Book or Act' shifts to the public realm, a tumult of the populace (through whose reactions we have hitherto viewed the events of private life) which presents 'a notable example how great dissipations monarchal governments are subject unto' (p. 320) and again comes to rest with Philanax, who counsels moderation.[31] With his partial resolution of the problems of state, sunset comes: 'the sun, I think, a-weary to see their discords, had already gone down to his western lodging.' (p. 326.)

The narrator's presence is not strongly felt in Book IV, and when he does intervene it is not to produce the suspense proper to interlacing strands of action but instead to insist on the presence of divine justice beneath all the events. This book is more closely dominated by theme than any other, and the projection of that theme into narrative method is to bind together a great many unrelated actions both purposeful and accidental and then to point

[29] For an analysis of these positions, see Davis, *A Map of Arcadia*, pp. 80–1.
[30] The meeting of Pyrocles and Musidorus leads to another solemn debate on heaven in Book V; see Davis, *A Map of Arcadia*, pp. 81–2.
[31] See Davis, *A Map of Arcadia*, pp. 154–6, on disorder in the state.

to that binding as evidence of divine justice. Each phase of the action proceeds so as to lead the reader to discover design, and the coming to rest of each phase in the firm hands of Philanax helps draw that design into the open. Whereas in Book III comic and tragic double plots interlaced, here we observe a neat progression from comic causes to tragic effects. The growing closeness with which narrative segments interrelate is stressed by the unity of the book—its theme asserted, demonstrated, discussed, all of its actions occurring within one day defined by a sunrise and sunset that express the heavens' half-noticed control over human affairs.

The Fifth and Last Book or Act intensifies our sense of control as it draws all strands of action together. It is dominated by a single scene, a trial that represents the ceremonial public muster of the newly unified state operating in conformity with its own laws. The populace of Arcadia sees it all and reacts to it like a chorus; Philanax the voice of harsh divine punishment presents the action to the judge and the court crowd; and the whole is presided over by Euarchus, at one and the same time the just ruler and father and uncle to the accused. Euarchus serves as the central intelligence here, for what we readers receive is what events he sees and hears of and how he judges them; and to pass from Philanax to Euarchus as centres is to move from a mind passionate with desire for revenge to a steady, settled mind dominated by the humility proper to humanity.[32] This single scene, a final act of order, is designed to highlight elements of pattern in the events in Arcadia and to redefine these events in accord with that pattern. Through Euarchus' eyes and ears, it tries to answer questions about what it is that has happened and how we are to evaluate it.

The narrative method changes to pure summary. The action is over, and what is needed is to compact, interrelate, and interpret events, so that what Sidney here is, in effect, offering the reader is several different possible versions of his romance. Three possible summaries of the plot of *Arcadia* are offered here, and, since they are quite different kinds of stories, they call up questions about what sort of thing fiction is. The characters have become story-tellers, and their Arcadian audience a surrogate for the reader.

The first version is Philanax's. For him, the events in Arcadia were connected from beginning to end by a single clear purpose,

[32] On Euarchus see Davis, *A Map of Arcadia*, pp. 101–2.

that being Pyrocles' regicidal plot; his original disguise was meant to beguile the king, Gynecia was a party to the plot, and even the ravishment of Philoclea was meant to cover up usurpation by marriage. Philanax's version of the story is totally political in theme; it is like a moral exemplum ('a short and simple story', he calls it, p. 388) designed to illustrate rather than test a precept; and its characters are drawn like caricatures in black and white. Philanax's story is most formal in its presentation, the *Narratio* section of a forensic oration in fact, and it is a melodrama formed by rigid selection therefore. He is a very self-conscious narrator— 'I shall need to be but a brief recounter and no rhetorical enlarger, of this most harmful mischief,' he avers (p. 386)—and therefore constantly refers to his story in stage terms (p. 389, for example), and attempts to counter audience disbelief in its rigid symmetry: 'neither do I think your virtuous ears will be able to endure the report of them, but will rather imagine you hear some tragedy invented of the extremity of wickedness than a just recital of a wickedness indeed committed.' (p. 386.)

To this didactic tale Pyrocles opposes a first-person narrative with his own inside view, in the plain style (p. 392). For him, it has been a love-story, and, far from being a simple purposeful plot, it has no order but is composed of starts, mistakes, failures, and new starts—a tangled skein of purpose and accident. He criticizes Philanax's simple version as 'having mingled truths with false-hoods, surmises with certainty, causes of no moment with matters capital, scolding with complaining' (p. 392), and he offers at best 'the thread to guide you in the labyrinth this man of his tongue had made so monstrous' (p. 393). Pyrocles' is a more realistic narrative than Philanax's, but not as useful forensically, because it baffles the judgement of its auditors—necessarily so because it is a story about love, 'a passion far more easily reprehended than refrained' (p. 392).

Pyrocles' was a counter-oration to Philanax's, but with the accusation and reply of Musidorus the speeches lapse into informality and even scurrility. Musidorus' version avoids both a theoretical singleness of scheme on the one hand and a welter of unexamined experience on the other, and in doing so presents us with a plot (and a concept of plot) as incomplete pattern. He moves away from vexed questions of purposiveness, refuses to analyse motives, and instead focuses on effects, stressing the good results of actions no matter what their motives, and pleads the 'just excuses of love's force'; 'our doing', he says, 'in the extremest interpretation is but a human error' (p. 402).

The three versions of the action of *Arcadia*—as single purposeful act, as mixture of purpose and accident, and as bewildering ambiguous experience—offer us what might be termed progressively more sophisticated versions of what fiction is, for they move out to accommodate more and more uncontrolled experience and to make it acceptable, if not understood, to human purposes.

The reader's reactions to these stories are indicated by those of the Arcadian audience that, in the frame of this book, hears the stories. And those reactions are increasingly favourable; after Musidorus' version, for example, the populace is astonished, Sympathus compassionate, and Kerxenus diversely moved (p. 403). After the revelation of their true identities, 'Even Philanax's own revengeful heart was mollified' and he 'had already unclothed his face of all show of malice' (p. 410) and Euarchus' sentence moves all 'to roaring lamentations' (p. 412). These responses by chorus are made thematically meaningful for the reader (hence allowing him intellectual consent as well as emotional response) by the several redefinitions of justice that fill Book V. At the beginning of the trial it is human justice that receives stress, as Musidorus invokes the rule of equity and cries out, 'where is that justice the Arcadians were wont to flourish in, whose nature is to render to every one his own?' (p. 378.) Gradually, though, the appeals shift to divine justice: 'Euarchus, whom the strange and secret working of justice had brought to be the judge over them—in such a shadow or rather pit of darkness the wormish mankind lives that neither they know how to foresee nor what to fear, and are but like tennis balls tossed by the racket of the higher powers . . .' (pp. 385–6.) Human justice becomes seen as an inadequate attempt to interpret the divine, so that it seems to Gynecia that in Philanax 'truth doth make thee deal untruly, and love of justice frames unjustice in thee' (p. 381). And, as the book comes to rest, it insists on the kind of complete ambiguity that dominated Musidorus' version of the action: 'so uncertain are mortal judgements, the same person most infamous and most famous, and neither justly.' (p. 416.)

Richard Lanham presents the theme of the *Old Arcadia* as ambivalence—the ambivalence of rhetorical formulations, of the power of love, of the certitude of standard precepts in a world 'by love possessed'.[33] Certainly Sidney's romance (like the old Greek romance) offers the reader at one and the same time a proof of design in existence and a demonstration of human inadequacy to define or even perceive that design.[34] Two facts about the narrative method of the last Book or Act are appropriate to that final sense of design. First, all hitherto unrelated and dissimilar episodes are pulled together in various ways and for various purposes here, so that interrelations are much closer than ever before. Second, plot is presented as material for analysis; heroes and readers are positioned as interpreters of the action, faced with summaries whose significance they and we are asked to envision and revise as our knowledge grows clearer. Thus Sidney ends his romance by asking us to interpret it. The whole is left open-ended, for even the interpretation of the just Euarchus is overturned in comic irony by the accident of Basilius' rise from supposed death. Not even the noblest and most comprehensive interpretation of the action can stand as final.

The changes in narrative method we have observed in the process of this essay allow the reader to partake in the sense of growing design as well as to accept it as a premiss of the action, to take, in fact, the sorts of realization the heroes acquire into his own experience of the romance. For what we observe as we read is a closer and closer interweaving of actions unrelated in probability, so that we experience the growth of an unlikely design. At first, we find analogical segmentation, entirely separate actions that resemble each other and that the heroes perceive with a sense of the irony of things; then contrastive segmentation, separate actions forming meaningful contrasts that only the reader sees; then contrasting actions interlacing one with the other and hence acquiring influence one with the other; then contrasting actions forming strange, tight interrelations as causes or effects for each other; and finally all actions compacted together in plot summaries so as to present some view of human affairs as rational or absurd.

---

[33] Lanham, p. 331; see also Davis, *Idea and Act*, pp. 64–7.

[34] For a subtle account of the interplay of providential design and human ignorance, see M. E. Dana, 'The Providential Plot of the *Old Arcadia*', *SEL* 17 (1977), 39–57 (see above pp. 83–102).

A Defence of Poetry (*An Apology for Poetry*)

5. SIDNEY'S FEIGNED *APOLOGY*

Ronald Levao

Any attempt to discuss Sidney's theory of poetic fictions proves to be something of a paradox, since *An Apology for Poetry* opens with a warning not to take theories too seriously. There Sidney compares himself to his master in horsemanship, John Pietro Pugliano, who, not content to teach his young students the practical side of his profession, 'sought to enrich [their] minds with the contemplations therein.' So mighty does his art appear, thanks to the light of his self-love, that, Sidney observes, 'if I had not been a piece of a logician before I came to him, I think he would have persuaded me to have wished myself a horse' (p. 95).[1] Following his master, Sidney opens with a theoretical justification of his own vocation, poetry, but with such a precedent, readers may wonder whether Sidney will persuade them to wish themselves poems (which is, in fact, where Sidney's Astrophil ends up in *AS* 45).

If the opening of the *Apology* is not paradoxical enough, the *Apology* itself is filled with contradictions and shifts of emphasis. Despite these, it does make certain significant gestures toward theorizing. I argue that Sidney's readers have long mistaken his intellectual affinities because of the oblique and self-conscious way he echoes traditional philosophical and critical positions. A closer view of his performance will, I think, reveal the *Apology* as one of the most daring documents of Renaissance criticism, in keeping with the most original thought of its time.

I

Sidney's purpose seems obvious enough: to justify poetic fictions against the charge that they are unreal and irresponsible fantasies. For the sake of clarity, I begin by dividing my examination into two parts, following the line drawn by Sidney's own argument:

Reprinted by permission of the Modern Language Association of America from *PMLA* 94 (1979), 223–33.

[1] All quotations of Sidney are from *An Apology for Poetry or The Defence of Poesy*, ed. and introd. G. Shepherd (London and New York, 1965, repr. Manchester 1973), hereafter cited as *Apology*.

any understanding knoweth the skill of the artificer standeth in that *Idea* or fore-conceit of the work, and not in the work itself. And that the poet hath that *Idea* is manifest, by delivering them forth in such excellency as he hath imagined them. Which delivering forth also is not wholly imaginative, as we are wont to say by them that build castles in the air; but so far substantially it worketh, not only to make a Cyrus, which had been but a particular excellency as Nature might have done, but to bestow a Cyrus upon the world to make many Cyruses, if they will learn aright why and how that maker made him. (p. 101.)

What is striking about this defence is that Sidney seeks to justify poetry by turning towards the two extremes it mediates, first to its source in the poet's 'Idea' and then to the moral effect it has on the reader's world; it becomes a conduit, leading the ideal to flow into the actual. To understand how Sidney puts his argument together, we must take a closer look at these two extremes and their relations.

First, what is the Idea or 'fore-conceit'? Modern critics are nearly unanimous in pointing to it as an example of Renaissance Neoplatonism and/or Augustinianism. The reasons for this are clear: both traditions helped to fulfil a central need for sixteenth-century theorists of the artist's Idea by giving it a fixed ontological basis.[2] Panofsky's discussion of the revival of Neoplatonism is instructive:

the Idea was reinvested with its apriori and metaphysical character. . . . the autocratic human mind, now conscious of its own spontaneity, believed that it could maintain this spontaneity in the face of sensory experience only by legitimizing the former *sub specie divinitatis*; the dignity of genius, now explicitly recognized and emphasized, is justified by its origin in God.[3]

---

[2] For Sidney as a Renaissance Platonist, see F. Krouse, 'Plato and Sidney's Defence of Poesie', *CL* 6 (Spring 1954), 138–47; W. Wimsatt and C. Brooks, *Literary Criticism: A Short History* (New York, 1957), p. 174; A. C. Hamilton, *The Structure of Allegory in the Faerie Queene* (Oxford, 1961), pp. 15–29; and W. R. Davis, *Idea and Act in Elizabethan Fiction* (Princeton, 1969), pp. 31, 37. Besides the obvious metaphorical difference, Augustinian illumination is different from Platonic inspiration; the former deals with the general nature of cognition, the latter with a special poetic gift. But both fulfil similar functions in Renaissance poetics. The argument for Sidney's Augustinianism is derived from Mornay and Hoskins's hierarchy of inner 'words', leading to the divine Logos. See *Apology*, pp. 59, 157–8; *An Apology for Poetry*, ed. and introd. F. G. Robinson (Indianapolis, 1970), p. 17 n. 63; and F. G. Robinson, *The Shape of Things Known: Sidney's Apology in Its Philosophical Tradition* (Cambridge: Mass., 1972), Ch. 3.

[3] E. Panofsky, *Idea: A Concept in Art Theory*, trans. J. Peake (New York, 1968), pp. 91–2.

Rosemond Tuve thinks this kind of justification is essential to Renaissance poetic theory. The poet, she argues in her influential *Elizabethan and Metaphysical Imagery*, 'simply has no nervousness dealing overtly with universals'. She attributes this confidence to 'the pervasiveness of Platonic and Neo-Platonic conceptions of reality . . . imitating Plotinus' ideal form and order'.[4] As Kristeller had previously noted, for the Neoplatonist, the 'true poet does not follow the arbitrary impulse of human thought, but is inspired by God'.[5]

Sidney seems to need this justification as much as any other theorist. Like the boldest Neoplatonists before him, he praises the poet as a free creator 'lifted up with the vigour of his own invention . . . freely ranging only within the zodiac of his own wit' (p. 100). He is free of nature and of any given subject matter; he does not derive 'conceit out of a matter, but maketh matter for a conceit' (p. 120). But in the *Apology*, Sidney tends to regard the protection the Platonic–Augustinian argument would afford as part of a voice that he self-consciously affects, a voice he asks us to think about critically, even as he uses it to provide terms for the poet's creativity.

Sidney's discussion of poetic inspiration, for example, is deliberately tangled and ambivalent. He starts by examining the Roman term for poet, *vates*: he translates this 'heavenly' title as 'diviner, forseer, or prophet' and says that the Romans attributed the power of prophecy to Virgil. Sidney then gives us two contradictory reactions to this information. First he condemns the Romans for their 'vain and godless superstition' (p. 98), and then he tells us they were 'altogether not without ground'. He softens his criticisms because 'that same exquisite observing of number and measure in words, and that high flying liberty of conceit proper to the poet, did seem to have some divine force in it' (p. 99). The poet, then, is not really inspired; his heavenly and divine nature is at best metaphorical. It is an illusion, but an understandable one, based on verbal artifice and the 'high flying liberty of conceit'. The irony is clear: inspiration is not the *cause* of the poet's conceit but the *effect* that the conceit has on the reader.

[4] R. Tuve, *Elizabethan and Metaphysical Imagery* (Chicago, 1947), pp. 41–2.
[5] P. O. Kristeller, *The Philosophy of Marsilio Ficino*, trans. V. Conant (1943, repr. 1964), p. 308.

Where Sidney does mention poets who were truly inspired by
God (David, Solomon, *et al.*), he is careful to set them apart from
'right poets', his subject.[6] He makes so many motions in distinguishing these right poets from philosophical and historical poets
(those who follow a 'proposed subject' instead of their own
'invention') that another distinction is easily missed.[7] It can,
however, be deduced easily enough, and it is equally important to
his argument. Sidney is interested in a poetic grounded entirely in
the human mind, and inspiration would compromise its autonomy.
As Sidney tells us later, Plato in his *Ion* 'attributeth unto Poesy
more than myself do, namely, to be a very inspiring of a divine
force, far above man's wit' (p. 130).

Sidney's use of metaphysics can be deceptive. Though he uses
its terms to praise the poet's creativity, he then dismisses them
before they can compromise the mind's autonomy. The same
pattern recurs immediately after the *vates* discussion, when Sidney
turns to the word 'poet': 'It cometh of this word *poiein*, which is "to
make".' Sidney's use of Greek etymology, like Landino's, serves as
an occasion to praise the poet, and Sidney follows with his famous
celebration of poetry's golden world and the poet's creation of a
new nature. Sidney then defends his claims:

Neither let it be deemed too saucy a comparison to balance the highest
point of man's wit with the efficacy of Nature; but rather give right honour
to the heavenly Maker of that maker, who having made man to His own
likeness, set him beyond and over all the works of that second nature:
which in nothing he showeth so much as in Poetry, when with the force of
a divine breath he bringeth things forth far surpassing her doings, with no
small argument to the incredulous of that first accursed fall of Adam:
since our erected wit maketh us know what perfection is, and yet our
infected will keepeth us from reaching unto it. (p. 101.)

---

[6] See A. C. Hamilton, 'Sidney's Idea of the "Right Poet"', *CL* 9 (Winter 1957), 41–59.

[7] This silence is part of Sidney's rhetorical strategy. He wants us to be able to say, as
does John Buxton, that 'Sidney describes the poet as a combination of vates, divinely
inspired seer, and poet, or maker'. (*Sir Philip Sidney and the English Renaissance* (1954
(2nd edn. 1964, repr. 1965), p. 4). But Sidney is careful to leave us enough evidence to
deduce a more precise set of theoretical distinctions. A disenchantment with, or
distancing from, arguments for poetic inspiration in the later Renaissance has been
noted by other critics. See, for example, B. Hathaway on Fracastoro, *The Age of Criticism:
The Late Renaissance in Italy* (1962, reprinted, Westport, Conn., 1972), pp. 405–6, and
R. Durling, *The Figure of the Poet in Renaissance Epic* (Cambridge, Mass., 1965), pp. 199–
200, where Tasso's yearning for inspiration and his view of poetry as 'rationalistic,
autonomous *techne*' are seen to be in conflict.

Our position in the universe is a gift of God, and we are fitted into a hierarchical series of makers, beginning with God, who surpasses us, and nature, which we surpass. But if the gift explains our capacity, it does not control our use of it or bind it to the fixed order of things. After the *vates* argument, the 'divine breath' must be metaphorical, referring to our own efforts to bring forth our own creations, perhaps echoing Scaliger's claim that man 'transforms himself into a second deity'. We reveal our divinity through our own effort.

But, more important, there is no clear transition from the mind's operations to its transcendental source. Sidney's 'highest point of man's wit' is *not* a mystical *apex mentis* directly sparked by the divine. It is the faculty that creates fictions, the faculty that creates another nature and so reveals our divinity to ourselves. In order to demonstrate 'erected wit' we must be 'lifted up with the vigour of [our] own invention' (p.100). We know our Ideas, not by tracing them back to an eternal logos, but by making them 'manifest, by delivering them forth in such excellency as [we have] imagined them' (p. 101).

Furthermore, the above quotation on the hierarchy of makers is a defence of one possible metaphor, an attempt to show that it is not 'too saucy'. After his magnificent praise of the erected wit, Sidney tells us: 'But these arguments will by few be understood, and by fewer granted. Thus much (I hope) will be given me, that the Greeks with some probability of reason gave him the name above all names of learning.' (p. 101.) All is suddenly qualified as Sidney reminds us that the passage is part of a voice he has assumed for the sake of a few debatable arguments. He is not concerned with establishing their objective validity, and he neither affirms nor denies them. He is satisfed with showing that, at best, they point to 'some probability of reason'. Indeed, the entire argument for the poet as maker is not so much a *justification* of the wit as a *demonstration* of it. It is a bold 'comparison' which, according to Aristotle and Renaissance rhetoricians, is a prime way of exhibiting wit.[8]

[8] W. G. Crane, *Wit and Rhetoric in the Renaissance* (New York, 1937), p. 14. There are, to be sure, religious themes sounded in the passage, from the exhortation to give 'right honour to the heavenly Maker' to the mention of 'that first accursed fall of Adam'. But these references are keyed to rhetorical ends; the emphasis in the *Apology* is on man as the maker of images, not man as the image made. Acknowledgement of the Fall and the

II

If the poet is 'lifted up with the vigour of his own invention', so too is the reader. Poetry is the best teacher, the 'first light-giver to ignorance', and the first study to show us a 'pleasure in the exercises of the mind' (pp. 96, 98). The separation of the Idea from a fixed ontology, moreover, makes poetry a special kind of exercise. In a fascinating article, A. E. Malloch argues that, for Sidney, it is only in poetry that reason finds an object properly proportioned to its capacities. But Malloch sees this in a Thomist light: the fallen world is deficient, while poetry's golden world reveals a 'fullness of being' which fully actualizes the act of cognition.[9] I would argue, on the contrary, that the poetic object is best proportioned to our reason because that object is a projection of our reason. Jacopo Mazzoni made this very argument in Italy, only a few years after the *Apology* was written. The object of poetic imitation is one that is consciously framed to fit the poet's intellectual needs.[10]

The more autonomous the poet's Idea becomes, however, the more insistent the need to attach it to something outside itself. And if a metaphysical foundation is lacking, then a practical and ethical application becomes all-important. The function of poetry is to reform the will, as well as to perfect the wit, since 'no learning is so good as that which teacheth and moveth to virtue' (p. 123). Using a suggestive pun, Sidney writes, 'the poet . . . doth draw the mind more effectually than any other art doth' (p. 115). The poet both depicts the mind and leads it to action. And this brings us to the second part of Sidney's theory, that poetry is justified not only by the brilliance of the Idea but by the way it works in the world, bestowing a 'Cyrus upon the world to make many Cyruses'.

Sidney echoes the humanists' rhetorical interpretation of poetry, and, following Minturno's transference of Cicero's 'teach, delight, and move' from the orator to the poet, he writes that poets

infected will does not draw the discussion into the orbit of theology—although diverging claims have been made for it as evidence of Sidney's Calvinism, Thomism, or semi-Pelagianism—so much as it advertises the way poetry can grant an argumentative edge over the 'incredulous'.

[9] A. E. Malloch, '"Architectonic" Knowledge and Sidney's *Apology*', *ELH* 20 (1953), 181–5.
[10] See A. Gilber, ed., *Literary Criticism: Plato to Dryden* (1940, repr. Detroit, 1962), pp. 358–403, and Hathaway.

'imitate both to delight and teach: and delight to move men to take that goodness in hand' (p. 103). According to Paul Alpers, this is the distinctive mark of Sidney's 'golden world'. It is not a self-consistent 'heterocosm', a 'self-contained universe of discourse'. Rather, Sidney stresses the didactic efficacy of the poet's moral exempla.[11]

But if poetry makes a rhetorical address to the reader, it does so only in a way that conforms to Sidney's radical conception of the status of a poet's Idea, a way that Sidney defines by opposing poets to philosophers and historians.

A philosopher claims that, by teaching what virtue is, his discipline makes clear 'how it extendeth itself out of the limits of a man's own little world to the government of families, and maintaining of public societies' (p. 105). According to Sidney, a philosopher never extends himself; he is trapped within the closed world of his fellow philosophers: 'the philosopher teacheth, but he teacheth obscurely, so as the learned only can understand him; that is to say, he teacheth them that are already taught.' (p. 109.) A philosopher depends on others coming to him, into his own exclusive world. While pretending to point out the limitations of philosophers, Sidney parodies the circularity of their discourse: 'Nay truly, learned men have learnedly thought that where once reason hath so much overmastered passion as that the mind hath a free desire to do well, the inward light each mind hath in itself is as good as a philosopher's book: seeing in Nature we know it is well to do well.' (p. 113.) The learned learnedly discuss how it is well to do well, but their terms only point to themselves: 'happy is that man who may understand [them], and more happy that can apply what he doth understand.' (p. 107.) The same charge reappears indirectly, if a bit more cruelly, during a later discussion of love: 'some of my masters the philosophers spent a good deal of their lamp-oil in setting forth the excellency of it.' (p. 125.) Lamp-oil, Sidney suggests, is all a philosopher usually 'spends' in love. A philosopher fails in teaching and seduction because his definitions 'lie dark before the imaginative and judging power, if they be not illuminated or figured forth by the speaking picture of poesy' (p. 107).

---

[11] See P. J. Alpers, *The Poetry of the Faerie Queene* (Princeton, 1967), pp. 19–20. Tuve's final chapter in *Elizabethan and Metaphysical Imagery* has a brilliant summary of didactic theory, though it depends on some questionable platonizing and an idealized psychology that Sidney rarely, if ever, realized.

Poetry extends itself into the world in peculiar ways, as Sidney's argument with history makes clear. If philosophy gives us reason devoid of external application, history is caught in the external world, one devoid of any inherent rationality. The historian is 'bound to tell things as things were' and 'cannot be liberal ... of a perfect pattern' (p. 110): 'the historian, being captivated to the truth of a foolish world, is many times a terror from well-doing, and an encouragement to unbridled wickedness. For see we not valiant Miltiades rot in his fetters? the just Phocion and the accomplished Socrates put to death like traitors? the cruel Severus live prosperously?' (pp. 111–12.)

Not only is the historian's world one of moral chaos, but history, in recording it, lacks logical coherence. The example of history 'draweth no necessary consequence', and so the historian follows the logic that, 'because it rained yesterday, therefore it should rain to-day' (pp. 107–110). The historian cannot understand the nature of examples and how the mind uses them: 'but if he know an example only informs a conjectured likelihood, and so go by reason, the poet doth so far exceed him as he is to frame his example to that which is most reasonable ... where the historian in his bare *was* must tell events whereof he can yield no cause; or, if he do, it must be poetical.' (p. 110.)

The poet knows that the mind must work through conjectures and that examples can lead only to 'a conjectured likelihood'. Thus the poet is freed from imitating things as they have been, the 'bare *was*', and is able to concentrate, instead, on the modes of understanding themselves, the lines of connection or consequence that the mind attempts to draw in making sense out of the world. Examples in poetry are framed according 'to that which is most reasonable', not according to any external *res*. It is of small importance that the historian can boast of bringing us 'images of true matters, such as indeed were done, and not such as fantastically or falsely may be suggested to have been done' (p. 109). The historian knows better 'how this world goeth than how his own wit runneth' (p. 105). The poet, by contrast, having no law but wit, can frame examples into purified types of moral ideals: 'If the poet do his part aright, he will show you in Tantalus, Atreus, and such like, nothing that is not to be shunned; in Cyrus, Aeneas, Ulysses, each thing to be followed.' (p. 110.) The poet faces a brazen world, a foolish world of moral disorder that snares the historian in its senselessness, but delivers a golden world, another nature structured by reason.

Sidney is often seen as a Platonist because this theme of reshaping the world echoes Neoplatonic claims, just as Sidney's Idea does. Ficino writes: 'What, then does the intellect seek if not to transform all things into itself by depicting all things in the intellect according to the nature of the intellect? . . . the universe, in a certain manner, should become intellect.'[12] As in the first part of his theory, Sidney both advances metaphysical claims and refuses to rely on them for protection. If there is any justification for the poet's inventions, it must lie in their didactic efficacy.

If we look back to the Idea–Cyrus passage, we can see how insistently Sidney attempts to join his golden world and his didacticism in a bond of dialectical necessity. The poet's fiction, the delivering of the Idea, is 'not wholly imaginative, as we are wont to say by them that build castles in the air; but so far substantially it worketh, not only to make a Cyrus, which had been but a particular excellency as Nature might have done, but to bestow a Cyrus upon the world to make many Cyruses . . .' (p. 101.) A poet's effect on the world is as important to him as it is to the world he affects. It is the only way he can grant substance to his creations, the only way he can be sure that his poetry is not a sign of his estrangement. For Sidney suspects, as Danielle Barabaro and others did, that eloquent fantasies must be carefully directed to prevent the teacher of the many from becoming the frenzied and solitary builder of castles in the air (Hathaway, *Criticism*, p. 332).

At crucial junctures in the *Apology*, where Sidney would have found a metaphysical argument most useful, we discover, instead, claims for didactic efficacy. Forrest Robinson, in keeping with his argument that the poet has access to absolute patterns, suggests that the fore-conceit is a pre-verbal mental diagram, which, because of its participation in absolute truth, serves as a universal frame to ensure a uniform response in all readers (*Shape of Things Known*, p. 118). But when Sidney comes to discuss how this frame works, he simply tells us that, when readers of poesy are 'looking

---

[12] Ficino, 'Five Questions concerning the Mind', in *Renaissance Philosophy of Man* (Chicago, 1948), pp. 201–2. For an argument that Sidney's notion of poetic feigning may have been influenced by Ficino, see C. M. Dowlin, 'Sidney's Two Definitions of Poetry', *MLQ* 3 (1942), 579.

but for fiction, they shall use the narration but as an imaginative ground-plot of a profitable invention' (p. 124). Sidney does not claim that there is any true or universal Idea embodied by, or hidden in, the ground-plot. 'Invention' carries its full ambiguity here, and we cannot tell whether readers come upon a pre-established meaning or simply create their own.[13] All we do know is that it ought to be profitable. We are not guaranteed a fixed unity between speaker and hearer; the most we can aim for is some ethical utility.

A similar development appears in the all-important icastic-fantastic opposition. As William Rossky has shown, the fear of imaginative distortion was a powerful theme in Renaissance England, and English texts are filled with admonitions to control the imagination.[14] George Puttenham's *Arte of English Poesie* (1589) relies heavily on the Platonic theme of controlling our represen-tations by carefully fitting the mind to objective truth. Despite his earlier echo of Sidney, that the poet 'contrives out of his owne braine' without 'any foreine copie or example', Puttenham insists that the orderly imagination must represent things 'according to their very truth. If otherwise, then doth it breede Chimeres and monsters in mans imaginations and not only in his imaginations but also in his ordinarie actions and life which ensues.'[15] The useful life must be 'illuminated with the brightest irradiations of knowledge and of the veritie and due proportion of things'.

Sidney, by contrast, avoids such Augustinian metaphysics. More decisively committed to poetic feigning, he welcomes the mind's ability to create such new forms 'as never were in Nature, as the Heroes, Demigods, Cyclops, Chimeras, Furies' (p. 100). He reduces the icastic–fantastic dichotomy from a metaphysical to an ethical distinction: 'For I will not deny but that man's wit may make Poesy, which should be *eikastike*, which some learned have defined, "figuring forth good things", to be *phantastike*, which doth contrariwise infect the fancy with unworthy objects.' (p. 125.) There is no question here of approximating an image to an

[13] See M. W. Bundy, '"Invention" and "Imagination" in the Renaissance', *JEGP* 29 (1930), 535–45, and B. Hathaway, *Marvels and Commonplaces* (New York, 1968), p. 56.

[14] W. Rossky, 'Imagination in the English Renaissance: Psychology and Poetic', *Studies in the Renaissance* 5 (1958), 49–73.

[15] G. Puttenham, *The Arte of English Poesie*, facsimile of 1906 reprint, ed. Edward Arber (Kent, Ohio, 1970), p. 35.

external model, of a faithful likeness being opposed to a mere semblance. For Sidney, as for Mazzoni, who actually placed the fantastic over the icastic, this approximation has become too restrictive. But instead of reversing the distinction, Sidney redefines it; 'good' and 'unworthy' are purely ethical. Thomas Wright was to warn his English audience in 1605 that the distorted imagination 'putteth greene spectacles before the eyes of the witte, to make it see nothing but greene' (Rossky, p. 56). But for Sidney, one can never take away the spectacles. All cognition implies some filtering or refraction; we can only hope to control the lenses we use.

But what is this hope based on? As the preceding quotation admits, man's wit has made irresponsible poetry. Sidney hopes by this admission to answer those who see poetry as a corrupting influence: we should 'not say that Poetry abuseth man's wit, but that man's wit abuseth Poetry' (p. 125). This closes one problem but opens a larger one. Poetry depends on the wit, it is born in the fore-conceit, and poets follow no law but wit. Without a direct argument of inspiration or illumination, how can we tell whether light-giving poets themselves have the proper light? What is the foundation for their claims? Some critics, borrowing from the rhetorical tradition, argue that good poets must also be morally good, but this only begs the question, rather than answers it.

The problem with Sidney's double justification is that both sides are problematic: Sidney wants to make the kinds of claims that traditionally have been supported by some metaphysic but tries to make them without recourse to such support. The poetic Idea, as we have seen, points to perfection only by pointing back to itself. It justifies itself only by repeating its own act of creation.

The other side of the argument, the attempt to translate poetic effects into moral ones, is pursued with perhaps greater urgency. Sidney would very much like to present poetry as the instrument of the moral, active life, but the very process of making the argument exposes its gaps, indeed, it faces a similar dilemma. Wimsatt notes: 'Sidney, like most of those who have maintained that poetry is (and ought to be) moral, has not been able to resolve an ambiguity of the word ought as used in the formula. Is this a poetic "ought", or is it in fact only a moral "ought"? In the second sense, "ought to be moral" is a tautology—since moral is what all our works ought to be.' (p. 171.) The easiest way out for Sidney would have been to repeat Boccaccio's claims for the unity of poetry and theology or to claim some metaphysical universal at work, as many did who turned Aristotle's 'ought' into a moral term (Hathaway, *Criticism*, p. 130). As Sidney's argument stands, it comes close to telling us that poetry ought to be what it ought to be, and, like the moral philosophers he parodies, Sidney finds his terms pointing back to themselves.

III

One of the reasons there is such difficulty on both sides of the justification is the paradoxical nature of the poetic fictions that lie between them. Unlike some rhetorical critics, who magically derived true conclusions from false elements, Sidney tells us:

> Now for the poet, he nothing affirms, and therefore never lieth. For, as I take it, to lie is to affirm that to be true which is false; so as the other artists, especially the historian, affirming many things, can, in the cloudy knowledge of mankind, hardly escape from many lies. But the poet (as I said before) never affirmeth. The poet never maketh any circles about your imagination, to conjure you to believe for true what he writes. (pp. 123–4.)

Insisting on the fictional nature of poetry, Sidney argues that its essential feature is the poet's 'feigning', 'not rhyming and versing' (p. 103).[16] Poetry appears to inhabit a special realm of discourse, one that eludes the strict laws of verification. Sidney's claim may not be unique to the Renaissance, but the route by which he arrives at his claim and the consequences he draws from it have an important effect on the way we read the *Apology*, giving us a more general sense of what all discourse implies for Sidney.

Poetic fictions, for Sidney, are the result of a coincidence of conventional opposites. Poetry fuses the two extremes of philosophy and history, as it 'coupleth the general notion with the particular example'. It is clearly *not* an Aristotelian mean between them, as some Italian theorists have reckoned it on a scale of abstractions.[17]

---

[16] For arguments that Sidney's radical insistence on the poet's free feigning sets Sidney apart from such Italian sources as Scaliger and Minturno, see C. M. Dowlin, 'Sidney and Other Men's Thought', *RES* 20 (1944), 257–71, and Hamilton, 'Sidney's Idea of the "Right Poet"'.

[17] For poetry as a mean, see B. Weinberg, *A History of Literary Criticism in the Italian Renaissance* (Chicago, 1961), p. 31. By contrast Jacob Bronowski has noted that in the *Apology* poetry appears to be straining in two directions at once, towards liberated

Sidney includes both extremes within the synthesis, which gives rise to an entirely new mode of discourse, one that, he claims, goes beyond conventional limits. It is, in a sense, more abstract than metaphysics, because it is completely free from nature, unlike the 'metaphysic, though it be in the second and abstract notions, and therefore be counted supernatural, yet doth he indeed build upon the depth of Nature' (p. 100). At the same time, it is more concrete than history, since its speaking pictures and shining images are able to instruct and move men immediately.[18]

There is something unsettling in Sidney's comparison between this special mode and the others. He does not argue the claims of fiction over fact, but he does suggest that *all* attempts to make sense out of the world are based on illusion; poetry is only a special instance of the fictionality that pervades all discourse. The most casual observations show that other disciplines use fictions to enhance their effectiveness: lawyers use such fictitious names as 'John a Stile' and 'John a Noakes' in their cases for the sake of making 'their picture the more lively', while chess players call a piece of wood a bishop. So too historians, despite their claims of truthfulness, still give 'many particularities of battles, which no man could affirm' and invent 'long orations', which historical figures never pronounced (p. 97).

In a profounder sense, any attempt at rational communication leads to fiction making. Our only choice is whether or not to acknowledge the pretence. So the historian is described as 'loaden with old mouse-eaten records, authorising himself (for the most part) upon other histories, whose greatest authorities are built upon the notable foundation of hearsay'. Any art that purports to rest on the foundation of external verities finds that its support quickly disintegrates. Even those who go beyond books to nature find themselves in this vertiginous plight: 'There is no art delivered to mankind that hath not the works of Nature for his principal object, without which they could not consist, and on which they so depend, as they become actors and players, as it were, of what Nature will have set forth.' (pp. 99–100.) They pretend to 'follow

ideality and a forced application to the concrete. See Bronowski, *The Poet's Defence* (Cambridge, 1939), esp. pp. 39–56.

[18] For the argument that Tasso likewise defines a new realm of poetic discourse through a coincidence of opposites, the 'Intellectual fantasy', see P. Damon, 'History and Idea in Renaissance Criticism', in P. Damon, ed., *Literary Criticism and Historical Understanding* (New York, 1967).

nature' but find themselves on a stage, their words turned into players' lines, their deeds transformed into mere theatrics.

A. C. Hamilton has argued that Sidney's paradox is borrowed from Agrippa's sceptical attack on the vanity of human studies.[19] However much we attribute to Agrippa's influence, whether on the basis of his mocking tone or of his argument that nothing can be affirmed, it is clear that Sidney carries the sceptical argument to its conclusion, that our only access to reality is through fiction and conjecture. As Montaigne writes: 'Have I not seen this divine saying in Plato, that Nature is nothing but an aenigmaticall poesie? As a man might say, an overshadowed and darke picture, inter-shining with an infinit varietie of false lights, to exercise our conjectures ... philosophy is nothing else but a sophisticated poesie.'[20] Sidney would object, however, that the only real 'poesie' is poetry itself. It is the greatest of the arts because it is the only one to realize that it is not anchored to a fixed and objective Truth. Sidney does not let this realization force him back to a passive fideism: poets recognize the necessity of conjecture and so boldly set about inventing their own.

This claim inevitably doubles back to affect the status of the *Apology*. If the only choice is between those who unconsciously live fictions and those who act their own, then Sidney, as the speaker of the *Apology*, makes it clear that he thinks of himself as one of the latter.

At the beginning of the *Apology*, Sidney tells us that he is following the example of John Pietro Pugliano, the master horse-man and self-promoter, and that in order to defend his own craft, poetry, he needs 'to bring some more available proofs'. He is alluding to Aristotle's definition of rhetoric as the 'faculty of observing in any given case, the available means of persuasion', and so is signalling us that he is about to adopt the role of rhetorician. Kenneth Myrick's book on Sidney helps us to see just how self-conscious an actor Sidney is, as he closely models his work after the 'judicial oration in behalf of an accused client'.[21] Sidney, furthermore, seems to remind us continually of the role he

[19] A. C. Hamilton, 'Sidney and Agrippa', *RES* ns 7 (1956), 151–7. Similar claims are made in Hamilton's book on Spenser, cited in n. 2.

[20] Montaigne, *Essays*, trans. John Florio (London, 1919, repr. 1938), ii. 244–5.

[21] K. Myrick, *Sir Philip Sidney as a Literary Craftsman* (Cambridge, Mass., 1935, repr. Lincoln, 1965), p. 53.

is playing. As Myrick demonstrates, Sidney not only follows the seven-part form of an oration as he found it described by Thomas Wilson, but does so in elaborate detail, following the recommended subject matter and style for each section and even marking the transitions between them with conspicuous phrases (pp. 54–5).

This is a fitting role for Sidney, considering the highly rhetorical role he imagines for poetry. But the paradox thickens when we realize that Sidney is playing not only the rhetorician but the poet as well. He tells us at the start that he has slipped into the title of poet, and he often demonstrates the appropriateness of that title in the *Apology*. After describing poetry as 'feigning notable images of virtues, vices, or what else', Sidney proceeds to 'feign notable images' of the poet's competitors, including the moral philosphers, whom he envisions approaching him 'with a sullen gravity', and the historian, staggering under a load of mouse-eaten records. Before they have a chance to speak, Sidney gives us a notable image of them as hypocrites and buffoons and, in the process, characterizes himself as one who acts out his own theories.

Sidney leads us to recognize his arguments for his craft as examples of his craft by showing us that they are in the same realm of discourse, the realm of feigned images and self-conscious conjectures. I have already mentioned the discussion of the poet as maker as a kind of conjecture. Later, during a crucial argument with those who claim that fictions are mere daydreams or toys, Sidney counters, 'if to a slight conjecture a conjecture may be opposed, truly it may seem, that as by him [Homer] their learned men took almost their first light of knowledge, so their active men received their first motions of courage' (p. 127).

There are, of course, advantages to adopting this role. Sidney can demonstrate, even as he describes, the persuasive force of poetry. And by treating his arguments as conjectures, he can arrange a variety of them without strict regard for consistency. He presents us with 'something for everyone', aiming different claims at different readers, hoping that all will find something to serve as 'an imaginative ground-plot of a profitable invention'. We often find, in fact, running counter to what I have described as the central theory, the testing of more conservative possibilities, aimed at those who may be unhappy with the more daring claims for the poet's creativity. We can see this, for example, in the notion of poetic 'fitness'.

Early in the *Apology*, when praising the poet's creativity, Sidney argues for the peculiar 'reverse adequation' found in critics like Mazzoni. The mind does not fit its concepts to externals but, rather, invents forms to fit its own faculties. Poets are like painters, who, 'having no law but wit, bestow that in colours upon you which is fittest for the eye to see' (p. 102). If verse is used in poetry, so much the better, because of the 'fitness it hath for memory' (p. 122). But later, when discussing stage productions, Sidney moves far away from the freedom of Mazzoni's idols and closer to the unimaginative literalness of Castelvetro. Unity of place is essential because no audience could believe a rapid change of location. Playwrights are attacked for being too 'liberal' with time as well. There must be a correspondence between the imitation and the action imitated. The play should be 'fitted to the time it set forth' (p. 134).

These reversals are not restricted to specific questions of dramaturgy. At one moment the poets are free of the works of nature, not enclosed by its 'narrow warrant'; at another, they must rely on the 'force truth hath in nature' and their proper effects are endangered if the matter is 'disproportioned to ourselves and nature' (p. 136). We may even suspect that Sidney is allowing himself to act out his own ambivalence about the poet's 'high flying liberty of conceit'. Late in the *Apology*, Sidney tells us that 'the highest-flying wit [must] have a Daedalus to guide him', and that this Daedalus has three wings, 'Art, Imitation, and Exercise': 'Exercise indeed we do, but that very for-backwardly: for where we should exercise to know, we exercise as having known; and so is our brain delivered of much matter which never was begotten by knowledge.' (p. 133.) Sidney more strictly regulates the poet with a firmer objective orientation. The next sentence, in fact, complains, 'For there being two principal parts—matter to be expressed by words and words to express the matter—in neither we use Art or Imitation rightly.' (p. 133.) Sidney does not openly contradict his earlier idealistic claim that the poet 'bringeth his own stuff, and doth not learn a conceit out of a matter, but maketh matter for a conceit' (p. 120), but he is clearly suggesting a safer *res/verba* distinction, as used by the Horatian critics to direct poetry outward, toward the solidity of things.[22]

---

[22] Weinberg, pp. 77, 93, 99–100, 158, 801. For later developments of this controlling of the imagination through *res/verba* distinctions, see A. C. Howell, '*Res et verba*: Words and Things', *ELH* 13 (1946), 131–42.

Sidney can take these liberties because of the nature of the *Apology*. But his retreat to more conservative themes does not solve his dilemmas; rather, their conjectural quality serves only to remind us of those dilemmas. The claim that poetry neither affirms nor denies may not have been unprecedented in the Renaissance, but the suggestion that one's own defence of poetry follows the same pattern questions the very possibility of making such a defence.

Sidney's theory requires that he take an affirmative stand somewhere, that he find some first premiss from which to deduce his conclusions. Sidney himself makes this need explicit by reducing his argument to a syllogism: 'if it be, as I affirm, that no learning is so good as that which teacheth and moveth to virtue, and that none can both teach and move thereto so much as Poetry, then is the conclusion manifest that ink and paper cannot be to a more profitable purpose employed.' (p. 123.) Sidney makes this statement just after he has given a lesson in logic to the poetry haters, laughing at their argument that 'doth (as they say) but *petere principium*' (p. 123.) But, immediately after his own argument, he undermines the clause on which the entire syllogism rests, 'I affirm'. For it is here that he chooses to place the already quoted passage on how the poet 'never affirmeth', unlike the others who, 'affirming many things, can, in the cloudy knowledge of mankind, hardly escape from many lies' (p. 124). Even as he points out the logical mistakes of his opponents, Sidney seems to be deliberately committing his own, making any first premiss impossible and so exposing himself to an inevitable infinite regress.[23] To put the matter more simply, if the best the mind can accomplish is conjecture, then its justification is also a conjecture.

Sidney reminds us of this problem in the peroratio, or conclusion:

I conjure you all that have had the evil luck to read this ink-wasting toy of mine . . . to believe, with Aristotle, that they were the ancient treasurers of the Grecians' divinity; to believe, with Bembus, that they were first bringers-in of all civility; to believe, with Scaliger, that no philosopher's

---

[23] Sidney violates an essential principle of Aristotle's *Posterior Analytics*, on the intuitive acceptance of first principles. From the thirteenth century on, this work, which shows what a body of knowledge should 'look' like and deals with the use of syllogisms, became increasingly important in describing an art. See É. Gilson, *History of Christian Philosophy in the Middle Ages* (New York, 1955), p. 312.

precepts can sooner make you an honest man than the reading of Virgil; to believe, with Clauserus, the translator of Cornutus, that it pleased the heavenly Deity, by Hesiod and Homer, under the veil of fables, to give us all knowledge, Logic, Rhetoric, Philosophy natural and moral, and *quid non*?; to believe, with me, that there are many mysteries contained in Poetry, which of purpose were written darkly, lest by profane wits it should be abused; to believe, with Landino, that they are so beloved of the gods that whatsoever they write proceeds of divine fury; lastly, to believe themselves, when they tell you they will make you immortal by their verses. (pp. 141–2.)

The facetious tone is unmistakable, from opening self-depreciation to insistence that we believe the love-poet's favourite seduction line. But we also find a summary listing of nearly all the arguments made in the *Apology*, now paraded without distinction. We are conjured to believe arguments that Sidney has made essential, namely, for poetry as a civilizing force and for its didactic efficacy; those he has rejected, such as Landino's for poetry as an emanation of divine fury; and those he has deliberately minimized or ignored, such as the view of poetry as a veil of allegory or as a mystery for the initiated. All are brought out like actors at the end of a play, taking their bows.

Sidney cannot expect that his readers will believe so many conflicting points of view, and the lack of distinction among them hurts their credibility. Even his insistence that we do believe them, when he 'conjure[s us] . . . to believe', is a self-parody, teasing us with verbal echoes of a previous denial: 'The poet never maketh any circles about your imagination, to conjure you to believe for true what he writes.'

Myrick, who gives an excellent survey of Sidney's rhetorical strategies, argues that this kind of playfulness adds to the *Apology*'s persuasiveness. It is a sign of Sidney's *sprezzatura*, a 'courtly grace which conceals a sober purpose' (p. 298). Sidney does praise the courtier who finds a style 'fittest to nature' and who 'doth according to art, though not by art', and contrasts him to the pedant who uses 'art to show art, and not to hide art' (p. 139). But Sidney is not that courtier. Little is hidden by the style of the *Apology*. His adopted role is announced as an adopted role, and nearly all his persuasive tricks and witty anecdotes are relished as persuasive tricks and demonstrations of wit. We rarely lose sight of the self-conscious fashioning of the *Apology* and cannot forget that Sidney is, in Myrick's terms, a 'literary craftsman' constructing a 'literary artifact'.

It would be tempting to conclude that the *Apology* acts out its own argument, that the work itself moves us through images and fictions while praising the power of poetry to move us through images and fictions. But if this were so, there would be no real argument to act out, only a fiction that neither affirms nor denies, taking as its subject still other fictions. The *Apology* requires another *Apology* to justify it, and so on without end.

What the *Apology* does act out are the tensions characteristic of the most adventurous Renaissance thought. Sidney's intellectual affinities lie not so much with Ficino and the Neoplatonists as with thinkers like Nicholas of Cusa. Cusa, in his most famous work, *De docta ignorantia*, tells us that previous philosophers erred in their attempts to understand the nature of things because of the illusion that their systems could precisely represent some fixed structure. With his doctrine of 'learned ignorance', he attempts to free his readers from this mistake by short-circuiting traditional logical categories, teasing his readers with puzzles that lead to a co-incidence of opposites. The technique does not close the gap between human representation and precise truth, but does bring them to recognize its inevitability, allowing them to manipulate it consciously. Cusa calls this free play 'conjecture', which encourages the mind to project its own forms of thought—mathematical, symbolic, and metaphorical—on to a world that lacks any fully apprehensible rationality.[24] Like Sidney, Cusa argues that conjecture, while neither true nor false, has a practical value: it erects the wit and energizes the will, leading man to the Good. Yet even this claim, because it is made discursively, must be taken as yet another conjecture.[25]

This is the kind of play that is going on in Sidney's *Apology*. Sidney's friend Hubert Languet had little patience with such

[24] Of equal importance is Cusa's second major work, *De coniecturis*, which complements the first. I am not arguing that Sidney read Cusa's works: if he heard of him at all, it was probably from chance comments made by Giordano Bruno. I am interested here more in pointing out conceptual parallels that will help to trace a Renaissance theory of fiction than in ascribing sources.

[25] The essential studies of Cusa are in E. Cassirer, *The Individual and the Cosmos in Renaissance Philosophy*, trans. Mario Domandi (New York, 1963), and M. de Gandillac, *La Philosophie de Nicholas de Cues* (Paris, 1942). The best treatment of this paradox in Cusa's thought, however, is in K. Jaspers, *The Great Philosophers*, trans. Ralph Manheim (New York, 1962), ii.

protracted ambiguities, and Sidney enjoyed teasing him about it. In his correspondence with the older humanist, Sidney praises the joys of mental exercise: 'I am never less a prey to melancholy than when I am earnestly applying the feeble powers of my mind to some high and difficult subject.'[26] Languet approves of his enthusiasm but is forever warning him not to spend too much time on studies that do not lead directly to a life of action. He recommends Cicero's letters 'not only for the beauty of the Latin but also for the very important matter they contain' (p. 20). But he is guarded about those who practise a double translation method, turning Latin into a modern language and then closing the book to translate it back again. This exercise in style is considered useful by some, but it smacks too much of what Languet later calls 'literary leisure'. Sidney responds: 'I intend to follow your advice about composition thus: I shall first take one of Cicero's letters and turn it into French; then from French into English and so once more by a sort of perpetual motion . . . it shall come round into Latin again. Perhaps, too, I shall improve myself in Italian by the same exercise.' (p. 23.)

Like Languet, Sidney wants to direct his learning outwards, to energize the will through the wit. That the transition can be made is confidently, even aggressively, asserted in the *Apology*. But for Sidney, there always seems to be another game to be played by the wit, yet another circuit to be made by its self-circling energies, before it can make that transition.

---

[26] *The Correspondence of Sir Philip Sidney and Hubert Languet*, ed. and trans. S. A. Pears (1845), p. 29.

6. OLD MOUSE-EATEN RECORDS: HISTORY IN SIDNEY'S *APOLOGY*

Elizabeth Story Donno

Some forty years ago Marguerite Hearsey[1] made the valuable suggestion that, among the various sources proposed for Sidney's *Defence of Poesy*, Bishop Amyot's Preface to his translation of Plutarch's *Lives* (published 1559; in Thomas North's translation, 1579) should be accounted as one, and she went on to demonstrate the similarity of argument in the two works by juxtaposing a number of passages. Though the validity of her suggestion cannot be questioned by anyone who looks at the two texts, the 'anti-history' motivation she offers for Sidney's appropriation of this material seems to me very open to question. She suggests that in 1579 Sidney 'may have been more or less definitely formulating a sort of refutation', prompted, on the one hand, by Amyot who had set forth his 'eloquent and even impassioned eulogy of history, raising it above all the other arts and sciences', and, on the other, by North who had also set forth his 'confident assertion of the superiority of history over all other "bookes"' in his address to the reader. Thus Amyot's Preface, in North's translation, could be seen as one of 'two incentives' for Sidney's writing his *Apology*; the other was Stephen Gosson's *School of Abuse*.

Despite the plethora of sources proposed over the years for ideas found in the *Apology*—Plato, Aristotle, Cicero, Horace, Scaliger, Minturno, Castelvetro, Fracastoro, Agrippa, Sibilet, and so on—saner minds now acknowledge that many of these ideas were Renaissance commonplaces and that Sidney's use of them was indeed eclectic and selective. But the notion that he was 'anti-history' is still to be met with. In his admirable edition, even Geoffrey Shepherd,[2] who devotes a section of his introduction to

Reprinted by permission of the University of North Carolina Press from *Studies in Philology* 72 (1975), 275–98.

[1] M. Hearsey, 'Sidney's *Defence of Poesy* and Amyot's Preface in North's Plutarch: A Relationship', *SP* 30 (1933), 535–50.

[2] *An Apology for Poetry or the Defence of Poesy*, ed. G. Shepherd (London and New York, 1965, repr. Manchester, 1973), to which my references and citations are keyed; I refer to Sidney's work throughout by this title.

'The Debate with History', suggests that Sidney 'had a theoretical distrust of any over-insistence on the value of history' and that he probably shared 'a residual scepticism' about that value 'with other men of the late sixteenth century'.[3]

Of these two claims, the one, relating to Sidney's use of the arguments brought together in Amyot's Preface, is now generally acknowledged though, it seems to me, its implications have not been properly understood. The other—largely a corollary of the first—relating to the belief that the *Apology* reflects Sidney's anti-historical (as well as anti-philosophic) propensity, is also generally acknowledged though, I believe, on dubious grounds. In review of these claims, the ordering of my discussion must necessarily fall in two parts. I shall first consider Sidney's attitudes towards history as they are reflected in his correspondence, where they are divested of literary guise, as they are not in the *Apology*. To read a consciously fashioned sixteenth-century literary text as if it were straightforward exposition tends, in general, to distort its author's views and, in the case of the *Apology*, in particular, to distort that most accomplished of critical works. I shall secondly reconsider the question as to why Sidney took occasion to make such close and obvious use of the arguments deployed in Amyot's Preface, albeit wresting them to his own ends. The result, I trust, will be to set the *Apology* in a new perspective, yet one that is in harmony with Sidney's intellectual outlook and his proposed intention. Only by so doing can we grasp the degree of his literary achievement.

To find Sidney 'anti-history' is to mark him out as holding a point of view quite out of accord with that of his contemporaries. While anyone familiar with the period will readily admit it offers diversity of ideas (among them, recognition of the Aristotelian

[3] pp. 41–2. It is to be noted that both Hearsey and Shepherd make their 'anti-history' observations somewhat tentatively—'may have', 'suggests that', 'probably shared'—a mode of expression that (perhaps) suggests their uneasiness at hazarding the notion. For a discussion of the *Apology* as compatible with a 'new' conception of history typified in Camden, Hayward, and Bacon, see also F. J. Levy's 'Sir Philip Sidney and the Idea of History', *Bibliothèque d'Humanisme et Renaissance* 26 (1964), 608–17. The notion that Jean Bodin's attempt to introduce 'method' into the study of history may have struck a response in Sidney (*Apology* pp. 39, 176n.) is countered by his comment to his brother Robert in 1580: 'You may reade him and gather out of many wordes some matter.' (*The Complete Works of Sir Philip Sidney*, ed. A. Feuillerat (4 vols., Cambridge, 1912–26, reprinted, with much of the verse omitted, as *The Prose Works of Sir Philip Sidney* (Cambridge, 1962, etc.), iii. 130.)

distinction between poetry and history or, in Spenserian terms, the 'Poet historicall' and the 'Historiographer'), he will also, I think, readily admit that certain doctrines, however individually modulated, seem omnipresent in the Tudor literary scene. One of these is a repeated insistence on the utility and pleasure deriving from the study of history—whether it be Greek, Roman, or English (let alone, sacred) history.[4]

Surviving historical texts, as well as their poetic derivatives, all attest to a keen and practical awareness of its values—for authors (providing matter or invention); for readers (providing pleasure as well as practical application); for the government (providing political indoctrination: 'Turne over and read the histories of all Nations, looke over the Chronicles of our owne country . . .'[5]). One need only recall the widespread diffusion of historical matter: translations of classical and continental historians, 'original' compilations of chronicles and histories, tragical legends, tragical complaints, historical epistles, chronicle and history plays, and, finally, that most esteemed of all literary forms whether translated or original, the heroic poem.

Clearly, in the sixteenth century the utility of history was acknowledged in sweeping fashion. How then, may we ask, did Sidney, so attuned to his era that he set a fashion for three literary modes (sonnet, criticism, romance), come to hold it in derogation? The answer of course is that he did not. The evidence is to be found in his letters where he speaks *in propria persona*. It may also be discerned in the *Apology*, despite its ostensible denigration of history and philosophy, when that work is seen in perspective, with due recognition of the strategies Sidney employed in achieving his stated aim: the *defence* of poetry.

If we turn to the surviving correspondence to elicit his intellectual outlook, and in particular his attitudes towards history, we can trace the development of certain of his ideas from the time he was a student protégé of Languet to the point when, at the age of twenty-six, he was in turn to give counsel to his younger brother Robert and to Edward Denny, seven years his senior. During his

---

[4] See the marshalling of witnesses in Herschel Baker's lectures on Renaissance historiography, *The Race of Time* (Toronto, 1967).

[5] 'The fourth part of the Homily against *disobedience and wilfull rebellion*', *Certaine Sermons or Homilies*, ed. M. E. Rickey and T. B. Stroup (Gainesville, Florida, 1968), p. 301.

three years' study abroad and in the years following that formative period, Sidney adjusts his views from those of a 'raw' eighteen-year-old to ones more in accord with those of his mentor. In 1579 and 1580, he began to sound like a junior Hubert Languet.

As a student at Shrewsbury School under its famed headmaster, the ardent Protestant Thomas Ashton, and during his time at Oxford, Sidney was exposed, as we know, to the standard Roman, as well as some of the Greek authors, including of course the historians. This early familiarity with history is attested to by his correspondence. Advising him on his studies in January 1574, Languet observes that he need not speak to him of the importance of reading history, 'by which more than anything else men's judgements are shaped', because, he explains, 'you are brought to it of your own accord, and you have made great progress in it'. Writing to him six years later, he again remarks on the fact that Sidney has been 'diligently engaged in the reading of history'.[6]

Allusions to specific texts show that while abroad Sidney was reading in the recent historians, and his familiarity with them is later shown by his correspondence after he returned to England when he refers to French, Italian, German, and English near-contemporaries.[7] Though he asks Languet to obtain Plutarch's works (*opuscula*) in French for him,[8] his concern with recent writers would indicate that he already owned or had read the earlier authors he was later to recommend to his brother and to Denny—Xenophon, Thucydides, Livy, Tacitus, Justin, and so on: all in all, he recommends to them more than twenty classical and medieval historians. But in December of 1573, he is concerned with timely works, offering to send Languet 'choice' books by Giovanni Tarchagnoto (*Delle historie del mondo*, 1562 and ff.), Gasparo Contarini (*De magistratibus et republica Venetorum libri quinque*, 1543 and ff.), and Donato Giannotti (*Libro de la Republica*

---

[6] For ease of reference, citations are to *The Correspondence of Sir Philip Sidney and Hubert Languet*, ed. and trans. S. A. Pears (1845), pp. 26, 169 (22 Jan. 1574; 30 Jan. 1580). I have, however, consulted the first edition of the correspondence (*Viri clarissimi epistolae politicae et historicae* (Frankfurt, 1633)) and in some instances modified the translation.

[7] See note 24.

[8] Hearsey (p. 539) assumes he was referring to the *Lives*; W. Ringler (*The Poems of Sir Philip Sidney* (Oxford, 1962), p. xxiii) to the *Morals*. A later reference to his request by Languet (1 Jan. 1574), discussed below, suggests it was the *Morals*. They had appeared in 1572; the *Lives* after the first edition in 1559 in five further editions up to 1572. From the frequent allusions in the *Apology* to derivative material, one concludes that Sidney was patently well read in both.

de'Vinitiani, 1540 and ff.).[9] In June 1574, he purchases a copy of Guicciardini in Padua,[10] and in the fall he queries a friend about Carlo Sigonio's *Historiarum de regno Italiae libri quindecim*, a work that was not to appear until the following spring.[11] Thus the extant correspondence confirms his interest in both modern and earlier periods of history.[12]

While in Venice and later in Padua, Sidney toyed with a number of intellectual possibilities—'learning the sphere, and a little music'[13] and considering the study of geometry and Greek. Invariably adopting a pragmatic approach to the education of his protégé, Languet commends him for learning the elements of astronomy, for those ignorant of it cannot know geography, and those who read history without geography are 'like men who make journeys in the dark'.[14] Three weeks later, however, he recommends that he proceed no further in the subject since he would derive no great benefit in return, and he expresses some dubiety about his continuing the study of geometry since to learn 'the rudiments of many arts for display rather than for use is foolish'. As for his study of Greek, he hesitates to advise him, urging him first to concentrate on essential matters suitable for his calling. He then goes on to enunciate a scale of values for his study: the most necessary is that provided by the Holy Scripture, the second by 'that branch of moral philosophy which teaches right and wrong', and the third by the study of history, concerning which, as mentioned above, he felt no need to convince him since he was brought to it of his own accord.[15]

---

[9] 19 Dec. 1573, Feuillerat, iii. 81; Pears, pp. 9–10.

[10] W. L. Godshalk, 'A Sidney Autograph', *Book Collector* 13 (1964), 65.

[11] Letters quoted in J. M. Osborn, *Young Philip Sidney, 1572–1577* (New Haven and London, 1972), pp. 259–61, 290.

[12] Of works dedicated to Sidney during his short lifetime, three were historical. In 1581, Henri Estienne dedicated to him his edition of the two late Greek historians Herodian and Zosimus (J. Buxton, *Sir Philip Sidney and the English Renaissance* (1954; 2nd edn. 1964, repr. 1965), p. 58). In 1584 David Powell dedicated to him a translation of Caradoc, *The History of Cambria, now called Wales*, STC 4606. Its translator was the same Humphrey Lhuyd who was the butt of a jocular exchange between Sidney and Languet for his *Commentarioli Britannicae descriptionis Fragmentum*, published in Cologne, 1572 (Osborn, pp. 140–4). In 1585 he received a dedication by the editor of a part of the three-part *Pontici Virunnii Britannicae historiae libri sex*, STC 20109 (F. B. Williams, *Index of Dedications and Commendatory Verses* (London, 1962)).

[13] 19 Dec. 1573, Feuillerat, iii. 80; Pears, p. 8.

[14] 1 Jan. 1574, Pears, p. 20.

[15] 22 Jan. 1574, Pears, pp. 25–8.

In addition to being pleased to give up the study of astronomy (though still uncertain about geometry), Sidney responds that he wishes to absorb only so much of Greek literature as will suffice to understand Aristotle well, and he asserts that he considers the *Politics* to be the most worth reading, mentioning the fact in order to offset Languet's advice that he should apply himself to *moral* philosophy.[16] While acknowledging Aristotle as a most excellent writer, in reply, Languet none the less observes that his concise and pointed style makes him 'obscure' even to those who have spent whole lifetimes reading him, and he suggests that Plutarch and other writers of that sort would better suit his purpose.[17] Of other writers of that sort, Languet clearly has Cicero in mind, for, as he had commented earlier, once Sidney began to read the *Letters* he would perhaps not require the French edition of Plutarch.[18]

Five years later his brother Robert accompanied Languet to the Continent. In an undated letter, Sidney counsels him about his travels and his studies, and his advice now echoes that of his mentor. He points out that 'Aristotles Ethicks' are 'the begyning, and foundacion of all his workes, the good ende [to] which everie man doth and ought to bend his greatest actions'.[19] The following year in counselling Edward Denny (22 May), he recommends that he too study 'some parts of Morall Philosophy': 'And therof are many bookes written; but to my pleasing Aristotles Ethickes passe; but he is somethinge darke ... Tullyes offices next if not equall, and truly for you and my selfe beyond any. With him you may joyne some of Plutarcks discourses, as of Refreining anger, of curiosity [etc.], and soe by peeces as your leysure serves.' Sidney then goes on to enunciate to Denny a scale of values for *his* study: first comes 'the foundation of foundations, and Wisdome of Wisdomes ... the holy scripture'; next Tully as the foundation 'for that mater', and finally matter relevant to his profession. This last is to be found in books dealing with 'arte' (or theory, 'what should be done') and in histories. For 'historicall maters' he suggests that before proceeding to the historians proper Denny should first read 'a litle' of Sacro Bosco's *De sphaera* and the geography of some modern

---

[16] 4 Feb. 1574, Feuillerat, iii. 84; Pears, pp. 28–9.
[17] 19 Feb. 1574, *Epistolae*, Sig. BII; Osborn, pp. 148–9.
[18] 1 Jan. 1574, Pears, p. 20; 'read both volumes of Cicero's letters, not only for the elegance of the Latin, but also for the weighty matters they contain.'
[19] Feuillerat, iii. 124.

writer, and he urges him to consult an Ortelius (*editio princeps*, 1570) so that in reading about any locale he may 'finde it out' and have it 'as it were' before his eyes. Yet he cautions him to spend only a month or a little more doing so, since he does not want 'an artificers wadinge into it'.[20]

What seems to have happened in these six or seven years is that, in accord with the view of Languet, Sidney has adopted the position of emphasizing private over public virtue (Aristotle's *Ethics* over his *Politics*), motivated in part perhaps by a sense of his own untapped potential. Three years after he was back in England he was to write bitterly to Languet: 'For to what purpose should our thoughts be directed to various kinds of knowledge, unless room be afforded for putting it into practice, so that public advantage may be the result, which in a corrupt age we cannot hope for?'[21]

Support for this new emphasis on private virtue also comes from the undated letter to Robert where to illustrate the distinction between practical knowledge and the knowledge of good and evil, he cites a line from Homer: *Qui multorum hominum mores cognovit et urbes*. By *mores*, Sidney says, Homer meant moral philosophy, 'the true discerning of mens myndes, both in vertuous passions and vices'. By *cognovit urbes*, he meant 'the knowing of their religions, pollicies, lawes, bringing upp of their children, discipline both for Warr, and Peace, and such like'. These comments, it would seem, recall comments of Languet: as early as 22 September 1573, he had commended Sidney's 'noble eagerness' to '"observe the manners and cities of many men" (as the poet says), for by this means more than anything else mens judgments are shaped'.[22] Again in 1574, while Sidney was still in Padua, he advised him on acquiring the

---

[20] J. Buxton, 'An Unpublished Letter from Sir Philip Sidney', *TLS* (24 Mar. 1972), pp. 343–4. (Here and elsewhere I expand Elizabethan abbreviations and adopt modern typographical conventions.) Sidney suggests that Denny allot an hour to Sacro Bosco and to Valerius (*De sphaera*) or another writer on astronomy as the basis for geography and then take up his history of England and his Ortelius 'to knowe the places' he reads of. Five months later in writing to Robert (18 Oct., Feuillerat, iii. 132), he says: 'I thinke yow understand the sphere, if yow doe, I care litle for any more astronomie in yow.'

[21] 1 Mar. 1578, Feuillerat, iii. 119; Pears, p. 143.

[22] *Epistolae*, Sig. AI; Osborn, p. 103. This, it should be emphasized, is exactly the same statement he makes in commending the study of history (Sig. B4), which has been quoted above (p. 150). In Languet's view, history is thus equated with the providing of both an ethical and a practical guide to human affairs; in Sidney's view, both history and philosophy provide such guides.

knowledge to live correctly. 'Keep in mind ... that to have observed the manners and cities of many men, as that other poet says, serves this purpose very well.'[23]

Concern with private virtue, concern with a pragmatic approach to learning—what he later records in the *Apology* as the Aristotelian distinction between *gnosis* and *praxis*—and a persistent concern with history reflect Sidney's outlook in 1579 and 1580, and these concerns underlie the letters to Robert and to Denny. To Robert, setting out on his travels, he points out, as mentioned earlier, the distinction between the knowledge of good and evil and practical knowledge and enjoins him to gain knowledge of such things as may be 'serviceable' to his country and 'fitt' for his calling. In conjunction with this advice he makes a revealing statement in disparagement of the study of languages, 'for wordes are but wordes, in what language soever they bee'. To the older Denny he likewise points out the distinction between knowledge 'of our selves' and the 'outward application of our selves' and then goes on to outline the scale of values for learning discussed above, taking due cognisance of his years ('this age you nowe pass in') and his profession of 'souldiery'. To both he enjoins the study of history.

Apart from the recommendation to both of specific historical texts which overlap, Sidney's letter to Robert in 1580 is the most illuminating of the three in that it gives the fullest exposition of his views. He distinguishes two approaches to historical writing: history ('story') and history set forth as a 'treatise' which goes beyond the recording and analysis of data. The first is a chronological narration of 'things done, with the beginings, cawses, and appendences [concomitants] therof' which must be studied very exactly, '*seriem temporum*', from Herodotus to Thucydides, to Xenophon, etc., through the Roman historians down to historians of the present monarchies.[24] In this study he is to note 'the

---

[23] 28 Jan. 1574, *Epistolae*, Sig. B5^v; Osborn, p. 140. While the reference is to the opening of the *Odyssey*, the verse must have been exceedingly familiar to a Renaissance reader since Horace quotes it both in the *Ars poetica*, i. 141 (*qui mores hominum multorum vidit et urbes*) and in *Epist.* I. ii. 19–20. Whereas Sidney may depart from a Horatian text in quotation (*cognovit* for *vidit* or *inspexit*), Languet quotes precisely, on occasion tacitly correcting his protégé's words in reply. For an example, see note 42.

[24] To Denny he specifies among recent historians Commines, Paulo Emilio, Guicciardini, Thomas Languet, Polydore Vergil, Melanchthon, and Holinshed. To Robert he recommends, among others, the chronology of Tarchagnoto he had earlier commended to Languet.

examples of vertue or vice, with their good or evell successes, the extablishments or ruines of greate Estates, with the cawses, the tyme and circumstances' of laws, of the beginning and ending of wars, including the stratagems of the enemy and the discipline of the soldiers. This is the approach of a 'very [true] Historiographer', a systematic presentation of 'thinges done'.

In addition to this orderly setting forth, the Historian proper 'makes himselfe a discourser [exhibiting the capacity for reflection and reason][25] for profite and an Orator, yea a Poet sometimes for ornament'. First he shows himself an Orator in 'making excellent orations *e re nata*'—as has been observed, the 'soul' of Thucydides' history—which are to be marked in the Table of Remembrance he advises Robert to keep with the 'note' of 'rhetoricall remembrances'. Secondly, he shows himself a Poet in painting forth 'the effects, the motions, the whisperings of the people', which taste of a 'poeticall vaine'. These also ought to be gallantly noted. Sidney then pointedly comments that, even though such attributions of cause and effect 'perchance' were not so, 'it is enough they might be so'.[26]

[25] cf. *Hamlet*, IV. iv. 36–9: 'Sure he that made us with such large discourse, / Looking before and after, gave us not / That capability and godlike reason / To fust in us unused.' The phrase 'discourse of reason' was in use from the fifteenth century on. For the less frequent term 'discourser', the *OED* offers applicable synonyms only as 'preacher' and 'orator', but, as the rest of his statement makes clear, Sidney is using the term to signify something other than either a divine or an orator. In the earlier letter to Robert, he uses the term more loosely: 'although some Italians in deede be excellentlie lerned, yett are they all given to soe counterfeit lerning, as a man shall learne of them more false groundes of thinges, then in anie place ells that I doe knowe for from a tapster upwardes they are all discoursers.' He then advises him to take pains in getting 'excellent men' to speak with him. cf. Languet's comments on the Italians: 'You will admire the wit and sagacity of the people. They are in truth sharp and quickwitted; yet most of them carry more on the surface than they have within, and they generally mar their attainments by too much display and become offensive.' (21 Dec. 1573, Pears, p. 12.)

[26] In commenting in his *History of the World* on the difficulty of ascertaining second causes, Ralegh alludes to Sidney's remark (*Apology*, p. 97) that historians borrow from the poets 'not onely much of their ornament, but somewhat of their substance'. None the less, he points out that they quite properly seek to ascertain 'particular humours', 'affections', 'most likely motives', and 'so figuring as neere to the life as they can imagine', they 'judiciously consider the defects in counsaile, or obliquitie in proceeding'. And he concludes that the Historian 'does not faine, that rehearseth probabilities as bare conjectures; neither doth he deprave the text, that seeketh to illustrate and make good in humane reason, those things, which authoritie alone, without further circumstance, ought to have confirmed in every mans beliefe' (II. xxi. 6, ed. C. A. Patrides (Philadelphia, 1971), pp. 213–17).

In referring to this passage, Shepherd (*Apology* p. 177n.) says that Sidney would be

The third and final merit of a Historian in teaching profit is as a Discourser, the name Sidney gives 'to who soever speakes *non simpliciter de facto, sed de qualitatibus et circumstantiis facti*'. Again it is this particular merit, Sidney says, which prompts him and many like him to 'note much with our penn then with our minde'. For the interpretation of such complex matters ('not tyed to the tenor of a question as Philosophers use') cannot be left to the 'confused trust' of memory.

As a Discourser, the Historian sometimes plays the Divine 'in telling his opinion and reasons in religion', sometimes the Lawyer 'in shewing the cawses and benefites of lawes', sometimes a Natural Philospher 'in setting downe the cawses of any strange thing' which the history compels him to speak of, but 'most commonly' a Moral Philospher 'either in the ethick part when he setts forth vertues or vices and the natures of Passions, or in the Politick when he doth (as often he doth) meddle sententiouslie with matters of Estate'. As a result, 'not professing any art', the Historian deals with 'all arts' as his matter leads him, and in displaying 'the life of a lively exemple, it is wonderfull', Sidney affirms, 'what light it gives to the arts themselves'.[27] Witness the use made of 'the discourses of the Historians' by civil lawyers ('the greate Civillians'), by Soldiers, even indeed by Philosophers and Astronomers.

Sidney then directs Robert (with the help of Henry Savile,[28] later the translator of Tacitus) to keep a Table of Remembrance, not only of what art is touched upon but also 'the next member and parcell of the art' in logical subdivisions. He should likewise

'dissatisfied' with this position, 'for he looked for a more certain truth and some knowledge of perfection'. It seems to me that, once one allows for his tactical procedure in the *Apology*, his overall point of view is very much in accord with Ralegh's.

[27] In referring to this letter, Shepherd (*Apology* p. 41) misconstrues its tenor by placing together nonsequential statements: 'Sidney in instructing his brother does not entirely commend this diffused amateurishness of the historian, who "not professing any art, as matter leades him, he deals with all arts". "And that it is which makes me and many others rather note much with our penn that with our minds."'

[28] Thomas Zouch, *Memoirs of the Life and Writings of Sir Philip Sidney* (York, 1808), p. 170n., followed by Pears, p. 199. Though circumstantial, the evidence that his mentor was *Henry* Savile seems fairly conclusive: while at Oxford, Savile established a reputation for being as able a mathematician as any of his time; in 1578 he went to the Continent where he collected manuscripts and met the most eminent scholars. In this same letter, Sidney urges his brother to 'take delight likewise in the mathematicalls, Master Savell is excellent in them' (*DNB*; John Aubrey, *Brief Lives*, ed. A. Clark (Oxford, 1898), ii. 214).

include the 'rhetoricall remembrances' remarked on before—be they witty words from Tacitus, sentences from Livy, or similitudes from Plutarch, classified accordingly as they are military ('or more spetiallie defensive militarie, or more perticulerlie, defensive by fortification').[29] He should also classify 'politick matters', conjoining with them the 'historical part', that is, an example of some stratagem or good counsel, and he should especially consider and note wherein the particular historian excels, as Dio Cassius in searching the secrets of government and Tacitus in pithily opening 'the venome of wickednes, and so of the rest'.

Thanks to the evidence provided by the extant correspondence, including the letters when he is speaking *in propria persona* and those when he is being addressed by Languet, we conclude that Sidney did indeed acknowledge the pleasure and, above all, the utility to be derived from reading the historians—ancient, medieval, and modern—a conclusion that is supported by his predilections, his general familiarity with the subject, and his specific recommendations to his brother and to Denny.

In turning to the *Apology*, one can only be struck by the way that, given its strategical method, its views cohere with those expressed in the correspondence. We note that the 'noblest scope' to which any learning is directed is 'goodness' or moral doctrine, 'the chief of all knowledges'. Learning, 'under what name soever it come forth' or 'to what immediate end soever it be directed', has as its final purpose to draw us to 'as high a perfection as our degenerate souls, made worse by their clayey lodgings, can be capable of'.

The focus of the treatise, then, is to establish poetry as the most efficient of the several arts in attaining this end. Sidney cites four—history, philosophy, divinity (quickly excepted from secular learning), and law—as the only ones that deal in the 'consideration of men's manners' (the Homeric *multorum hominum mores* or the 'true discerning of mens myndes both in vertuous passions and vices' he had set forth in the earlier letter to Robert). Other kinds of learning—astronomy, music, mathematics, as well as 'natural and supernatural' philosophy—while having a private end in themselves (hence practical and relating to the 'outward application of our

---

[29] In the earlier undated letter he had also enjoined him to note the fortifications and garrisons of each country visited, advice again reflecting his own experience: in 1573 he took occasion to make a side trip from Strasbourg in order to inspect the fortifications under construction at Phalsbourg (Osborn, p. 90).

selves', as he put it in the letter to Denny) are directed to the 'highest end of the mistress-knowledge' which is the knowledge of ourselves in its 'ethic and politic consideration' but with the end of 'well doing and not of well knowing only'. In his account of the 'architectonic arts', Sidney is of course drawing on Aristotle's discussion in the *Nicomachean Ethics*, with the difference that he joins ethics *with* politics (as in the 1580 letter to Robert) whereas for Aristotle the 'mistress-knowledge' (or 'master art') is politics.[30]

In order to exalt the poet above his 'other competitors' in the learned arts, Sidney has only, he states, to reckon with the four concerned with 'men's manners'. Having dismissed the divine, he easily discounts the lawyer (who endeavours not 'to make men good' but rather to see that 'their evil hurt not others'). But in dispensing with the philosopher and the historian, he faces a more difficult task. This justifies the more extensive treatment accorded them as well as the sharp vignettes of each he provides (the one appearing 'with a sullen gravity', the other 'loaden with old mouse-eaten records'). With the perspective afforded by Sidney's letters, the reason is not far to seek: he rejects them only as a tactical device.

As is to be expected from the letters, one of the tactics he adopts is to declare that both the philosopher and the historian make use of poetry. For the former (his burden great), he names Plato in somewhat sophistical fashion—whom 'of all philosophers I have ever esteemed most worthy of reverence, and with great reason: since of all philosophers he is the most poetical'.[31] The philo-

---

[30] Sidney's conjoining of ethics with politics is still of course Aristotelian as in the *Rhetoric* (I. ii. 1356a), just as the connection of rhetoric with ethics and politics is also Aristotelian (I.viii. 1366a). For Sidney's familiarity with the *Rhetoric*, see p. 161.

[31] Although some profess to find Sidney reflecting Platonism in the *Apology* (e.g. I. Samuel, 'The Influence of Plato on Sir Philip Sidney's *Defence of Poesie*,' *MLQ* I (1940), 383–91 and F. M. Krouse, 'Plato and Sidney's *Defence of Poesie*', *CL* VI (1954), 138–47), he is, so far as I can see, Aristotelian at heart. When it comes to *defending* poetry, he obviously must reckon with the most notorious rejection of the poets as he attempts to do in the passage dealing with the '*Idea* or fore-conceit'. He later again counters Plato's rejection of poets, this time by means of the flat assertion that he banished the abuse and not 'the thing' itself. His justification: it would 'full evil' become him to put such words against the poets in the mouth of his master—'the only wise man' by confirmation of Apollo. For (it is said) Socrates too was a poet. Sidney's manifest technique, candidly acknowledged, is to enlist Plato at strategic moments as 'patron', not to confront him as 'adversary'.

Yet, in accord with his dextrous shifts of strategy, he feels free to include the Platonic 'especially' among the 'farfetched maxims of Philosophy', since they require a

sopher, we accept, is consequently successful in inciting to well doing only when he borrows the 'masking raiment of Poesy'— witness Plato (p. 128), Cicero (p. 107), and Boethius (p. 114).

Equally, since he is 'bound to tell things as they were'[32] (though one recalls his statement to Robert that for second causes it is enough that 'they might be so'), the historian is able to set forth a 'perfect pattern' only when he is being poetical. Plutarch, who 'trimmeth' *both* the garments of history and philosophy 'with guards of Poesy', is the prime example.

Sidney, furthermore, acknowledges that the philosopher provides doctrine relating to virtues and vices as well as to 'matters of public policy or private government', doctrine that remains 'dark', however, until figured forth in poetry. The historian likewise provides examples of virtue and vice, as we remember from the 1580 letter to Robert (though, significantly, Sidney does not say so here, p. 107). To exalt the poet above both his competitors, he has consequently to emphasize the imaged particularity of philosophic precept and historical example in his definition: the poet is the *feigner* of notable images of virtues and vices which issue in 'delightful teaching'. Admitting that so far as 'teaching' (or *gnosis*) is concerned, the philosopher may be superior and, so far as rendering a particular example truly, history is superior, Sidney asserts that in pragmatic terms (*praxis*) the feigned example is of the more 'use and learning'. As opposed to the obscure teaching provided by the philosopher (though not necessarily by the historian—a point Sidney, significantly, also does not make here since he has earlier acknowledged the 'force' of a true example to teach, p. 110), the poet is seen as 'the right popular philosopher',

grounding in geometry. He feels free to remark derisively on Plato's inability to deal with Dionysius effectively, on the 'abominable filthiness' which he authorized in the *Phaedrus* and the *Symposium*, on the 'community of women' which he allowed in the commonwealth from whence he banished the poets; lastly, he freely discounts the doctrine of divine inspiration. In contrast, apart from the implication in the remark that Alexander left his schoolmaster (the living Aristotle) behind while taking dead Homer with him, all the references to Aristotle are endorsements.

[32] In stressing the 'bare *was*' of the historian which necessitates his allowing of 'that which we call fortune' to overrule wise actions, Sidney parallels a passage in Amyot where he explains that fortune is 'nought else' but a 'fained devise of mans wit' to account for his ignorance of first causes ('Gods infinite power and incomprehensible wisdome'), a view with which Sidney obviously would have agreed. In contrast to the asseveration in the *Apology*, Amyot then candidly admits that wise actions do not always eventuate in happy outcomes (Sig. A6, 1603 edition of North's translation, where the Preface occupies Sigg. A4–A8).

providing, in accord with the sugared pill theory, 'food for the tenderest stomacks'. None the less, he unerringly places his stress on the power of the feigned example to move the reader to 'right action' since it may be tuned to the highest key of passion. And he attributes the effectiveness of the individual poet to 'that forcible-ness or *energia*' wherein 'the highest point of man's wit' may be compared 'with the efficacy of Nature'.[33]

None the less, Sidney is not quite willing to surrender 'the life of a lively exemple' (1580 letter to Robert) even for forensic purposes. Thus he acknowledges that, whatsoever action or faction, or counsel, policy, or war stratagem the historian 'is bound to recite', the poet may 'if he list' make it his own, 'beautifying it both for further teaching, and more delighting, as it pleaseth him' (p. 111).[34] As the different genres are good if severed, conjunction cannot be hurtful. Hence the Elizabethan 'Poet historicall'.

Concerned in the main with the art and not the artificer, since it is, after all, not Poetry that 'abuseth man's wit' but rather 'man's wit that abuseth Poetry', Sidney offers a prescription for the correction of these abuses: Art, Imitation, and Exercise provide the wings of the true Daedalian art, and the prescription itself provides Sidney with an easy introduction to his survey of the current state of English poetry.

Though the *Apology* was not to become generally known until its appearance in the two editions of 1595, it obviously had circulated in manuscript—as John Harington's 'Briefe Apologie' prefacing his translation of Ariosto (1591) attests; its composition has been variously assigned to a date between 1579 and 1583.[35] Ever since the 1808 publication of Thomas Zouch's *Memoirs of the Life and Times of Sir Philip Sidney*, the notion that he was responding to

[33] For a survey of this vexed critical term, frequently confused with *enargia*, and the frequent misinterpretation of critics, see W. Gibson, 'The Energy Crisis: *Enargia and Energia*', unpublished Master's Essay, Columbia University, 1974.

[34] This statement is, of course, a modification of his earlier assertion that, in imitating, the *right* poet borrows 'nothing of what is, hath been, or shall be', but ranges 'only reined with learned discretion, into the divine consideration; of what may be and should be' (p. 102). See also note 43 for another statement of this point of view which is at odds with the authority of 'Aristotle himself', earlier cited with approval.

[35] On the basis of the so-called digression on English poetry, O. B. Hardison has recently argued ('The Two Voices of Sidney's *Apology for Poetry*', *ELR* 2 (1972), 97–9) for composition in two 'phases', the 'newer material . . . incompletely harmonized with the old'.

Gosson's *School of Abuse* has been generally current. This stage attack with its dedication to Sidney was entered in the Stationers' Register 22 July 1579, and, though Spenser was to declare in a letter written a few months later that he was scorned for his action, Gosson was shortly to dedicate a second volume to him (the *Ephemerides of Phialo* with an appended 'Apologie' of the *School of Abuse*, entered 7 November). Whether or not his 'pitiful defence' is seen as a direct reply to Gosson among other poet whippers, it is certain that Sidney knew the work dedicated to him.[36]

It is equally certain that he knew Amyot's defence of history prefacing North's fine translation of Plutarch's *Lives*, with its dedication to the Queen, which was also published in 1579 in two issues (entered 6 April). While the new correspondence (brought together in *Young Philip Sidney*) is conspicuous for its almost total lack of reference to contemporary poetry, by 1580 Sidney had slipped into his 'unelected vocation', having written *The Lady of May* (performed in 1578 before the Queen at Wanstead), experimented with classical metrics according to Spenser, and progressed sufficiently on the *Arcadia* so that he could promise Robert, in October 1580, 'with Gods helpe' to send him his 'toyfull booke' by the following February.

Similarly, since the 1935 publication of Kenneth Myrick's *Sir Philip Sidney as a Literary Craftsman*, recognition of the generic basis of the *Apology* as a judicial oration has also been generally current. Though questions have been raised as to its several divisions,[37] no one, I think, questions its intent to persuade. Certainly some of the techniques Sidney uses are analysed in Aristotle's *Rhetoric*, 'the directest' source of knowledge, according to John Hoskyns, 'to describe, to move, to appease, or to prevent [anticipate] any motion whatsoever, whereunto whosoever can fit his speech shall be truly eloquent', and Hoskyns points out that Sidney's knowledge of the *Rhetoric* was manifest to him even before he knew of his translation of the first two books.[38]

Attuned, as we are, to its forensic nature, I should like now to

---

[36] In his *Stephen Gosson* (1942, repr. New York, 1972), pp. 116–22, W. Ringler, accepting the *Apology* as, in part, a reply, offers a reconciliation of interpretations and facts variously seen in conflict in this matter. See note 12 for reference to another dedication to Sidney of a work, the translator of which had been jocularly abused in an exchange between Languet and Sidney.

[37] See *Apology* pp. 12–3 and, more recently, Hardison.

[38] *Directions for Speech and Style*, ed. H. H. Hudson (Princeton, 1935), p. 41.

consider Sidney's substantial use of Amyot's Preface. Since most of the borrowings (though by no means all of the parallel views) have been well catalogued in the notes to Shepherd's edition, it is sufficient for my purpose to point out that, while many of the ideas are to be found in either one or another source or are Renaissance commonplaces, the essential configuration of Amyot's defence appears in Sidney's, albeit wrested to other ends. There was no need for him to go far afield in search of a pattern of argument.

Amyot begins with a general defence of literature—which, if pleasurable only, is misliked; if profitable only, seems harsh to delicate wits; and he endorses the Renaissance Horatian blend, the one 'profiting the more because of the delight', the other 'delighting the more because of the profit'. Of literary kinds history is the best. In support, he offers three arguments: its antiquity— even pre-literate men delivered in song the 'remembrance of things past'[39]—its immortalizing quality, and its truth in treating the greatest and highest things that are done in the world. History, furthermore, is superior to moral philosophy in grace, efficacy, and speed of precept because examples are of more force 'to move and instruct';[40] it is likewise superior to poetry in weight and gravity, and it is superior to civil laws and ordinances in both grace and modesty since it is better to teach and instruct than to chastize or punish (or, obversely stated in Sidney's Horatian words, serving 'to make men good rather *formidine poenae* than *virtutis amore*'). Yet, since history punishes, as it were, by reproach of 'everlasting infamie' and rewards by 'immortall praise and glorie', it is a lively spur, leading to the end of 'good doing' (Sidney's 'right action'). For it is by the example of the heroical deeds of the wise and valiant that the spirit of emulation is aroused in men. To delight, to teach, and to move by the power of the particular example is Amyot's essential justification; in the *Apology* this becomes of course the power of the *feigned* example.

Amyot's answer to the argument of experience (called 'the schoolemistris of fooles') issues in Sidney's stress on the harmlessness of fiction—which enables one to save his nose in the bargain—

---

[39] However well known to us from Shakespeare's Sonnet 30, North could have been recalling the phrase either from the Great Bible, the Bishops' Bible, or the Geneva Bible (Book of Wisdom 11: 12; 11: 10).

[40] In his note on sources for Sidney's 'moving to well doing', Shepherd (*Apology* p. 181), curiously, ignores Amyot though Hearsey does not.

a merit of reading history, according to Amyot. In North's translation, the passage has, in fact, a very Sidneian ring: 'Therefore we must not tarie for this wit that is wonne by experience, which costeth so deare, and is so long in comming, that a man is oft times dead in the seeking of it before he have attained it, so as he had need of a second life to employ it in, because of the overlate comming by it.' (Sig. A6.)

He next prescribes the three means whereby princes can acquire knowledge to govern in peace and war—the conventional triad of Nature (innate ability), Art (gotten by the examples and the 'wise discourses' in good histories), and Practice; and he then goes on to point out that its abuse should be ascribed to the practitioner, not to the art itself.

One can only be struck by the similar deployment of persuasive argument in the two works. As we have seen, in his personal correspondence Sidney did not reject either the appeal or the utility of history. Why then should he have so obviously wrested the arguments brought together by Amyot to the justification of poetry in the *Apology*, as Elizabethan readers familiar with North's translation in the early 1580s would have noted? Though one may doubt his considered endorsement of the commonplace notion that, next to *ratio*, *oratio* is the greatest gift bestowed on mortals ('wordes', opposed to 'right action', are 'but wordes, in what language soever they bee'). Sidney clearly polished his 'speech' and considered his 'words' in writing the *Apology* (pp. 121–2). In fact, his ease of accomplishment has led many to accept its cast of ideas—some useful only in terms of argumentation, which he surely would have been the first to concede—as revealing his strong commitment to an exalted view of poetry among the several liberal arts. Even when one allows for the derogation of his own literary efforts as a courtly pose, his letters show him motivated by a profoundly serious concept of personal and patriotic duty (however much the latter aim was to be frustrated).[41]

[41] As early as 1578, Sidney complains to Languet that his pen has fallen into disuse and that his mind, 'if it ever were active in anything', is now beginning by reason of his fruitless leisure to lose its vigour and to become lax; he then goes on to express his frustration at his lack of service to the state to which I have referred above (p. 153). On several occasions Languet rallied him to forego an easy escape from tempestuous affairs of state (22 Oct. 1578; 24 Sept., 22 Oct. 1580). After his visit to England when he had seen him functioning in a courtly milieu, he rebuked him for wasting the flower of his life, expressing fears lest he take pleasure in pursuits that would only enervate his mind (14 Nov. 1579, Pears, p. 167).

The anecdote with which he begins the work derives from his (unfeigned) experience at the court of Maximilian II—John Pietro Pugliano's extolling of horses and horsemen (the former 'peerless' among beasts, the latter, like 'peerless' poets, triumphant both in camps and courts). A 'piece of a logician', Sidney implies that in following his master Pugliano he too undertakes his task motivated by 'self-love' which is better 'than any gilding to make that seem gorgeous wherein ourselves are parties'. Acknowledging that his master's 'strong affection and weak arguments' may not be satisfactory, he offers the 'nearer example' of himself, thus allowing the reader, who may also be a piece of a logician, to extrapolate that this defence in behalf of poetry may in its turn represent 'strong affection and weak arguments'.

This attractive introduction is generally accounted for as part of the recognized judicial method of capturing the good will of an audience by humorous anecdote or mock expostulation (Shepherd, p. 13). In addition, of course, it skilfully sets the tone of the total work as persuasive demonstration of how 'honey sweet' eloquence may be directed to achieving its designated end.

Sidney then proceeds with the argument of poetry's antiquity, its universality (used by the earliest philosophers and historians), and its etymology—as Hardison shrewdly points out, a kind of proof based on the names for 'poet' in several languages. Before proceeding to his first very syncretic (Aristotelian, Horatian, and Simonidean–Plutarchan) definition of poetry, he offers his notable answer to Plato, an answer that should not be 'jestingly conceived' even though 'the works' of Nature are 'essential' and those of the poet are 'imitation or fiction'. It is to declare that the knowledge ('skill') of the artificer 'standeth' in the '*Idea* or fore-conceit of the work' and not 'in the work itself'.

Neither let this be jestingly conceived, because the works of the one be essential, the other an imitation or fiction; for any understanding knoweth the skill of the artificer standeth in that *Idea* or fore-conceit of the work, and not in the work itself. And that the poet hath that *Idea* is manifest, by delivering them forth in such excellency as he hath imagined them. (p. 101.)

This is of course an argument by good intentions unless the poet can indeed deliver 'them forth'—the antecedent must be 'works'— 'in such excellency as he hath imagined them'. With the force of a 'divine breath',[42] Sidney says, the poet is able to surpass the doings of Nature and thus provide the 'perfect pattern' of exemplary action.[43]

Consequently, by the end of the *confirmatio* (p. 120), we are persuaded that of all the (formerly denigrated) serving sciences, it is indeed poetry, though never so labelled, that is chief. Directed to attaining the 'mistress-knowledge'—the knowledge of man's self in the ethic and politic consideration—it is poetry itself that must be reckoned 'in the most excellent work' of teaching and inciting to virtue as 'the most excellent workman' (p. 115).[44] Accordingly, when we come to evaluate the theoretical basis of this most accomplished of critical works, the essential point, I think, is not whether the evidence warrants the conclusion or even whether that conclusion would have been fully endorsed by the Sidney of the letters. Rather it is to recognize that we accede to its validity without unduly questioning the multiple strategies used, so adroitly has its author handled his proofs.

[42] In the 1 Mar. 1578 letter referred to above, Sidney describes the individual mind as a 'particle of the divine mind' (*divinae mentis particula*, a phrase which Languet (2 May 1578) commends (*et tu eleganter scribis*) but then rephrases, following Horace, as *divinae particula aurae* (*Epist.* Sig. L2; *Sat.* II. ii. 79).

[43] Since Sidney, like most Elizabethans, recognized in practice the dubious aesthetic results of depicting an 'unmixed' character, his term 'perfect pattern' must refer to the 'right action' a paradigmatic figure ultimately achieves. In enunciating the view that a poet names a Cyrus or Aeneas only to show 'what men of their fames, fortunes, and estates should do' (pp. 124–5), Sidney is modifying a passage of Aristotle he had earlier quoted with approval: '"the universal weighs what is fit to be said or done, either in likelihood or necessity."' (p. 109; *Poetics* 1451b.) Later, it is true, Aristotle describes things as 'they ought to be' as one possible class of representation (1460b). See also note 34 for another instance of a modified point of view relating to this same aesthetic problem. Such later modifications of ideas proposed earlier do not, I submit, reflect on Sidney as a 'piece of a logician' but rather represent conscious shifts of strategy for forensic ends: in Horatian terms, to 'say at the moment what at that moment should be said' (*Ars poetica*, i. 43, trans. H. Rushton Fairclough, Loeb Classical Library, 1955).

[44] In sixteenth-century generic terms, this means of course it is that most esteemed of literary forms, the heroic poem, whether written in verse or prose, that most aptly conforms to this requirement. As Spenser was to put it in the letter to Ralegh, the intention of the 'Poet historicall' is to set forth the example of 'a good governour and a vertuous man'. In accord with excellent literary precedent, ancient and modern, they may be 'ensampled' either in a single figure (like Orlando) or two (like Rinaldo and Godfredo), the one representing 'that part which they in Philosophy call Ethice, or vertues of a private man', the other representing that part called 'Politice'. In determining on the 'most plausible and pleasing' way of achieving his purpose in *The Faerie Queene*, Spenser says that he selected a 'historicall fiction' (Sidney's 'imitation') because 'the most part of men' take delight in such reading for the 'variety of matter' rather than for the 'profite of the ensample'. *In propria persona*, Sidney no doubt would have concurred.

It is, however, in answering the several traditional charges directed against poetry that Sidney is seen at his most dazzling verbal best, arguing by affirmation, concession, denigration, denial, authority, and what have you. And it is the citation of authorities, including exponents of views he opposes, that makes for the happy mockery of the peroration, which descends to the appeal to self-interest: your name shall flourish in the printers' shops; you shall be of kin to many a poetical preface. Counterposing this appeal is the double anathema pronounced on the enemies of poetry: to live in love and never get favour for lacking skill of a sonnet—a far cry from the high claims that have been made for the 'peerless poet'—and to be forgotten after death for want of an epitaph, a reductive parallel to Amyot's claim for the historian's immortalizing words, which 'neither picture, nor pillar, nor sumptuous sepulcher' can match.

Myrick has rightly observed that Sidney's technique is a display of courtly *sprezzatura*. This is certainly true. Not only is Sidney artful in a seemingly artless fashion, he is also brilliantly illogical ('a piece of a logician'), mustering the necessary tactics for the necessary reasons. It is especially true, moreover, when we recognize, as Elizabethan readers in the early 1580s would have recognized, that throughout the *Apology* Sidney has very eloquently turned Amyot's pattern of eloquent argument to his own ends. While not, in fact, opposing history (or even philosophy), he adapted the configuration of Amyot's Preface in order to underscore his own forensic performance: the use of 'honey sweet' eloquence to achieve a designated aim—the *defence* of poetry. Skilfully manipulating matter and words (*res et verba*) and thus illustrating the *right* use of Art and Imitation, in contrast to current practice, he made the *Apology* itself a demonstration of his proposition that a 'fiction' indeed has the power to move, to instruct, and, above all, to delight.

Seen in perspective, then, the *Apology* is not only in harmony with Sidney's intellectual outlook as evidenced in the correspondence; it is also in harmony with his other major achievements, and it should be classed with them as a literary construct. In writing his 'toyfull booke' he undertook to present his Arcadian heroes in actions relating to an ethical and political consideration—the highest end of the 'mistress-knowledge'. In writing *Astrophil and Stella*, he undertook to present 'strong affection and weak arguments' deftly manipulated to the intent of winning favour by 'skill' of a sonnet. As a result, both of these may be said to illustrate the practical application of Sidneian criticism even though that too is a 'fiction'.

Astrophil and Stella

7. SIDNEY AND THE SUPPLE MUSE: COMPOSITIONAL PROCEDURES IN SOME SONNETS OF *ASTROPHIL AND STELLA*

Germaine Warkentin

PHILISIDES. But when I first did fal, what brought most fall to my hart?
ECHO.   Arte.

In the first sonnet of *Astrophil and Stella*, the poet–lover's self-condemnation is shaped for us by the problem afforded by the composition of the poem itself. In this, the *excusatio* of his collection, Sidney sets to one side the retrospection of Petrarch's 'Voi ch'ascoltate in rime sparse il suono' (the archetype of most such opening poems), but he does not entirely abandon his original. In the *Canzoniere* Petrarch admits that 'che quanto piace al mondo è breve sogno', and enters the plea for pity that is, finally, the only defence the peccant lover can make. In Sidney's sonnet sequence Astrophil demonstrates his imperfection in the poem itself: as everyone knows, he mistakenly turns to the example of others for guidance in composition, instead of looking to the image of Stella graven on his heart which ought to have provided him with his point of departure, the ground of his invention. His plight cannot have been an uncommon one; as Leonard Cox wrote in 1524, 'whomsoever desyreth to be a good oratour or to dyspute and commune of any maner thyng' will discover that 'the most difficile or harde is to invente what thou must saye wherfore of this parte the Rhetoryciens which be maysters of this arte have written very moche and diligently'.[1] Astrophil does not appear to have read any of these masters, though we can be sure that Sidney had; his own command of the art of the oration is evident in *The Defence of Poesy*, and his interest may have been fairly technical, for he is reputed to have translated the first two books of Aristotle's *Rhetoric*.[2] Whatever the case may be, it is clear

Reprinted by permission of Georgia State University from *Studies in the Literary Imagination* 15 (1982), 37–48.

[1] Leonard Cox, *The Arte of Rhetoryke* (1524, repr. Amsterdam, 1977), Aiiii^r and Aiiii^v.
[2] *The Poems of Sir Philip Sidney*, ed. W. A. Ringler Jr. (Oxford, 1962), p. xix.

that, in handling his introductory poem in this way, Sidney is issuing an explicit invitation to consider this poem, and possibly the rest of his collection, in the light of its compositional procedures, and taking for granted what no audience of his day needed to have pointed out, that these are the procedures of classical rhetoric.[3] In this essay, I take up the poet's invitation, first by looking closely at three sonnets of *Astrophil and Stella*, and then by examining the implications for a reading of the sequence as a whole of the approach to composition which I argue they represent.

For a Renaissance poet, freely applying the categories of public oratory to his poetic practice in the phenomenon George Kennedy calls *letteraturizzazione*,[4] invention or 'finding' is the step which initiates the process moderns call 'composition'. The operations of this process are determined by whether the orator/poet conceives of his task as argumentation or display; that is, whether rhetoric for him is philosophical or sophistic. This has an important effect both on the way a poem is generated, and on the way it is developed for the reader. The 'philosophical' orator/poet isolates the agreed-upon issues—the *stasis*—in a problem, so that he can then elaborate an argument. The sophistic too seeks a stable point from which to begin—a *topos*, a 'place'—but he is likely to find it in the accepted wisdom of his age (we still term this kind of knowledge 'commonplace') and to develop it as a display of his skill in embellishment. George Gascoigne's much-quoted remarks on invention illustrate the difference:

The first and most necessarie poynt that ever I founde meete to be considered in making of a delectable poeme is this, to grounde it upon some fine invention. For it is not inough to roll in pleasant woordes, nor yet to thunder in *Rym*, *Ram*, *Ruff* by letter (quoth my master *Chaucer*) nor yet to abounde in apt vocables or epythetes, unless the Invention have in it also *aliquid salis*. . . . If I should undertake to wryte in prayse of a gentlewoman, I would neither prayse hir christal eye, nor hir cherrie lippe, etc. For these things are *trita et obvia*. But I would either finde some supernaturall cause wherby my penne might walke in the superlative degree, or

---

[3] It seems clear that statements like this about the primacy of rhetoric no longer need extended defence; see, for example, T. O. Sloan and R. B. Waddington, *The Rhetoric of Renaissance Poetry from Wyatt to Milton* (Berkeley, 1974), p. 1, and also Sloan's essay in that volume, 'The Crossing of Rhetoric and Poetry in the English Renaissance', pp. 212–42.

[4] G. Kennedy, *Classical Rhetoric and Its Christian and Secular Tradition from Ancient to Modern Times* (Chapel Hill, 1980), pp. 16–17 and *passim*.

els I would undertake to aunswere for any imperfection that shee hath, and thereupon rayse the prayse of hir commendacion.[5]

Against the epideictic effect of externally applied embellishment—alliteration, the blazon, the ornamental epithet—Gascoigne poses the *aliquid salis* of a treatment which seeks a cause, and an answer, and thus makes possible a direct and argumentative entry into the subject matter itself. The difference—for the poet, since here we must leave behind the orator—is the difference between poetry which canonizes accepted wisdom, 'categorical' poetry, as Leonard Nathan calls it, and poetry which is much more investigative, the kind Nathan calls 'relational'.[6]

It is the conflict between these two methods which Sidney exploits in his opening sonnet. The first line of the poem flatly establishes the facts of the case, which are nowhere controverted: Astrophil loves 'in truth'. But it is not until the last line that Astrophil himself succeeds in recognizing—literally 'finding'—the 'place' where this truth is situated, and out of which he can develop the proofs that will persuade Stella to love him. Instead, he uses a method extrinsic to the material before him, leafing through the poems of others in the fashion of a schoolboy with his commonplace book. This is not Invention, but Study; Invention is 'Nature's child', says Sidney, attributing to it something of that priority in the order of things with which Spenser endows Nature herself, in his portrait of the

> . . . great Grandmother of all creatures bred
> Great Nature, ever young yet full of eld,
> Still mooving, yet unmoved from her sted;
> Unseene of any, yet of all upheld.
>
> (*Faerie Queene*, VII. vii. 13.)

Gabriel Harvey was making the same point in his own inimitable way when he wrote briskly in the margin of his copy of

[5] George Gascoigne, *Certayne Notes of Instruction* (1575), in *Elizabethan Critical Essays*, ed. G. G. Smith (2 vols, Oxford, 1904), i. 47, 48.

[6] L. Nathan, 'Gascoigne's "Lullabie" and Structures in the Tudor Lyric', in Sloan and Waddington, pp. 58–72. Nathan discusses (n. 15) the same passage from Gascoigne I quoted above, but remains unsure about the extent to which Gascoigne possesses an adequate terminology for differentiating between the two approaches. For a useful treatment of the same kind of problem from a different perspective, see the discussion of 'Normal' and 'Prudential' method in Ramist rhetorics by J. Webster, ' "The Methode of a Poete": An Inquiry into Tudor Conceptions of Poetic Sequence', *ELR* 11 (1981), 22–43.

Gascoigne, 'the Invention must guide & rule the Elocution: non contra'.[7]

By insisting on the priority of 'Nature' over 'Study' in inventing, Sidney is rejecting all that is represented by the schoolroom stress on the systematic assembling of a useful repertoire of common-places—traditional wisdom in sententious form—which was encouraged by the compilers of 'Nizolian paper books' and which is dazzlingly demonstrated by even so discriminating a rhetorician as Erasmus in *De copia*. Always 'a piece of a logician', Sidney returns to Aristotle's emphasis on the priority of the reasoning process in all rhetorical art (and in so doing, illustrates why it is so tempting to class him with the Ramists). Yet if we examine very carefully the compositional devices, rhetorical and otherwise, used by Sidney in *AS* 1, we shall find that, in his own writing, the boundary between 'relational' and 'categorical', between argument and accepted wisdom, is by no means clearly drawn.

As we have seen, the *stasis* established in line one of *AS* 1 is that Astrophil loves 'in truth'. The poem which develops from this starting-point is structured as a demonstrative enthymeme, a procedure in rhetorical reasoning in which conclusions are drawn from the premises admitted in the *stasis* (Aristotle, *Rhetoric*, II. xxiii). The result has the character that a syllogism would have in dialectic: '*since* such-and-such was the case, *therefore* I did such-and-such, *but* things fell out as follows, *thus* in the end . . .' Aristotle listed twenty-eight topics appropriate for initiating the development of such enthymemes; if Sidney were using the *Rhetoric* for guidance he may have had in mind the twenty-seventh, for this topic 'consists in making use of errors committed, for purposes of accusation or defence' (*Rhet*. II. xxiii). If this is indeed the case, the poet has a double opportunity in *AS* 1, for, in accusing Astrophil of a vice, he can at the same time establish the praiseworthiness of the opposing virtue, and thus exhibit that skill in recognizing the opposites of propositions which is essential to a speaker who must anticipate every strategy of his opponent. Thus in this poem the resources of rhetoric as Sidney conceives it yield,

---

[7] Gabriel Harvey, *Marginalia*, ed. G. C. Moore Smith (Stratford-upon-Avon, 1913), p. 169. The marginal note is not on the Gascoigne passage I have quoted, but concerns Gascoigne's remarks on 'auncient English Wordes' (Smith, p. 51). Harvey's complete entry is: 'A pithie rule of Sir Philips Apologie for Poetrie. The Invention must guide & rule the Elocution: non contra.'

as we can see, a compositional method which, while sure and principled, is at the same time open to deft and unexpected manœuvre.

Yet, if the compositional procedures of *AS* 1 open the poem to the searching method of dialectic, they also draw on certain more closed and formal structures which come to Sidney from the schoolroom exercises of the *progymnasmata*, and are represented in the work of such rhetoricians as Thomas Wilson, whose *Arte of Rhetorique* Sidney must have been familiar with, since he had known its author from boyhood.[8] It is under such influence that Sidney would have, for example, acquired skill in the kind of embellishment which Abraham Fraunce savoured in the *gradatio* of the first lines of the sonnet.[9] Paradoxically, part of the poem's energy comes from just such a set piece of rhetorical art: the enthymeme is presented as a narrative in the past tense, and the sonnet thus becomes one of several examples in *Astrophil and Stella* of Fable or Apologue. The attraction of such brief tales, says Erasmus, 'is due to their witty imitation of the way people behave, and the hearers give their assent because the truth is set out vividly before their very eyes'.[10] Nothing more congenial to the vivid Sidneian mode can be imagined, and the interweaving of rhetorical argument and rhetorical set piece is so adeptly managed as to be invisible, except in its delightful effect. Nevertheless, the presence of the set piece is as important to the composition of the poem as its argumentative method.

But there is more to be said about Sidney's 'inventing' in this poem, and it throws new light on his relationship with his sources. I began by calling *AS* 1 an *excusatio*. As such it represents a vigorous Renaissance tradition, one based on Petrarch's 'Voi ch'ascoltate' but with earlier analogues in Boethius and the Latin elegists.[11] But *AS* 1 is also related to the twentieth sonnet of Petrarch's *Canzoniere*, though in a way not immediately apparent. Petrarch's poem is as follows:

---

[8] *Poems*, p. xix.

[9] Abraham Fraunce, *The Arcadian Rhetorike*, ed. E. Seaton (Oxford, 1950), pp. 38–9.

[10] Erasmus, *De copia*, trans. Betty I. Knott, in *Collected Works of Erasmus*, v. 24, *Literary and Educational Writings*, ed. C. R. Thompson (Toronto, 1978), Pt. 2, p. 631. Other examples of Fable or Apologue in *Astrophil and Stella* include *AS* 8, 13, 16, 17, 20, and several other poems in which the device plays an important role like *AS* 73, 92, and 105.

[11] G. Warkentin, ' "Love's sweetest part, variety": Petrarch and the Curious Frame of the Renaissance Sonnet Sequence', *Renaissance and Reformation*, 11 (1975), 14–23.

Vergognando talor ch'ancor si taccia,
Donna, per me vostra bellezza in rima,
ricorro al tempo ch'i' vi vidi prima,
tal che null'altra fia mai che mi piaccia.

ma trovo peso non da le mie braccia,
ne ovra da polir colla mia lima:
però l'ingegno che sua forza estima
ne l'operazion tutto s'agghiaccia.

Più volte già per dir le labbra apersi,
poi rimase la voce in mezzo 'l petto:
ma qual son poria mai salir tant'alto?

Più volte incominciai di scriver versi,
ma la penna et la mano et l'intelletto
rimaser vinti nel primier assalto.[12]

    Ashamed sometimes at having ceased to speak
About your beauty, Lady, in my rhyme,
I think back to the time I saw you first,
For nothing else will ever please me more.
    That weight I find ill-suited to my strength
And not for my file's polishing that work;
However shaping skill esteems its power,
In practice everything is turned to ice.
    How often when I part my lips to speak
My voice remains in silence in my breast—
Though what sound ever could ascend so high?
    How many times I've started to write verse,
To find that pen and hand and intellect
Remain still conquered by the first assault.

            (J. W. Cook and G. Warkentin 1983.)

In both sonnets, the poet–lover complains of an inability to write, but the Petrarchan poem is meditative in cast; it lacks the rigorous cause-and-effect structure of the Sidneian one. Furthermore, Petrarch attributes his failure to write adequately of Laura to the height of his subject matter; it is a paradoxical effect of Laura's beauty that it freezes the poet's art, rather than freeing it. Yet the two poems seem to share a common ground, or rather to revolve around the same axis. On the one hand, the poet is possessed of

---

[12] Francesco Petrarca, *Canzoniere*, ed. G. Contini (Torino, 1968), p. 22. (All further references to Petrarch's text are to this edition.) The translations are from a forthcoming translation of the *Canzoniere* by J. W. Cook and G. Warkentin.

a vision of his lady (in Petrarch's retrospective mode, 'al tempo ch'i' vi vidi prima'; in Sidney's more immediate one, the picture graven on Astrophil's heart). On the other hand, the poet is faced with the question of how 'la penna et la mano et l'intelletto' can turn this vision into art. His problem is that he cannot bring the two together. For Petrarch, this is because his topic is quite literally 'inexpressible'. For Sidney, however, it is because Astrophil himself is 'incapable of expression'. The fact that Astrophil's problem is different from Petrarch's should not prevent us from recognizing that it is, nevertheless, a variation of the same notion. The *topos* with which it begins is the conventional one of 'inexpressibility'; it is simply that the cause of the failure of expression has been relocated in the poet himself. And, in so far as Sidney's poem has a source, it is the *topos*, and not Petrarch's poem (though that may enter in as well), for both sonnets begin in the same 'place' in the exact, technical sense of that term.

Astrophil's address to the moon in *AS* 31 is a good instance of Sidney's use of a familiar commonplace as the ground of an invention, one noted by Erasmus in *De copia* as particularly suited for a similitude or *collatio* involving several different comparisons: 'for example the frequent changes of the moon can be used for the vicissitudes of fortune, or the mutability of human life, or the irresolution of the foolish.'[13] Sidney's *collatio* is initially a simple one; in the wanness of the moon, the sorrowing poet–lover recognizes the symptoms he already acknowledges in himself. But the analogy is 'unfolded' or developed for us in two ways peculiar to Sidney. The first is the process of interrogation that slowly reveals the truth of the comparison between pale moon and pale lover:

> With how sad steps, ô Moone, thou climb'st the skies
> How silently, and with how wanne a face,
> What, may it be that even in heav'nly place
> That busie archer his sharpe arrowes tries?
> Sure, if that long with *Love* acquainted eyes
> Can judge of *Love*, thou feel'st a Lover's case. . . .[14]

These lines share in the argumentative quality of *AS* 1, yet here the effect comes not from the syllogistic drive of an enthymeme, but from a familiar rhetorical embellishment, the figure of *erotema*,

---

[13] Erasmus, *De copia*, p. 641.
[14] *Poems*, p. 180. (All further references to Sidney's text are to this edition.)

or *interrogatio*. Sidney, however, does not employ this figure merely as an epideictic structural schema (as, for example, Petrarch did in the famous 'S'amor non è, che dunque è qual ch'io sento?'). Rather, the interrogation leads to an unexpected conclusion, which comes from the contrary way that Sidney exploits the *topos* of inconstancy that the similitude of the moon opens up. The plight both of lover and of moon has been caused by the fact that they are faithful in love, not wavering. Indeed, the final question which the lover addresses to the moon asks whether in heaven where the Moon resides 'ungratefulness', that is, the scornful rejection of that fidelity, is deemed a virtue. Thus by the end of the poem, the process of interrogation has exploited the contrary of the *topos* of inconstancy so fully that the lover and the moon are joined in a fellowship which has become, paradoxically, an icon of constancy.

AS 100, 'O teares, no teares, but raine from beautie's skies', is one of a group of three sonnets Vanna Gentili describes as 'encomi costruiti con tutti i possibili espedienti retorici'.[15] Again, we can identify a source by noting the Petrarch poem to which its *topos*, 'the plaint of the beloved', is most closely related. This is *Canzoniere*, 157:

> Quel sempre acerbo et onorato giorno
> mandò sì al cor l'imagine sua viva
> che 'ngegno o stil non fia mai che 'l descriva;
> ma spesso a lui co la memoria torno.
>
> L'atto d'ogni gentil pietate adorno
> e 'l dolce amaro lamentar ch' i' udiva,
> facean dubbiar se mortal donna o diva
> fosse che 'l ciel rasserenava intorno.
>
> La testa ór fino, et calda neve il volto,
> ebeno i cigli, et gli occhi eran due stelle
> onde Amor l'arco non tendeva in fallo;
>
> perle et rose vermiglie ove l'accolto
> dolor formava ardenti voci et belle,
> fiamma i sospir, le lagrime cristallo.
>
> That day—forever bitter and revered—
> Conveyed its living image to my heart
> So that no skill or style can capture it;
> Often I turn to it in memory.

[15] Vanna Gentili, ed., *Astrophil and Stella* (Bari, 1965), p. 483.

Her manner, with all noble mercy graced,
Those bittersweet laments I listened to,
Made me unsure if mortal lady she
Or goddess were, who brightened heaven all round.
Her head was purest gold, her face warm snow,
Her eyebrows ebony, her eyes two stars
In which Love did not aim his bow amiss;
Pearls and vermilion roses, where that woe
Was gathered, shaped those ardent, lovely words;
Her sighs were flame, and crystalline her tears.

(J. W. Cook and G. Warkentin 1983.)

Constrained as it is within the strictness of correlative verse, Sidney's poem is, if anything, more 'medieval' than Petrarch's; the enumerative scheme which Petrarch has gracefully eased into his sestet has taken over and rigidly organizes the entire poem. The three signs that show the beloved laments are listed—her tears, her sighs, and her plaints—and then each is expanded upon through the figure of *epanorthosis* or *correctio*: 'O teares, *no* teares, *but* raine from beautie's skies.' In line 12, these signs are 'collected', as the correlative scheme requires, but collected with a difference: 'Such teares, sighs, plaints, no sorrow is, but joy.' The signs that have been enumerated seem like sorrows, but Sidney subverts this assumption by an *epanorthosis* of the whole: the sorrows are in fact joys.

The rhetorical elaboration has a further dimension yet, for *AS* 100 belongs to a venerable generic type, the *enueg* or *noia*, a type of poem first found among the Provençals and as energetically practised in Italy in Sidney's day as in Petrarch's. The *enueg* is a poem which lists, in a disconnected, epigrammatic fashion, a series of things the poet does not like, and which is marked by a repeated phrase such as 'mi noia' which expresses the poet's attitude and serves to unify the list.[16] Its rhetorical opposite is the *plazer*, a list of things which please the poet; the conjunction of the two forms in a single poem leads to the ubiquitous 'joy/annoy' of so many Italian sonnets, a rhyme which crops up at the end of *AS* 100, as at the end of the sequence itself. Sidney's awareness of what the genre of the *enueg* could yield him is clear in the skilful variation practised in

[16] See Kenneth McKenzie's essay 'The "Noie" as a Literary Form', prefaced to his edition of Antonio Pucci's *Le Noie*, Elliott Monographs 26 (Princeton and Paris, 1931), pp. liv–cxxvii.

AS 100: the mandatory list (here the signs of sorrow threaded like beads on the string of the correlative scheme) and then the *epanorthosis* which transforms *enueg* into *plazer*. But a further transformation takes place in the couplet, where the poet considers the possibility that these 'joys' may well prove to be sorrows indeed: if Stella is ill (as the following two sonnets will suggest), then 'All mirth farewell, let me in sorrow live'. In a dazzling feint, the poem has become what Kenneth McKenzie calls a 'reversed *plazer*',[17] a list of things which fail to please the poet, and Astrophil has yet further subverted our assumptions by insisting that this condition is the one he would *prefer* to live in.

In these three poems (a different selection would have served my purpose just as well) we have seen Sidney composing with utter indifference to the boundary line between philosophical and sophistic rhetoric, a boundary line which certainly existed in his day, as contemporary debate (and indeed the very enterprise of Ramism) testifies. The most surprising result of this indifference is the role which customary wisdom—the normative, the axiomatic—plays in his poetic method. All three of these sonnets begin in conventional 'places': with the *topos* of inexpressibility, with that of inconstancy, or that of the lady's tears. And to develop them Sidney draws easily on techniques which, if they had not been employed with such verve and sophistication, might well have seemed *trita et obvia* indeed. Those in doubt should take a moment to compare Sidney's *AS* 103, 'O happie Tems, that didst my *Stella* beare', with George Turberville's attempt at the same subject, 'The Lover to the Thems of London to favor his Ladie passing thereon'. Recognizing the pervasive presence of such *topoi* in *Astrophil and Stella* opens afresh the question of Sidney's sources. This has seemed a closed subject since Ringler concluded that Sidney's imagination was essentially assimilative and that he neither had nor required very many 'models'.[18] Although it is true that Sidney almost never imitated another poet directly, it is also true that the poems of *Astrophil and Stella* are linked in a dense network to those of many other Renaissance *canzonieri* by the *topoi* which they share.

A second effect of the presence of conventional *topoi* is the lack of metaphysical insight which haunts Sidney's work. This lack has seemed to relegate him forever to a place just slightly to the rear of

[17] McKenzie, p. lv.   [18] *Poems*, pp. xxxv–xxxvi.

the great vatic presences of English poetry: the Spensers, the Shakespeares, the Miltons. But if Sidney is no metaphysician, he is philosophical in another way, one which affects his craft as poet rather than his vision. In that craft, the logician finds his metier: Sidney's sonnets are structured syntactically, with a powerful sense of the need for 'cause' and 'answer' which Gascoigne had also sought. This syntagmatic quality, however, must be seen for what it is: it gives to a poem a firm armature which makes it possible for Sidney to escape the extrinsic structuring mechanisms of much verse before his time. (Paradoxically, it also makes it possible for him to exploit extrinsic schemata with detachment and energy, as he does in *AS* 100, simply because they are not his only resource.) But if Sidney escapes entrapment by a kind of poetry that the *Defence* makes clear he was anxious to set behind him, he does so, not in a revolutionary gesture, but by returning to the fountainhead of philosophical rhetoric: Aristotle and his stress on debating the issues of a case. As such, the argumentative strain in *Astrophil and Stella* is as profoundly normative as his use of *topoi*; it is a channelling of discourse so as to win a debate, not an invitation to subversion.

Why then is Sidney so persistently and delightfully a subversive poet? The answer is complex, but one part of it is to be found in the management of the three poems we have looked at. Although the result we shall find there sends us back once more to the resources of traditional rhetoric, it is with a difference. In each of the cases I have examined, Sidney both exacts from his *topos* all that the tradition of that *topos* affords him, yet at the same time manages to turn it back upon itself in some way. In *AS* 1, it is not the lady who cannot be described, but Astrophil who cannot describe her. In *AS* 31, both moon and lover are constant rather than vacillating. And in *AS* 100 he plays with the fundamental stubbornness of the figure of *correctio* in ways which extract from it all its capacity for contention.

In so doing, Sidney is practising a humanist technique of schoolroom simplicity but of real consequence when it operates within the Petrarchan tradition: the searching out of contraries. For, as Douglas Kelly notes perceptively, 'in rhetoric every commonplace includes its opposite'.[19] As we have already seen, the

[19] D. Kelly, *Mediæval Imagination: Rhetoric and the Poetry of Courtly Love* (Madison, 1978), p. 6.

enthymeme which helps to structure *AS* 1 is one which can be used for purposes of accusation *or* defence. In the rhetorician's arsenal, accusation and defence are wedded as surely as demonstration and refutation or praise and blame; even the drudges assembling lists of commonplaces are aware that no collection of maxims of *sententiae* is complete without their opposites. Erasmus' advice on *contraria* is very practical:

The same considerations apply to maxims, which one may not only extract from authors but invent according to one's requirements. If you contrast each of these with its opposite, and subjoin related ideas to both headings, you can see what a vast store of speech will be laid up. As all this has so many applications ... there is nothing which you will not be able to apply somehow to the enrichment of your speech. Even opposite ideas can be brought in through irony, or by the adducing of a contrast, or by a comparison.[20]

'I curst thee oft, I pitie now thy case,' says Sidney in *AS* 46, exploiting just such an opportunity for drawing out the *contraria* in his subject. The inversions we have seen in the three poems under discussion are the result of real insight into the rhetorical fertility of the *contraria*, and real expertness in their deployment.

This insight into the contrariness of things has always been recognized by students of Sidney, though the reasons for it are much controverted. To moderns, it provides a basis for our sense of the mischievous self-destructiveness and temperamental variability that seems to characterize Astrophil. In the sixteenth century it seemed a source of abundance or *copia*; as Sir John Davies put it in *Orchestra*:

> Yet *Astrophell* might one for all suffize,
> Whose supple Muse Camelion-like doth change
> Into all formes of excellent devize[21]

Here we can look into only two ramifications of this issue, which, if they do not resolve it, at least point out some directions we might take in doing so.

First, a practical consequence of the rhetorical method in general, and the exploitation of *contraria* in particular, is that in tracing the relationship between poems in *Astrophil and Stella* we

---

[20] Erasmus, *De copia*, pp. 646–7.
[21] Sir John Davies, *Orchestra*, st. 30, in R. Krueger, ed., *The Poems of Sir John Davies* (Oxford, 1975), p. 125.

should always be aware that sonnets invite just such variation, and thus the compositional unit is as likely to be the group as it is to be the individual poem. For example, it makes sense to treat *AS* 41, 'Having this day my horse, my hand, my launce' and *AS* 53, 'In Martiall sports I had my cunning tride' as alternative treatments of a conventional subject matter that goes back at least to Ovid (*Amores*, III. ii). That these poems are dispersed in the sequence matters only to those with a naïve sequential view of its composition: one of the most dispersed 'groups' in the sequence is the fine set of variations on the *topos* of solitude, *AS* 23, 27, 54, and 104, which probably originates, as Vanna Gentili suggests of *AS* 23, in Petrarch's beautiful and influential 'Solo e pensoso i più deserti campi (*Canz.* 35).[22] On the other hand, there are several obvious groupings that have been kept close together, perhaps to display their rhetorical variety: the 'sleep' sonnets, *AS* 32 and 38–40; the 'kiss' sonnets, *AS* 73, 74, and 79–83; the 'absence' sonnets (deeply implicated in the Petrarchan tradition) of the last part of the sequence.

A second and even more important consequence of recognizing Sidney's use of traditional rhetoric as a principle of composition is that it makes it possible for us to identify very precisely the kind of access Sidney had to the radical dividedness of the Petrarchan tradition, and to the rhetorical expression of that dividedness. As I have argued elsewhere at greater length,[23] in Petrarch's *Canzoniere*, the poet's submission to an unworthy form of loving expresses itself as that disruption of the poetic process we have seen in *Canzoniere* 20: hand, pen, and intellect are vanquished by the first assault of *Amor*, and the lyrics the poet produces are thus the scattered rhymes alluded to in his *excusatio*. They are 'seguaci de la mente afflitta' (*Canz.* 127), and Petrarch makes their resistance to the imposition of compositional method an integral part of the drama of the *Canzoniere*: 'quai fien ultime, lasso,' he writes in the same *canzone*, 'et qua' fien prime?' The result is the famous Petrarchan *dissidio*, that dissolution of the moral self into separate parts which leaves the poet–lover in perpetual search of the upward movement that might heal this fissure. As Giuseppe Mazzotta notes, each of Petrarch's lyrics is a new attempt at that upward

---

[22] Gentili, p. 266.
[23] G. Warkentin, 'The Form of Dante's "libello" and its Challenge to Petrarch', *Quaderni d'Italianistica* 2 (1981), 160–70.

movement.[24] Each new beginning—precisely because it starts again—recreates the rupture yet once more.

As a consequence, the rhetorical strategy of searching out contraries becomes one of the primary compositional devices of any Petrarchan *canzoniere* or sonnet sequence. Petrarch's scattered rhymes compose a series of individual attempts at the consolidation of multiple aesthetic material, and into each one is packed immense possibilities for invention by poets mastering—as Petrarch did himself—the application of classical rhetoric to poetry in the emerging vernaculars. For many of his heirs the *Canzoniere* functioned quite literally as a commonplace book,[25] in which all that could be said about love was collected under a single 'head', ready for their art to unpack. Sidney's genius was to have grasped the essential connection between the visionary experience of the Petrarchan poet and his rhetorical method. In the *Old Arcadia*, Philisides (in one of Sidney's early, unhappy struggles with the Latin hexameter), asks, 'But when I first did fal, what brought most fall to my hart?' To which Echo, with her habitual succinctness, replies 'Arte'. That he understood this from the beginning was what qualified Sidney more than any of his mid-Tudor contemporaries for the laurel crown of the 'English Petrarke'.

[24] G. Mazzotta, 'The *Canzoniere* and the Language of the Self', *Studies in Philology* 75 (1978), 271–96.

[25] That topical methods of composition may have facilitated *copia* in sonnet-writing has already been hinted at by Sister Joan Marie Lechner, *Renaissance Concepts of the Commonplace* (New York, 1962), p. 110.

8. *ASTROPHIL AND STELLA*:
A RADICAL READING

Thomas Roche Jr.

Angels enjoy the heaven's inward choirs:
Stargazers only multiply desires.

(*Caelica*, 17.)

I

Sidney's *Astrophil and Stella*, although the third to be published, holds pride of place as the most influential of the English sequences. Its author was a young nobleman who died a hero's death in 1586; its heroine a beautiful lady of the court. The story it told of Astrophil's love for Stella was well known through circulated manuscripts before it appeared in 1591 in a pirated edition by Thomas Newman and in 1598 in an edition authorized by Sidney's sister, the Countess of Pembroke, which contained 108 sonnets among which are interspersed eleven songs.[1]

The appreciation of Sidney's achievement over that of his predecessors is clearly announced by his first critic, Thomas Nashe.[2] And *Astrophil and Stella* became a quarry for pickpurses of others' wits: indeed its 108 sonnets themselves came to symbolize Sidney's achievement to other poets, and they paid him the compliment of using 108 structurally in their writings.[3] Spenser's elegy for Sidney, *Astrophel*, to which is added the *Doleful Lay of Clorinda* (presumed by some to be the work of the Countess of Pembroke) contains 216 lines (2 × 108). Mute tribute is also paid by the 108 poems of the anonymous *Alcilia* (1595) and of Alexander Craig's *Amorous Songs, Sonnets, and Elegies* (1606), some of which are

Reprinted (with revisions) by permission of AMS Press from *Spenser Studies* 3 (1982), 139–91.

[1] The 1591 quarto edition contains 107 sonnets (*AS* 37, punning on Lord Rich's name, omitted) and ten songs (xi omitted). The order of the poem is different; *AS* 55 and *AS* 56 are reversed, and the ten songs appear as a block at the end. The many verbal differences are cited in *The Poems of Sir Philip Sidney*, ed. W. A. Ringler Jr., (Oxford, 1962), to which edition all further citations of the poems are made (see pp. 447–57).

[2] Thomas Nashe, preface to *Syr P. S. His Astrophel and Stella* (1591; reprinted Menston, 1970), Sig A.3. For a text, see above, pp. 11–12.

[3] A. Fowler, *Triumphal Forms* (Cambridge, 1970), pp. 175–6. See also note 32.

addressed to Sidney's 'Stella'. The 109 poems of *Caelica*, with their numerous borrowings from Sidney, may also be an acknowledgement of praise from Fulke Greville. Of such emulative influence there can be no question; the excellence of Sidney's wit guaranteed that, as Nashe foresaw.

What is surprising is that a story of such moral bleakness should have found such welcome from the moral Elizabethans. Alongside Nashe's noted description of this 'theatre of pleasure' (so often cited by later critics) should be read the equally instructive dedication by Thomas Newman; like Nashe he appreciates Sidney's achievement in 'the famous deuice of *Astrophel and Stella* which carrying the generall commendation of all men of judgement, and being reported to be one of the rarest things that euer any Englishman set abroach', but nevertheless worries that 'the Argument perhaps may seeme too light for your graue viewe' (i.e. the view of Frauncis Flower, to whom it is dedicated). Both Newman and Nashe unequivocally praise the excellence of the poetry, but Newman's concern for the possible lightness of the argument in the grave view of Mr Flower should alert us to the discrepancy between Sidney's excellence and his argument, a discrepancy implicit in Nashe's description. His 'theatre' is nothing more or less than a 'paper stage . . ., an artificial heau'n to ouershadow the fair frame' in which 'the tragicommody of loue is performed by starlight . . . The argument cruell chastitie, the Prologue hope, the Epilogue dispaire.' Sidney's rival creation is filled with shadows and false lights and ends in the darkness of despair, facts that have not deterred modern critics from finding cause to praise Astrophil's pursuit of desire. But to the Elizabethans who firmly believed that 'all the world's a stage', the pleasures of such theatres lay in their just imitation of nature to teach true morality. As Sidney himself writes in the *Defence*:

that imitation whereof *Poetrie* is, hath the most conveniencie to nature of al other: insomuch that as *Aristotle* saith, those things which in themselves are horrible, as cruel battailes, unnatural monsters, are made in poeticall imitation delightful. Truly I have knowne men, that even with reading *Amadis de gaule* which God knoweth, wanteth much of a perfect *Poesie*, have found their hearts moved to the exercise of courtesie, liberalitie, and especially courage.[4]

    [4] *The Complete Works of Sir Philip Sidney*, ed. A. Feuillerat (4 vols.; Cambridge, 1912–26, reprinted, with much of the verse omitted, as *The Prose Works of Sir Philip Sidney* (Cambridge, 1962, etc.)), iii. 20.

Poetry teaches the lessons of morality; but what kind of morality does Astrophil's despair teach? It teaches us about a man pursuing a married woman for whom he has conceived a passion, 'Not at first sight', a man who steals a kiss from her while she is asleep, worrying all the while about her anger and later chiding himself for not being more adventurous (Song ii), a man who frankly propositions her despite her gentle, 'No, no, no, no, my Deare, let be' (Song iv), and then churlishly vilifies her because she has not given in (Song v), a man who once more tries rather gawkily to seduce her (Song viii), is again repulsed and retires into pastoral exile (Song ix), only too soon to be found under her window still refusing to accept her refusal until she sends him packing (Song xi) to the despair of the final sonnets. In a theatre this would be viewed as morally reprehensible behaviour. And yet most modern critics feel a necessity to praise Astrophil's actions because he is, after all, driven by love. The poetic success of Astrophil's failure to win Stella has captivated these critics into believing that we should follow his lamentations and praise of Stella with total sympathy for his endeavours. These lenient modern assessments of Astrophil, it seems to me, miss the point of Sidney's poem. I think that Sidney wanted us to be delighted by Astrophil's wit and to be instructed by the image of a man whose reason gives way to his will and whose hopeful desires finally lead him into despair.[5] Astrophil is not a hero, and he is not a hero precisely because he succumbs so

---

[5] For example, L. L. Brodwin, 'The Structure of *Astrophel and Stella*' *MP* 67 (1979), 25–40, in a very perceptive study leaves Astrophil in a thoroughly untenable situation:

> In the first section [*AS* 1–35], Astrophel sought a virtuous resolution of the conflict between *ideal reason* and desire caused by a love which had no hope of reciprocation. In the second section [*AS* 36–85], Astrophel's internal struggle is displaced by the 'new warre' of *external* struggle with Stella following upon her unexpected show of favour to him. This wrecks the *virtuous* resolution toward which he had struggled so painfully in the first section and leaves him in the third section [*AS* 87–108], with no *moral* armor against the unrelieved despair *caused* by Stella's final rejection of his love. (p. 27, emphasis added.)

I do not accept the *virtue* of Astrophil's dilemma. With A. R. Howe, 'Astrophil and Stella: Why and How?' *SP* 61 (1964), 150–69, I can recognize much poetic talent in Astrophil but no virtue. I do not want to restructure the sequence as she would, nor do I want to divide the persona of Astrophil into pure and impure persuasion as does R. A. Lanham, '*Astrophil and Stella*: Pure and Impure Persuasion', *ELR* 2 (1972), 100–15. J. J. Scanlon, 'Sidney's Astrophil and Stella: "See what it is to love" Sensually' *SEL* 16 (1976), 65–74, is closer to my position, but I would like to trace Sidney's use of sonnet themes back to pre-Bembo sources, since Neoplatonism tends to becloud the basic Christian issues at stake. A reading closer to mine is A. Sinfield, 'Astrophil's Self-Deception', *EIC* 28 (1978), 3–17.

wholeheartedly to the pursuit of his desires. He teaches morality by negative example. The vacancy at the heart of Sidney's poem proclaims in chorus with all the other English sequences: Go, and do not likewise.

The most explicit statement of the virtues of negative example is the advice of the anonymous 'gentleman friend' Philaretes to the author of *Alcilia*:

In perusing your Loving Folly, and your Declining from it; I do behold Reason conquering Passion. The infirmity of loving argueth you are a man; the firmness thereof, discovereth a good wit and the best nature: and the falling from it, true virtue. Beauty was always of force to mislead the wisest; and men of greatest perfection have had no power to resist Love. The best are accompanied with vices, to exercise their virtues; whose glory shineth brightest in resisting motives of pleasure, and in subduing affections . . . Yet herein it appeareth you have made good use of Reason; that being heretofore lost in youthful vanity, have now, by timely discretion, found yourself!

Let me entreat you to suffer these your Passionate Sonnets to be published! which may, peradventure, make others, possessed with the like Humour of Loving, to follow your example, in leaving; and move other *Alcilias* (if there be any) to embrace deserving love, while they may.[6]

This context makes sense of Newman's hesitation about the lightness of Sidney's argument and shows that Nashe's accurate description does not necessarily imply approbation or praise. The

---

[6] *Some Longer Elizabethan Poems*, ed. A. H. Bullen (Westminster, 1903), pp. 321–2. Alexander Craig, another follower of Sidney, makes the same point: '*So haue I in middest of my modest Affections, committed to the Presse my vnchast Loue to Lais, that contraries by contraries, and Vertue by Vice, more cleerely may shine.*' ('To the Reader', *Amorose Songes, Sonets, and Elegies* [1606], [Glasgow, 1873], p. 11.) The basic critical issue is whether one achieves the moral purpose of literature by writing strict doctrine or by slyly using ironic techniques while implying the opposite. The most ancient and common version of the issue is whether Ovid was a lewd or a moral poet: more recently the same problem has been debated on the meaning of Andreas Capellanus' *De Amore*. See D. W. Robertson Jr., 'The Subject of the *De amore* of Andreas Capellanus', *MP* 50 (1953), 145–61. An interesting example of the problem, roughly contemporaneous with Sidney, is Robert Greene's *Vision*, where the supposedly dying author reflects on his own literary practice and has both Chaucer and Gower tell a tale on how to drive out jealousy, Chaucer taking the ironic, witty route and Gower taking the straightforward moral route. Greene describes the business of the true writer not 'in painting out a goddesse, but in setting out the praises of God; not in discovering of beauty, but in discovering of virtues, not in laying out the platforms of love, nor in telling the deep passions of fancy, but in perswading men to honest honorable actions, which are the steps that lead to true and perfect felicity' (*Life and Works of Robert Greene, MA*, ed. A. B. Grosart (15 vols.; 1881–6), xii. 189). The further irony of Greene, very lively, writing about his death and repentance, deserves further study.

'paper stage' betrays the lack of a firmer foundation; the 'artificial heau'n' does 'ouershadow the faire frame' of God's intended creation; the 'tragicommody of loue is performed by starlight' only for lack of better light. The argument is *cruell* chastitie' only because that chastity will not respond to Astrophil's desires. Sidney, as I hope to prove, is using Astrophil's journey from hope to despair as a fictional device for the analysis of human desire in Christian terms.

Most commentators on Sidney find an irresistible impulse to draw into *Astrophil and Stella* the final two sonnets of *Certain Sonnets*, 'Thou blindman's mark' and 'Leave me, O love, which reachest but to dust'.[7] The impulse is entirely understandable not only because those two sonnets analyse the inadequacies of human desire within a context that accounts for the inadequacy but also because the ending of *Astrophil and Stella*, if read as a justification or glorification of Astrophil's actions, is grievously inconclusive and uninstructive. Those two explicitly Christian poems cry out to be included unless one sees that beneath the witty surface of Astrophil's lamentations and selfish demand lies the old battle of the 'erected wit' and the 'infected will' that, as Sidney assures us in the *Defence*, continues to deprive us of the golden world that was once ours by right. Nevertheless, it would be a great mistake to include those two poems in the sequence. They show a repentance and a knowledge of desire that Astrophil never achieves. The brilliance of Sidney's negative example is that he realized that Astrophil must end in despair because he never learns from his experience. The reader is meant to supply the Christian context that will make sense of the insufficiencies of Astrophil's insights into his predicament.

Astrophil and Stella are separate from the moment the title is read, for what possible union is there for a star-lover and a star? The tragicomedy of love performed by starlight is inadequately lighted. Stella's eyes, 'nature's chiefest work', are black, 'that sweete blacke which vailes the heav'nly eye' (*AS* 20). Astrophil's starlit stage is dark and perilous. His theatre is of the mind that 'sought fit words to paint the blackest face of woe' (*AS* 1). The face can be none other than his own face, his own rejected desires. Astrophil, in calling for 'some fresh and fruitfull showers upon my

---

[7] For example, see D. Kalstone, *Sidney's Poetry: Contexts and Interpretations* (Cambridge, Mass., 1965), p. 178.

sunne-burn'd braine' (*AS* 1), is sounding a retreat from the light of
common day, a retreat that will engulf him in the blackness of his
own mind as figured by the blackness of Stella's eyes. Who ever
heard of black stars before the discovery of black holes?[8]

The metaphor of blackness expands under Astrophil's preoccupations. He reaches out to the common sunlit world he has
rejected to find the metaphors to describe the blackness he now
recognizes as his world:

> I call it praise to suffer Tyrannie;
> And now employ the remnant of my wit,
>> To make my selfe beleeve, that all is well,
>> While with a feeling skill I paint my hell.
>
>> (*AS* 2.)

His painting of the scenery of his starlit world draws upon the
common Christian opposition of heaven and hell, but no lover has
ever thought that a denial of what he considers heaven is anything
else but a hell. By *AS* 86 he has transferred the responsibility for
his fate to Stella:

> Use something else to chast'n me withall,
>> Then those blest eyes, where all my hopes do dwell,
>> No doome should make one's heav'n become his hell.[9]

Astrophil at this point is playing a more skilfully feeling game in
drawing in other common words from Christian eschatology.
'Doome' carries a heavy overtone of Christian damnation, of
judgement against the speaker, but in point of fact, the 'doome' is
merely Stella's judgement of his love suit, which has turned his
heaven into his hell. Astrophil has inverted every image he uses.
Black has replaced light. Heaven is Stella's submission to him,
Hell her refusal of her grace. Astrophil exploits every ambiguity of
common Christian imagery to paint his own case in the most salutary light, which he calls 'the blackest face of woe'. He constantly
uses spiritual meanings for physical ends:

> So while thy beautie drawes the heart to love,
>> As fast thy Vertue bends that love to good:
>> 'But ah,' Desire still cries, 'give me some food.'
>
>> (*AS* 71.)

---

[8] For a different interpretation of the star imagery, see R. Stevenson, 'The Influence
of Astrophil's Star', *TSL* 17 (1972), 45–57.   [9] See note 25.

These lines are the mid-lines of the entire sequence, a matter to which I shall return. Meanwhile we need only say that Astrophil is painting most skilfully but only feelingly, that is, selfishly.

This simple technique of inversion is evident even in the light imagery used to describe Stella. The single star her name implies becomes by *AS* 7 two black stars, her eyes, which Astrophil would have us believe to be Nature's 'chiefe worke'. By *AS* 68 Stella has become 'the onely Planet of my light, / Light of my life, and life of my desire', and by *AS* 76 his star has been metamorphosed into his sun: 'But now appeares my day, / The onely light of joy, the onely warmth of *Love*.' By the end his sun is only memory because of Stella's absence from him (*AS* 88, 89, 91, 96, 97, 98).

> But soone as thought of thee breeds my delight,
>   And my yong soule flutters to thee his nest,
>   Most rude dispaire my daily unbidden guest,[10]
> Clips streight my wings, streight wraps me in his night,
>   And makes me then bow downe my head, and say,
>   Ah what doth *Phoebus'* gold that wretch availe,
>   Whom iron doores do keepe from use of day?
>
> (*AS* 108.)

The imagery of light associated with Stella's eyes is, to say the least, contradictory: 'When Sun is hid, can starres such beames display?' (*AS* 88.) The contradiction should alert us to the confusion of Astrophil's apprehension, climaxed most explicitly in *AS* 89, the only sonnet in the sequence to employ just two rhymes:

> Now that of absence the most irksome night,
>   With darkest shade doth overcome my day;
>   Since *Stella's* eyes, wont to give me my day,
> Leaving my Hemisphere, leave me in night,
> Each day seemes long, and longs for long-staid night,
>   The night as tedious, wooes th'approch of day;
>   Tired with the dusty toiles of busie day,
> Languisht with horrors of the silent night,
> Suffering the evils both of the day and night,
>   While no night is more darke then is my day,
>   Nor no day hath lesse quiet then my night:
> With such bad mixture of my night and day,

---

[10] The phrase 'daily unbidden guest' seems to me to foreshadow Milton's 'worthy bidden guest' of *Lycidas*, 118, derived from Matthew 22: 8: 'Truely the wedding is prepared but they which were bidden were not worthie.'

> That living thus in blackest winter night,
> I feele the flames of hottest sommer day.

Every possible inversion of day and night is wrung out of this infernal litany of the lover's despair. The literary sources are Virgil, *Aeneid*, iv. 522–32 and more directly Petrarch's *Canzoniere*, 22, but Sidney complicates the issue by having Astrophil confuse both inner and outer day and night. They have become all one to him, and hereafter the sequence is shrouded in darkness both physical and moral.

The permutations of Stella's light-giving qualities in these later poems are anticipated in an earlier block of sonnets (*AS* 31–40), which also describe the lover's night world. *AS* 32, the central sonnet of the first unbroken block of sonnets (*AS* 1–63), is an invocation to Morpheus, and requires elucidation. Morpheus, the son of Somnus, god of sleep, is most elaborately described in Ovid's story of Ceyx and Alcyon (*Metamorphoses*, xi. 591 ff.). He is the god who appears to dreamers in human shape, and it is he who appears to the grieving Ceyx to inform her of her husband's death. Ovid describes him:

> At pater e populo naturum mille suorum
> excitat artificem simulatoremque figurae
> Morphea: non illo quisquam sollertius alter
> exprimit incessus vultumque sonumque loquendi;
> adicit et vestes et consuetissima cuique
> verba.[11]

Ovid emphasizes the artifice of the verisimilitude. Sidney undoubtedly knew the Ovidian story (he imitates lines 623–6 in *AS* 39), but he would also have known Chaucer's use of it in *The Book of the Duchess* where this beneficent dissimulator's ambivalence is more apparent. And Spenser has Archimago send to the house of Morpheus to fetch him evil spirits to deceive Una and Red Crosse (*Faerie Queene*, I. ii. 36–44). Thus, an invocation to Morpheus should not be read as a simple request for sleep:

> *Morpheus*, the lively sonne of deadly sleepe,
> Witnesse of life to them that living die:

---

[11] 'But the father rouses Morpheus from the throng of his thousand sons, a cunning imitator of the human form. No other is more skilled than he in representing the gait, the features, and the speech of men, the clothing also and the accustomed words of each he represents.' (Text and translation from the Loeb edition by F. J. Miller.)

> A Prophet oft, and oft an historie,
> A Poete eke, as humours fly or creepe,
> Since thou in me so sure a power doest keepe,
>   That never I with clos'd-up sense do lie,
>   But by thy worke my *Stella* I descrie,
> Teaching blind eyes both how to smile and weepe. . . .
>
>   (*AS* 32.)

Morpheus' power over Astrophil is that he is the bringer of Stella's image, but even Astrophil appreciates the artifice. I am not so sure that he is aware of the double edge of those 'blind eyes' or of the earlier 'Witnesse of life to them that living die'. Sidney's invocation of Morpheus implies the hellish nature of Astrophil's infatuation. He has closed out every consideration of the waking world. In *AS* 30 he enumerates the great political problems of his time and concludes:

> These questions busie wits to me do frame;
> I, cumbred with good manors, answer do,
> But know not how, for still I thinke of you.

In *AS* 31 he projects his wretched plight on to the moon ('With how sad steps, ô Moone, thou climb'st the skies') before succumbing to the blandishments of Morpheus in *AS* 32. Astrophil is busy enclosing himself in the night of his own desires under the dubious patronage of Morpheus.

The complex of metaphors I have been describing derives ultimately from a common Christian metaphor, most forcefully stated in Romans 13: 10–14 (Geneva version):

Love doeth not euil to his neighbour: therefore is loue ye fulfilling of the law.
And that considering the season, that it is now time that we shulde arise from slepe: for now is our saluation nerer, then when we beleued it.
The night is past, & the day is at hand: let vs therefore cast away the workes of darkenes, and let vs put on the armour of light,
So that we walke honestly, as in the day: not in glotonie, and dronkennes, neither in chambering and wantonnes, nor in strife and enuying.

Paul's injunction to put on the new man of spirituality and to put away the old man of bondage to sin, couched here in metaphors of light and dark, sleep and waking, occurs also in 1 Thessalonians

5: 5–6: 'Ye are all the children of light, and the children of the day: we are not of the night neither of darknes. Therefore let vs not slepe as do other, but let vs watch and be sober.' The Genevan gloss is instructive: 'Here slepe is taken for contempt of saluation, when men continewe in sinnes, and will not awake to godlinesse.' 'Watch' is glossed: 'And not be ouercome with the cares of the world.' Astrophil's concerns throughout the sequence lock him up in his 'sleep of the senses' and prevent his seeing that worship of the idol he himself has created has imprisoned him in his hellish night. Sidney's brilliant inversion of traditional imagery cries out for the Christian context, which finally endows meaning to Astrophil's negative example of what a lover should be.

II

The negative example of Astrophil's wit is not restricted to inversions of explicitly biblical metaphors. The informing spirit of Christian charity extended itself to include even the epic tales of Homer. We have long accepted that the Stella of the sonnets is a fictionalized account of a supposed romance between Sidney and Lady Penelope Rich.[12] More recently it has been argued that her first name suggested to Sidney a structural device, with the 108 sonnets representing the Homeric Penelope's 108 suitors, who played a game of trying to hit a stone called the Penelope stone to decide who would win her. The structure of *Astrophil and Stella* truncates that game, fruitlessly invoking an absent Penelope. I would like to propose an additional submerged Homeric metaphor in the structure of the sequence: its 119 poems are one short of the number of months Ulysses spent returning to Penelope; thus Astrophil's 119 attempts to win his Stella are doomed by the very form of the sequence.[13] Astrophil is a negative example of the fortitude and fidelity of Ulysses, who was proposed as an exemplar of both 'wisdom and wariness' by Roger Ascham, towards the end of

---

[12] On the identification of Stella with Lady Penelope Rich, see *Poems* pp. 440–7 and H. H. Hudson, 'Penelope Devereux as Sidney's Stella', *Huntington Library Bulletin* 7 (1935), 89–129; J. Stillinger, 'The Biographical Problem of *Astrophil and Stella*', *JEGP* 59 (1960), 617–39; and E. G. Fogel, 'The Mythical Sorrows of Astrophil', *Studies in Language and Literature in Honour of Margaret Schlauch* (Warsaw, 1966), pp. 133–52. I cannot accept A. C. Hamilton's suggestion of strong autobiographical impulse in the sequence (*Sir Philip Sidney: A Study of His Life and Works* (Cambridge, 1977), pp. 80–6).

[13] See final section of this essay.

the first book of *The Scholemaster*, in his tirade against the Italianate Englishman:

Which wisdom and wariness will not serve neither a traveler except Pallas be always at his elbow, that is, God's special grace from heaven, to keep him in God's fear in all his doings, in all his journey. For he shall not always, in his absence out of England, light upon a gentle Alcinous and walk in his fair gardens full of all harmless pleasures; but he shall sometimes fall either into the hands of some cruel Cyclops or into the lap of some wanton and dallying Dame Calypso, and so suffere the danger of many a deadly den, not so full of perils to destroy the body as full of vain pleasures to poison the mind. Some Siren shall sing him a song, sweet in tune, but sounding in the end to his utter destruction. If Scylla drown him not, Charybdis may fortune swallow him. Some Circe shall make him, of a plain Englishman, a right Italian. And at length to hell, or to some hellish place, is he likely to go, from whence is hard returning, although one Ulysses, and that by Pallas' aid and good counsel of Tiresias, once escaped that horrible den of deadly darkness.[14]

Ascham concludes by enumerating four effects of such ungodly journeying:

The first, forgetfulness of all good things learned before; the second, dullness to receive either learning or honesty ever after; the third, a mind embracing lightly the worse opinion and barren of discretion to make true difference betwixt good and ill, betwixt truth and vanity; the fourth, a proud disdainfulness of other good men in all honest matters.[15]

Ascham's Platonic terms may be used to gloss the actions and speeches of Astrophil throughout the sequence. We need not repine at the moral strictures of the man chosen to be tutor to Queen Elizabeth. His allegorization of Ulysses as exemplar rests firmly on an allegiance to virtue and wisdom, the right use of the reason to control temptations, and a firm belief that the fear of God is the beginning of wisdom. Ascham's terms are the insights of a learned and pious Christian humanist. His often quoted remarks on the 'open manslaughter and bold bawdry' as the 'whole pleasure' of Malory's *Morte d'Arthur* often cause him to be dismissed as a simplistic moralizing critic, but his comments require their context, the Horatian *utile et dulce*: 'This is good stuff for wise men to laugh at or honest men to take pleasure at.'[16] Wise

---

[14] *The Schoolmaster* (1570), ed. L. V. Ryan (Ithaca, NY, 1967), pp. 62–3.
[15] *The Schoolmaster*, p. 64.   [16] *The Schoolmaster*, pp. 68–9.

men, one assumes, would laugh at the follies that destroyed
Arthur's kingdom: honest men would take pleasure in the negative
example that Malory's Arthurian world presents. Ascham knew
what he was about, and his analysis of the effects of the unheroic
inversion of Ulysses' voyage back to his wife can act as a gloss to
the upstart, surrogate Ulysses that Sidney is postulating to make
obvious Astrophil's absurdities of wit in that most Italianate poetic
form, the sonnet sequence.

Astrophil's forgetting what he and every other Renaissance
schoolboy has learned needs no further investigation than *AS* 1,
where he completely inverts the sequence of the laws of rhetorical
composition: *inventio, dispositio, elocutio.* As Ringler notes: 'Astrophil began in the wrong order with an inadequate method. He first
sought words (*elocutio*) rather than matter, and tried to find words
through imitation of others rather than by the proper processes of
invention.' Sidney, the first major theoretical literary critic of the
English Renaissance, could hardly have been unmindful that his
Astrophil was breaking a primary rule of composition: it is not,
despite Kalstone's eloquent defence,[17] Sidney's attempt to
discover the new eloquence of love poetry. Sincerity and dramatic
energy are far from the point of the final tercet:

> Thus great with child to speake, and helplesse in my throwes,
>   Biting my trewand pen, beating my selfe for spite,
>   'Foole,' said my Muse to me, 'looke in thy heart and write.'

There is as much wit and probably more sincerity in Sidney's
rendition of Psalms 7: 14:

> Lo he that first conceiv'd a wretched thought,
>   And great with child of mischeif travail'd long,
>   Now brought abed, hath brought nought foorth, but nought.

The Genevan version of this same verse provides an interesting
comparison: 'Beholde, he shal trauaile with wickednes: for he
hathe conceiued mischief, but he shal bring forthe a lye.' The similarity of Sidney's imagery in both *AS* 1 and Psalm 7 suggests that
we pay attention to the matter rather than the manner of his
utterance. Renaissance commentators on the heart suggest that it
is not the most reliable or discriminating of the natural organs.

---

[17] *Poems*, p. 459; Kalstone, pp. 124–30.

Thomas Wright in his *The Passions of the Minde* cites the heart as the 'place where passions lodge' and concludes:

Yet supposing the Passions principally reside in the heart, as we perceiue by the concourse of humours thereunto . . . the humours concurre to help, dispose and enable the heart to worke such operations: for as we proue by experience, if a man sleepe with open eyes, although his sight be maruelous excellent, yet he seeth nothing, because in sleepe, the purer spirits are recalled into the inner parts of the body, leauing the eyes destitute of spirits, and abandoned of force, which presently in waking returne againe: euen so I conceiue the heart, prepared by nature to digest the blood sent from the liuer yet for diuers respects, not to haue the temperature which all passions require; for loue dilateth; the heart therefore which was to be subject to such diuersities of Passions, by Nature was depriued of al such contrary dispositions.[18]

Wright was a respectable medical authority, and his verdict on the capacity of the heart invites us to ask two further questions of the final lines of *AS* 1. What muse would direct a poet to such an inadequate touchstone? What nurse would call her poet a fool? Considering Astrophil's other references to muses and his apparent poetic self-sufficiency, we can hardly take the muse's command in *AS* 1 as a beneficent beginning for this sequence or even as the beginning of the romantic movement.

Astrophil's forgetfulness of all he has learned appears again in *AS* 3: 'Let daintie wits crie on the Sisters nine, / That bravely maskt, their fancies may be told.' If he has learned anything from his Muse in *AS* 1, it is that he must rely on the passions of his heart, yet here he rejects as mere artifice the attempts of other love poets, and in *AS* 6 he has already put aside the whole pretence of Muses: 'Some Lovers speake *when they their Muses entertaine*, / Of hopes begot by feare, of wot not what desires.' But we need not restrict our catalogue of Astrophil's forgetfulness to the lessons of the Muses. He has forgotten the precepts of Virtue (*AS* 4), of Christian morality (*AS* 5), of Reason (*AS* 10), of Truth (*AS* 11), of friends (*AS* 14, 21), and of literary convention (*AS* 15). One should not require a full catalogue of the poems in which Astrophil's desires blind him to the dictates of the outside world, which he has learned but put aside as impediments to his desires. Seneca, Plato,

---

[18] Thomas Wright, *The Passions of the Minde in Generall*, intro. Thomas O. Sloan (1604; reprinted Urbana, 1971), Sigs D^v–D2 (pp. 34–5).

Socrates, all that he has learned has been superseded by his love for Stella.

This forgetfulness is climaxed in *AS* 63 when he addresses that most basic of learning tools: 'O grammer rules' and triumphantly concludes:

> But Grammer's force with sweet successe confirme,
> For Grammer sayes (ô this deare *Stella* weighe,)
> For Grammer says (to Grammer who sayes nay)
> That in one speech two Negatives affirme.

His conclusion is based on the simple fact that Stella 'twise said, No, No'. As Ringler rightly notes: 'Astrophil's argument is doubly sophistical: (a) in the sixteenth century the double negative was a common and accepted English usage, so that his "grammer rules" apply only to Latin and not to English; and (b) grammatically "no, no" is a repetition for emphasis and not a double negative at all.'[19]

Astrophil's inability to learn anything new can be illustrated by the juxtaposition of *AS* 72 and Song ii:

> Desire, though thou my old companion art,
> And oft so clings to my pure Love, that I
> One from the other scarcely can descrie,
> While each doth blow the fier of my hart. . . .
> But thou Desire, because thou wouldst have all,
> Now banisht art, but yet alas how shall?

This apparent repentance on Astrophil's part is immediately countered by his discovery of Stella asleep: 'Have I caught my heav'nly jewell?' The irony of that 'heav'nly' cannot be unintentional on Sidney's part. One is reminded of Lady Wishfort's 'What's integrity to an opportunity?' But Astrophil, the slow learner, his integrity lost, cannot seize the opportunity and blames himself in the last stanza for not overachieving:

> Oh sweet kisse, but ah she is waking,
> Lowring beautie chastens me:
> Now will I away hence flee:
> Foole, more foole, for no more taking.

---

[19] *Poems*, p. 478. For a full treatment of Sidney's misuses of grammar, see M. de Grazia, 'Lost Potential in Grammar and Nature: Sidney's *Astrophil and Stella*', *SEL* 21 (1981), 21–35.

His callousness is staggering. The intellectual decision of *AS* 72 (clearly difficult to implement as the pathetic 'but yet alas how shall' (l. 14) shows) is followed immediately by a course of action that negates it. Such a contradiction fits well Ascham's third effect: 'a mind embracing lightly the worse opinion and barren of discretion to make true distinction betwixt good and ill, betwixt truth and vanity.'

This effect is illustrated in Astrophil's words as well as his actions: he constantly chooses the more material sense of a word, thinking to deplete it of its spiritual meaning. A simple example occurs in *AS* 1:

> Loving in truth, and faine in verse my love to show,
> That the deare She might take some pleasure of my paine:
> Pleasure might cause her reade, reading might make her know,
> Knowledge might pitie winne, and pitie grace obtaine.

The skilful use of the figure *gradatio* leads up to the climactic word 'grace', which here can only mean 'favour', or even 'sexual union', but so early in the sequence we can hardly accuse Astrophil of indecorous suggestions or even of misappropriating a theological term. Nevertheless, the insinuation is there, as it is in *AS* 77.[20] After a partial *blazon* of looks, face, presence, grace, hand, lips, skin, words, voice, conversation, he concludes:

> [They make] me in my best thoughts and quietst judgement see,
> That in no more but these I might be fully blest:
> Yet ah, my Mayd'n Muse doth blush to tell the best.

The *blazon* is partial: it omits details of a fleshy nature, unlike, say, Spenser's *Amoretti*, Sonnet 64, and *Epithalamion*, stanza 10. Spenser includes eyes, forehead, cheeks, lips, breast, paps, neck,

> And all her body like a pallace fayre,
> Ascending uppe, with many a stately stayre,
> To honours seat and chastities sweet bowre.

Sidney's *blazon* anatomizes an animated conversation, hand gestures included. We can only assume then that the 'best' is Stella's body, undescribed, but clearly present in Astrophil's imagination.

---

[20] See A. Sinfield, 'Sexual Puns in *Astrophil and Stella*', *EIC* 24 (1974), 341–55. I think we would have to agree that one reader's pun is another's poison. On the relation of *AS* 1 and 77, see note 41.

The same levelling of experience to the physical occurs in
AS 76.

> She comes, and streight therewith her shining twins do move
>   Their rayes to me, who in her tedious absence lay
>   Benighted in cold wo, but now appeares my day,
> The onely light of joy, the onely warmth of *Love.*
> She comes with light and warmth, which like *Aurora* prove
>   Of gentle force, so that mine eyes dare gladly play
>   With such a rosie morne, whose beames most freshly gay
> Scortch not, but onely do darke chilling sprites remove.

Stella, his sun, has come like Aurora, to light his world and warm
his spirits, but, as his day increases in light and heat, he complains
of the heat, 'it burnes', and then turns in the concluding couplet to
a desire that 'my sunne go downe with meeker beames to bed'. The
image continues the progress of the sun of Astrophil's world, but
he wants those burning beams to be meeker in 'bed'. Astrophil is
not referring to the sun sinking in the west; the bed he is suggesting
is his own, and the meekness he requires is Stella's submission to
him.[21]

[Roche proceeds to argue in detail that Astrophil is shown constantly—
and unintentionally—revealing the material, at times grossly physical,
quality of his desire for Stella. The section concludes with a study of
AS 45, whose final line, 'I am not I, pitie the tale of me', is proposed as a
pun whose coarseness displays Astrophil's inability 'to distinguish
between a response to literature and a response to life'. (D.K.)]

The dissociation of Astrophil's being and his growing concentration on his sexual desires as the central issue of his fable to
Stella is matched by his hybris, Ascham's fourth effect derived
from Plato. Ascham's rendition of Plato's term ὕβρις restricts it to
'a proud disdainfulness of other good men in all honest matters'.
Ascham could not envision that Astrophil would carry his hybris to
the ultimate deification of his idol, blasphemy. Once more Sidney
undercuts his plangent hero, and of this latter type of undercutting
Song i is a perfect example.

---

[21] Sinfield (p. 344) relates Astrophil's remark in l. 9, 'But lo, while I do speake, it
groweth noone with me', to Mercutio's 'for the bawdy hand of the dial is now upon the
prick of noon' (*Romeo and Juliet*, II. iv. 108) and to Barnabe Barnes's imitation of Sidney
in *Parthenophil and Parthenophe*, Sonnet 23, which ends, '*Still smiling at my dial, next
eleven!*'; Barnes, *Parthenophil and Parthenophe. A Critical Edition*, ed. V. A. Doyno
(Carbondale, Ill., 1971), p. 16.

III

The poem has been unjustly neglected by the critics, presumably because of the extravagance of the praise, unusual even for Astrophil's heady rhetoric. The poem is circular, with identical first and ninth stanzas. Each stanza begins with two lines of question, which are answered by the last two lines. The third line is identical throughout:

> Doubt you to whom my Muse these notes entendeth,
> Which now my breast orecharg'd to Musicke lendeth?
> To you, to you, all song of praise is due,
> Only in you my song begins and endeth.

The self-conscious smugness of the question should infuriate the reader barraged by unceasing praise of Stella for the preceding sixty-three sonnets. Astrophil is so 'oercharg'd' that the sonnet form will not contain his passion and he bursts into song. But what is the purpose of that rhetorical question? And is the question addressed to Stella or to the reader? In either case the answer to the question is, of course, 'Stella', as Astrophil's triumphant answer in lines 3 and 4 should assure us of both his intense devotion and the circularity of his argument mirrored by the circularity of his poem. The reader, however, should see that Astrophil's lyrical outburst is nothing but blasphemy. Only to God all song of praise is due; only in God do we begin and end. Astrophil is both infatuated and fatuous. Sidney was neither of these, and has furthermore told us in his other works how he viewed the relationship of poetic utterance and Christian belief.

In the *Defence* he describes the three most general types of poetry:

The chiefe, both in antiquitie and excellencie, were that they did imitate the unconceivable excellencies of God. Such were *David* in his Psalmes; *Salomon* in his songs of songs, in his *Ecclesiastes*, and *Proverbes*. *Moses* and *Debora* in their Hymnes; and the wryter of *Jobe* ... against these none will speake that hath the holie Ghost in due holy reverence.... And this *Poesie* must be used by whosoever will follow *S. Paules* counsaile, in singing Psalmes when they are mery, and I know is used with the fruite of comfort by some, when, in sorrowfull panges of their death bringing sinnes, they finde the consolation of the never leaving godnes.

Sidney is referring to Paul's advice in Ephesians 5, to which no modern editor of the *Defence* has seen fit to give so much as a reference.[22]

Sidney's reference is not restricted to the muscularious merriment of hymn-singing. Ephesians 5 is one of the crucial passages of Paul's epistles for establishing the hierarchical principles in medieval and Renaissance society. Sidney could not have been unaware of the import of his allusion, to the metaphors of light and dark, to the overriding allegiance of man to God, of the further consequences of this allegiance, the obedience of the wife to the husband. Milton used this passage as the biblical source of his 'He for God only, She for God in him'. I am not suggesting for a

---

[22] Feuillerat, iii. 9. Most modern editors follow the Olney and Penshurst texts which read 'James', a reference to James 5: 13; later folios read 'Paul', a reading that should at least have a hearing:

> Be ye therefore followers of God, as dere children,
> And walke in loue, euen as Christ hathe loued vs, and hathe giuen him self for vs, *to be* an offring and a sacrifice of a swete smelling sauour to God.
> But fornication, & all vnclennes, or couetousnes, let it not be once named among you, as it becommeth Saintes,
> Nether filthines, nether foolish talking, nether iesting, which are things not comelie, but rather giuing of thanks.
> For this ye knowe, that no whoremonger, nether vncleane persone, nor couetous persone, which is an idolater, hathe any inheritance in the kingdome of Christ, & of God.
> Let no man deceiue you with vaine wordes: for of suche things commeth the wrath of God vpon the children of disobedience.
> Be not therefore companions with them.
> For ye were once darkenes, but are now light in the Lord: walke as children of light,
> (For the frute of Spirit *is* all goodnes, and righteousnes, and trueth)
> Approuing that which is pleasing to the Lord.
> And haue no fellowship with ye vnfruteful workes of darkenes, but euen reproue them rather.
> For it is shame even to speake of ye things, which are done of them in secret.
> But all things when they are reproued of the light, are manifest: for it is light that maketh all things manifest.
> Wherefore he saith, Awake thou that slepest, & stand vp from the dead, & Christ shal giue thee light.
> Take hede therefore that ye walke circumspectly, not as fooles, but as wise,
> Redeming the time: for the dayes are euil.
> Wherefore, be ye not vnwise, but vnderstand what the wil of the Lord is.
> And be not drunke with wine, wherein is excesse: but be fulfilled with the Spirit,
> Speaking vnto your selues in psalmes, and hymnes, and spiritual songs, singing, and making melodie to the Lord in your hearts,
> Giving thankes alwaise for all things vnto God euen the Father, in the Name of our Lord Iesus Christ,
> Submitting your selues one to another in the feare of God.
>   (Eph. 5: 1–21, Geneva version.)

moment that Sidney had this chapter in mind as he wrote *Astrophil and Stella*, although it is a source remote. I do want to suggest that it provides a context both for his comments about the Psalms and for his understanding of what I have called the blasphemy of Astrophil's answer to his rhetorical question in Song i.

Sidney's reverence for the Psalms as divine praise extended to his translating a good portion of them into English metres, to make them available to English readers. The translation was completed by the Countess of Pembroke after his death, but the part that he assuredly did bears strong metaphorical resemblance to metaphors used in *Astrophil and Stella* and to the argument that I would like to present about the nature of Astrophil's witty eroticism. Take Sidney's metrical version of Psalm 10:

1.   Why standest Thou so farr,
       O God our only starr,
       In time most fitt for Thee
       To help who vexed be!

2.   For lo with pride the wicked man
       Still plagues the poore the most he can:
       O let proud him be throughly caught
       In craft of his own crafty thought!

3.   For he himself doth prayse,
       When he his lust doth ease,
       Extolling ravenous gain:
       But doth God' self disdain.

4.   Nay so proud is his puffed thought
       That after God he never sought,
       But rather much he fancys this
       That Name of God a fable is.

5.   For while his ways do prove,
       On them he sets his love:
       Thy judgments are too high
       He cannot them espy,

6.   Therfore he doth defy all those
       That dare themselves to him oppose
       And sayeth in his bragging heart,
       This gotten blisse shall never part. . . .

It is interesting to note that the author of *Astrophil and Stella* compares God to 'our only starr', especially so since it is Sidney's addition to the psalm. The Genevan version of verse 1 reads: 'Why standest thou farre off, O Lord, & hidest thee in *due* time, *even* in afflictions?' Sidney's paraphrase reads almost like a gloss on the figure of Astrophil I am trying to present. The proud man of the psalm has turned away from the proper song of praise and has substituted an idol of his own making for the true God. The gloss to the Genevan version is uncompromising in its condemnation: 'The wicked man rejoyceth in his owne lust: he boasteth when he hathe what he wolde: he braggeth of his wit & welth & blesseth himselfe, and thus blasphemeth the Lord.'

Sidney's technique in Song i is to choose descriptive details that apply to Stella only as self-seeking, demented hyperbole, the very extravagance of which turns the reader to the only One to whom they rightly belong:

Only for you the heav'n forgate all measure.	8
Onely by you *Cupid* his crowne maintaineth.	12
Onely to you her Scepter *Venus* granteth.	16
Onelie through you the tree of life doth flourish.	20
Onely at you all envie hopelesse rueth.	24
Only of you the flatterer never lieth.	28
Only with you not miracles are wonders.	32

This litany of praise, when applied to Stella, is crass. What unwillingly sought-after woman would want to be reminded that she is the 'tree of life'? One could, I suppose, accept the Cupid and Venus praises just as we accept the mythological extravagance of *AS* 13, but it is more satisfactory to acknowledge that human desire (Cupid) and beauty (Venus) are both maintained and surpassed by God, the beginning and end of all creation, through whom the tree of life really does flourish. It also seems an odd choice of praises to introduce envy and the flatterer into a verbal evocation of desire, envy, and flattery being perversions of human desire and verbal truth. Envy is hopeless with God as his object because God is all and transcendent; flattery cannot lie about God because He is ineffable. Ringler suggests that the enigmatic last answer is really an inversion, that is, 'only with you miracles are not wonders', a suggestion that makes perfect sense if one is urging the reader to see beyond the one addressed to Another One.

The idolatrous blasphemy of the answers is duplicated in the questions that form the first two lines of each stanza. Here the poetic technique is that of the riddle, in which one is asked a question about a thing but is given its attributes. One might almost say that the riddle is the ultimate test of metaphor: all of the vehicle (in I. A. Richards' terminology) is presented to the reader, and the test is to find the tenor, the concept or substantive that unites them. Sidney devised a formulaic pattern (who hath the eyes, lips, feet, breast, hand, hair, voice) followed by relative clauses that further complicate the description of the attributes. There seems to be no pattern to the ordering of the physical details, which is perhaps another indication of Astrophil's disordered mind. He cannot get Stella straight. In fact, the whole poem can be seen as a dismemberment.

> Who hath the eyes which marrie state with pleasure,
> Who keepes the key of Nature's chiefest treasure?

Immediately, other questions arise. What is the meaning of the marriage of 'state' with 'pleasure'? What have 'eyes' to do with this marriage? What is the 'key' of 'Nature's chiefest treasure'? What is 'Nature's chiefest treasure'? With the circularity of doubt that constitutes the poem, none of these questions can be answered with any ready certainty. Let us begin with the last question. Nature's chiefest treasure for Astrophil is Stella, and she perforce must be the keeper of the key to herself, but in what sense are we the readers to understand this conundrum? If the 'who' of the question is the lady who keeps the key to nature's chiefest treasure, then it is her portion to unlock or disclose that treasure to Astrophil, an unmistakably physical act of submission. But then we must ask, as we should with Astrophil's abjurations of virtue, philosophy, and morality of friends in the sonnets preceding this song, what is Nature's chiefest treasure? In *AS* 7 Stella's eyes are Nature's 'chief work'; but I think it would be naïve of us to think that that is the answer that Astrophil's 'breast orecharg'd' would expect. The object of this 'song of praise' is unusually crass even for Astrophil. The riddle turns on our seeing that ostensible praise is actually a prurient, fawning sensuality that dehumanizes its subject by turning it into an idol, a 'sex object' in modern parlance. Or we might recall an earlier manifestation in Pygmalion's fevered fantasies of the life his desires have inspired in his created idol.

Katherine M. Wilson has reminded us that 'taken seriously sonnet talk would be blasphemous',[23] and that is certainly the case with Song i. Astrophil is taking himself seriously, and unfortunately

---

[23] K. M. Wilson, *Shakespeare's Sugared Sonnets* (1974), p. 24.

so have the critics. In each of the riddling questions (unless we are persuaded by Astrophil's rare logic) we will see that the hyperbole applies only to the ineffable fullness of God, the Creator, and is ultimately demeaning to the creature. Would any Christian reader not have answered the riddle, 'Whose grace is such, that when it chides doth cherish', with Paul's advice in Ephesians 5: 28–9 (Geneva version):

So oght men to loue their wiues, as their owne bodies: he that loueth his wife, loueth him selfe

For no man euer yet hated his owne flesh, but nourisheth & cherisheth it, euen as the Lord *doeth* the Church.

One need not even seek the biblical sources of other riddles:

> Who long dead beautye with increase reneweth?   22
> Who makes a man live then glad when he dieth?   26

No satisfactory glosses of the lines I have quoted have been given by Sidney scholars; for the most part they are ignored in all modern editions—presumably because Astrophil's praise is accepted as right and proper.

IV

In fact, the songs have played no part in modern critical commentary on Sidney's sonnet sequence.[24] Only the numerologists have given them their rightful place in the structure of the poem, but they understandably but unfortunately do not discuss their meaning. Astrophil's Song i, as I have indicated, is both idolatrous and blasphemous. In Song ii Astrophil steals that kiss from his sleeping Stella. Song iii is a praise of the power of music. Song iv is the colloquy between Astrophil and Stella, in which she refuses his advances with her constant, 'No, no, no, no, my Deare, let be'. Of the group of five Songs v–ix, only the narrative Song viii has elicited comment, but the substance of that group of songs is the key to the desperate meaning that Sidney intended. It is not enough to rely on the narrative content of Songs ii, iv, and viii and to relegate the other lyrical outbursts to earlier poems included to

[24] The one exception I have found is J. F. Cotter, 'The Songs in *Astrophil and Stella*', *SP* 67 (1970), 178–200. Our basic disagreements will be apparent; our readings are fundamentally different even when we seem to agree on individual points.

fill out the sequence. Fill out what? Poets of Sidney's stature do not fill grab-bags of scraps. This used to be the answer to the bewildering array of tales that form the middle books of Spenser's *Faerie Queene*, but it is not so. Songs v, vi, and vii are of major importance in determining the meaning of Astrophil's struggle with Stella.

Song v is the second longest song in the sequence. It is a simple vilification of Stella for her 'change of lookes' in the preceding poem, and attempts to undo all the praise heaped on her throughout the sequence. Its text is the conclusion of *AS* 86:

> Use something else to chast'n me withall,
>   Then those blest eyes, where all my hopes do dwell,
>   No doome should make one's heav'n become his hell.

And it is hellish vilification that he resorts to.[25] The poem is a one-sided lover's quarrel. The first five stanzas are a legalistic brief of all the benefits he has conferred on Stella through his love expressed in poetry. The sixth stanza introduces the true subject: revenge for his injured feelings:

> Revenge, revenge, my Muse, Defiance' trumpet blow:
> Threat'n what may be done, yet do more then you threat'n.
> Ah, my sute granted is, I feel my breast doth swell:
> Now child, a lesson new you shall begin to spell:
> Sweet babes must babies have, but shrewd gyrles must be beat'n.

Astrophil's infernal heroics mask a basic childishness, which he transfers immediately by making his idol Stella into a child to be whipped into shape. In a crescendo of vilifying names she is a thief, a murderer, a tyrant, a rebel, a witch, and finally a devil (presumably the one presiding over his private hell):

> You then ungratefull thiefe, you murdring Tyran you,
> You Rebell run away, to Lord and Lady untrue,

---

[25] It seems to me significant that *AS* 86 is important as a structural referent. Its final rhyme word 'hell' is meant to support the kind of allusive reading I have been suggesting as a means of giving a Christian context to Sidney's poem. The word 'hell' appears four times in the sequence, three of those times as rhyme words: in 2. 14: 'While with a feeling skill I paint my hell'; in 74. 7: 'And this I sweare by blackest brooke of hell, / I am no pick-purse of another's wit'; and the last line of *AS* 86. The fourth occurrence is line 83 of the fifth song. Putzel comments on Song v in his edition of *Astrophil and Stella* (p. 193) as to 'tone and burden' and finds it 'unrelated to any other poem'. Then relying on Ringler's regress to earlier Arcadian composition, Putzel seems to me to beg the question of artistic integrity, of which Sidney was a master: when a poem does not match one's expectations as to tone, throw it back into the court of juvenilia.

> You Witch, you Divill, (alas) you still of me beloved,
> You see what I can say; mend yet your froward mind,
> And such skill in my Muse you reconcil'd shall find,
> That all these cruel words your praises shall be proved.

The irony of this stanza, and the whole process of vilification, is that he has used virtually every one of these terms to praise Stella in earlier sonnets: ungratefulness (*AS* 31), murdering, thief (applied to Love, *AS* 20), tyrant (*AS* 2, 47), rebel (*AS* 5).

Song v is the low point of Astrophil's songs of praise, and it introduces the reader to two songs that have perplexed critics mainly because, as in Song v, they are determined to make Astrophil into the lover as hero. Song vi is a debate between beauty and her music.[26] I propose that the debate, in the long tradition of debates about the primacy of the ear or the eye, has broader implications for the sequence and is between Stella's beauty and Astrophil's music, that is, between Stella as object and Astrophil as poet. To reduce the poem to a debate over whether Stella is more beautiful or sings more beautifully is to narrow our reading. The poem's logic is more complicated. Beauty is to the eye what music is to the ear. That is the start, but Astrophil writes poems and songs about the beauty of Stella's eyes, thus introducing a third and particularizing item into the basic equation, and the opening lines of the poem generate further complication by introducing the reader's response:

> O you that heare this voice,
> O you that see this face,
> Say whether of the choice
> Deserves the former place:
> Feare not to judge this bate,
> For it is void of hate.

The directive of these opening lines is clearly aimed at the reader, who can only hear the voice or see the face through the words of the poems he has been reading. The final line of the stanza equally clearly refers obliquely to the vilification of Song v and in characteristic Astrophiliac manner contradicts what he has just said.

If we read this simply as another poem with Astrophil as 'barker', we diminish its impact. Our training in finding their

---

[26] *Poems*, p. 485; Putzel, p. 195.

'dramatic situations' falsifies the moral intent of many Renaissance poems. Again we as readers are placed in a situation created by Astrophil's words. In particular we should be aware of the abstract diction.

> This side doth beauty take,
> For that doth Musike speake.

Are we to see a scene in court with various parties taking sides? Are we to see the divided apprehension of Astrophil as 'This side' and 'that'? Or are we to understand a generalized debate on the power of visual images and that of words? The poem is inconclusive in its findings, and as with most debate poems the reader must already know the moral answer to the riddle if the poem is to sit with any certainty in his mind. In this case Astrophil is presenting a well-known argument about the primacy of either hearing or sight, but he presents the argument in terms of the agent (beauty–music) rather than of the sense perceiver (eye–ear) except for the first stanza. The abstraction of the debate reaches a climax in the seventh:

> Musike doth witnesse call
> The eare, his truth to trie:
> Beauty brings to the hall,
> The judgement of the eye,
> Both in their objects such,
> As no exceptions tutch.

Not Stella's song but 'Musike'; not Stella's beauty but 'Beauty' calls in, not the Court's nor Astrophil's ear or eye but 'The Eare' and 'The judgement of the eye'. The putative dramatic or pictorial quality of the poem becomes abstract and generalized. The real dramatic impact comes from the conflict of ideas, and here once more Astrophil's presentation of the facts must be called into question.

Renaissance psychology is unremittingly clear on the facts that the senses are mere receivers of perceptions, not judges, and that the 'common sense' is the receiver only of these sense impressions and thus cannot be, as Astrophil suggests, an 'arbiter' of this debate:

> The common sence, which might
> Be Arbiter of this,

> To be forsooth upright,
> To both sides partiall is:

The debate must be referred to the proper mental faculty, reason, which Astrophil, even in his benighted condition, finally does:

> Then reason, Princesse hy,
> Whose throne is in the mind,
> Which Musicke can in sky
> And hidden beauties find,
> Say whether thou wilt crowne,
> With limitlesse renowne.

The sudden change to the second person pronoun prepares us for the transition to the seventh song, which is not the words of Astrophil but the words of reason, following Petrarch's example (*Canzoniere*, 119). The seventh song leads us from the realm of philosophy and virtue that Astrophil's sonnets have tried to disparage and keep at bay into that very citadel of enigmatic clarity. Song vi has taken the debate of beauty and words to the limits of Astrophil's perverted apprehension. Song vii is another outburst of Sidney's poem that brings the reader into the realm of integrity that Astrophil has been playing with throughout the sequence through a glass darkly. It begins:

> Whose senses in so evill consort, their stepdame Nature laies,
> That ravishing delight in them most sweete tunes do not raise;

These heptameter lines of the seventh song could not be spoken by Astrophil. They occupy a central place in the sequence, as I shall demonstrate, and they are too critical and acute an assessment of Astrophil's condition for him to make in his own voice. The syntax of the lines is complex and confusing, but they may be paraphrased: who have senses in such bad harmony and make songs to their stepdame Nature that most sweet tunes do not raise in them ravishing delight? The lines are clearly a question, not a statement, and parallel the question which begins the second stanza: 'Who have so leaden eyes, as not to see sweet beautie's show, / Or seeing ...'. The syntactical parallel also continues the debate of the preceding poem by having stanza one deal with music and stanza two with beauty (ear and eye). The conclusion of stanza one proceeds logically:

Or if they do delight therein, yet are so cloyed with wit,
As with sententious lips to set a title vaine on it:
O let them heare these sacred tunes, and learne in wonder's schooles,
To be (in things past bounds of wit) fooles, if they be not fooles.

The lines both develop an argument and depict one, whose senses are in 'evill consort / . . . so cloyed with wit / As with sententious lips to set a title vain on it: / To be . . . fooles.' The image projected is that of Astrophil, who has been called 'foole' by his Muse (*AS* 1), by Morpheus (*AS* 32), by Cupid (*AS* 53) and by himself (*AS* 43, 83, Song ii), whose wit so pleases him that he puts it in opposition to will (*AS* 4), reason (*AS* 10), Stella (*AS* 12) and himself (*AS* 33, 34). Reason seems in these lines to be describing Astrophil's predicament, and also to be suggesting that there are two kinds of songs (stepdame Nature's lays and sacred tunes) and two kinds of fool ('To be . . . fooles, if they be not fooles'). The latter tradition is derived from 1 Corinthians 3: 18–19: 'Let no man deceiue himself. If anie man among you seme to be wise in this worlde, let him be a foole, that he may be wise. For the wisdome of this worlde is foolishness with God: for it is written, He catcheth the wise in their own craftines.' The man who is wise in the things of this world is a fool in the eyes of God. The distinction lies in one's attitude towards God and the things of the world. Nature becomes a stepdame only when one has in mind a heavenly Father and a spiritual home. To perceive naturally is to perceive only partially. Stepdame Nature's lays must be heard as sacred tunes for the reader to understand them truly. One must hear not only the letter but the spirit.

A similar kind of opposition is developed in the two following stanzas. The progression in the second is from 'leaden eyes' that do not perceive beauty, to 'wodden wits' that do not know its worth, to 'muddy minds' that knowing are not in love with beauty, to 'frothy thoughts' of those lovers who are easily moved to another object. The stanza ends by advocating that these four kinds of deficient perceivers of beauty amend their ways:

O let them see these heavenly beames, and in faire letters reede
A lesson fit, both sight and skill, love and firme love to breede.

The progression of the images from 'leaden' to 'frothy', while not including Astrophil's particular kind of idolatrous devotion, expands the vision of the deficiency of human lovers, as a speech of Reason should.

The third stanza is an attempt to amalgamate the two kinds of love and the various oppositions in Songs vi and vii.

> Heare then, but then with wonder heare; see but adoring see,
> No mortall gifts, no earthly fruites, now here descended be:
> See, do you see this face? a face? nay image of the skies,
> Of which the two life-giving lights are figured in her eyes:
> Heare you this soule-invading voice, and count it but a voice?
> The very essence of their tunes, when Angels do rejoyce.

The voice of reason tells of something in ordinary perception that is beyond even her ken: nature gives us only an 'image of the skies', a 'figure'. The upshot of Reason's speech is that there is in fact no opposition between the senses if we trace the lineage of the senses to their ultimate source. Eye and ear are one, likewise beauty and music, if we could but see them truly in their fleshly manifestations, 'when Angels do rejoyce'. The perception is never a request for a denial of natural existence but a true apprehension of the reality of what human love and nature is in terms of its sources. Sidney, in the *Defence*, considered these things in his passage on the poets' golden world and the erected wit and infected will of poet and reader, but 'these arguments will by few be understood and by fewer granted'. The double vision required of Christian readers—the proper use of their stepdame Nature and their proper use of that nature to their true allegiance to God—is the subject of Sidney's depiction of Astrophil. Song vii leads us to a vantage point where we are urged to take a proper view of the worth and wonder of humanity and to assess Astrophil's fevered desires.

The increasing abstraction and distancing of Astrophil's plight in Songs vi and vii lead to the most dramatic depiction of the love affair in Song viii, the longest poem in the sequence. Song vii insists that we view Astrophil's problem outside the frame of his own editorializing wit, and Song viii is, uniquely, a third-person narrative. It is as if Reason's Song vii has taken us into another realm where we may observe the plangent lover's story from a different perspective, in which for the first time Stella's responses are fully enunciated.

Though all but forgotten in the hyperbolic onslaught of Astrophil's rhetoric, Stella's responses, more than the arguments of virtue, reason, or friends, present the case for positive Christian morality. The first important statement, in *AS* 62, explains the simple oppositions we have been noting. Sidney's strategy is to play with the two meanings of the word 'love'. Stella speaks of a love that is not blind (6), a love considerate of the merits and possibilities of the other (7–8), a love based in virtue (11); Astrophil hears of a love that is blind and naked, of a love that exists in the flesh and extends itself whenever it can. The two loves described are the most common of Christian metaphors. They are the *caritas* and *cupiditas* that St Augustine taught to the world of the Middle Ages and Renaissance as the two faces of human love. The juxtaposition gives added point to the colloquial disappointment of line 5: 'I joyed, but straight thus watred was my wine'. Astrophil hopes that Stella's declaration of 'true love' in line 4 will bring the heady intoxication of wine, a hope soon watered by the sobering expansion of meaning (lines 6–11). But the homely image gives Sidney the opportunity to outwit his creation through an irony that Astrophil is not allowed to understand. Watered wine is a disappointment physically, but spiritually water and wine symbolize the Eucharist, the food of charity. The water that Stella's words add to Astrophil's wine is nothing less than the possibility of his spiritual regeneration into charity, a possibility that he unknowingly rejects in the almost patronizingly witty conclusion of the sonnet.

> Alas, if this the only metall be
> Of *Love*, new-coind to helpe my beggery,
> Deare, love me not, that you may love me more.

Astrophil thinks that he has made a point here with his witty and falsely gracious abjuration of her kind of love so that she may fall into the trap of his kind, but, although he can see that two definitions of love are at stake, he understands them both exclusively in terms of his desire's goal. His is the true love; hers can be merely active cruelty or passive fear, soon to be conquered by his superior love and wit.

Stella's voice is next heard in Song iv, again refusing Astrophil's demands with her understated but comprehensive 'No, no, no, no, my Deare, let be', but her most extended exposition of her reaction to Astrophil occurs in Song viii. Sidney plans the scene carefully.

In a grove most rich of shade,
Where birds wanton musicke made,
May then yong his pide weedes showing,
New perfumed with flowers fresh growing,

Astrophil with *Stella* sweete,
Did for mutuall comfort meete,
Both within themselves oppressed,
But each in the other blessed.

Him great harmes had taught much care,
Her faire necke a foule yoke bare,
But her sight his cares did banish,
In his sight her yoke did vanish.

The poem has been most often understood as a lover's tryst in a conventional May-time setting, but in view of the development of both Astrophil's and Stella's speeches (stanzas 8–16, 19–25, respectively) a more important consideration is the nature of the 'mutuall comfort' they are seeking. We know why Astrophil is there, but Stella's presence needs some explanation. Why should a married woman meet in a secluded place a young man who loves her, especially if her marriage is a 'foule yoke'? The obvious answer is of course adultery, but that, the poem assures us, is not the answer. At the opposite extreme is the answer Sidney might have used if he had been writing a different poem: Stella could have been turned into a Boethian Lady Philosophy to guide Astrophil to the proper path of virtue. But Stella is clearly neither erring woman nor allegorical figure. Her presence in that 'grove most rich of shade' is most comparable to those ladies in Book VI of *The Faerie Queene* who with the best intentions find themselves in rather murky moral situations that harm their social reputations but not their inner virtue. Stella is unhappy. Although she knows that Astrophil is unhappy, the poem explicitly states that *only* 'In *his* sight her yoke did vanish'. She meets him for that mutual comfort that grows out of the charitable love she has tried to explain to him in *AS* 62, but the possibilities of the situation are immediately exploited by Astrophil: 'There his hands in their speech, faine / Would have made tongue's language plaine:' (lines 65–6). Stella's response to this 'pass' has been often misinterpreted as a teasing half-acceptance, an interpretation that Sidney did not intend. To understand the extreme delicacy of Stella's response we can compare it to Fulke Greville's imitation in *Caelica*, 75:

> Philocel, if you love me,
> For you would beloved be,
> Your own will must be your hire
> And desire reward desire.
> Cupid is in my heart sped,
> Where all desires else are dead
> Ashes o'er love's flames are cast,
> All for one is there disgraced.
> Make not then your own mischance
> Wake yourself from passion's trance,
> And let reason guide affection
> From despair to new election
>
> (95–106.)

Caelica's rather testy Lady Philosophy is giving sound advice, advice that Stella will give to Astrophil in Song xi, but here in Song viii her response, although it has the immediate effect of staying Astrophil's advances and dampening his hopes, is compassionately gentle:

> Then she spake; her speech was such,
> As not eares but hart did tuch:
> While such wise she love denied,
> As yet love she signified
>
> '*Astrophil*' sayd she, 'my love
> Cease in these effects to prove:
> Now be still, yet still beleeve me,
> Thy griefe more then death would grieve me'.
>
> (69–76.)

Sidney sets the stage for her response by once more invoking the two loves of *AS* 62: she is simultaneously denying Astrophil his cupidity and signifying charity. It is wrong to read lines 71–2 as if Stella were merely restraining her passion for Astrophil. She is quite clear that her love for him cannot be tested in the ways he has proposed. She then cites in five conditional statements her love for him, ending:

> If thou love, my love content thee,
> For all love, all faith is meant thee.
>
> (91–2.)

If Astrophil, rather than the narrator, had related this episode to us, we would be convinced that he had lost the battle but won the

day; that is indeed the point that Sidney makes explicit in the final
two stanzas of Stella's response. She does love him:

> Trust me while I thee deny,
> In my selfe the smart I try,
> Tyran honour doth thus use thee,
> *Stella's* selfe might not refuse thee.

She does want him and 'might not refuse' him if it were not for
'Tyran honour'. Stella's reply is the triumph of reason over
passion, which converts her desire to the charity she is now
offering Astrophil. Critics have universally given Stella's voice too
little credit. 'Tyran honour' is read as 'I would if I could', but this
reading does a disservice both to Stella and to sixteenth-century
morality. 'Honour' is the operative word; 'tyran' is her mere
concession to Astrophil's obsession, her grace to the grieving
lover. Stella's love for Astrophil is one of Sidney's most brilliant
strokes. It serves two purposes. It removes Stella immediately from
the category of proud and aloof sonnet lady so that Astrophil will
be forced to reconsider his lost possibilities in the knowledge that
he might once have won his goal, just as in *AS* 33 he ruefully
surveyed the possibilities lost through his own failure of initiative.
It also serves as an exemplum of the proper discipline of the
passion of desire by reason, which she serves up to Astrophil as the
conclusion to the long string of conditional statements:

> Therefore, Deere, this no more move,
> Least, though I leave not thy love,
> Which too deep in me is framed,
> I should blush when thou art named.
>
> (96–100)

The blush would come, not only from embarrassment about her
passion but also from the attendant dishonour.

Stella has presented a case that Astrophil cannot refute on the
basis of either of their definitions of love. She has vanquished
passion and has learned to offer him charity. He has been overcome by passion and cannot comprehend what Stella's love means.
His reaction is a retreat to the pastoral world in Song ix, the last of
the central group of songs. He is left alone in the false Eden he has
created for himself, like Colin Clout in Spenser's January and
December eclogues:

> Go my flocke, go get you hence,
> Seeke a better place of feeding,
> Where you may have some defence
> From the stormes in my breast breeding,
> And showers from mine eyes proceeding.

Within the conventions of pastoral poetry Astrophil is simply abdicating his responsibility and indulging himself in self-pitying incomprehension of his situation:

> Yet alas before you go,
> Heare your wofull maister's story,
> Which to stones I els would show:
> Sorrow onely then hath glory,
> When tis excellently sory.

The poem's humour may have been lost on the sheep, as it has on the critics. The sudden recall of the flock to hear his story is only to keep Astrophil from giving sermons to stones. That sorrow should have any glory is surprising enough, but that it must be 'excellently sory' to gain this reward shows Astrophil at his wonted task of overachieving. The picture he gives of his love for Stella is ludicrously inappropriate:

> *Stella* hath refused me,
> *Stella* who more love hath proved,
> In this caitife hart to be,
> Then can in good eawes be moved
> Toward *Lamkins* best beloved.

Even if we grant Astrophil his comparison of mother love, I am not certain that ewes do in fact single out particular lambs for especial affection. He is equally ignorant of what Stella has told him in Song viii:

> Why alas doth she then sweare,
> That she loveth me so dearely,
> Seing me so long to beare
> Coles of love that burne so clearely;
> And yet leave me helplesse meerely?
>
> Is that love? Forsooth I trow,
> If I saw my good dog grieved,
> And a helpe for him did know,
> My love should not be beleeved,
> But he were by me releeved.

Argument from analogy is the weakest form of argumentation, as Sidney undoubtedly knew, which is probably why he allowed Astrophil this unfortunate excursion into animal imagery.

From this point on in the sequence Astrophil retreats to memory for his only satisfactions, for his Stella is absent. Song x is a deliberate sexual fantasy, which he sends off to persuade the absent Stella:

> Thought see thou no place forbeare,
> Enter bravely every where,
> Seaze on all to her belonging;
> But if thou wouldst garded be,
> Fearing her beames, take with thee
> Strength of liking, rage of longing. . . .

This unabashed exercise in sensuality ('Joying til joy make us languish') ends in the recall of the thought:

> My life melts with too much thinking;
> Thinke no more but die in me,
> Till thou shalt revived be,
> At her lips my Nectar drinking.

Sidney allows Astrophil one more sight of Stella. Song xi is a dialogue between them.

> 'Who is it that this darke night,
> Underneath my window playneth?'
> It is one who from thy sight,
> Being (ah) exild, disdayneth
> Every other vulgar light.
> 'Why alas, and are you he?
> Be not yet those fancies changed?'

Being assured of his unswerving devotion, she must resort to the conventional arguments to conquer desire: absence (11), time (16), new beauties (21), reason (26), wronged love (31). Stella's list resembles Caelica's, but the suggestions are delivered more gently. To no avail. Astrophil's wit is still about its old tricks of seizing on the outer senses of Stella's words and using them to support his own desires. Since he will not, or cannot, grasp the reasonableness of her arguments, she must resort to an angry dismissal lest the neighbours see or hear them:

'Well, be gone, be gone I say,
Lest that *Argus* eyes perceive you.'
O unjustest fortune's sway,
Which can make me thus to leave you,
And from lowts to run away.[27]

Where reason fails, prudence prevails, and Astrophil is left, disgruntled and unenlightened, contemplating an empty window (*AS* 105, 106), and totally impervious to Stella's classical allusion.

Juno sent Argus, a hundred-eyed monster, to guard Io, a love of Jupiter's, whom he changed into a white heifer to escape Juno's jealous anger. Seeing Io's unhappiness, Jupiter sent Mercury to kill the monster and was reconciled to Juno on condition that she allow Jupiter to return Io to human shape. Stella's allusion suggests that she is the Io in this situation, with Lord Rich assigned the role of the jealous Juno. Her dismissal of Astrophil precludes the possibility of her seeing Astrophil in the role of Mercury, who got control of the monster through the power of his music. Sidney does not leave Astrophil a chance of winning such control, and the sequence ends in the despairing night world of *AS* 108.

Astrophil, as I hope I have made abundantly clear, in allowing his reason to let his erected wit free rein, has succumbed to the indulgence of the 'sleep of the senses'. He has become demented; he is no longer in control of his desires; he does not understand what Stella tells him. The flagrant logical and moral inconsistencies of his words push him closer and closer to the despair that finally engulfs him at the end of the sequence. Sidney consistently gives him futile verbal victories, but beneath the surface of lover's bravado exists an authorial subtext in the elaborate disposition of the poems, and even parts of poems, asserting Sidney's complete control of this outburst of mad love.

v

The external features of *Astrophil and Stella*'s formal structure provide a clue to the structure that Sidney intended. The 1598 edition of the poem included 108 sonnets and 11 songs, interspersed with apparent irregularity. The sonnets are all conventional

---

[27] For Argus reference see *OA* 8, in *Poems*, pp. 20–2.

fourteen-line sonnets except that six (1, 6, 8, 76, 77, and 103) are hexameter rather than pentameter. The songs are written in iambic (i, iii, v, vi, vii) or trochaic (ii, iv, viii, ix, x, xi) metre and range in length from 18 to 104 lines. As with Petrarch, the apparent artlessness of the arrangement reveals on closer examination an ingenious artistry that organizes the substantive chaos of the individual poems into a coherent unity. The order of the poem is:

Sonnets 1–63	(63)
Song i	
Sonnets 64–72	(9)
Song ii	
Sonnets 73–83	(11)
Song iii	
Sonnets 84–5	(2)
Song iv	
Sonnet 86	(1)
Songs v–ix	(5, or 63 stanzas)
Sonnets 87–92	(6)
Song x	
Sonnets 83–104	(12)
Song xi	
Sonnets 105–8	(4)

The sonnet groups range from the largest group (63 sonnets) to the single sonnet, *AS* 86, flanked by groups of 9, 11, and 2 sonnets (*AS* 64–85) and of 6, 12, and 4 sonnets (*AS* 87–108). The songs follow a more complicated but similarly formal pattern. The total number of stanzas in the songs is 108, corresponding to the number of sonnets. The stanza total of the unbroken block of Songs v–ix is 63, repeating the number of the unbroken block of sonnets, *AS* 1–63, producing the following symmetry:

63 sonnets	(1–63)
1 song	(i)
25 poems	(64–85, ii, iii, iv)
1 sonnet	(86)
63 stanzas	(v–ix)
24 poems	(87–108, x, xi)

Sidney is clearly relying on the number 108 to serve some structural and symbolic purpose.[28] The number has been given a most ingenious and convincing explanation by Adrian Benjamin as reported by Fowler. We know that Sidney's Stella was Penelope Devereux, daughter of the first Earl of Essex. Some time after her marriage to Lord Rich, Sidney metamorphosed her into his Stella, recalling that other chaste Penelope in Homer, who by keeping her suitors at bay for twenty years became the type of chaste married love. Homer tells that Penelope's suitors whiled away their time in a game, resembling the Elizabethan game of bowls (*Odyssey*, i). Sir Thomas Browne, drawing upon the comments of the scholiasts Athenaeus and Eustathius, describes the 'prodigal paramours' at their game of Penelope: 'For being themselves an hundred and eight, they set fifty four stones on either side, and one in the middle, which they called *Penelope*, which he that hit was master of the game.' Fowler concludes that 'the absence of a 109th or Penelope sonnet-stone from Sidney's sequence confesses Astrophil's failure as a lover'.

In spite of the brilliance of this explanation a simple question arises: why does the sequence contain 119 poems instead of 108? The answer is to be found again in the Homeric story. Astrophil is not just another suitor but rather the inversion of the wise and wary Ulysses returning to his chaste wife. The 119 poems are meant to symbolize the ten years of Ulysses' journey home: the total number of poems is one short of the 120 months of that epic voyage. I do not want to push the Ulysses analogy too far because Sidney is as silent about Ulysses as about Penelope. I do think, however, that the group of poems *AS* 84–5, song iv, and *AS* 86 may be a covert allusion to the return of Ulysses. This sequence, concluding one of the major blocks, is one of the most tentatively narrative sections. *AS* 84 addresses a highway through which Astrophil is approaching Stella. *AS* 85 focuses on a house in which Astrophil will seize on his treasure. Song iv is the meeting of Astrophil and Stella, who refuses his advances. *AS* 86 complains of 'this change of lookes', and introduces the block of Songs v–ix that send Astrophil into his despairing decline.

[28] It may also be of significance that Sidney's Song viii is the one hundred and eighth poem in *England's Helicon* (1600). Whether the compilers of anthologies were also numerologists is a question that should be looked into. The fact that the word 'love' is used precisely 108 times *in the sonnets* suggests the degree of ingenuity expended on the composition of sonnet sequences.

The ninth song has two details that suggest further Odyssean analogies. Ulysses returns to Ithaca and is received by the swine-herd Eumaeus. If it is not a pastoral retreat, it is still not home, and Ulysses must move from the country to the town where his palace is. On the way he meets his old dog Argus, who recognizes him and dies (*Odyssey*, xvii). In the second stanza Astrophil laments (emphasis added):

> Merry flocke, such one forgo,
> Unto whom mirth is displeasure,
> Only *rich* in mischiefe's treasure.

Surely this is another reference to Lord Rich (as in *AS* 37) and the reason that not even '*Nestor's* counsel can my flames alay' in *AS* 35. This love is an inversion, an invasion of Rich's marriage to Penelope, but Astrophil sees himself as rightfully dispossessed in the next stanza (emphasis added):

> Yet alas before you go,
> Heare your wofull maister's story,
> Which to *stones* I els would show:
> Sorrow onely then hath glory,
> When tis excellently sory.

It might seem appropriate to have Astrophil turn from his sheep, like the despondent Colin Clout, to stones, but I think that the stones referred to here are an explicit reference to the Penelope game, especially since the line about the stones in the fourth stanza is the fourth time the number 108 is repeated. Hence the 'Sorrow [that] only then hath glory', which is not to be, occurs in the fourth 109th line of the line number of the songs.

The fifth and final such occurrence is in the last stanza of the eleventh and final song ('"Well, be gone, be gone I say, / Lest that *Argus* eyes perceive you."') The 'Argus eyes' have always been interpreted as the eyes of the monster set to watch Io, but I think that Sidney is playing another trick on Astrophil. Argus is the dog who first recognizes Ulysses on his return; Stella may be saying that Astrophil may be recognized by Ulysses' faithful hound as the false suitor he is, playing with his 108 stones to win the Penelope game. The possibility is strengthened by reference to the eighth stanza of song ix:

> Is that love? forsooth I trow,
> If I saw my good dog grieved,

> And a helpe for him did know,
> My love should not be beleeved,
> But he were by me releeved.

The stanza says explicitly what a deceitful Ulysses would say on his return about the dog that was not his.

Many readers will be unwilling to accept both Fowler's and my readings of the numbers 108 and 119 as symbolically significant parts of the meaning of the sequence. For them the jump from number as quantitative measure to number as meaning will be too great. But Fowler notes the conclusion of Song viii:

> Therewithall away she went,
> Leaving *him* so passion rent,
> With what she had done and spoken,
> That therewith *my* song is broken.[29]

The shift from third- to first-person pronoun is important. It would appear to be Sidney speaking *in propria persona*, showing his control over his creation. Such a reading suits well my earlier suggestion that Song viii is the answer of Reason to the debate of Song vi. That is, both vii and viii take us outside the narrating voice of Astrophil to a more objective vantage-point.

Fowler's brilliant but short account of the numerological complexities of *Astrophil and Stella* does not deal with several problems that require further elaboration: the organization of *AS* 1–63, the hexameter sonnets, and the meaning of the sequence as a poem.[30]

---

[29] Astrophil alludes primarily to his grief: but his 'broken' song stops just short of the twenty-seven stanzas needed for a line total of 108, and just short of bringing the Songs' overall stanza total to 109 (which would have represented victory in the Penelope game); see Fowler, *Triumphal Forms*, p. 178.

[30] On the meaning of the sequence Fowler writes: 'For the authors of many sequences of love sonnets mannered their eroticism with a cool deliberation arranging individual sonnets—themselves often ardently passionate yet highly structured—in intricate symmetrical patterns or according to relatively *recherché* number symbolisms.' On *AS* 1–63: 'Now by Sonnet lxii *Astrophil and Stella* has certainly reached a critical phase of heightened intensity, marked in the form by interposition of lyrics, in the narrative by Astrophil's outbursts of passion, by his dishonourable suggestion of Song VIII and by his consequent loss of Stella.' On the alignment of the stanza totals of the Songs (i–iv = 28; v–ix = 63; x–xi = 17): 'The number 28, a "perfect" number, signified virtue: 63 denoted a life crisis: and 17 was a familiar Pythagorean number symbolic of misfortune and grief.' On the pair of 22 sonnets surrounding *AS* 86: 'We find a symmetry about Sonnet lxxxvi, the sonnet concerned with a "change of looks" in Stella the "sweet judge", who thus occupies a central seat of judgment in the formal structure in

Fowler rightly points out that the first sixty-three sonnets form a symbolic unit based on the ancient notion of the Grand Climacteric year 63, a crisis of both mind and body.[31] The sequence of these sonnets begins with a total misapprehension of basic rules of rhetoric[32] and ends with a misapplication of the rules of grammar ('For Grammer sayes ... That in one speech two Negatives affirme'). The sequence thus reverses the traditional order of the trivium (grammar, logic, rhetoric) just as *AS* 1 reverses the order of rhetorical composition, logic being misapplied through the entire sequence. Although Astrophil seems to think that both *AS* 1 and *AS* 63 are significant triumphs in his pursuit of love, we as readers should know that he has turned the ordinary process of education in using words upside-down. Grammar playing as rhetoric is illogical. The midpoint of this sequence is *AS* 32, the invocation to Morpheus, another inversion, since Astrophil is asking for a kind of sleep that will further delude his already deluded senses.

The sequence proceeds to a second invocation of the Muses at *AS* 55, another inversion of traditional knowledge, in which Astrophil refuses the support of the Muses. *AS* 55 is also the midpoint of the 108 sonnets, and, as Fowler points out, would have been the Penelope stone if the sequence had been carried out successfully for Astrophil.[33]

The interlocking elaboration of the groupings of sonnets around the songs is further complicated by the placement of the hexameter sonnets: *AS* 1, 6, 8, 76, 77, and 102. Why should Sidney have chosen to begin his sequence with an hexameter sonnet and why place other hexameter sonnets throughout the sequence at the places he did? To insert songs or any forms other than the usual fourteen-line pentameter sonnet in sequences was common from the time of Dante and Petrarch, but to vary the expected pentameter sonnet is Sidney's innovation. Certainly to begin his sequence with a hexameter sonnet was to alert the reader to an

the midst of numbers signifying chastity (22, 22).' Especially for those who find numerological symbolism unconvincing, some further correlation between the numbers and the text is required (Fowler, pp. 174–7).

[31] Fowler, p. 176, cites the 63 sonnets of Constable's *Diana* (1592) and Drayton's *Idea* (1619). The number is the product of 7 (body) × 9 (mind). The complexities of the climacteric are spelled out in Wright's appendix to *The Passions of the Minde in Generall* (1604), *A Succinct Philosophicall declaration of the nature of Clymactericall yeeres, occasioned by the death of Queen Elizabeth*, Sigs A3–C3.

[32] See *Poems*, pp. 458–9, 478.

[33] The fact that *AS* 55 and 56 were reversed in 1591 seems to me of little importance.

innovative undertaking. Whether that reader followed the signs of metrics and placement of poems cannot be determined, since none of Sidney's contemporaries commented on the structure of his poems.[34] Perhaps Sidney wanted the reader to see that Astrophil was at sixes and sevens.[35]

Alongside the complexities of the numerical patterns I have been suggesting, and in spite of the overlapping symmetries, a basic structure does emerge, which supports the reading I gave the sequence at the outset. I suggested that a formal division could be made as follows: 63 sonnets (1–63), Song i, 25 poems (64–85), one sonnet (86), 63 stanzas (v–xi), 24 poems (87–108): 63/1/25/1/63/24. The repetition of the climacteric number seems to me important. Most of the studies of *Astrophil and Stella* are postulated on the assumption that Astrophil changes dramatically as the sequence progresses. They try to demonstrate the progress of the lover through various stages of love, but neither these stages nor when they occur is agreed upon.[36] My reading of Sidney's poem is based

[34] See J. J. Yoch, 'Brian Twyne's Commentary on *Astrophel and Stella*', *Allegorica* 2 (1977), 114–16. Twyne's comment on *AS* 63, I think, supports Ringler's suggestion and my reading of that sonnet. 'His loue Stella saide, no, no whenes he concludes yt accordynge to gramer rules 2 negatiues make an affirmatiue.'

[35] The relationship between *AS* 7, 'When Nature made her chiefe work, Stella's eyes' and the two hexameter sonnets which flank it, suggests confusion, perhaps delusion, on Astrophil's part. Sidney uses the same rhyme pattern for the hexameter sonnets, *AS* 1 and 77, 8 and 76. On the possible hints of structure from similarity of form and rhyme scheme (as in *AS* 1 and 77, 3 and 61, 4 and 62, 5 and 75, 8 and 76, 22 and 76), see Ringler, *Poems*, pp. 570–1, and Fowler, *Triumphal Forms*, p. 177.

[36] In response to the proposed tripartite division of the poem by earlier critics, A. C. Hamilton in his article 'Sidney's *Astrophel and Stella* as a sonnet sequence', *ELH* 36 (1969), 59–87, makes both a poignant and witty assessment of the critical situation: 'Since critics have placed the end of the first section of Sidney's poem variously at sonnets 32 [Buxton], 40 [Rudenstine], 43 [Young], and 51 [Ringler], one may fairly conclude that it does not possess 'a clearly discernible three-part structure.' (p. 66.) This astute observation does not prevent Hamilton from throwing his hat in the ring with a new tripartite structure of *AS* 1–35, 36–71, Song ii–*AS* 108, with strong arguments to enforce the dramatic or narrative development of the persona of Astrophil [*sic*]. Hamilton's division of the sequence did not deter others from dividing up the sequence in different ways. Brodwin suggests a division *AS* 1–35, 36–86, 87–108. Stevenson, reverting to Young, divides it *AS* 1–43, *AS* 55–Song ix, *AS* 85–108. A. Weiner ('Structure and "Fore Conceit" in Astrophil and Stella', *TSLL* 16 (1974), 1–25) decides on a five-part structure: *AS* 1–20, 21–45, 46–68, 69–Song vii, Song viii–*AS* 108; and B. F. Harfst ('*Astrophel and Stella*: Precept and Example', *PPL* 5 (1969), 397–414) urges the seven-part structure of a classical oration. Weiner's justification is that we are dealing with a 'dynamic process and not a static definition' (p. 1). I think that Sidney would not have understood the dynamic of the process. Not one of these critics acknowledges what Sidney wants us to see Astrophil doing to himself: verbal talent in the service of desire defeating itself through its own cleverness and basic desire.

on a different assumption: there is no progress in this sonnet sequence. Astrophil is sadly in love in *AS* 1 and sadly in love in *AS* 108. All the intervening sonnets are songs and recapitulations of the same crisis: human desire and its effects. As Rosemond Tuve remarks, 'We meet the Beast in a thousand guises and recognize him each time for the first time.'[37] One might almost say that in English sequences there is not progression, only regression into the selfish nightworld of desire unfulfilled. The crises occur again and again and are met with the same response:

> So while thy beautie drawes the heart to love,
> As fast thy Vertue bends that love to good:
> 'But ah,' Desire still cries, 'give me some food'.
>
> (*AS* 71.)

These lines are literally at the midpoint, or heart of the whole sequence. All that comes before and after is mere descant and recapitulation. No progress is possible; no reasonable outcome can be expected. The Penelope stone is absent from the beginning, hence the twenty-four rather than twenty-five poems at the end of the sequence. Whether in song or sonnet Astrophil repeats his crises, by invoking Morpheus (*AS* 32) or renouncing the Muses (*AS* 55) or grammar rules (*AS* 63), by observing 'changed looks' (*AS* 86) or by retreating into a false pastoral world (Song ix). Once the desire is codified into idolatrous blasphemy (Song i) there is no hope that the voice of reason (Song vii) will be understood, and Astrophil must sing his way to a 'conclusion in which nothing is concluded'.

[37] R. Tuve, *Allegorical Imagery* (Princeton NJ, 1966), p. 108 n.

9. STRUCTURE AND SYNTAX IN
ASTROPHIL AND STELLA

COLIN WILLIAMSON

When in the *Defence* Sidney wrote that the poets of his day should 'exercise to know', not 'as having known',[1] he meant, I take it, that his contemporaries had much to learn about their language and its poetic resources, and that they should write in order to discover what could and what could not be done with the materials available to them. That Sidney practised what he preached has been extensively demonstrated over the past thirty years, and he is now recognized as probably the most versatile and innovatory of the Elizabethan poets. Not apparently concerned to ground his own standing with posterity on his writings, he saw them to a great extent, I believe, as technical experiments which might be useful to contemporary and later writers. For the twentieth century, of course, the technical problems Sidney addressed are no longer topical, and it is inevitable that critical emphasis should have fallen increasingly on what he said rather than how he said it. With regard to *Astrophil and Stella* such matters as the critique of Petrarchism or the complex interrelation between Sidney/ Astrophil/Penelope/Stella have tended to absorb most critical attention, although of course there has been no lack of concern with the techniques he employed in handling these themes.

Sidney would have considered it an impertinence for him to attempt to teach other poets *what* they should write. The discovery of some fine invention, whether in his own heart or elsewhere, was the business of the individual author. But the demonstration of the capabilities of a particular form, for whatever purpose, was exactly the kind of contribution to English poetry that exercise, as Sidney understood it, could properly make. By focusing attention on a very limited aspect of his work I hope to show that formal considerations had a greater importance for Sidney in *Astrophil and Stella* than has generally been recognized. My area of concentration is his handling of the sestet, particularly in its English form

Reprinted from *RES* ns 31 (1980), 271–84.

[1] *Miscellaneous Prose of Sir Philip Sidney*, ed. K. Duncan-Jones and J. van Dorsten (Oxford, 1973), p. 112.

with the characteristic final couplet. The interest and variety of Sidney's sestets have often been commented on, but not in sufficient detail to reveal their full significance.

While experimenting more widely with the sonnet form than any other Elizabethan poet, Sidney showed throughout his career a predilection for the final couplet; he used it in fifteen out of the eighteen sonnets in the *Arcadia*, in all but one of the sonnets in *Certain Sonnets*, and in eighty-five of the 108 sonnets in *Astrophil and Stella*. Now the closing couplet has been generally regarded as perhaps the most important formal feature of the English sonnet in the sixteenth century, with its natural tendency to detach itself somewhat from the rest of the poem, thus inviting the poet, for better or for worse, to provide an epigrammatic ending, clinching or commenting on the first twelve lines of the poem. But when Sidney began writing, this form had not achieved the ascendancy that it was to gain in later years through Shakespeare's adoption of it. Wyatt had favoured a rhyme scheme based on his Petrarchan models, and although J. W. Lever sees Wyatt's sonnets as developing steadily towards but never quite reaching the English rhyme scheme as a kind of inevitable consummation ('Had he lived he would almost certainly have discovered this for himself in his next sonnet or two'),[2] this development seems to be much less regular and its hypothetical conclusion a good deal less inevitable than Lever allows for. It was of course left for Surrey to evolve what Lever (p. 46) describes as 'the staple late-Elizabethan sonnet-form', a form which must have established itself thanks more to Surrey's reputation than to the number of sonnets he wrote. Nevertheless, by 1575 its dominance was sufficiently clear for Gascoigne, whose opinion and practice were probably fairly representative, to be quite unequivocal in *Certayne Notes of Instruction* in saying of the sonnet's fourteen-line structure: 'The firste twelve do ryme in staves of foure lines by crosse meetre, and the last two ryming together do conclude the whole.'[3] In the couplet sonnets in the *Arcadia* and *Certain Sonnets* Sidney appears for the most part quite content to follow this pattern, but there is one interesting exception in *Certain Sonnets*, No. 31, 'Thou blind man's marke'.[4]

[2] J. W. Lever, *The Elizabethan Love Sonnet* (London, 1966), p. 34.

[3] George Gascoigne, *Certayne Notes of Instruction* (1575), in *Elizabethan Critical Essays* ed. G. G. Smith (2 vols., Oxford, 1904), i. 55.

[4] All quotations are from *The Poems of Sir Philip Sidney*, ed. W. A. Ringler Jr. (Oxford, 1962).

Thou blind man's marke, thou foole's selfe chosen snare,
Fond fancie's scum, and dregs of scattred thought,
Band of all evils, cradle of causelesse care,
Thou web of will, whose end is never wrought;

Desire, desire I have too dearely bought,
With price of mangled mind thy worthlesse ware,
Too long, too long asleepe thou hast me brought,
Who should my mind to higher things prepare.

But yet in vaine thou hast my ruine sought,
In vaine thou madest me to vaine things aspire,
In vaine thou kindlest all thy smokie fire;

For vertue hath this better lesson taught,
Within my selfe to seeke my onelie hire:
Desiring nought but how to kill desire.

Here Sidney uses a rhyme scheme which is clearly aimed at reducing if not entirely eliminating the expected breaks between the internal units. The potential quatrains of the octave are dissolved by the repeated but reversed rhymes; the 'ought' rhyme of the octave is carried over into the sestet, and the new rhyme introduced in line 10 is used for a final couplet that is also part of a triplet, giving a total pattern

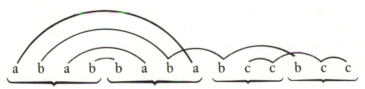

Considered in isolation from the sense, the rhyme scheme of the sestet could be regarded either as a quatrain plus couplet—bccb/cc—or as two triplets—bcc/bcc.[5] Syntax, however, and the fourfold repetition of 'vaine' in lines 9–11 establish the triplet pattern as primary, although the 'hire/desire' rhyme makes it impossible to exclude some sense of lines 13 and 14 as a couplet. The rhyme-link back to lines 10–11, however, counteracts any tendency for the two closing lines to detach themselves from the rest of the poem, whereas the use of in effect the rhetorical figure epanelepsis in

[5] This is a common Petrarchan rhyme scheme and is similar to Wyatt's favoured sestet pattern, but Petrarch and Wyatt do not link octave and sestet by rhyme, and Wyatt almost invariably introduces a new rhyme in the couplet.

line 14 gives the final line a kind of emphatic self-sufficiency, although the rhyme marries it fast to line 13 and so back to the rest of the sestet. A further small point is worth noting. The pattern of the opening words of lines 1–4—'Thou/Fond/Band/ Thou'—(-ond/-and, while not identical, are phonetically closely related) comes very close to setting up a head-rhyme pattern abba—that is, the characteristic Italian pattern—in contrast to the abab tail rhyme here employed. I do not intend to dwell on this poem, merely to draw attention to the use of rhyme patterns which interlace and interact with each other and with other structural elements (syntax, word repetition, head rhyme) to an extent which cannot be accidental and which clearly reveal Sidney as concerned to explore the possibilities of such formal counterpointing. In this the poem serves to direct attention to an important but neglected aspect of *Astrophil and Stella*.

When we turn to the first sonnet of the sequence it is after all with a formal feature that we are likely to be immediately struck—the bold departure in the use of the alexandrine from what Wyatt and Surrey had early established as the metrical norm for the sonnet in England. It would not be surprising if this departure was intended to alert the reader to be on the look-out not only for a new view of love but also, and quite as important, for a new adventurousness in the handling of the sonnet form.

The sestet of *AS* 1 has been often discussed and as often praised, so that it is impossible to comment on it without repeating what has been said by other critics, but it cannot be omitted since it draws attention to so many important features in the rest of the sequence.

> But words came halting forth, wanting Invention's stay,
> Invention, Nature's child, fled step-dame Studie's blowes,
> And others' feete still seem'd but strangers in my way.
> Thus great with child to speake, and helplesse in my throwes,
> Biting my trewand pen, beating my selfe for spite,
> 'Foole,' said my Muse to me, 'looke in thy heart and write.'

The rhyme scheme of the sestet is of the conventional English 4/2 pattern—cdcd/ee—but we at once notice that the arrangement of syntactic units cuts across this. The full stops at the ends of lines 11 and 14 (although the punctuation of the standard editions cannot always be relied on to give guidance in this matter) establish a 3/3 pattern which, amongst other things, has the effect of counteracting any tendency for the final couplet to break away from the rest of the poem. But there are further sub-divisions to be noted. The repetition of 'invention' links lines 9 and 10 to give just a hint of 2/1 division within this triplet, although the conjunction 'And' prevents the possibility from becoming actual-ized. What is merely hinted at in lines 9–11 is, however, fully realized in lines 12–14 where, as has often been remarked, line 14, the sudden intrusion of the voice of the Muse, is effectively isolated from what has gone before; but the exact nature of the device by which Sidney achieves this effect seems to have escaped most critics; R. L. Montgomery, for example, reveals he has missed the point when he writes 'the ending of Sonnet 18 uses exactly the same construction'.[6] Kalstone comes nearest to recognizing what Sidney is up to here, but even he does not quite nail the point.[7]

In his literary works Sidney shows perhaps more explicit consciousness of grammar and its workings than any other poet of his day. He bases *AS* 63 on 'grammer rules', he uses grammatical concepts in imagery ('Let me, therefore, receive a clear under-standing, which many times we miss while those things we accounted small, as a speech or a look, are omitted, like as a whole sentence may fail of his congruity by wanting one particle,' says Musidorus at the end of Chapter 12 of the First Book of the *New Arcadia*); and he draws attention to a lapse by Dorus from third to first person narrative, in those terms, as a crucial self-revelation in his discourse with Pamela (*New Arcadia*, Book II, Chapter 8). It is not to be supposed, then, that Sidney was unaware of how perilously close the construction of his final sentence comes to the classic solecism of the hanging participle. The octave of the sonnet—'Loving in truth . . . I sought fit words . . .'—which gets the construction right, creates a half-conscious expectation that the pattern will repeat itself in the sestet, following 'Biting my trewand pen . . .'. The whole point, however, is that this expectation is defeated as Sidney indulges in a little verbal brinkmanship to snatch a grace beyond the reach of preferred usage by creating the

[6] R. L. Montgomery, *Symmetry and Sense: The Poetry of Sir Philip Sidney* (Austin, Texas, 1961), p. 79.

[7] D. Kalstone, *Sidney's Poetry, Contexts and Interpretations* (Cambridge, Mass., 1965), p. 129. The last line, he says, has 'only a tenuous syntactical connection to what precedes it'.

sense of syntactic dislocation characteristic of the hanging participle and then retrieving the situation with the appearance of the indirect object 'to me', which gives the present participles of line 13 something to relate to, and establishes that 'Fool' refers to the poet and is not, say, the Muse's protest to Apollo at being lumbered with such an unlikely protégé. Sidney manages in effect to eat his cake and have it. The lurch from the implied first-person subject of the opening phrases to the third-person subject of the main clause isolates the last line, so stressing the new voice and with it the completely new approach breaking in on the poet's cogitations; but this is achieved in such a way as not to offend the grammatical purist. That so few readers appear to have noticed exactly what happens here is a tribute to Sidney's poetic tact in using syntactic dislocation to enact a radical shift of viewpoint.

So in the final three lines the 2/1 pattern barely suggested in lines 9–11 becomes explicit to create the tapering structure ('pointed' might even be a better word) that was a favourite with Sidney in the English-type sestets in the sequence, setting against the 4/2 rhyme pattern a 3/2/1 pattern of sense or syntax, isolating the last line in sense, relating it firmly to the preceding structure by rhyme, separating the last two lines by rhyme, linking them to the preceding lines by sense and syntax. Again, Sidney's use of this 3/2/1 structure has been remarked on, but its frequency and the variety of devices Sidney uses to achieve it have not received the attention they deserve.[8]

There is, of course, nothing novel in organizing the sestet of a sonnet as two triplets—it is after all the standard procedure in the Italian form.[9] What is suggestive, however, is an examination of the very different frequency of this and other patterns established by sense or syntax in the Italian and in the English types of sestet. I have already referred to the generally recognized tendency for the English form to encourage the use of a clinching, often epigrammatic couplet, yet there are surprisingly few of these in *Astrophil*

---

[8] Lever, pp. 61–2; see also Kalstone, p. 123.

[9] As Lever points out (p. 90) some of Wyatt's sonnets make use of interlocking rhyme scheme and syntax. Indeed, Wyatt's favourite sestet scheme, cddcee, lends itself to such an effect, since it can be taken as a quatrain plus couplet (cddc/ee) or two triplets (cdd/cee). Wyatt usually allowed his Italian originals to dictate a 3/3 syntactic division, and I see no evidence that he was systematically exploiting the rhyme/syntax tension. The disposition of Sidney's sestets, since they are not translations, was entirely a matter of the poet's choice.

and Stella, although they are common in the *Arcadia* sonnets and in *Certain Sonnets*. Its concluding couplet, on the other hand, means that the English form does not lend itself to last-line isolation, yet this feature occurs in nearly a third of the English sestets in *Astrophil and Stella*. On the other hand, while most of the rhyme schemes characteristic of the Italian form *do* lend themselves to last-line isolation, this is rare (less than one in ten) in the Italian sonnets in the sequence, whereas, somewhat surprisingly, the incidence of syntactically self-contained concluding couplets is about the same in both English and Italian types.

This somewhat unexpected situation is hardly to be explained simply on the grounds that Sidney enjoyed the fascination of what is difficult (although doubtless he did). He seems rather to have been interested in and experimenting with a kind of structural counterpoint: like other poets of the period, he discovered how to play off speech rhythms against metrical patterns. I would suggest that Sidney set out in *Astrophil and Stella* to explore ways in which syntactic or sense units might be counterpointed against the units created by rhyme.

What is more, the relative incidence of these features in the English and Italian forms suggests that Sidney's concern may have been less expressive than formal. As we have seen, in the sequence he overwhelmingly favoured a sestet division into two triplets, and had a strong preference for dividing the second triplet 2/1. If he considered that a 3/3 or a 3/2/1 division was *in itself* more expressive than the characteristic English 4/2 division, one would expect the favoured pattern to occur at least as often in the Italian as in the English sestets, indeed rather more often since the Italian rhyme scheme could be expected to emphasize or enhance the effect. That this is not what we find suggests that other considerations were at work. The practice in *Astrophil and Stella* of avoiding—and the statistics justify the term 'deliberately'—self-enclosed final couplets in the English sestets but introducing isolated last lines in them roughly four times as often as in the Italian forms suggests that Sidney may have recognized what his contemporaries either did not notice or did not regard: the danger of a couplet or single line becoming *too* detached if both rhyme and syntax co-operated in an isolating effect and so threatening the unity of a poem.

To argue, however, that formal considerations were important, even dominant, in this matter is not at all to imply that expressive

considerations were disregarded. Sidney's aesthetic ideal, articulated especially cogently in the description of Kalander's house
(*New Arcadia*, Book I, Chapter 2) involved a perfect accommodation of form and function. And it was only by exploring the formal
resources and limitations of the sonnet that he could realize for
himself and make available to others its expressive possibilities.

Let me return to the poems themselves, and the evidence they
contain that Sidney was aiming to complement and counterpoint
the rhyme patterns of his sonnets by the use of other devices, and
particularly to link the final couplets of his English-type sestets
with the preceding lines. The evidence can be divided broadly into
two categories, negative and positive. Some features in the poems
could be taken to indicate no more than that Sidney was not
actively concerned to maintain the characteristic break after the
twelfth line. Such an attitude would reveal itself most obviously in
a readiness to allow syntactic units to run on from line 12 to line 13,
and this we certainly find; but so frequently—in seventy-three out
of the eighty-five English sonnets—that it begins to look suspiciously like deliberate choice rather than mere accident. Even
more suggestive are those cases where Sidney uses a parenthetical
construction, a kind of syntactic loop, to avoid the conventional
break before the concluding couplet. In *AS* 12, for example, line
13, 'So fortified with wit, stor'd with disdaine', merely expands on
'such' in the previous line; the self-sufficient syntactic unit is made
up of lines 12 and 14:

> O no, her heart is such a Cittadell . . .
> That to win it, is all the skill and paine.

An even more striking example is *AS* 24, the first of the 'rich'
sonnets, which concludes:

> Let him, deprived of sweet but unfelt joyes,
> (Exil'd for ay from those high treasures, which
> He knowes not) grow in only follie rich.

Here the contemptuous main clause 'Let him . . . grow in only follie
rich' sandwiches two syntactic units parallel in that they begin with
the similar words, 'deprived' and 'Exil'd'. This parenthetical structure achieves an effect not dissimilar to that already discussed in
AS 1. The parenthesis cuts off the subject of Astrophil's venom
syntactically as it does literally from those delights from which we

are told he is cut off by natural incapacity. Again syntax has been used artfully to enact meaning. An effect like this does not just happen. It indicates a Sidney consciously organizing the last three lines as a structural unit within which a significant pattern could be created.

It is interesting and perhaps not wholly accidental that Sidney uses a variation on this procedure in another 'rich' sonnet, *AS* 37.

> Rich in the treasure of deserv'd renowne,
> Rich in the riches of a royall hart,
> Rich in those gifts which give th'eternall crowne;
> Who though most rich in these and everie part,
>   Which make the patents of true worldly blisse,
>   Hath no misfortune, but that Rich she is.

Here, of course, Stella is the subject, and the enclosing clauses in the last three lines 'Who . . . Hath no misfortune, but that Rich she is', set Stella's fortune off against her excelling personal qualities which are summed up in the parenthesis 'though most rich in these and everie part, / Which make the patents of true worldly blisse'. The contrast between the gifts of Nature in which Stella is truly rich and those of Fortune which have made her rich in name alone is reinforced, like the contrast in *AS* 24 between the name Rich and the poverty of spirit it represented, by the parenthetical construction of the last three lines of the poem.

A technique which is in a way the reverse of the parenthesis or syntactic loop to hold together the closing lines is found in *AS* 91. This is an unusual poem in that instead of the usual octave the main opening statement comprises the first nine lines, line 9 answering to the 'If' of line 5—another example of Sidney's readiness to vary the standard form. But that by the way. We are now all familiar, thanks to Professor Ricks, with Milton's way of giving a word a dual function, linking it both backwards and forwards, as in the classic instance '. . . her hand / Soft she withdrew'. In this sonnet Sidney uses a somewhat similar device in the placement of line 12.

> They please I do confesse, they please mine eyes,
> But why? because of you they models be,
> Models such be wood-globes of glistring skies.
> Deere, therefore be not jealous over me,
>   If you heare that they seeme my hart to move,
>   Not them, O no, but you in them I love.

The heavy punctuation—the full stop (which may well not be authorial) at the end of line 11—slightly obscures but by no means destroys the effect. As we read the poem, our first impulse is to understand the 'therefore' of line 12 as referring back to what has gone before—'Don't be jealous because in fact those to whom I have been attracted were only models of you'; but as we read on we sense that the 'therefore' points forward too, as indeed the punctuation of the standard edition implies, to provide the logical introduction of lines 13 and 14. Thus, in contrast to the use of parenthesis to place a syntactic loop around the units to be joined, here Sidney achieves what seems to be his usual objective of linking the final couplet to the rest of the sestet by the use of a line whose sense links it equally with the lines that precede and follow it.

A parallel effect occurs in *AS* 107.

> And as a Queene, who from her presence sends
> Whom she imployes, dismisse from thee my wit,
> Til it have wrought what thy owne will attends.
> On servants' shame oft Maister's blame doth sit;
> O let not fooles in me thy workes reprove,
> And scorning say, 'See what it is to love.'

Line 12—'On servants' shame oft Maister's blame doth sit'—appears initially to be warning Stella of the consequences of not allowing Astrophil to achieve whatever it is that her 'will attends'; but again (and again Ringler's punctuation invites the forward linkage) the line can be read equally well as introducing the admonition of the final couplet. Thus in both these poems the twelfth line is artfully contrived at once to complete the sense of the quatrain in the conventional 4/2 pattern and to initiate a further step in the development of the sestet as the first line of the second triplet in Sidney's favourite 3/3 structure.

To return, however, to *AS* 37. The reader will almost certainly be struck not by the parenthetical structure of the closing lines but by the repetition, particularly at the beginning of lines 9–11, of the word 'Rich'—indeed we are likely to notice this on the page even before we begin to read the poem. Sidney frequently uses patterns of head rhyme to counterpoint the conventional rhyme scheme; and it is here that we pass from the negative evidence—features which Sidney at least did not go out of his way to avoid—to the positive, features which are clearly deliberate and can therefore be taken to reflect some positive intention on the part of the poet. In *AS* 37 the effect of the repeated 'rich' is to mark off lines 9–11 as a triplet with an identity of its own, balanced against the syntactic unity of lines 12–14. This use of repetition as a means of demarcating a structural unit is found also, again perhaps not accidentally, in the preceding poem.

> With so sweete voice, and by sweete Nature so,
> In sweetest strength, so sweetly skild withall,
> In all sweete stratagems sweete Arte can show,
> That not my soule, which at thy foot did fall,
>> Long since forc'd by thy beames, but stone nor tree
>> By Sence's priviledge, can scape from thee.

Although head rhyme is not used, the repetition 'sweete ... sweete/sweetest ...sweetly/sweete ... sweete' holds lines 9–11 firmly together by internal patterning. Here repetition and syntax are used together to create an emphatic 3/3 structure, cutting right across the traditional 4/2 rhyme scheme.

The repetition of word or phrase, either as head rhyme or internally, is in fact one of Sidney's favourite devices—it occurs in almost a quarter of the sonnets in the sequence—but more often than not word-play and patterning go hand in hand with structural effect, although by no means always to establish simple 3/3 patterns as in *AS* 36 and 37. For example, the Italian type *AS* 4 has lines 13 and 14 beginning 'That'—the same word though in different grammatical categories—so that head rhyme almost turns the lines into a couplet, creating the pattern: head rhyme xyy/tail rhyme ddc, an interesting reversal of Sidney's more frequent practice of modifying the English form by the use of triplets in the sestet.

A more remarkable example of the use of head rhyme and repetition for structural purposes is *AS* 5.

> It is most true, that eyes are form'd to serve
> The inward light: and that the heavenly part
> Ought to be king, from whose rules who do swerve,
> Rebels to Nature, strive for their owne smart.
>> It is most true, what we call *Cupid's* dart,
>> An image is, which for our selves we carve;
>> And, fooles, adore in temple of our hart,
>> Till that good God make Church and Churchman starve.

> True, that true Beautie Vertue is indeed,
> Whereof this Beautie can be but a shade,
> Which elements with mortall mixture breed:
> True, that on earth we are but pilgrims made,
>   And should in soule up to our countrey move:
>   True, and yet true that I must *Stella* love.

Here the two opening quatrain units are thrown into relief by their identical beginnings—'It is most true . . .'. The compression of the whole phrase to the single word 'True' at line 9 gives a feeling of urgency, almost impatience, which is reinforced by the accelerated recurrence of 'True' at line 12, at first sight to demarcate two triplets in the sestet; but the acceleration continues, as line 14 not only begins 'True' but continues 'and yet true that I must *Stella* love'. Here then word and phrase repetition has been used with a threefold effect: to unify the whole structure of the sonnet, at once defining and yet linking its units; to create the tapering 3/2/1 sestet already discussed; and by the progressive reduction of the intervals between the repetitions to suggest a state of mind growing increasingly impatient with traditional platitudes in view of the overwhelming and inescapable fact of Stella's power. It would not be extravagant, I think, to claim that the increasing independence of the orthodox 4/2 sestet created by the punctuating 'true's mimics the speaker's dissatisfaction with orthodox attitudes to morality and love.

AS 14 represents a further use of these devices of repetition.

> If that be sinne which doth the maners frame,
> Well staid with truth in word and faith of deed,
> Readie of wit and fearing nought but shame:
> If that be sinne which in fixt hearts doth breed
>   A loathing of all loose unchastitie,
>   Then Love is sinne, and let me sinfull be.

The obvious one is the repeated 'If that be sinne' opening lines 9 and 12 to establish the familiar triplet pattern, further broken down to a 3/2/1 structure by the 'If . . . If . . . Then' logical organization. But this arrangement is complicated by the repetition of 'sinne' and 'sinfull' in line 14, so that, while the logical pattern isolates the final line, the recurrence of the key root 'sin' points back to lines 9 and 13, offering an unexpected identification of sin, love and virtuous conduct in defiance of the 'Rubarb words' of the poet's critic. Again, the interlacing of the conventional rhyme units with the unconventional units created by syntax and verbal patterning constitutes a formal (as the poem does a logical) challenge to established orthodoxies.

The sestet of *AS* 18 is unusual in that it comes very close to the quatrain plus striking final couplet so common elsewhere but so unusual in this sequence, and it is therefore of particular interest to see Sidney using head rhyme to counteract the conspiracy of tail rhyme and sense units to isolate the final couplet.

> My youth doth waste, my knowledge brings forth toyes,
> My wit doth strive those passions to defend,
> Which for reward spoile it with vaine annoyes.
> I see my course to lose my selfe doth bend:
> I see and yet no greater sorrow take,
> Then that I lose no more for *Stella's* sake.

The triplet pattern created by 'My youth doth waste' and 'My wit doth strive' of lines 9 and 10 and 'I see my course' and 'I see . . .' of 12 and 13 is sufficiently striking to overlay the 4/2 structure and bind this sestet into the complex unity of quatrain plus couplet alongside two triplets which it seems Sidney was throughout the sequence concerned to explore and exploit.

The famous 'Moon' sonnet, *AS* 31, provides a further variant.

> Then ev'n of fellowship, ô Moone, tell me
> Is constant *Love* deem'd there but want of wit?
> Are Beauties there as proud as here they be?
> Do they above love to be lov'd, and yet
> Those Lovers scorne whom that *Love* doth possesse?
> Do they call *Vertue* there ungratefulnesse?

The rhyme scheme is the regular 4/2 arrangement, but the syntax creates a counterpointing pattern of two triplets each in turn subdivided into a question taking up two lines followed by one occupying a single line; but the second of these divided triplets is further organized by head rhyme—'Do they . . . / Do they . . .'—to give three levels of patterning:

tail rhyme:	ababcc
head rhyme:	. . . xyx
syntax:	ddedde

Thus, while the final line is so isolated as to be a sufficiently striking climax, it is integrated with the rest of the sestet by tail rhyme with line 13, by head rhyme with line 12, and by syntactic parallelism with line 11. The unobtrusive elegance of this inter-locking pattern is the kind of thing that enables Sidney to give his sonnets their outstanding formal coherence while his speaker propounds attitudes often positively iconoclastic.

AS 85 shows how far the use of head rhyme and phrasal repeti-tion was from becoming a merely formal device:

> But give apt servants their due place, let eyes
> See Beautie's totall summe summ'd in her face:
> Let eares heare speech, which wit to wonder ties,
> Let breath sucke up those sweetes, let armes embrace
> The globe of weale, lips *Love's* indentures make:
> Thou but of all the kingly Tribute take.

Here by combining repetition with enjambment Sidney has achieved couplet patterns cutting across the orthodox rhyme scheme without the repetition ever becoming mechanical. Lines 9 and 10 form a unit by virtue of the run-on 'let eyes / See . . .'; lines 11 and 12 are linked by the head rhyme 'Let eares . . . / Let breath . . .'; lines 12 and 13 are unified again by enjambment; while, in so far as line and syntactic units coincide, the structure is an unusual 2/3/1 arrangement. Since enjambment may be regarded as the refusal of units of meaning to submit to metrical constraints, this is a fine example of Sidney's recognition of the need to achieve and success in achieving a balance between pattern and freedom, the artificial and the natural.

One final example of the use of head rhyme and repetition for a rather different effect. *AS* 105:

> But cease mine eyes, your teares do witnesse well
> That you, guiltlesse thereof, your Nectar mist:
> Curst be the page from whome the bad torch fell,
> Curst be the night which did your strife resist,
> Curst be the Cochman which did drive so fast,
> With no worse curse then absence makes me tast.

The repeated 'Curst . . .' opening of lines 11, 12, and 13 echoed by the assonantal 'no worse curse' of line 14 works powerfully to create a sense of the speaker's anger and frustration, but the intensity is contained by the way in which these emphatic line openings are linked phonetically with the second rhyme of the quatrain and also the couplet rhyme: 'mist/Curst/Curst/resist/

Curst/fast/tast'. One should notice in addition that, while lines 9 and 10 constitute a syntactic couplet, the 'curse' repetition holds lines 11–14 together as an emotionally unified quatrain to create a 2/4 structure in the sestet, counterpointing the usual 4/2 rhyme pattern.

Without the benefit of external evidence there must always be some uncertainty in making a case for systematic experimentation where others may see only accidental variation. The repetition of some novel feature of form or mode of expression may give a clue; what happens twice in quick succession is perhaps more likely to be deliberate than fortuitous. The juxtaposition of the sonnets using the repetition of 'sweet' and 'rich' has already been remarked on, and there are other instances of adjacent sonnets containing formal parallels. In *AS* 21 and 22, for example, last-line isolation is achieved by the use of the similar phrases 'now tell me this' and 'the cause was this'; *AS* 27 and 28 have sestets in which the sense units, unusually in Sidney, create a 2/4 pattern against the 4/2 rhyme scheme (and it is suggestive that the Italian 29 imposes a 4/2 sense pattern on a cddece rhyme structure); while *AS* 61 and 62 use similar paradoxical conclusions (which were to bear fruit in Herbert's 'Affliction')—'That I love not, without I leave to love' and 'Deare, love me not, that you may love me more'. There may be evidence here, although one would not wish to press it, that Sidney was sufficiently pleased with the success of the device in question to feel inclined to repeat it immediately. There cannot be much doubt that he was aware of these repetitions and although, particularly in the pairs 36/37 and 61/62, it could be argued that the determining factor was thematic parallelism, it seems unlikely to be the complete explanation.

Another clue may be found in the practice of Sidney's major contemporaries. A statistical comparison of the relative frequency of, say, a 3/3 structure in the English-type sestet suggests itself, or even of apparent attempts to bridge the gap between lines 12 and 13, but a brief survey of the incidence of these features outside Sidney's work shows them to be so rare as to be insignificant. This suggests that it was not enough to be a poet of skill and originality, a Shakespeare, Spenser, Daniel, or Drayton, to hit on the formal variations that abound in *Astrophil and Stella*. A conscious experi-mentalism had to be present. That Sidney believed in experiment—'exercise to know'—we have his own word in the

Defence; but even without it I believe the internal evidence of which I have given but a few examples in *Astrophil and Stella* is sufficient to demonstrate Sidney's preoccupation with the form of the sonnet, and particularly with the effects that might be created by the superimposition of an unusual pattern—of syntax or head rhyme or what else—on another more familiar. Reflection on the matter of the sequence indicates that this preoccupation was no mere verbal game played for its own sake. The strength of the sequence lies in its exploration of the tension and conflict between different codes of conduct, different loyalties, between reason and desire, spiritual and physical love, private and public life, and so on. It is entirely in keeping with Sidney's aesthetic belief that form and function should go hand in hand, that the exploration of these overlapping and interacting areas of human feeling and conduct should issue in poetry characterized by interlocking and contrasting formal patterns, and it is this accommodation which established *Astrophil and Stella* as the boldest and most self-conscious exploration of the formal and expressive resources of the sonnet in our greatest age of sonneteering.

The *New Arcadia*

10. STRUCTURE AND RHETORIC IN SIDNEY'S *ARCADIA*

John Carey

Sidney's *Arcadia*, to a modern reader, can seem an ornate and frivolous work. We find it hard to account for its seventeenth-century reputation. In the seventeenth century it was regarded as not only the greatest English literary work, but also a work that could match the classics of world literature. It was thought worthy of comparison with Homer and Virgil. George Hakewill, in his *Apology of the Power and Providence of God* (1627), selects the *Arcadia* to support his argument (p. 236) that the modern excels all previous eras in its cultural achievement.

It was the way the *Arcadia* was written, as much as its content, that compelled admiration. It seemed a miracle of verbal craft—so that John Hoskins, in his *Directions for Speech and Style*, was moved to illustrate all the rhetorical figures he wished to recommend with examples from the *Arcadia* alone. If we are to understand the work, we must regain a sense of its vital rhetorical operation—must see its rhetoric as part of its life. I shall argue that the prolific display of figuring in which Sidney's narrative is embodied is not ornate but functional, a linguistic equivalent of a particular and tragic world view, and that its plotting, likewise, is not frivolous, but holds in equipoise a bleak vision of man's fate with a delicate response to the agitations of the human psyche. Study of the *Arcadia* is made easier, of course, by the fact that we have got two versions, the original version and a rewritten, though unfinished, version, the 1590 *Arcadia*.[1] From a comparison of these two we can deduce the organizing principles behind Sidney's thought and expression—the set of concepts which, when we read the *Arcadia* rightly, the whole complicated extension of the work can be seen to be endorsing. For the rhetoric of the *Arcadia* is not haphazard. It

This is a revised version of an article which appeared in *Poetica* 18 (1984), 68–81, copyright material reprinted with permission of Shubun International Co. Ltd.

[1] All quotations from and all references to the new or revised *Arcadia* are to *The Complete Works of Sir Philip Sidney*, ed. A. Feuillerat (4 vols., Cambridge, 1912–26), reprinted with much of the verse omitted, as *The Prose Works of Sir Philip Sidney* (Cambridge, 1962, etc.), i. Quotations from and references to the *Old Arcadia* are to *The Countess of Pembroke's Arcadia (The Old Arcadia)*, ed. J. Robertson (Oxford, 1973).

emphasizes, cumulatively, a single pattern—a pattern that remains discernible despite the multiple variations it is spun into. Hoskins can help us to perceive this, for of the figures he discusses two are given special prominence by the space he allots to them—antimetabole and synoeciosis—and both show the pattern in a seminal form. An example Hoskins quotes of antimetabole (a figure which, he observes, Sidney is addicted to) is: 'If any for love of honour, or honour of love'; and, illustrating synoeciosis (defined as 'a composition of contraries'), he cites Sidney's comment on mingled smiles and tears: 'a man could not tell whether it were mourning pleasure or delightful sorrow.'[2]

What these two examples, and the figures they stand for, have in common is a basic structure, akin to chiasmus, which first advances from A to B and then, after the hinge word 'or', steps back from B to A. The phrasing loops round elegantly on itself, returning in a circle or figure-of-eight to its starting-point. So we have love–honour–honour–love, and, with a little more variation, mourning–pleasure–delightful–sorrow. It is this circling or to-and-fro motion that I take to be dominant in the rhetoric of the *Arcadia*, and essential to the work's meaning.

It will help, before proceeding, to look at a few other, and slightly less obvious, instances of its operation, and I shall choose all of them from the *Old Arcadia*, since it is part of my argument that this has the same basic structure as the new. An example of the to-and-fro rhetoric being endorsed by narrative action is Pamela's breath (p. 201) which 'seemed loath to leave his contentful mansion: but that it hoped to be drawn in again to that well closed paradise'. Breath, incessantly leaving and returning, acts out Sidney's principle of stasis within motion, as does his periphrasis ('contentful mansion' and 'well closed paradise' both meaning the same thing). Periphrasis, a favourite device of Sidney's, is committed to showing sameness (stasis) underlying apparent difference (motion). Structurally similar are the frequent figures that set repeated words against one another, e.g.: 'with extraordinary boldness to overcome boldness, and with danger to avoid danger.' (p. 129.) Boldness and danger come into operation, here, only to negate themselves and restore the status quo. Often this assertion of stasis is brought about by contraries cancelling each

    [2] J. Hoskins, *Directions for Speech and Style*, ed. H. H. Hudson (Princeton, 1935), pp. 14, 36.

other, as in: 'the joy would have carried his life from him, had not the grief he conceived to see her in such case something diminished it.' (p. 52.) The partnered opposites, joy and grief, perform a brief dance—joy tending to kill, grief to save—and so prevent anything happening.

This constant impulse towards deadlock in the rhetoric, produced by opposites pitted equally against each other, is often elaborated by Sidney into insoluble questions, where the two possible answers are so balanced that you cannot choose between them. Pyrocles' hair provides an instance, its locks: 'some curled, and some, as it were, forgotten, with such a careless care, and with an art so hiding art, that he seemed he would lay them for a paragon whether nature simply, or nature helped by cunning, be the more excellent.' (p. 26.)

The universe of the rhetoric is designed to evolve such locked problems, transmitting a version of nature as debate, but debate in which contraries artfully co-operate to maintain stability. The landscape offers neatly deadlocked dispute: 'the meadow itself yielding so liberally all sorts of flowers that it seemed to nourish a contention betwixt the colour and the smell whether in his kind were the more delightful.' (p. 46.) What all these rhetorical mannerisms assert is the principle of binary opposition—the world splitting incessantly into paired qualities; and the principle of frustrated motion—advance is followed by withdrawal, to by fro.

As we shall see, these are vital aspects of Sidney's subject in the *Arcadia*. But to demonstrate this we must briefly summarize his plot, and the alterations he made in plotting when he rewrote.

The plot of the original *Arcadia* is relatively simple and tightly planned, and has a comparatively small cast of characters. Basilius, Duke of Arcadia, frightened by the prophecy of an oracle, retires into the country, accompanied by his wife Gynecia and daughters Pamela and Philoclea. Two foreign princes, Musidorus and Pyrocles, fall in love with the princesses, and join them in the country in disguise. Musidorus is disguised as a shepherd, Dorus; Pyrocles, as an Amazon, Cleophila. The first half of the plot is largely comic, because both Basilius and Gynecia fall in love with the disguised Pyrocles, Basilius thinking Pyrocles really is a woman (Cleophila), Gynecia realizing he is a man. Pyrocles has a difficult time fending off these two, and he manages to trick them so that they both go to a dark and secret place of assignation and climb into bed together, each thinking that the other person in the bed is Pyrocles (alias Cleophila). Meanwhile Pyrocles is actually in bed with their daughter Philoclea.

While all this is happening Musidorus, the other lover, reveals his true identity to Pamela, and they elope together hoping to get back to his own country. At this point we have reached the end of the third act, as it were. The work is divided into five acts, or sections, and in between these there are sets of eclogues, where the Arcadian shepherds meet and hold song contests. These eclogues are like the choruses of a classical tragedy, and the themes of the shepherd songs can be shown to bear an oblique relation to the main action.

By the end of the third act there have been only two hints of danger, when Pyrocles and Musidorus rescue the princesses first from a wild lion and bear, then from some rebellious Arcadians. In neither case is the danger much more than an excuse for the princes to show their courage. But at the start of the fourth act, things turn sour. Basilius and Gynecia wake up in the morning, realize they are in bed together, and mutual reconciliation takes place. But unfortunately Basilius drinks a love-potion Gynecia has brought along, and falls dead. Gynecia, distraught and over-whelmed with guilt, goes and confesses to Philanax, the regent whom Basilius appointed when he went into the country, and Gynecia is accordingly arrested on a charge of regicide. Pyrocles is also arrested, in Philoclea's bedroom, and, since the punishment for fornication in Arcadia is death, they both face a capital charge. Meanwhile Musidorus and Pamela are also captured, on the borders of Arcadia, by some bandits, at a point when Musidorus, his feelings having got the better of him, was about to rape Pamela. The two of them are brought back to court by the bandits, where Musidorus faces a charge of abducting the princess.

The trial of all the defendants is presided over by Euarchus, King of Macedon, who happens to be passing through Arcadia, and who is actually the father of Pyrocles and the uncle of Musidorus, though because they are disguised he does not recognize them. He pronounces death sentences on both Pyrocles and Musidorus, and also on Gynecia, who is to be buried alive with her husband's corpse. The true identity of the two princes now emerges, but Euarchus refuses to change his sentence, despite his relationship to the accused. However, before the executions can be carried out, Basilius comes back to life. He had just been drugged by the love-potion, it emerges, not poisoned. So all is well.

What are the ruling principles behind this action? We can pick out two dominant and persistent features, and it is worth doing so because they are basic to the new or rewritten *Arcadia* of 1590 as well. The first of these is the idea of the blindness of humankind, which makes human actions and endeavours produce the opposite of what was intended. This is the prime philosophical concept behind Greek tragedy, which is, I think, Sidney's model. The tragic irony so prevalent in Sophocles depends on the actors not realizing how their words and actions will actually turn out; and the peripeteia or reversal, which Aristotle in the *Poetics* selects as a crucial element in Greek tragic plot, also results from people urgently pursuing courses of action which produce the opposite result to what they intended. Sidney directly voices this view of human affairs towards the end of the first version of the *Arcadia* (p. 385): 'In such a shadow or rather pit of darkness the wormish mankind lives that neither they know how to forsee nor what to fear, and are but like tennis balls tossed by the racket of the higher powers.'

It might be objected that Sidney was a Christian, so could not really have believed this. But the dominant mode of Christian thought in Sidney's England was Calvinism, which, like Sophoclean fatalism, encouraged a belief in the blindness and ignorance of mankind and the irretrievable wrongness of human reason. It was this aspect of Calvinism that made it a favourable climate for pagan modes of feeling—as the revival of classical scepticism and the flourishing of neo-Stoicism in the late Renaissance illustrate.

The plot of the *Old Arcadia* manifests peripeteia both in major and minor incidents. Basilius, for instance, brings all the trouble about by trying to avoid trouble. He hopes to evade what the oracle foretells but actually precipitates it. The self-defeat inherent in Basilius' action is pointed out at the start when he discusses with Philanax his plan of going into the country. Referring to the oracle's prediction that a foreign state would take over Arcadia (as of course does happen when Basilius is thought dead and Euarchus presides at the trial), Philanax says (p. 7) 'Why should you deprive yourself of governing your dukedom, for fear of losing your dukedom, like one that should kill himself for fear of death?' That neatly locked rhetorical pattern is, as we have seen, one of

Sidney's characteristic figures. The language steps forward, and steps back. In this way Sidney creates in the rhetoric of the *Old Arcadia* a linguistic equivalent to his tragic world view. The counteraction inherent in action, the repercussion of acts upon the agent, is figured in these elegant turnarounds of language. The whole linguistic atmosphere is stained with circularity and self-defeat. So are the actions of the characters, right through to the end when Euarchus, quite ignorant of what he is doing, condemns his own son and nephew to death, in what is almost a copybook example of Greek peripeteia—the urge for justice rebounding upon the giver of justice, so that his sentence falls on himself.

This, then, is one principle behind the plot-structure of the *Old Arcadia*. The second is the principle of conflict, of divided loyalties, of tension and struggle within the soul. The key figure here is Gynecia, but what is true of her applies to almost all the main figures in lesser degree. Gynecia is a tragic heroine, torn between lust and duty, between desire for Pyrocles and fidelity to Basilius. She is presented as a maelstrom of warring emotions, seeing her own degeneracy clearly, but helpless to combat it. Reason and passion wrestle within her. 'Reason', writes Sidney, 'began to cry out against the filthy rebellion of sinful sense, and to tear itself with anguish' (p. 279). The other characters share Gynecia's inner division. They are forced into subterfuge, disguise, furtiveness, and disgrace by the heat of their desires, and Sidney keeps reminding us of their split psyches, of reason and passion warring. When Philoclea yields to Pyrocles, she is torn between joy and fear, and Sidney draws a general moral: 'such contradictions there must needs grow in those minds which neither absolutely embrace goodness, nor freely yield to evil' (pp. 120–1). All men and women, he shows, are caught in this middle state, and from that their struggles ensue.

One thing worth adding before we turn to the *New Arcadia* is that these two basic narrative principles of peripeteia (or reversal) and passion warring against reason are linked, because passion is shown by Sidney as a prime cause of the blindness that conceals from people the results of their actions. He is intent as a narrative artist on constructing passionate situations which also involve a turnaround in intention. For example, the bandits capture Musidorus and Pamela just as he was about to rape her, and Sidney rhetorically encapsulates this clash of events and aims in a typical cluster of balanced opposites: 'But a greater peril preserved her [Pamela] from the less, and the coming of her enemies defended her from the violence of a friend' (p. 306). The bandits, too, suffer from peripeteia in this episode, for when they approach the Arcadian court with their prisoners they are themselves put to death by a search party looking for Pamela and Musidorus (p. 317), and again Sidney transforms the reversal of fate into a rhetorical performance: 'such an unlooked-for end did the life of justice work for the mighty-minded wretches, by subjects to be executed that would have executed princes, and to suffer that without law which by law they had deserved.' The style perpetuates a cosmic pattern, a circular justice, or fate, governing the lives of the people caught up in Sidney's world.

Turning now to the plot of the revised *Arcadia* of 1590: the initial situation is the same as in the *Old Arcadia*, and the first two episodes or acts follow roughly the same pattern. Basilius and his family retreat into the country to avoid the oracle. The two princes join them, in disguise, although this time Pyrocles, disguised as an Amazon, calls himself Zelmane not Cleophila. We have the episodes of the lion and the bear and the rebellion among the Arcadians, more or less as before. But it does not seem at all the same when we read it, and that is because of the first major change Sidney has made in his narrative method, which is to break up the main story with interspersed flashbacks to other adventures Pyrocles or Musidorus have taken part in, entailing loves and wars and betrayals and disasters and mistaken identities, and introducing crowds of new characters, as well as involving and perplexing the story-line in a way that deliberately makes it hard to follow. The point of this vast extension and diversification of the narrative is that it gives the workings of fate and the struggles of passion and reason that Sidney portrays a seemingly endless validity and complication. His moral landscape stretches now as far as the eye can see, restless, tormented, full of pain and unlooked for catastrophe. The inset stories parade an anthology of mishaps. Thus Queen Andromana's devouring passion for Pyrocles and Musidorus leads to the death of her beloved son Palladius (Book II, Chapter 21), and his death is, typically, a mistake—one of his mother's guard takes him for an enemy and slays him. When Andromana sees what she has brought about, she commits suicide—the ultimate self-negating act, which brings into the open the inner motive of

Sidney's self-negating rhetorical antitheses. Likewise the loving brothers Tydeus and Telenor (Book II, Chapter 22) who are tricked into killing each other in combat and die clasped in each other's arms, each craving pardon of the other, display in human form the warring yet reconciled, opposed yet self-defeating elements of the typical Sidneian rhetorical figure, as well as the boomerang of fate which such figures emblematize.

The other major innovation in the plotting of the *New Arcadia* becomes apparent at the end of the second act. Instead of the story of the love-potion and the seeming death of Basilius, Sidney introduces a new character, the wicked Cecropia, aunt to the princesses and Basilius' sister-in-law, and a whole new set of events which she instigates. By a trick she captures the princesses and Zelmane and locks them in her castle. Her son Amphialus is in love with Philoclea, and Cecropia subjects the sisters to a variety of mental and physical tortures to try to get Philoclea to marry him. Meanwhile Basilius lays siege to the castle, and there are many bloody combats as Amphialus sallies out to assault the besiegers. In this part, with its persistent presentation of the horror and beauty of war and warriors, and the blood-dimmed tide of carnage, Sidney seems to have Homer's *Iliad* clearly in mind: but, because the minds of the women are particularly closely studied, as well as the fortunes of war, it is a modern *Iliad*, involving a whole new level of sensibility. Eventually Amphialus meets the disguised Musidorus in battle, and is nearly killed. When he recovers, he is horrified to find what tortures his mother has been subjecting the princesses to. On the roof of the castle he approaches Cecropia with a sword in his hand, and she falls to her death, whereupon Amphialus tries to kill himself, and is carried off mortally wounded. His friend Anaxius vows to revenge him, and execute the princesses, but Zelmane (the disguised Pyrocles) snatches a sword, kills Anaxius' brothers and is fighting with Anaxius himself when the narrative suddenly stops in mid-sentence. The principle of self-negation overtakes the work itself.

If we ask who the key figure is in this second, rewritten part of the *New Arcadia*, the answer, I think, is not Cecropia but her son Amphialus. Cecropia is a monster of vice and cruelty, but she is a relatively simple, unexamined creature, chiefly important for plunging the other characters into suffering. It is Amphialus around whom the interest centres: he is in a sense the new hero, or anti-hero of the whole work, for Musidorus and Pyrocles become relatively muted—Pyrocles shut away in prison and his woman's disguise; Musidorus far off among the besiegers, unable to participate in the main action in Cecropia's castle. All the responsibility devolves upon Amphialus, and it is easy to see why Sidney has given this prominence to him in the *New Arcadia*, because Amphialus personifies the human dilemmas—the peripeteia and the self-conflict—which we have identified as Sidney's foremost structural principles.

Just before he kills himself Amphialus has a long speech (Book II, Chapter 24, pp. 492–4) where he works it out that everything he has done in his life has turned out disastrously, against all his intentions. As we read this speech, we can see that Amphialus' life has been carefully constructed by Sidney as an extended peripeteia. When we first hear of him, in one of the flashbacks, Amphialus was loved by Helen, Queen of Corinth, and, though he did not return her love, this led to his being challenged by his friend and foster-brother Philoxenus, Helen's lover. Philoxenus forces the unwilling Amphialus to fight him, and is killed. Further, Philoxenus' father Timotheus dies of grief when he hears of his son's death (Book I, Chapter 11). So Amphialus, quite unintentionally, has killed his foster-brother and foster-father for the sake of a woman whom he detests.

The next adventure of Amphialus' we hear about is also mined throughout with unmeant catastrophe. In the flashbacks of the *New Arcadia*, two of the major new characters are a pair of lovers, Argalus and Parthenia. We learn of the early trials of their love, and of their eventual wedded happiness. But, when Basilius besieges Cecropia's castle, he sends for Argalus to help. Parthenia begs him not to go, but honour forces him to. He leaves his wife, engages Amphialus in combat, and is killed, though Amphialus, who loves and admires him, does all he can to persuade him to save himself. Worse, after Argalus' death, an unknown challenger called the Knight of the Tombs arrives to fight Amphialus. After their first encounter it is clear that this new knight is no match for Amphialus, and he courteously and honourably offers his opponent peace. But the Knight of the Tombs insults him and insists on fighting, so Amphialus mortally wounds him. But when he strips the helmet from his bleeding enemy, long golden hair falls about the shoulders of the dying knight and Amphialus realizes with horror that he has killed Parthenia, who chose this way of dying, rather than surviving her husband. The moment when the helmet comes away and reveals the golden hair is a graphic emblem of peripeteia from Amphialus' viewpoint—victory turns to defeat, man to woman, dead foe to dead friend, all in an instant. It is an epitome of Sidney's major theme.

Even the minor episodes of Amphialus' life are arranged to bring about these devastating turnarounds of fortune, defeating Amphialus' noble purposes. One of the most gruesome battle scenes (Book III, Chapter 7) has an incident where Agenor, a young and beautiful Greek warrior, charges Amphialus, and Amphialus, pitying the youth's beauty, deliberately aims at the hand-guard of his lance, meaning to give a harmless blow. But by an unlucky accident Amphialus' lance breaks, and the splintered end of it hits Agenor in the face, not only killing him but destroying the very beauty which Amphialus had wanted to spare.

Amphialus' life, then, is a mass of unmeant fatalities, and, as he says in his suicide speech, his love for Philoclea is equally disastrous. He means her nothing but good, yet his love leads to her imprisonment and torture. The suicide speech also tells us that Amphialus did not even mean to kill his mother. When he approached her with the drawn sword it was only to remonstrate: she fell to her death by mistake, though it was his fault. Ironically, the last act we see him perform also rebounds on him—his suicide attempt. For, though he stabs himself, he does not die. Appropriately, within the Sidneian rhetoric, this is a suicide which suicides itself—like Pyrocles' attempted suicide (Book III, Chapter 22) which fails because he is in too much of a hurry to commit it ('the haste to doo it, made the doing the slower'). Amphialus' body, horribly wounded, is carried off by a queen famed for her knowledge of medicine, and this queen is none other than Helen of Corinth, whom Amphialus, at the start of his misfortunes, left in disgust after being trapped into killing Philoxenus for her. So fate has wound itself in a circle, and Amphialus, though he has tried everything, even suicide, is back where he least wants to be, with Helen.

But, if this major new character in Sidney's rewritten *Arcadia* is a walking proof of the ironic inscrutability of human destiny, of the capacity of events for doubling back on themselves and defeating intention, he also embodies the second of Sidney's master themes, inner conflict, indecisiveness, the dilemma of the torn psyche. It is his love for Philoclea that sets him at war with himself. She is his and his mother's prisoner, and her happiness demands that he set her free. But his desire for her forbids that. Sidney examines his quandary in Book III, Chapter 3, in the scene where Amphialus confronts Philoclea in her cell. She begs to be released, and Amphialus is simply immobilized by the ensuing inner conflict. Love urges him to set her free. But love also insists that he keep her in his power. He is trapped, powerless to act, 'neither able to grant, nor denie', as Sidney puts it. He tries, in his dilemma, to make Philoclea see that she is really the cause of it all, that she is imprisoning herself: 'I am not the staye of your freedome,' he tells her, 'but Love, Love, which ties you in your owne knots. It is you your selfe, that imprison your self: it is your beautie which makes these castle-walles embrace you: it is your owne eyes, which reflect upon themselves this injurie.' This desperate exposition of back-to-front logic is, of course, an attempt on Amphialus' part to project his own quandary on to Philoclea. It is really Amphialus who is tied by love in his own knots. In being so, he conforms to the *Arcadia*'s dominant pattern. It is a work which demonstrates, in detail as well as grand design, self-frustration. We can pick this up both in incidental flourishes like Zelmane's luckless fishing—'the taker was so taken that she had forgotten taking' (Book I, Chapter 15)—and in Sidney's persistent distortion of physical reality to make it support his vision—as when he presents even the simple operation of sailing a boat as a self-cancelling intention—'the arte of catching the winde prisoner, to no other ende, but to runne away with it' (Book II, Chapter 7).

At the start of Book III, Chapter 3, Sidney shows us Amphialus' crippling ambivalence when he tries to decide what clothes he will wear to visit Philoclea in her prison. He is afraid that, if he is too sumptuously dressed, he will seem to be glorying in her misery. but if he dresses mournfully, it may make her think something awful is about to happen to her. So in the end he dresses indecisively, both sumptuously and mournfully at once. He wears a black velvet robe, set with pearls, so that it resembles, says Sidney, dark clouds with stars showing through. And he wears a collar which also symbolizes irreconcilable conflict:

About his necke he ware a brode and gorgeous coller; whereof the pieces enterchangeably answering; the one was of Diamonds and pearle, set

with white enamell, so as by the cunning of the workman it seemed like
shining ice, and the other piece being of Rubies, and Opalles, had a fierie
glistring, which he thought pictured the two passions of Feare and
Desire, wherein he was enchayned. (p. 356.)

So the struggle between opposing passions spreads out from
Amphialus' soul and imprints itself on his clothes, which become a
sort of placard for his dilemma. Clothes, badges, escutcheons, and
other emblems offer a way of simultaneously representing and
stabilizing (i.e. negating) conflict, rather as the stilled pattern of a
rhetorical figure does, and Sidney seized this opportunity from the
start. In the *Old Arcadia* Pyrocles wears an ambivalent jewel which
represents 'an eagle covered with the feathers of a dove' (p. 27),
and Philoclea's clothes, a few pages later, achieve a poised uncertainty between revealing and concealing: 'so near nakedness as
one might well discern part of her perfection, and yet so apparelled
as did show she kept the best store of her beauties to herself.'
(p. 37.) In no other author would clothes need to be made to appear
so indecisive.

Indecision spreads out into the countryside. Sidney uses his
rhetoric to make the landscape of Arcadia, the space in which the
characters move, full of vacillation and ambivalence. It is no
accident that the book starts with a shipwreck in which a ship
catches fire and burns out on the water. This is the vessel that
brings Pyrocles and Musidorus to Arcadia, and its fate, the confusion of water with fire, the warring elements, is, like Amphialus'
collar, a picture of the fate the heroes will endure.

In Arcadia natural objects are repeatedly made to seem, by the
twists of Sidney's rhetoric, to hover between irreconcilable alter-
natives. In Book I, Chapter 19, we find a brook which 'did both
hold the eye open with her azure streams, and yet seeke to close the
eie with the purling noise it made upon the pebble stones it ran
over'. The brook makes you want to stay awake to look at it, but
also puts you to sleep: it is not so much a natural object as a natural
dilemma. There is another indecisive brook in Book II, Chapter
11, which 'ranne upon so fine and delicate a ground, as one could
not easily judge, whether the River did more wash the gravell, or
the gravel did purifie the River'. Sidney does not keep tying these
rhetorical knots for decoration, but to inundate his setting with the
moral and intellectual quandaries that control his action.

The figures, like Gynecia, caught between lust and honour,

enact the same vacillation that we saw in the *Old Arcadia*, but it is much more intense here. First, because there are many more figures, crowded into the flashback insertions, who are tormented by their own split desires. Second, because Sidney makes his people explicit about their conflicts, as they were not in the *Old Arcadia*. This keeps happening. Zelmane playing a lute in Book II, Chapter 1 compares the discord of her thoughts with the concord of its strings. In Book I, Chapter 12, Musidorus lectures Pyrocles about the contest between passion and reason in the human soul, and Pyrocles expands on this subject himself in Chapter 14. Musidorus sees inner conflict as the essential factor in the human condition, distinguishing men from beasts. He expounds this idea in Book II, Chapter 2, as he watches his grazing sheep: 'O wretched mankind ... in whom witte (which should be the governer of his welfare) becomes the traitor to his blessedness. These beasts, like children to nature, inherite her blessings quietly; we, like bastards, are layd abroad even as foundlings, to be trayned up by griefe and sorrow.'

This idea that there is some primal fault in human nature, which debars us from the unselfconscious joy of animals, has always been a powerful element in anti-intellectual movements, starting with the Greeks and prominent in the Romantics and moderns like D. H. Lawrence. Sidney makes his character voice it, but we have no sense that as an author he merely concurs in it. Things are not so simple, he wants to show us, and their not being simple is part of the tangle human beings find themselves in. Part of the split in human consciousness is not being able to decide whether the split is an advantage, or the contrary. Vacillation is what makes us human. To compound indecisiveness in the *New Arcadia*, Sidney persistently declines to offer comment in his own person, putting comment and narrative instead into the mouths of often untrustworthy characters. So, for example, the description of Philoclea's beauty in Book I is now done, not, as in the *Old Arcadia*, by Sidney, but by Pyrocles, with an obvious loss of objectivity and dependability. Sometimes the change is quite glaring. When Cleophila's oratory pacifies the rebels, Sidney in the *Old Arcadia* offered a moral observation (p. 131): 'O weak trust of the many-headed multitude, whom inconstancy only doth guide ...'. But in the *New Arcadia* these seemingly wholesome reflections are attributed to a much less creditable source: 'So said a craftie felow among them, named *Clinias*, to himselfe.' (Book II, Chapter 26.) It is now Clinias, not Sidney, who tells the story of the confused start of the rebellion (Chapter 27), and Clinias is a fraud. It is later revealed (Book III, Chapter 2) that he started the rebellion himself. The change in the narrative voice removes authority from the work and furthers the interests of confusion and multiple viewpoint. In the *New Arcadia* Sidney keeps bringing his readers into open, explicit confrontation with this factor, as well as letting it melt into and permeate the action.

Another important instance of it being made explicit comes in the big debate in Book III, Chapter 10, between Cecropia and Pamela. The subject of this debate is the existence of God, and Cecropia puts the case for atheism. What is significant, from our angle, is that Pamela's argument for the existence of God hinges entirely on the obsessive Sidneian theme of conflict versus unity. The whole created universe, just like the human psyche, is naturally a theatre of endless, internecine conflict, Pamela argues. By nature the elements war against one another: water quenches fire; water drowns earth. The principle of self-destruction is written into the cosmos. And this proves, Pamela contends, that there must be a God, who unifies what would otherwise be end-lessly discordant. 'There must needes have bene a wisedome which made them [the elements] concurre: for their natures beyng absolute contarie, in nature rather woulde have sought each others ruine, then have served as well consorted partes to such an unexpressable harmonie.' So Sidney's universe is essentially discordant, unified only by God's omnipotent interference. Musi-dorus saw discord as the native property of the human soul; Pam-ela sees it as the natural property of all matter.

A third set of thematic statements shows discord as indissoluble from man as a social animal. Society, Sidney demonstrates, is a frail equipoise of inevitably warring interests. The *New Arcadia* is a work about political theory, among other things, and its most prominent piece of political anatomy comes in Book II, Chapter 26 with the rebellion in Arcadia. Sidney gives a breakdown of the social grievances the rebels encompass, showing that their aims, dictated by occupation, class, and income source, are mutually irreconcilable. On questions like food prices, taxes, education, rank, the Arcadian rebels split up into smaller and smaller factions, impelled by individual self-interest. Sidney's point is that civilized society is not natural, but fragilely imposed. Naturally, human beings in the mass are chaotic and self-destroying. The constant battles, tournaments, civil wars, armed risings in the *New Arcadia* enforce this gloomy truth.

To make it clearer, Sidney keeps inventing battles where the combatants start killing not the enemy but their own side. Pyrocles in Book II, Chapter 24, relating the incident where the ship caught fire, tells how the mutineers and the crew fought panic-stricken in the darkness, killing friends as well as foes. In the Arcadian rebellion, too (Book II, Chapter 27), no one knows, in the confusion, who is on which side, and an orgy of indiscriminate killing breaks out: 'each one killing him that was next, for feare he should do as much to him.' These outbursts of blind, murderous self-preservation are images for society in its natural state—the counterpart of the unremitting conflict in the individual human psyche that Sidney depicts.

In the scenes between the lovers, what the inner conflicts lead to is persistent indecision. Torn between opposing impulses, the characters vacillate and oscillate helplessly. Numerous scenes in the *New Arcadia* illustrate this: indecision is the work's psychological climate. A prominent example comes in Book III, Chapter I, in the scene where Musidorus offends Pamela, by too passionately pressing his suit, is angrily dismissed, and tries to compose a letter of apology:

Pen did never more quakingly performe his office; ... never the *Muses* more tired, then now with changes and rechanges of his devises: fearing howe to ende, before he had resolved how to begin, mistrusting ech word, condemning eche sentence. This word was not significant, that word was too plain: this would not be conceived; the other would be il conceived ...

and so on, with Musidorus becoming increasingly entangled in second thoughts, and brought to a standstill by the collision between his nervousness and his desire.

When he at last gets the letter written, and delivered, there is an equivalent display of indecision from Pamela. She invents a series of arguments for not opening it, and conversely for opening it; then she opens it and immediately throws it away without reading it; then she picks it up and reads it. Shakespeare borrowed much from the *New Arcadia*, and this scene seems to be the origin of Act I, Scene 2, of *The Two Gentlemen of Verona*, where Julia angrily tears

Proteus' letter to pieces, then gathers it up and fits it together to read it.

I have chosen this letter-scene as an example because it leads to my next point, which is about the kind of physical movement Sidney is repeatedly drawn to and fascinated by. He says about Musidorus that no pen ever more 'quakingly' performed its office—and quaking, trembling, shuddering are the kinds of movement that he keeps depicting in the *Arcadia* in scenes of stress, or of great and nervous delicacy between pairs of lovers, and it is clear that he means this to be a visible manifestation of their inner oscillation. Again, there are far too many examples to cite, but here are a few. The note is struck in the first chapter when Strephon says of Claius: 'I saw reverence and desire so devide thee, that thou didst at one instant both blushe and quake.' A similar symptom is observable in Pyrocles (Book I, Chapter 9) when he is trying to bring himself to tell of his love. Musidorus notices: 'the oft changing of his colour, with a kind of shaking unstayednes over all his body.' Pyrocles (disguised as a woman) is 'taken with such a quivering', as he watches the girls undress, that he has to lean against a tree overcome by the war between desire and restraint within him, and his agitation in this tremulous scene finds an echo within Philoclea's flesh: 'the touch of the cold water made a prettie kinde of shrugging come over her bodie, like the twickling of the fairest among the fixed stars.' In Book II, Chapter 17, when Philoclea learns that Zelmane, whom she has fallen in love with, is really a man, she is smitten with contraries in true Sidneian fashion: 'sicke with a surfeit of joy, and fearefull of she knewe not what,' and this brings on a quivering fit—'a shrugging kinde of tremor through all her principall partes'.

Panting, the quick oscillation of breath, is another of these palpitating movements Sidney keeps drawing our attention to. Like the others, it is a sign of inner conflict. In Book III, Chapter 23, when Pyrocles thinks Cecropia has killed Philoclea, she comes alive into his prison cell, but she comes sorrowfully to predict her death, which she believes imminent. So Pyrocles is incapacitated by conflicting emotions of joy and grief, and it shows itself in physical palpitation: 'when he had a little taken breath from the panting motion of such contarietie in passions, he fell to consider with her of her present estate.'

It is worth noting this tendency of Sidney's characters towards tremulous movement, not only as an index of inner drama, but also because it can help us to understand the function of much of his rhetorical figuring. He frequently writes, in fact, in a style of verbal tremulousness, of figures that waver and oscillate and hover over redoubled antitheses—as, for instance, in the bathing scene, when he writes of Philoclea 'blushing, and withall smiling, making shamefastnesse plesant, and pleasure shamefast'. The shaking, delicate syntax there, and in many scenes of the *New Arcadia*, has the function of portraying in words, in wavering figures of speech, the fragility and delicacy of what is going on, of the lovers' inner disturbance and indecision and mutual embarrassment. The conjunction of smiling, blushing (and bathing) plainly relates to Spenser's wanton nymph in the Bower—'Withall she laughed, and she blusht withall' (*Faerie Queene*, II. xii. 68), but Sidney is more interested than Spenser in using it as an index of inner agitation. The same demure confusion ('her cheekes blushing, and withal when shee was spoken unto, a little smilyng') overcomes Parthenia on her wedding day (Book I, Chapter 8); and, when Musidorus tells of his 'confusion of thoughts' so confusedly as to let his identity slip by mistake (Book II, Chapter 8), the lovers plunge into an intensifying exchange of smiles and blushes: '*Dorus* blushed, and *Pamela* smiled: and *Dorus* the more blushed at her smiling, and she the more smiled at his blushing.' The way Sidney handles scenes of courtship is quite new in English literature, more subtle than anything that had been tried before, and in his delicately complicated syntax he creates a linguistic equivalent of that subtlety, mitigating, by his play of pattern, the crude force of ordinary language: making language sensitized enough for the task.

Finally, I should like to indicate two other factors in the *New Arcadia* that strengthen my feeling that indecision and inner conflict are its nodes. First, in a number of major scenes Sidney shows speakers breaking off in the middle of what they are saying, becoming speechless in the middle of speech, because the opposition between their words and their feelings overpowers them. In Book I, Chapter 9, Pyrocles is trying to conceal from Musidorus the fact that he has fallen in love by making up alternative and false reasons for being solitary and melancholy. He breaks off because he cannot stand the pretence: what he is saying is not what he wants to say, but to talk of his love seems to him to require something more refined, less embarrassing than language. Pyrocles looks 'with a countenaunce, as though he desired he [Musidorus] should know his minde without hearing him speake'. Pyrocles is caught between the pressure of feeling and the ordeal of articulation. Earlier, in Book I, Chapter 12, both friends had been reciprocally overcome by the same pregnant dumbness: Pyrocles reduced to tears by Musidorus' seeming unkindness; Musidorus, by remorse at causing such tears: '*Pyrocles* . . . with a silent look upon *Musidorus*, as who should say, And is it possible that *Musidorus* should threaten to leave me? And this strooke *Musidorus* minde and senses so dumbe too, that for griefe being not able to say any thing, they rested, with their eyes placed one upon another.' In Book II, Chapter I, Gynecia is robbed of words in the dramatic scene where she confesses her love to Pyrocles (disguised as Zelmane). She comes upon him unexpectedly one morning. At first she is speechless with astonishment and embarrassment, but then tries to make conversation:

at length returning to some use of her selfe, she began to aske Zelmane, what cause carried her so early abroad? But as if the opening of her mouth to *Zelmane*, had opened some great flood-gate of sorrow (whereof her heart could not abide the violent issue) she sanke to the ground, with her hands over her face, crying vehemently, *Zelmane* helpe me, O *Zelmane* have pittie on me.

The pressure of the opposition between concealment and love in Gynecia builds up and explodes, shattering her attempt at polite conversation. It happens to her again in Book II, Chapter 25, where she is torn between a desire to reveal Zelmane's sex to Basilius and a desire to keep the secret to herself: 'O but; cryed *Gynecia*, and therewith she stayed: for then indeede she did suffer a right conflict, betwixt the force of love, and rage of jealousie.' This is the first kind of incident—the occurrence of fractured speech—that helps to show Sidney's fascination with inner conflict and its manifestations and his awareness of the inevitable indelicacy of language. The second kind leads on from it. We notice that, in the interview with Zelmane, Gynecia sinks to the ground with her hands over her face. That kind of gesture, covering the face or shutting the eyes, as if to hide, in one's emotion or embarrassment, not only from other people but even from oneself, is recurrent in Sidney's narrative too. The characters go into themselves. They blot out the external world in a bid to eliminate the cruel divergence between inner and outer reality from which their own self-division springs. Like other features we have been studying, this kind of protective gesture—an intensification of dumbness into blindness—is found in the *Old Arcadia* as well as the *New*. When Philoclea, in the original version, believes herself betrayed in love, she shuts out externals, 'closing her eyes, as if each thing she saw were a picture of her mishap, and turning upon her heart side' (p. 209). Gynecia, joyous but ashamed to find Cleophila apparently returning her love, shrinks from visibility—'closing her eyes and letting her head fall' (p. 222). Pyrocles, appalled at Philoclea's unjust suspicions, reacts 'with a deathful shutting of his eyes' (p. 235); and later he shows his anger, shame, and helplessness before the accusing Philanax by 'closing his eyes and laying his hands over them' (p. 391). All these gestures arise from divided feelings: the characters feel the conflict within themselves—feel a part of themselves detached—so acutely that they shut out the external world as if they could, by so doing, eliminate that detached self and restore their own unity. Perhaps the best example comes in Book II, Chapter 4 of the *New Arcadia*, where it dawns irresistibly upon Philoclea that she is in love with Zelmane (i.e. the disguised Pyrocles) and, since, at this point, she still believes him to be a woman, she feels horrified and ashamed as well as desperately in love. She lies on the ground, hiding her face, as if 'she could have hidden her selfe from her owne fancies . . . and with that, embrasing the very grounde whereon she lay, she said to her self (for even to her selfe she was ashamed to speake it out in words) O my *Zelmane*, governe and direct me: for I am wholy given over unto thee'. Philoclea tries to hide from her own thoughts, she is so divided from herself. She cannot bear to put her love into words, but also she cannot bear to suppress it. The Sidneian inner conflict has become so intense that language and the character collapse together, giving way to the unspeakable and insupportable.

The massive rhetorical display of the *New Arcadia* is not, then, decorative but functional. The kind of figures Sidney chooses, constantly doubling back on themselves, enact a world view which is dominated by reversal of intention, tragic peripeteia. And the rhetoric also functions to create, by its subtle figurings, an atmosphere of delicacy and tentativeness in which inner conflict and indecision, which Sidney sees as vital human features, can be graphically communicated. The language of the *New Arcadia* is a lived experience of tentativeness, delicacy, and poise, which the reader is enclosed in and made, in the act of reading, to share.

11. 'UNDER . . . PRETTY TALES': INTENTION IN SIDNEY'S *ARCADIA*

Annabel Patterson

Sir Philip Sidney's *Arcadia* is an important test case for the joint study of interpretation and culture. Defined by C. S. Lewis as the paradigmatic literary representation of Elizabethanism,[1] the *Arcadia* is also, in more ways than one, a central Caroline and civil war text. It achieved extraordinary significance as a cultural symbol in the court and even the life of Charles I; it featured in the political debates over his execution; it became not only a model for later-seventeenth-century fiction but a symbol of a certain type of fiction—the romance—fiction with ideological content, whose very fictionality held an interesting and provocative relation to its engagement with history. As such, the *Arcadia* was crucial to the evolution of seventeenth-century genre theory.

But these facts also imply that the *Arcadia* was constantly being reread during the seventeenth century; that is, reinterpreted, as the historical context and needs of the audience changed. Sidney's friend and editor, Fulke Greville, provided one interpretation in his *Life of Sidney*, written between 1610 and 1612. In so doing, he raised explicitly the question of authorial intention. According to Greville, Sidney's 'intent and scope' in the *Arcadia* was 'lively to represent the growth, state and declination of Princes, change of Government, and lawes; vicissitudes of sedition, faction, succession'.[2] Greville was clearly unbothered by fears or even fine distinctions about representationalism in art, accepting without difficulty a principle of fictional displacement, along with belief, common to his age, that literature could and should carry messages. The message of the *Arcadia* was, Greville asserted, particularly directed at 'Soveraign Princes', especially those who, like Sidney's Basilius, 'put off publique action' in order to 'play

Reprinted by permission of Georgia State University and of the University of Wisconsin Press from *Studies in the Literary Imagination* 15 (1982), 5–21, and *Censorship and Interpretation* (Madison, Wisconsin, 1984), 24–43.

[1] C. S. Lewis, *English Literature in the Sixteenth Century Excluding Drama* (Oxford, 1954), p. 339.
[2] Fulke Greville, *The Life of the Renowned Sir Phillip Sidney* (London, 1652), p. 18.

with their own visions'. Such rulers should recognize themselves in Sidney's text, and understand that they 'bury themselves, and their Estates in a cloud of contempt' (pp. 13–14).

Greville might be supposed to have known something about Sidney's intentions; but if his reading were 'correct', how was it possible for Charles I so to 'misread' the *Arcadia* as to incorporate it into his own visions, his own programme of English arcadianism, the halcyon days of the 1630s? Greville's *Life of Sidney* was not published until 1652, when someone perceived its potential appeal to a Puritan and republican audience, the relevance of its message to the monarchy that had just been abolished; yet by 1658 the *Arcadia* had been reclaimed, as it were, by the royalists, who discovered in the romance a key to class solidarity, a language in which to express and assess their own recent history.

These facts make Sidney's *Arcadia* an unusually elegant test case for theories of interpretation, particularly those of authorial intention and reception. By authorial intention I choose to mean conscious intention, Sidney's motives in embarking on the work, his changes of intention (for which the many revisions of the *Arcadia* provide a potent source of evidence), his concept of its function and audience. By reception I choose to mean the *Arcadia*'s history of publication, adoption (by certain groups of readers), adaptation (for certain ends), any evidence that we can recover of the way it has been understood at different moments after it passed beyond Sidney's control.

Questions of interpretation and authorial intention lead directly to the *Arcadia*'s status as disguised discourse. It is well known that Sidney felt himself to have serious problems of communication in the Elizabethan court, that his known advocacy of a militant international Protestantism deprived him of effective address to the Queen. It is also known (though not so widely) that Sidney was directly involved in parliamentary debates about political censorship. In 1581 the House of Lords had introduced a harsh bill designed to repress any further public comment on the notorious French marriage controversy: Elizabeth's hopes, from late 1578 through early 1581, of marrying the duc d'Alençon. This project raised a storm of national and Protestant outrage involving, among others, John Stubbs, author of *The Discoverie of a Gaping Gulf, whereinunto England is like to be swallowed by another French marriage, if the Lord forbid not the banes* (1579). The punishment for Stubbs was the old punishment for seditious libel, the loss of the right hand. Sidney, who had written a private letter to Elizabeth arguing against the marriage, suffered temporary disgrace and exclusion from court.[3] The *Act against seditious words and rumours* (23 Eliz. Cap. II) sometimes referred to as the 'Statute of Silence', was introduced by the Lords in January 1581. It began with the premiss that in previous censorship laws there had not been specified 'sufficient and condign punishment' for those who spoke or published what the Queen did not wish to hear; and it proceeded to specify a scale of increasingly gruesome penalties, from loss of one ear for spreading rumours, to capital punishment for seditious *publication*. Sidney was not only a member of this parliament, as was Stubbs, but also sat on the Commons committee that amended the bill and softened its rigour. In particular, they managed to write in a saving clause, 'with malicious intent', to govern all offences.[4] The effect of this amendment was not only to complicate the business of proof in charges of sedition, but to bring explicitly into the political area a form of literary inquiry. The state had formally entered the business of textual interpretation, and had been forced to declare a respect for authorial intention. In the light of these facts, it is reasonable to ask what relation the *Arcadia* held to Sidney's known concerns and recent experience; and particularly in the light of political censorship, to what extent its fictionality, its generic affiliations, its plot and other textual procedures may relate to the problem of restricted or proscribed communication.

We should start, then, with what is known of the *Arcadia*'s genesis and production, something that the best editorial minds have had difficulty in reconstructing, and in which authorial intention and reception are already confused. Even here, there are signs that genetic mystery may be actually mystification. The text exists in three major versions, none of which was published by Sidney himself. The first version, that we now call the *Old Arcadia*, may have been begun soon after Sidney's return from his German embassy in June 1577 and completed in the spring of 1581.[5] On the

---

[3] *A Discourse of Syr Ph. S. To The Queenes Majesty Touching Hir Marriage With Monsieur* survives in a number of manuscripts, but was first published only in 1663. See *The Complete Works of Sir Philip Sidney*, ed. A. Feuillerat (4 vols., Cambridge, 1912–26, reprinted, with much of the verse omitted, as *The Prose Works of Sir Philip Sidney* (Cambridge, 1962, etc.)), iii. 51–60, 385–6.

[4] J. E. Neale, *Elizabeth I and Her Parliaments, 1559–1581* (New York, 1953), i. 393–8.

[5] Evidence for dating is discussed by William Ringler Jr., ed., *The Poems of Sir Philip*

other hand, it may have been entirely conceived and executed while Sidney was in rustication from the Elizabethan court during 1580. The difference is not small if we are considering Sidney's motives in writing, and to that end investigating the *exact* historical context of his work. In any case, Sidney apparently abandoned the *Old Arcadia* some time in 1582, and either then or in 1584 embarked on a massively expanded and substantially revised version, the *New Arcadia*, that he never finished. It breaks off in mid-sentence, part way through its third book. We do not know whether this was because of reasons internal to the text, or Sidney's own dissatisfaction with it, or whether its composition was simply interrupted when he left to take up his military commission in the Netherlands, where he died of gangrene. Nor do we know how much authorial instruction Sidney's friend Greville was working with when he published the revised version, in its incomplete state, in 1590.[6] Finally, we do not know why, in 1593, Greville and Sidney's sister, Mary, Countess of Pembroke, apparently agreed to bring out a composite text, under the nominal editorship of Hugh Sanford, the Pembrokes' secretary. In the 1593 text, the last two and a half books of the *Old Arcadia* were grafted upon the *New*, with predictable effects of disproportion and incongruity. It was this version that became 'the' *Arcadia*, for the seventeenth century and for all readers, until manuscripts of the *Old Arcadia* were discovered and a text was published at the beginning of this century.

The hints of authorial intention that survive seem to confuse the issue still further. They are, first, Sidney's mention of an unspecified 'toyfull booke' or 'books' in an October 1580 letter to his brother; second, an undated letter to his sister, entrusting her with the manuscript of an 'idle worke . . . done onelie for you, onely to you', a work whose 'chiefe safetie, shalbe the not walking abroad'.[7]

Sidney (Oxford, 1962), p. 365; and by J. Robertson, ed., *The Countess of Pembroke's Arcadia (The Old Arcadia)* (Oxford, 1973), pp. xv–xvii. On their painstaking analysis of the text and manuscript tradition all serious analysis of the *Arcadia* depends. Where they differ, as on the date of completion of the *Old Arcadia* and of the beginning of work on the *New*, I lean toward Robertson, whose edition I cite throughout this chapter.

[6] Greville reported in a letter to Walsingham that Sidney had left with him the only manuscript of the *New Arcadia*, along with directions for its editing, but did not specify further. Ringler, on the basis of manuscript evidence and the prefatory note to the 1590 edition, concluded that it was left entirely up to the editors to insert or delete the eclogues 'they considered appropriate' (p. 372). This conclusion can be accepted only with qualifications.

[7] Feuillerat, iii. 132; i. 3–4. All quotations from the *New Arcadia* are from Feuillerat, i.

This letter was published by Greville as a preface to the *New Arcadia* in 1590. It suggests a recreative exercise, a pastime, intended at most for a small private audience. We do not know, however, which version of the *Arcadia* it originally referred to. Some critics have felt that it fits the *Old Arcadia* better than the *New*, some that it fits neither. Few have remarked the obvious conflict between the discretion invoked in the letter, the emphasis on the text's 'safetie' in 'not walking abroad', and its appearance as the preface to a *published* work. It may be that the letter is only a clever and specious disclaimer, either written by Sidney himself, or constructed by Greville, who (as we shall see later) was quite capable of such disingenuousness.

Third, there is the preface to the 1593 composite text, which sets the problem of intention squarely before the audience, without making any gestures toward solving it: 'Though they find not here what might be expected, they may finde nevertheless as much as was intended, the conclusion, not the perfection of Arcadia: and that no further then the Authours own writings, or knowen determinations could direct. Whereof who sees not the reason, must consider there may be a reason which he sees not.'[8] This certainly sounds like intentional mystification, the kind of statement frequently found in the prefaces to seventeenth-century texts that provoke the suspicions or curiosity of the reader, inviting him to look closely.

Such a reader, denied explicit guidance, would probably look for authorial intention in the genre of the work before him. Now, the obfuscating textual history of the *Arcadia* has caused perhaps less dispute than its genre, not only because Sidney's recognizable models imply generic mixture, but also because he seems to have changed the generic emphasis of the work in revision. Without discussing for the moment the *Arcadia*'s romance and epic affiliations, we must surely agree that its first generic signal—its title—foregrounded a pastoral tradition, the kinship of the work to Sannazaro's *Arcadia*, and behind that to Virgil's *Eclogues*. In his *Defence of Poetry*, Sidney had articulated the standard Renaissance reading of Virgilian pastoral:

Is the poor pipe disdained, which sometime out of Meliboeus' mouth can show the misery of people under hard lords or ravening soldiers? And

[8] *The Countesse of Pembrokes Arcadia* (London, 1593), p. 4.

again, by Tityrus, what blessedness is derived to them that lie lowest from the goodness of them that sit highest; sometimes, under the pretty tales of wolves and sheep, can include the whole considerations of wrongdoing and patience.[9]

It is easy to assume that this passage could have very little bearing on a work as generically complex as the *Arcadia*; but the pastoral theory of the *Defence* is, if read carefully, both more complex itself and more germane to the *Arcadia* than it might seem. Lexical connections between it and crucial statements in the *Arcadia* suggest that Sidney himself not only connected the two, but intended the echoes to serve as a two-way gloss.

The passage from the *Defence* is distinctly cunning, both syntactically and semantically. It contains a condensed argument about the relationship between literature and socio-political experience. If you live 'under hard lords or ravening soldiers', you have to communicate 'under the pretty tales of wolves and sheep'. The prepositional symmetry ('under . . . under') supports the propositional irony of seeing pastoral as the genre in which writers 'lie lowest' in more senses than one. The central allusion is, of course, to Virgil's *First Eclogue*, in which the sad shepherd, Meliboeus, converses for a moment, before heading out into exile, with his more fortunate neighbour, Tityrus. The historical context of the poem was the last phase of the civil war and the expropriation of farm lands in Italy by Octavius, who wished both to reward his own soldiers and to punish those who had supported Brutus and Cassius. According to the ancient commentary of Servius, widely accepted during the Renaissance, Virgil's point was that the expropriated farmers were innocent victims. By representing himself as the fortunate shepherd exempted from their fate, he was able, however indirectly, to indicate the severity of Octavius' policy. The dominance of the *First Eclogue* over the *Eclogues* as a whole had the effect, also, of causing the other pastoral subjects—song contest and especially love complaint—to be measured by those larger standards of responsibility. This was something that Sidney's contemporary, George Puttenham, felt his audience needed to remember:

The Poet devised the Eglogue . . . not of purpose to counterfait or represent the rusticall manner of loves and communication; but under the vaile

[9] Sir Philip Sidney, *An Apology for Poetry or The Defence of Poesy*, ed. G. Shepherd (London, 1965), p. 116.

of homely persons, and in rude speeches to insinuate and glaunce at greater matters, and such as perchance had not bene safe to have beene disclosed in any other sort, which may be perceived in the Eglogues of Virgill, in which are treated by figure matters of greater importance then the loves of Titirus and Corydon.[10]

The connection between this theory and the *Arcadia* is made at the point where Sidney describes Arcadian mores. This point is differently located in the *Old* and *New* versions of the text. In the *Old Arcadia*, the description immediately precedes the First Eclogues, the first group of poems that interrupts the romantic narrative of Basilius and his daughters. 'The manner of the Arcadian shepherds', Sidney wrote, 'was . . . to pass their time', either in music or sports: 'But, of all other things, they did especially delight in eclogues, wherein sometimes they would contend for a prize of well singing, sometimes lament the unhappy pursuit of their affections, sometimes, again, under hidden forms utter such matters as otherwise were not fit for their delivery.' (p. 56.) In the *New Arcadia*, this passage was moved back to the opening description by Kalander of the unhappy state of affairs in Arcadia. The context is the news that Basilius has abandoned his responsibilities and gone into retreat on his country estate. The last phrase of the relocated passage was, moreover, significantly altered. Instead of 'under hidden forms utter such matters as otherwise were not fit for their delivery', Sidney wrote, 'under hidden forms uttering such matters, as otherwise they durst not deale with' (p. 28). By making the textual alteration, Sidney removed the possibility that he might have been referring merely to a theory of pastoral decorum, in which any kind of high subject or deep thought was out of bounds. By relocating the passage to Kalander's account, he placed it in a context that was already critical of Basilius, so that the theory of 'hidden forms' was connected to the problem of political expression, when a ruler is at fault. Further, to glance back at the passage from the *Defence* is to see that the crucial phrase— 'under hidden forms'—is an extension of the series 'under hard lords' and 'under the pretty tales', while an intentional connection between the two passages is further assumed by the 'sometimes . . . sometimes' formula in both.

But aligning the two passages also shows up the distinction

---

[10] George Puttenham, *Arte of English Poesie* (1589), eds. G. D. Willock and A. Walker (Cambridge, 1936), p. 38.

between them. In the *Arcadia*, the triple set of 'sometimes' introduces not, as in the *Defence*, a series of examples of arcane political comment, but a series of competing propositions about the function of pastoral. Writing 'under hidden forms' is distinguished both from song contest, i.e. 'wel singing' for its own sake or for fame, which we might call formalism, and from love complaint, i.e. 'lamenting their affections', in which we would recognize a poetry of self-expression. Moreover, all three possibilities are governed by the assumption that the Arcadians engage in the making of eclogues in order 'to pass their time', a phrase that creates a distinctly undermining, recreative context. It reminds us of those deprecatory references to a 'toyfull booke' and an 'idle worke'; and it suggests that the questions critics have asked about the *Arcadia* are questions Sidney was asking by means of it. Given that pastoral song is here, as it was in Virgil's *Eclogues*, a metaphor for literature both in the largest sense and specifically as its function was brought into question by events in Virgil's Rome, Sidney's analysis is recognizable as a poetics, its ostensible subject Arcadian culture, its real subject Elizabethan culture. The alternative theories of literature's function that he suggests—indirect didacticism, formalism, and expressivism—are, of course, still in competition today; but we do not easily credit Sidney and his contemporaries with such perception.

   In fact, the history of Sidney criticism during this century shows a marked tendency to argue from one of these positions at the expense of the others; and the alternation of those preferences is itself not without significance as part of the *Arcadia*'s history of reception. At the beginning of the century it was still possible to assume, as Greville had done, that literary texts could carry messages, and that those messages were determined by the original historical context of the work. In 1913 Edwin Greenlaw proposed a reading of the *Arcadia* as a sustained account 'under hidden forms' of Elizabethan politics. Basilius' defection from government, he suggested, was a metaphor for Elizabeth's foreign policy, whereby peace was purchased at the expense of the Protestant activism to which Sidney, Leicester, and Walsingham were dedicated. Similarly, the romantic misbehaviour in *Arcadia* was a figurative account, according to Greenlaw, of the French marriage controversy, which he saw as the historical origin of the *Arcadia*'s focus on romantic self-indulgence and excess.[11]

---

[11] E. Greenlaw, 'Sidney's Arcadia as an Example of Elizabethan Allegory', *Kittredge Anniversary Papers* (New York, 1913), pp. 327–37.

Greenlaw based his case on contemporary documents. One was Sidney's own letter to Elizabeth advising against the marriage. Then there was Sidney's correspondence with his mentor, Hubert Languet, a Huguenot refugee and ardent promoter of the Protestant cause in Europe. In their correspondence, both sides complained of a dangerous passivity among Protestant princes in the age of Spanish imperialism. That Sidney referred to this passivity as 'sleep' was, at the very least, suggestive in view of the *Arcadia*'s use of sleep—the extreme *otium* of Basilius' deathlike trance—as a central narrative device and moral emblem.[12] The third document, and the one on which Greenlaw relied most heavily, was Greville's *Life of Sidney*, with its assertions that the work was intended as a textbook for rulers, a taxonomy of political and ethical thought.

Greenlaw's argument was an interesting case of the old historical criticism at its intuitive best and with its methodological inadequacies plain. He drew attention to Sidney's demonstrable concerns, and suggested a plausible system for their displacement into fiction—that is, by broad analogy and symbolic transfer, rather than the tight system of equivalence we call allegory. At the same time, he made two serious mistakes. One was to invoke the historical context of the *Old Arcadia*, whereas Greville's *Life* refers unmistakably to the *New*, not begun until the French marriage crisis was clearly over. The other was to ignore the fact that Greville's *Life* was itself a 'text', with its own motives and strategies, rather than an authoritative account of Sidney's intentions. Writing not under Elizabeth, but under James, Greville held a view of Elizabethan foreign policy that was entirely different from that of Sidney in 1580. Much of the *Life* is devoted to a eulogy of Elizabeth, from a post-Armada perspective. Its moralism is, therefore, addressed to Jacobean 'visions' and failures, particularly the pro-Spanish policies and pacificism of James himself;[13] and for

---

[12] 'Then will the Princes of Christendom be forced to wake up from their deep sleep'; 'Our princes are enjoying too deep a slumber; nevertheless, while they indulge in this repose, I would have them beware that they fall not into that malady, in which death itself goes in hand with its counterpart.' Letters of 1 April and 7 May 1573, *The Correspondence of Sir Philip Sidney and Hubert Languet*, ed. S. A. Pears (London, 1854), pp. 48, 59. The Sidney–Languet correspondence was first published in Latin in Frankfurt in 1633. Translations were provided by Pears and by J. M. Osborn, *Young Philip Sidney, 1572—1577* (New Haven and London, 1972).

[13] The *Life*'s subtitle was 'The True Interest of England as it then stood in relation to all Forrain Princes: And particularly for suppressing the power of Spain'.

Greville, Sidney's own career illustrated the '*differences*, between the reall and large complexions of *those* active times, and the narrow salves of *this* effeminate age' (p. 11; italics added). Greville also makes it clear that the *Life* is his substitute for the history of Elizabeth's reign that he had wished to write, and that he was prevented from writing by Cecil's refusal to release the historical records to him, on the grounds that he might 'deliver many things done in that time, which might perchance be construed to the prejudice of this' (p. 239). The *Life*, then, has its own obliqueness, necessitated by the restraints against open historical reporting that Greville himself experienced. Its value as a guide to Sidney's intentions lies more in this, perhaps—their equally restrictive cultural environments—than in Greville's account of the *Arcadia*.

Greenlaw's arguments quickly disappeared from sight, as criticism since the 1920s became increasingly anti-historical. One could say that the latest phases of the *Arcadia*'s reception illustrated the rise and decline of formalism. Ringler's edition of the poems, with its elaborate stemma, emphasized the significance of textuality, while detaching the poems from their narrative, or any other, context. Rudenstine's teleological account of Sidney's career used metrical analyses of the Arcadian poems to prove their significance as apprentice work, a technical stage on the way to *Astrophil and Stella*.[14] Walter Davis and Richard Lanham transferred the formalist impulse from metrics to genre, a matter still of narrative and tonal relationships internal to the work; and Lanham explicitly declared that Sidney's intentions 'can reasonably be inferred from the text', and the text alone: 'We need not flee to biography.'[15]

In the 1970s, however, there began to be signs that formalism was proving too limited an approach to the *Arcadia*. In effect, the Greenlaw hypothesis was disinterred, though with important differences. Dorothy Connell, for example, applied the French marriage question, appropriately, to the *Old Arcadia*. She compared

---

[14] N. Rudenstine, *Sidney's Poetic Development* (Cambridge, Mass., 1967). Rudenstine's opening chapters do, however, relate the *Arcadia*'s contents to the Sidney–Languet correspondence, implying an expressive theory of literature. The *Arcadia* 'reveals itself ... as a fictional extension of Sidney's letters in defense of relaxation, reflection, and a life of dignified ease' (p. 46), in other words, as a fictional defence of pastoral *otium*, rather than a critique of it.

[15] R. A. Lanham, *The Old Arcadia*, in R. A. Lanham and W. R. Davis, *Sidney's Arcadia* (New Haven, 1965), p. 197.

Sidney's letter to Elizabeth to Philanax's opening advice to Basilius, and concluded that Philanax was a figure of Sidney's own role 'in trying to advise the Queen'.[16] Connell, however, resisted any implication that Sidney could have been opposed to Elizabeth's policies, as too subversive a notion; and she even more strenuously resisted the dreaded term 'allegory'. Yet she argued that the *Old Arcadia* carried an implied political message, and that its primary audience was intended to be the Queen herself.

Richard McCoy, on the other hand, attempted to combine a socio-political reading of the *Arcadia* with a psychological one. The text reflects, he argued, the 'social and personal predicament of an Elizabethan aristocrat, caught up in a tangle of diminishing feudal power . . . courtly dependence and intrigue, and a cult of devotion to a formidable, emasculating queen'.[17] In this reading, the dialectical tensions in the *Arcadia* are explained in terms of Sidney's own *ambivalences*, and McCoy's language implies an expressive theory of function, rather than a calculated act of persuasion. The text is described as 'an engaging diversion', a 'fictive exploration of the problems of sovereignty', 'an outlet', something that 'reflects' or 'illuminates' Sidney's personal conflicts which were also those of his class. That the illumination might have been intended for others was not, apparently, considered. For McCoy, Sidney was engaged in literary self-help, displacing his frustrations into fiction in order to acquire some emotional distance from them.

It is, of course, possible to argue, both from the dialectical nature of the *Arcadia* and from the diversity of critical opinion about it, that the work itself remains multivalent. There is a difference, however, between arguing that Sidney was himself responsible for the divisions among his readers, and that he had not himself made up his mind. The debate on the function of poetry is not, I think, left unsettled in the *Arcadia*. The early description of Arcadian culture, with its competing propositions, functions as a hypothesis to be complicated by later arguments. Any complete statement about what the *Arcadia* contributes to poetics or cultural analysis must certainly include a discussion of the role of Philisides in the text, Philisides who is clearly a figure for Sidney himself.[18]

---

[16] D. Connell, *Sir Philip Sidney: The Maker's Mind* (Oxford, 1977), pp. 102–13.

[17] R. McCoy, *Sir Philip Sidney: Rebellion in Arcadia* (New Brunswick, NJ, 1979), p. x.

[18] Compare D. Moore, *The Politics of Spenser's Complaints and Sidney's Philisides*, Salzburg Elizabethan and Renaissance Studies No. 101 (Salzburg, 1978).

If Philanax (king-lover, monarchist) stands for Sidney in his role
of would-be counsellor to Elizabeth, Philisides (star-lover,
idealist) stands for him in his role as a literary man, a maker of
texts. Yet there is reason to think that the roles of Philanax and
Philisides are not so far apart. Behind Philisides is Sannazaro's
Sincero, a figure for Sannazaro as a member of the Neapolitan
Academy; and behind Sincero, Tityrus, as Virgil's persona in the
Eclogues, and the figure who brings into question the function of
poetry in Rome.

Philisides first appears in the *Old Arcadia* during the First
Eclogues, as a lovesick youth in dispute with Geron (old man).
Geron's arguments are not only against lovesickness, arguments
which go back to, among other classical sources, the reproach of
Gallus in Virgil's Tenth Eclogue, but also against love complaint,
as something that makes matters worse: 'Up, up, Philisides, let
sorrows go,' cries Geron, 'who yields to woe doth but increase his
smart.' (p. 72.) Love complaint, in other words, represents an
abuse of poetry. In the next poem, formally connected to 'Up, up,
Philisides' by its opening line, 'Down, down, Melampus,' Geron's
anger at Philisides leads into another debate on appropriate
discourse, this time with the satirist Mastix (scourge). As Mastix
sees it, the behaviour of Philisides is symptomatic of a crisis in
Arcadia. Like the sheep-dog Melampus, who is supposed to
govern and protect the sheep, not fight with his fellow canines, the
greatest shepherds in Arcadia are misusing their position by
quarrelling with each other; and, if not infighting, they are 'asleep',
lulled by a false sense of security. Small wonder then that the
younger men waste their days in trivial occupations:

> At blow point, hot cockles, or else at keels,
> While, 'Let us pass our time', each shepherd says.
>
> (p. 77.)

This return of the concept of pastime is significant, as is the use of
'sleep' as a metaphor for irresponsibility, echoing as it does Sidney's
correspondence with Languet and foreshadowing the long sleep of
Basilius. In the mind of Mastix the satirist, Arcadian culture, with its
emphasis on *otium* and on pastime, is clearly decadent:

> . . . 'Let us pass our time', each shepherd says.
> So small account of time the shepherd feels,

And doth not feel that life is naught but time,
And when that time is past, death holds his heels.

(pp. 77–8.)

For Geron, however, a recourse to satire in this situation is not only too negative, but dangerous to the satirist. He proceeds to warn Mastix to keep quiet for his own good, producing as evidence a beast-fable, the tale of a swan who lost his voice for excessive social criticism. The swan having unwisely attacked all the other birds for various vices, they join ranks against him, summon a parliament, and mute him:

There was the swan of dignity deprived,
And statute made he never should have voice,
Since when, I think, he hath in silence lived.

(pp. 78–9.)

Now, the word *silence* had, in the *Old Arcadia*, clearly been given political connotations. In the last of the First Eclogues, Musidorus (as Dorus) had extended his complaints about unrequited love into a general discussion of failed communication; and, however deeply he deplored the ineffectuality of love complaint, that form of frustration is to be preferred, he declared, to the absolute restriction of discourse experienced at court:

Then do I think, indeed, that better it is to be private
In sorrow's torments than, tied to the pomps of a palace,
Nurse inward maladies, which have not scope to be breathed out,
But perforce digest all bitter juices of horror
In silence, from a man's own self with company robbed.
Better yet do I live, that though by my thoughts I be plunged
Into my life's bondage, yet may disburden a passion
(Oppressed with ruinous conceits) by the help of an outcry:
Not limited to a whisp'ring note, the lament of a courtier....

(p. 86; italics added.)

In the light of Sidney's own political experience, these lines provide both an intertextual and a contextual gloss on Geron's fable. Both poems derive their emotional force and point from the foregrounding of political censorship in 1579 through 1581, especially the case of John Stubbs; and the mention of both 'parliament' and 'statute' in Geron's beast fable made inevitable, one would think, a connection with the notorious 'statute of silence'.

This reading must affect our dating of the *Old Arcadia*, since the Geron–Mastix debate would seem to have been partly motivated by the events of January 1581. But it is also important to note what happened to this poem in the *New Arcadia*, conceived and executed in a less confrontational political atmosphere. The Geron–Mastix debate, along with its companion piece ('Up, up, Philisides'), disappeared from the First Eclogues, and there seems to have been no plan for their relocation. If one believes, as I do, that Sidney remained deeply interested in the function of the Eclogues in his revised conception of the work, then it follows that these poems were not simply lost in the shuffling of papers, but deemed no longer necessary. This was not, however, a gesture of conciliation. Mastix the satirist ('saying still the world was amiss, but how it should be amended he knew not') disappeared; but if we look closely at the *New Arcadia* we find that his critique of society, his outspokenness, survived him, that the echo even of his words has been carefully retained, and cunningly reconstructed.

In an important passage describing the state of Macedon before Euarchus took over, Sidney provided an indictment of a badly governed state. There was

a very dissolution of all estates, while the great men . . . grew factious among themselves: . . . olde men long nusled in corruption, scorning them that would seeke reformation; yong men very fault-finding, but very faultie . . . townes decayed for want of just and naturall libertie; offices, even of judging soules, solde; publique defences neglected; and in summe . . . witte abused, *rather to faine reason why it should be amisse, then how it should be amended.* (p. 186; italics added.)

The explicit echo, with corrections, of Mastix's position is vitally important here. Sidney's indictment of Arcadian government is not now contained within the point of view of one destructive personality, but generalized and aligned with the politically normative figure of Euarchus, antitype to Basilius. Still more to the point, its emphasis is cultural as well as political, its focus the role of the intellectual, the possessor of 'witte'. 'Witte [is] abused', or cultural energy dissipated, in a realm deprived of authority. It cannot be an accident, either, that this passage sets up another echo, with Sidney's own *Defence of Poetry*, and specifically with that moment where he admits that all is not well with Elizabethan literature: 'Say not that Poetry abuseth man's wit, but that man's

wit abuseth Poetry.' (p. 125.) We can follow Sidney's intentions
here as they become clearer to himself. Philisides (irresponsible
expressivism) has been corrected by Geron (moral didacticism)
and so has Mastix, the would-be conveyor of political messages,
though not, perhaps, in a sufficiently covert form; but in the final
version the impulse to a socio-political commentary is released
from its dialectical subordination. More or less objectified, it
becomes the dominant position.

Philisides, however, was to come into his own again, and in a
way that was compatible with the process just described. In the
middle of the *Old Arcadia*, during the Third Eclogues which cele-
brate a rural marriage, Philisides reappears, having now acquired a
mysterious presence and authority. Upon request, he sings to the
shepherds attending the wedding a song 'old Languet had [him]
taught', a statement that certainly encourages his readers to supply
a historical or autobiographical context. The song he sings is an
enigmatic beast-fable, whose subject has nothing whatever to do
with the concept of marriage that dominates the rest of the Third
Eclogues.

In Sidney's fable, all the animals appeal to Jove for a king. After
warning them that monarchy leads to tyranny, he grants their
request, on certain conditions:

> beasts, take heed what you of me desire.
> Rulers will think all things made them to please, . . .
>
> But since you will, part of my heav'nly fire
> I will you lend; the rest yourselves must give.
>
> (p. 257.)

When the divine spark is incarnate, and endowed with characteristics derived from each of the animals, the result is Man, the super-
beast. As Jove predicted, the new king quickly becomes a tyrant
over those who made him what he is. He foments hostility between
the great wild beasts and the lesser animals, driving the former into
exile and then preying himself on the meeker animals left without
protection. The fable ends with a double message:

> O man, rage not beyond thy need;
> Deem it no gloire to swell in tyranny. . . .
>
> And you, poor beasts, in patience bide your hell,
> *Or know your strengths*, and then you shall do well.
>
> (p. 259; italics added.)

Whatever this means, it is clearly not the appeal of an early ecologist. Modern critical opinion has attempted to decode the poem, using the reference to Languet as a key, but with various results. The fable has been read as an incitement to rebellion, in the line of Huguenot pamphlets like *Vindiciae contra tyrannos*;[19] as an expression of orthodox Tudor absolutism designed to ingratiate Sidney with the Queen;[20] as an assertion of the importance of a powerful aristocracy in maintaining the balance of power;[21] and as a Calvinist allegory on the fall of man.[22] While the last suggestion seems to have little merit, the text of the fable *is* capable of supporting any, or rather all, of the other three readings, and in ways that invite our careful scrutiny.

The story itself is, of course, a reworking of Aesop's fable of the frogs desiring a king.[23] As John Ogilby pointed out in his 1651 paraphrase of Aesop, the fable of the frogs had an ancient history of political meaning: 'Phaedrus will have this Fable to have been made by Aesop, upon occasion of Pisistratus his seising of the Port of Athens, and taking the Supreme Power into his own hands, as Tyrant.'[24] But Ogilby also noted that in Phaedrus's application of the fable the concluding moral reads:

> You, O Citizens, bear this, he said,
> Lest you a greater mischief do invade.

(p. 32)

Clearly this is the source of Sidney's conclusion, but with a significant variant; the insertion of an alternative to patient forbearance. '*Or* know your strengths', wrote Sidney; and for those who could

---

[19] W. D. Briggs, 'Political Ideas in Sidney's *Arcadia*', *Studies in Philology* 28 (1931), 137–61, and 'Sidney's Political Ideas', *Studies in Philology* 29 (1932), 534–42.

[20] I. Ribner, 'Sir Philip Sidney on Civil Insurrection', *Journal of the History of Ideas* 13 (1952), 257–65.

[21] Ringler, *Poems*, p. 413; endorsed by Robertson, *Countess of Pembroke's Arcadia*, p. 464.

[22] A. D. Weiner, *Sir Philip Sidney and the Poetics of Protestantism* (Minneapolis, 1978), pp. 135–8.

[23] Ringler, *Poems*, p. 414, points out that the tale combines Aesop's fable with the late-classical myth of how Prometheus created man, as told by Horace, *Carmina*, i. 16. Readers would also, no doubt, have assumed an allusion to 1 Samuel 8: 5 ff. Contrast, however, the account of Sidney's fable by M. N. Raitière, *Sir Philip Sidney and Renaissance Political Theory* (Pittsburgh, 1984), who downplays the Phaedrus source because it conflicts with his view that Sidney's poem *refutes* the monarchomachs.

[24] John Ogilby, *The Fables of Aesop Paraphras'd in Verse* (1668), ed. E. Miner (Los Angeles, 1965), p. 31.

recognize the original, he thereby signalled his desire for less stoical advice. Also, he ambiguated his message by addressing himself both to sovereign ('O man') and people ('O beasts'); while in its entirety his version of the fable implies a more subtle analysis of political tyranny than that available in Aesop. A ruler who combines Jove's 'heavenly fire' with a full set of animal characteristics is perceived both in ideal terms, kingship by divine right, and with a Machiavellian realism. Yet both these forms of absolutism are modified by hints of contract theory, since the animals agreed to what they got. Contract theory is also implied in these lines, crucial to the meaning and status of the poem:

> To their own work this privilege they grant:
> That from thenceforth to all eternity
> No beast should freely speak, but only he.

> (p. 257.)

The price they have to pay for a monarchy is their freedom of speech.

It seems clear that this fable is, like Geron's tale of the silenced swan, not only about repression and the restriction of free political commentary, but about itself, about fabling, and about equivocation in the interests of safety. It is worth remembering Sidney's point in the *Defence*, that living 'under hard lords' leads to writing 'under the pretty tales of wolves and sheep', a phrase that conflates pastoral and beast fable as those forms which can imply 'the whole considerations of wrongdoing and patience'. While Sidney's fable seems to remain ambivalent on these subjects (and hence, as we have seen, provocative of different interpretations), it does not remain ambiguous; for by pointing out the *need* for ambiguity, in a system where no one may 'freely speak' except the ruler, Sidney, in effect, makes plain his desire for reform.

Yet even this is not the end of the matter, and the note of certainty I have just sounded, the sense of superiority in having delivered the consummate reading, is immediately challenged by the text. For as soon as Philisides' song is over, the Arcadians themselves take to criticism:

According to the nature of diverse ears, diverse judgements straight followed: some praising his voice; others the words, fit to frame a pastoral style; others *the strangeness of the tale, and scanning what he should mean by it.* But old Geron ... took hold of this occasion to make his revenge and said he never saw thing worse proportioned than to bring in *a tale of he knew not what* beasts at such a banquet when rather some song of love, or matter for joyful melody, was to be brought forth. 'But', said he, 'this is the right conceit of *young men who think they speak wiseliest when they cannot understand themselves*.' (pp. 259–60; italics added.)

Everything in this passage dramatizes the problems of reception and interpretation that we, four hundred years later, continue to wrestle with.

Now, the source of this passage is Sannazaro's *Arcadia*. In Sannazaro's Tenth Eclogue, the Neapolitan poet Caracciolo sings a mysterious poem, with sharp echoes of Virgil's *First Eclogue*, that is obviously a lament for Naples under the oppression of France and Spain, in allusive, metaphorical terms. Caracciolo warns his audience: 'Great matter today I wrap in a thin veil.' After the song is finished, Sincero describes its reception. It was 'by divers men in divers manners interpreted' ('*da diversi in diversi modi interpretato*'), and 'even if by reason of the covert language it was little understood by us, nevertheless it did not follow that it was not heard by each man with the closest attention'.[25] The overt latency here, the well-advertised secrecy, is designed to provoke interpretative effort. But Sidney's quotation of this passage ('According to the nature of diverse ears, diverse judgements straight followed') seems to lead in a different, sadder direction. In his *Arcadia*, the inscrutability of the text is exaggerated by the audience, whose limitations—a formalist preoccupation with voice and style, a moralist concern with decorum—prohibit most of them from even considering 'what he should mean by it'. There may also be some irony directed at himself in Sidney's reference, even if it comes through Geron, to young men who 'cannot understand themselves'. It seems to me that Sidney was fully and tragically aware, as the *Arcadia* evolved, that he ran the danger finally of not being understood, because he had chosen the wrong medium. If he chose to write in a pastoral form because in Elizabeth's culture that form was privileged and so might get access to the queen where direct address had failed, he ran the danger that she would choose to read it, if at all, only as pastime, as entertainment. If he chose covert discourse because ambiguity gave him some protection, he ran the

---

[25] *Jacopo Sannazaro: Arcadia and Piscatorial Eclogues*, trans. R. Nash (Detroit, 1966), pp. 116, 118–19.

risk of going safe but unheard or misinterpreted. The hermeneutics of censorship create their own paradoxes. It may be that in
them lies the best explanation we are likely to produce for the
abandonment of the *Old Arcadia* and the beginning of the *New*.

The *Old Arcadia*, then, offers to anyone who would listen carefully an analysis of Elizabethan culture, finding it wanting. It also
presents (in the fable) conflicting theories and arguments about
the nature of monarchy and the rights and duties of subjects, but
leaves their consequences unspoken. The entire narrative offers
both the queen and her leading courtiers advice which could, if
taken, transform Basilius into Euarchus, combining the best of the
Arcadian ideals with public reforms and international imperatives.
By choosing to work within the system, Sidney, in the *Old Arcadia*,
still maintained his commitment to a principle of moderate
reformism. The consequences of being understood would have
been either success, in the sense of influence, or an enforced and
total silence.

Instead, we have the *New Arcadia*. For it, Sidney (or Greville)
dismantled the Eclogues, and we may speculate on what, if anything, the changes meant. Most important, the presence of Philisides in the work was much reduced. In particular, the two love
complaints for which he was responsible in the Fourth Eclogues
were reassigned respectively to Amphialus (pp. 394–9) and Musidorus (pp. 357–9). Philisides was also no longer said to be the
original composer of Pyrocles's erotic blazon. He becomes
throughout an anonymous young shepherd, though recognizable
still, for anyone who knew what to look for, in the allusion to
Languet which introduces his beast fable on monarchy. That
poem was transferred to the First Eclogues, a move consistent with
more frontal emphasis on politics throughout, and the dissociation
of Sidney himself from the erotic or amorous impulses of the work.
All of the other developments—the generic shift from pastoral to
chivalric romance, the massive expansion of the narrative to
broaden the political perspective of the work and create the taxonomy of political theory and example recognized by Greville—are
consistent with a loss of confidence in indirect or covert discourse,
or in messages accommodated to the forms of Elizabethan courtship. Only two of Sidney's additions will have to suffice here as
evidence. In Book III, Chapter 16, there appears the Knight of the
Tomb, at a moment when the rebellious forces of Amphialus

confront the loyalists, and when 'the horrour of Mars—his game' displaces the play world of romantic tournament. The Knight of the Tomb represents metaphor, figuration, and mystery, 'straunge not onely by the unlookedforness of his comming, but by the straunge maner of his comming', and 'Himselfe in an armour, all painted over with such a cunning of shadow, that it represented a gaping sepulchre' (p. 445). But unlike the artful emblematical entries in the earlier Tournament of Beauty, the Knight of the Tomb is a victim of his own metaphors. For him, interpretation is both necessary and fatal. Mortally wounded by Amphialus and uncased, he becomes Parthenia, following her husband to the grave.

If arcane representation in the *New Arcadia* leads to tragedy, direct counsel fares little better. Sidney's shift towards it, however, is expressed through his revision of the role of Philanax, a role scarcely compatible with that of the zealous prosecutor of the last two books of the *Old Arcadia*. Now Philanax both leads the loyalist forces against Amphialus, and, after the bloody battle, counsels Basilius against raising the siege, an act that would effectively render those already killed a useless sacrifice, merely in response to a threat against his daughters' lives. Philanax's speech here is notable for its advocacy, not only of a public code of conduct, but also of force and resolution; and it is delivered with manifest reluctance, in the certain knowledge that its message will be unacceptable: 'If ever I could wish my faith untried', he begins, '& my counsell untrusted, it should be at this time, when in truth *I must confesse I would be content to purchase silence with discredit*' (p. 467; italics added). It is a sad coincidence that Sidney's letters home from the Low Countries, after he had finally achieved his goal of a military commission, are burdened with allusions to the Queen's failure to support her own soldiers and commanders, and haunted by a conviction that nothing he or his friends at court may do will ever be correctly interpreted. In March 1586, for example, he wrote to Walsingham (now his father-in-law) a letter which alternates between religious dedication to the cause ('If her Majesty wear the fowntain I woold fear considring what I daily fynd that we shold wax dry, but she is a means whom God useth and . . . I am faithfully persuaded that if she shold withdraw her self other springes woold ryse to help this action'); practical cynicism ('If the queen pai not her souldiours she must loos her garrisons'); and personal irony

('How apt the Queen is to interpret everything to my disadvantage.')

In the local failure of hermeneutics, then, Sidney abandoned the *Arcadia* but stuck (literally) to his guns. He left the manuscript of the *New Arcadia* with Fulke Greville who, when he published it in 1590, attached to it the notorious prefatory allusion to 'idle worke'.

I trust that enough has been said by now to suggest how that phrase was intended to be read. But if there are any remaining doubts, it might be possible to remove them by referring one last time to Greville's *Life of Sidney*. In the *Life*, Greville describes the evolution of his own tragedies as media of political analysis, as another substitute, in effect, for the repressed history he was prevented from writing by Cecil. Greville contrasts his plans to Sidney's more radically fictional or poetic strategies of displacement; but the authorial anxieties he describes, the process by which restraint becomes a source of literary energy and motive, were equally applicable to Sidney. In particular, we should note the language in which he talks about the question of seriousness in literature and how an author may choose to conceal, or partly conceal, the seriousness of his intentions:

When I had in mine own case well weigh'd the tendernesse of that great subject; and consequently, the nice path I was to walke in between two extremities; but especially the danger, by treading aside, to cast scandall upon the scared foundations of Monarchy . . . a new counsell rose up in me, to take away all opinion of seriousnesse from these perplexed pedegrees; and to this end carelessly cast them into that hypocriticall figure Ironia, wherein men commonly (to keep above their workes) seeme to make toies of the utmost they can doe. (pp. 175–6.)

Greville's 'toies' and Sidney's 'pretty tales' have the same function: to allow their authors to keep faith with themselves, while creating a medium of expression that may, with luck, break through the political restraints and cultural assumptions.

Early Editions

12. SIR PHILIP SIDNEY, 1554–1586: A CHECK-LIST OF EARLY EDITIONS OF HIS WORKS

BENT JUEL-JENSEN

Twenty-five years ago I compiled a check-list of the early editions of Sir Philip Sidney's writings. It appeared in a series of articles, mostly about minor literary figures, whose writings at least temporarily had been forgotten. There is nothing minor about Sidney, but it had struck me, as an admirer of him as a poet and as a man, that there was not even a rudimentary guide to his writings in early editions. Seventeenth-century editions of the *Arcadia* were then still comparatively common. They offer as many bibliographical puzzles as one could wish for. New variants, none of great textual importance, but some of considerable bibliographical interest, have surfaced during the intervening years. A series of early editions of the *Arcadia* is representative of printing and editorial habits during a century and a half. My list was written for collectors, perhaps with the hope that it might also be of a little use to scholars. Some of Sidney's books are very rare indeed, and some of his works only circulated in manuscript until modern times.

Sidney and *Sidneiana* is a delightfully vague concept. I suspect that the main reason why Sidney is so rarely collected will be found in the practically total absence of any even tolerably complete bibliographical list of the editions of his *Arcadia*, let alone his other works. A complete run of all variants of the early printed editions of the *Arcadia* exists nowhere. But it is by no means impossible to assemble a nearly complete series of the fifteen editions. The real difficulties arise when the collection is extended to separate parts, continuations, adaptations, translations, and imitations of the *Arcadia*. Manuscripts are now nearly all in public collections. The other separate works span from Sidney's first book *The Trewnesse of Christian Religion*, from *Astrophel and Stella*, the *Defence of Poesie*, the metrical versions of the *Psalms*, to controversial writings and contributions to songbooks and miscellanies. Some works exist in

Reprinted (with corrections and additions) from 'Some Uncollected Authors XXXIV', *The Book Collector* (Winter 1962), 468–79; ibid. (Summer 1963), 196–202.

several early editions, some in MSS only. However impossible it may be to get the early printed books, a single contemporary manuscript (and there are several extant of many of the smaller works) will make even a small collection interesting. The small group of contemporary memorial verse on Sidney as well as the early lives naturally belong to a Sidney collection, as do also, though more remotely, the books dedicated to Sidney. For the last thirty-five years I have tried to collect such books, and I have found the absence of any guide very irksome. There is ample and excellent literature to help one appreciate all facets of Sidney, and in this brief preface I have deliberately not attempted to extol his many virtues. My check-list of *Sidneiana* is by no means complete. It includes all early English *Arcadias* known to me up to and including the fifteenth edition, and it attempts to give a list of early editions of the other works. I realize only too well the many short-comings, and I would welcome additions and corrections.

It had originally been the intention to include lists of known MSS, but with the publication of the *Poems* (ed. Ringler, Oxford, 1962), the *Arcadia* (ed. Jean Robertson, Oxford, 1973) and the *Miscellaneous Prose* (ed. Duncan-Jones and van Dorsten, Oxford, 1973), this has become unnecessary, for each contains admirable lists of the MSS known to the editors. There were numerous translations, and it would have been tempting to give details of all of them. I have included one representative example, the splendid German translation by Opitz from 1629/30, because of its remarkable series of engravings by Merian, and I have given brief notes on others known to me.

I am indebted to many individuals for pointing out errors in the original version of this list, in particular to Miss K. Pantzer, Mr John Buxton, Mr Paul Morgan, and Miss Katherine Duncan-Jones, all of whom have also added new information.

I have tried to locate as many copies as possible of the earliest editions, and I have given a representative list of locations of the later ones. The symbols used are those agreed upon for the revised *STC*. It seemed to be of some interest to have a near complete list of the extant copies of the 1590 *Arcadia*. The comparatively long list may convey a false impression of the frequency with which the book occurs. Very few additional copies will probably now be located. It is very strange that this book should be so rare whilst the *Faerie Queene*, published in the same year, by the same stationer, in the same format and of approximately the same length, by comparison is a common book. The list of copies of the first *Arcadia* also provides some salutary information about the frequency with which a famous book is rebound and tampered with in various ways, and it should be a warning to those in search of reliable bibliographical evidence.

CHECK-LIST OF EDITIONS OF *ARCADIA* TO 1739

1*a*. THE | COVNTESSE | OF PEMBROKES | ARCADIA, | WRITTEN BY SIR PHILIPPE | SIDNEI. | [*large coat-of-arms of the Sidneys*] LONDON | Printed for William Ponſonbie. | *Anno Domini*, 1590.

1*b*. [*Variant imprint. Title from the same setting of type up to and including* LONDON |. *The last line of the imprint is probably unaltered, but the last line but one is reset:*] . . . Printed by Iohn Windet for william [*sic*] Ponſonbie. | *Anno Domini*, 1590.

Collation: 4° (in eights). A⁴ B–Z⁸, Aa–Zz⁸. ff. [4], 1–38, 71, 40–328, 389–90, 331–60. First four leaves signed (–A1, –A2, –A4, +B5).

Contents: A1, blank; A2ʳ, title; A2ᵛ, blank; A3ʳ–A4ʳ, dedication by Sidney to the Countess of Pembroke; A4ᵛ, apology from the 'ouer-seer of the print'; B1ʳ–Zz8ᵛ, the text, ending abruptly . . . 'Whereat ashamed, (as having neuer done so much before in his life)'.

The ouer-seer was probably John Florio, see note to 2.

First edition, *STC* 22539a and 22539.

Copies: 1*a*.

1. *British Library.* G. 10440. (Grenville.)
2. *British Library.* C. 30. d. 22. (A4 in pen facsimile.)
3. *Keble College, Oxford.* Original vellum.
4. *Huntington.* 69441. (E. D. Church copy, 1909.) Contemporary calf.
5. *Pierpont Morgan.* (R. Farmer–Locker–Lampson–Van Antwerp.) Old half-calf.
6. *New York Public Library.* (Corser–Dunn–Gardner–Britwell–Clawson–Young.) Morocco by Clarke and Bedford.
7. *Chapin Library.* (Purchased from James F. Drake, 1918.) Brown morocco by Rivière.
8. *University of Texas.* (Catherine Cavendish, *c.*1600. Purchased from Robinson.) Calf *c.*1800.
9. *University of Indiana, Lilly Library.* (Bemis.) Contemporary calf, rebacked.
10. *Newberry Library.* (Lucia Hastings, 1624–Crocker–C. A. Stonehill) 12 leaves in facsimile: A2, A3, A4, B1, K8, V6, V7, V8, Cc2, Ll3, Zz1, and Zz8.
11. *Arthur J. Houghton, Jr.* Wye Plantation, Md. (Iohn Stodart: Coll. Iesu Oxon.–Henry Eyton.) Lacks A1, D3–D6 and Aa2 inserted from another copy; sold in Houghton Sale Pt II, Christie's 12 June 1980, lot 429, £7,000 to Fleming.
12. *H. Bradley Martin, New York City.* (John Borlase–Huth–Hogan–Greenhill.) A4 in facsimile, a genuine leaf A4 bought from a former owner of the Juel-Jensen copy in 1939 tipped in. Red morocco by Bedford.
13. *Sherman P. Haight, New York City.* (Hoe.) Part of A2, and A4 and B1 in facsimile.
14. *Bent Juel-Jensen.* (Jefferis, 1605–Yeamans–Eldridge–White–McLeish–Albert Ehrman–John Ehrman.) A2, 3, 4 and B1 facsimile by Emery Walker. Contemporary calf. A4 removed in 1939 and now in the Martin copy.
15. *Untraced.* (Shown in the Festival of Britain Exhibition, 1951, at the V. & A. Museum.)

Sold by Pickering & Chatto to C. A. Stonehill who made the imperfections up with
leaves from the Newberry copy with the exception of A4 which is in facsimile. Sold
to the Carnegie Bookshop who have since resold it.) A4 in facsimile and otherwise
made-up. (Leaves B1, K8, V6, V7, V8, Cc2, Ll3, Zz1 and Zz8 from the Newberry
Library copy. These leaves were still *in situ* when the latter was offered in Rosenbach's Poetry Catalogue, 1941, item 673.)

16. *Martin Bodmer*. Complete. Provenance unknown.

   1*b*.

   1. *Trinity College, Cambridge*, (Capell R.10).
   2. *Huntington*. 69442 (J. Crossley–Halsey). Title inlaid. Morocco. A4 has the verso
      blank; a second A4 from another copy with the usual note from the 'ouer-seer' has
      been inserted.
   3. *Pforzheimer Foundation*. (Bright–Heber–Crossley–Pearson–H. V. Jones.) Straight-
      grain morocco by Lewis.
   4. *Yale*. (James Hussey–Walter Thomas Wallace–Templeton Crocker.) Contem-
      porary calf.
   5. *Harvard*. Houghton Library. (Mrs R. W. Bliss, Dumbarton Oaks, Georgetown.–
      G. H. Armour.) Incorrectly listed under 1*a* in 1962.

   2. [*Within elaborate compartment, incorporating Sidney's crest at the top, and the pig-
and-marjoram device at the foot, McK. & F. 212.*] THE | COVNTESSE | OF
PEMBROKES | ARCADIA. | WRITTEN BY SIR | Philip Sidney Knight. |
NOW SINCE THE FIRST EDI- | tion augmented and ended. | LONDON. |
Printed for William Ponſonbie. | *Anno Domini*. 1593.

   Collation: fol. (in sixes), ¶⁴, A–Z⁶, Aa–Rr⁶, Sſ⁴. ff. [4], 1–43, 50, 45–8, 46, 50–243 [244].
(Var. 121 misprinted 115.) First four leaves signed (–¶1, –¶2, –Q4, –Sf4, H2 missigned I2).

   Contents: ¶1, blank; ¶2ʳ, title; ¶2ᵛ, blank; ¶3ʳᵛ Sidney's dedication to the Countess of
Pembroke, ¶4ʳᵛ *To The Reader*, signed H.S. (i.e. Hugh Sanford). A1ʳ–Ss3ᵛ, the text. Ss4
missing in copies seen, probably a blank.

   This edition reprints, with corrections, the 1590 *Arcadia*, adding, in order to complete
it, three books from the unrevised 'Old' *Arcadia*. The title-border was designed for this
book. The *impresa* invented by the editor, Hugh Sanford, gave rise to much ridicule.
Florio, who had been attacked by Sanford in the preface, alluded to Sanford as 'Huffe
Snuffe, Horse Stealer, Hob Sowter, Hugh Sot, Humfrey Swineshead. Now—Master H.S.
if this doe gaule you, forbeare kicking hereafter, and in the meane time you may make you
a plaister of your dride Marioram.' (*A Worlde of Wordes* (1598), a5ᵛ.) The border was used
again in the editions of 1598, 1613, in the London reissues of the 1621 edition, in the 1629
issue of the 1627 edition, and in the 1633 and 1638 editions. The border was probably
owned by Ponsonby and made available to Thomas Creede for use on the title of Machia-
velli's *Florentine History* of 1598 (*STC* 17162). It was also used in the 1611 and 1617 editions
of Spenser's *Faerie Queene*. (*STC* 23083.3–5).

   Second edition. *STC* 22540. (The printer was wrongly given as Thomas Creede in the
first *STC*. The book was printed by John Windet, see *The Library*, 5th Series, 12. 4
(1957), 274.)

   COPIES: L (C.21.d.21.). C.; F (2, one Bright–Britwell–Harmsworth). HD. HN. PML. NY.
HAVERFORD COLLEGE. WEL.; PENSHURST. WELBECK ABBEY (with arms of Henry, second Earl of
Southampton). BELVOIR CASTLE. JOHN BUXTON (imp.). MISS SYFRET. JJ. Minster Gate Books
of York in their cat. 2, item 157, 1974, advertised a copy in 17th-cent. calf for £1,450. JOHN
EMMERSON (2, imp.).

   3. [*Within the pig-and-marjoram compartment, McK & F.* 212] THE |
COVNTESSE | OF PEMBROKES | ARCADIA. | WRITTEN BY SIR |

PHILIP SIDNEY | Knight. | NOW THE THIRD TIME | publiſhed, with ſundry new additions | of the ſame Author. | LONDON | Imprinted for William Ponſonbie. | *Anno Domini.* 1598.

Collation: fol. (in sixes). ¶⁴, A–Z⁶, Aa–Zz⁶, Aaa–Bbb⁴. Pp. [8] 1–21, 20, 23–192, 219, 194–338, 341, 340–497, 496, 499–507, 404, 509–76. First four leaves signed (–¶1, –¶2, Oo3 and Oo4 signed Oiij and Oiiij).

Contents: ¶1, blank; ¶2ʳ, title; ¶2ᵛ, blank; ¶3ʳᵛ, Sidney's dedication to the Countess of Pembroke; ¶4ʳᵛ, Sanford's preface to the Reader; A1ʳ–Rr2ʳ, *Arcadia*; Rr2ᵛ–Sf5ᵛ, *Sonnets*; Sf6ʳ–Xx1ᵛ, *Defence of Poesie*; Xx2ʳ–Bbb3ʳ, *Astrophel and Stella*; Bbb3ᵛ–Bbb6ᵛ, *The May Day Masque.*

This is the first collected edition of the *Arcadia* and the *Poems*, *The May Lady*, and the *Defence of Poesie*. It was printed by Richard Field.

Third edition. *STC* 22541.

COPIES: L (2, C.21.d.16. and G.12956). L⁶. L¹⁸ (in a Queen Elizabeth Binding). L³⁰. O. O⁷ O¹⁴. C. C². (2, VI.3.69 with signature 'Mary Sidney' and VI.12.2.). C⁴ (Heber). C¹⁴. BIRM. M.; HN (69477, Hoe). HD. F (2, both imp.) CH. LC. Y.N. DAR. COR. TCU. WES. TEX. STAN. V. OREGON. PN.; TURNBULL LIBRARY; BUXTON. RINGLER (lacks tp., but Wordsworth's copy). JJ. Quaritch, Cat. 1043, item 23 (Lord Aldenham), Jan. 1985, $4000. Bodmer. JOHN EMMERSON.

4. [*Rectangular headpiece, including the arms of Scotland*] | THE | COVNTESSE | OF PEMBROKES | ARCADIA. | *WRITTEN BY SIR* | PHILIP SIDNEY | Knight. | *Now the third time publiſhed, with ſundry new*| *additions of the ſame Author.*| [*rectangular type ornament*] | EDINBVRGH. | *PRINTED BY ROBERT*| *walde-graue, Printer to the*| Kings Majeſtie. | *Cum priuilegio Regio*, 1599.

Collation: fol. (in sixes), π², A–Z⁶, Aa–Ee⁶, Gg–Zz⁶, Aaa⁶. ff. [2], 1–3, 7, 5–15, 12, 17–18, 29, 20–69, 40, 71–4, 74, 76–80, 94, 82–123, 123, 125–30, 121, 132–63, 165, 165–8, 173–89, 198, 191–7, 204, 199–212, 207, 214–31, 226, 233–7, 218, 239–42, 237, 244–74, 281, 267, 277–80. First three leaves signed (–π1, 2; sheets L–M, P–Dd, Ll, Pp–Zz all have the fourth leaf signed '4', and Nn is fully signed. The former curious signing is typical of Walde-grave. Ee2 is missigned Ee3, Aaa1 and Aaa3 are missigned Aa and Aa3. There is no signature Ff, and the foliation breaks down at this point. *Variant foliation:* '19' correctly printed, '64' for '60', '208' for '202', '259' for '260', '246' for '266'.

Contents: π1ʳ, title; π1ᵛ, blank; π2ʳ, Sidney's dedication to the Countess of Pembroke; π2ᵛ, *To the Reader*, preface by H. Sanford; A1ʳ–Qq5ᵛ, *Arcadia*; Qq6ʳ–Sf2ᵛ, *Sonnets*; Sf3ʳ–Vv4ᵛ, *Defence of Poesie*; Vv5ʳ–Aaa2ᵛ, *Astrophel and Stella*; Aaa3ʳ–Aaa6ʳ, *The May Day Masque*; Aaa6ᵛ, blank.

Although the title claims that this is the third edition, it is in fact the fourth. It was printed by Waldegrave. In 1597 one William Scarlett, a Cambridge bookbinder, had visited Edinburgh, probably to interest Waldegrave in the undertaking on behalf of various English booksellers. A curious lawsuit followed in the High Court of the Star Chamber, begun in November 1599 and instituted by Ponsonby against John Legatt the Cambridge printer, William Scarlett, and four London citizens. The court case is described at length by Plomer (*The Library*, Second Series, No. 2, 1 (1900), p. 195). Plomer found it hard to explain how Waldegrave could have printed the book during the seven or eight months that elapsed between Ponsonby's entry of *Astrophel and Stella* on 23 October 1598 and the following August when the Edinburgh edition was certainly on the market. If Scarlett's evidence is to be trusted, Waldegrave had said to him in 1597 that he intended printing an edition of the *Arcadia* with more additions. It may in fact be that he had started printing before Ponsonby's 1598 folio was ready, for the *Arcadia* is at least in part reprinted from the 1593 folio, and he may have intended to add *Astrophel and Stella* from one of the quarto editions, but before he had finished printing the *Arcadia*,

Ponsonby's 1598 edition conveniently appeared, and Waldegrave reprinted the Poems from that edition. That Ponsonby resented the piracy is understandable, for it sold at six shillings against the nine shillings which was the price of his edition. Ponsonby seized the copies of the piracy that had not been sold, and this may explain why this edition is the rarest of all the early *Arcadia*s.

Fourth edition. *STC* 22542.

COPIES: L (C.21. d.4.). C² (VI.3.70, title badly damaged). C¹³. E.; HD. F (Heber–Britwell–Harmsworth). PML. CH. NY. CHI.; JJ. BUXTON. PENSHURST (lacks all after Vv4).

Ramage lists: '(22541 after. Anr. ed?) printed f. M. Lownes, by H.L., 1599, KRH (imp).' This volume, in the Hurd Episcopal Library at Hartlebury Castle near Kidder-minster, is an imperfect copy of the 1613 *Arcadia* (no. 6), lacking the title and the inserts 'Ee5' and 'Sfii', bound in early 18th-cent. calf. Like a number of other books in the Library, it belonged to Alexander Pope, and has his name on a fly-leaf, and 'pr. 4s.' Pope has substituted for the absent title a beautifully drawn, calligraphic title, very similar in execution to other examples of titles from his hand. The title and imprint are wholly imaginary:

[*Within double rules*] THE | COUNTESS | OF | PEMBROKE'S | ARCADIA: | With other Works, | BY | ⟦Sir *PHILIP SIDNEY*: | [viz.] | The DEFENCE of POESIE. | SONGS AND SONETS. | ASTROPHEL and STELLA. | [*rule*] | *LONDON*. | Printed for *Matthew Lownes* by *H.L.* | Anno Domini; 1599.

5*a*. [*Within an elaborate compartment with figures representing Ptolemy, etc., signed IB✷F. McK. & F.* 99.] [*rule*] | THE | [*rule*] | COVNTESSE | OF PEMBROKES | *ARCADIA*. | [*rule*] | WRITTEN BY SIR | PHILIP SIDNEY | Knight. | [*rule*] | NOW THE FOVRTH TIME | PVBLISHED, WITH SVNDRY | NEW ADDITIONS OF THE | *fame Author*. | [*In separate panel, below:*] LONDON | Imprinted for SIMON WATERSON | *Anno DOMINI*. | 1605.

5*b*. [*Variant imprint. The title is from the same setting of type as 5a, but the imprint has been reset:*] | LONDON | Imprinted for MATHEW LOWNES | *Anno DOMINI*. | 1605.

Collation: fol. (in sixes), ¶⁴, A–Z⁶, Aa–Zz⁶, Aaa–Bbb⁶. Pp. [8], 1–192, 219, 194–6, 199, 198–267, 273, 269–72, 268, 274–6, 177, 278–314, 309, 316–38, 341–2, 341–93, 964, 395–501, 506, 503–11, 508, 513–25, 529, 527–76. First four leaves signed (−¶1, 2 −L4, −Hh4, Z2 printed 'Z2.')

Contents: ¶1, blank; ¶2ʳ, title; ¶2ᵛ, blank; ¶3ʳᵛ, dedication by Sidney to the Countess of Pembroke; ¶4ʳᵛ, *To the Reader*, signed H. S[anford].; A1ʳ–Rr2ʳ, *Arcadia*; Rr2ᵛ–Sf5ᵛ, *Sonnets*; Sf6ʳ–Xx1ᵛ, *Defence of Poesie*; Xx2ʳ–Bbb3ʳ, *Astrophel and Stella*; Bbb3ᵛ–Bbb6ᵛ *The May Lady*.

Although the title claims that this is the fourth edition, it is in fact the fifth, for the Edinburgh edition has not been counted. It is a page-for-page reprint of the 1598 folio. G. Eld printed A–Aa, Humfry Lownes the rest.

Three copies with the imprint 'H.L. for Mathew Lownes' are of particular interest. Two copies in the writer's collection have associations with the Sidney family. One, bound in a mid-nineteenth-century Janseniste binding by Thompson of Paris (formerly Quaritch: *Catalogue of English Literature*, 1915, item 3473, and again *English History and Literature*, cat. 369, 1922, item 994–Howard Pease of Otterburn Tower, Northumber-land–Maggs Cat. 858, *English Literature*, November 1958, item 3164, with illustration of the inscription on the title verso–Sotheby's, 22 July 1985, lot 8), has on the verso of the title the following autograph note by Anne Clifford, Countess of Dorset, Pembroke, and Montgomery: 'This Booke did I beegine to Red ouer att Skipton in Crauen aboutt the

Latter=ende of Januarey and I made an ende of Reding itt all ower in Apellbey Castell in Westmorland the 19 day of Marche folloing, in 1651: as the yeere beegines on Nwers= daye'. We know from the triptych of Lady Anne Clifford that she owned an *Arcadia*. It has few notes in her hand in the text, many underlinings, and several annotations in another hand, in one place signed 'E.D.' Edward Denny had been dead six years when the book appeared, and the hand does not appear to be that of Sir Edward Dyer. Another copy (in contemporary calf) has an autograph poem 'Ad Stellam et Philastrum amantes' by John Davies of Hereford (privately printed, Oxford, 1966). Davies wrote out the copy of Sidney's and the Countess of Pembroke's Paraphrase of the *Psalms* now at Penshurst, and possibly also the closely related MS in the writer's collection, once Sir Walter Aston's, from the Tixall library, and possibly the presentation copy to Queen Elizabeth (Ringler MSS A and J). A third copy of this issue (formerly Quaritch, cat. 1027, January 1985, item 194), now in the library of Miss Duncan-Jones, has the autograph of John Langford in three places, and 'whose [Sidney's] deayth was my undoinge'. Langford was mentioned in Sidney's will.

Fifth edition. *STC* 22543 and 22543a.

COPIES: 5*a*. L. L^{30}. O. O^{19}. C^4. BANGOR UNIVERSITY COLLEGE. LEEDS; Y. F (4, one imperfect). ILL. CHI. WEL. PFOR. (Hagen); BUXTON. JJ.

5*b*. L. C^4. GLOUC.; HN (Hoe). F. CH.; SYDNEY UNIV.; ROBERT TAYLOR. K. DUNCAN-JONES. JJ (3). BUXTON. PENSHURST.

6*a*. [*Within the pig-and-marjoram compartment, McK. & F.* 212] THE | COVNTESSE | OF PEMBROKES | ARCADIA. | WRITTEN BY SIR | PHILIP SIDNEY | Knight. | NOW THE FOVRTH TIME | publiſhed, with ſome new | Additions. | LONDON | Imprinted by *H.L.* for *Simon* | *Waterſon* 1613.

6*b*. [*Variant imprint. The title is from the same setting of type as 5a, but the imprint reset:*] LONDON | Imprinted by *H.L.* for *Mathew* | *Lownes*, 1613.

Early issue, before Alexander's Supplement was ready:
Collation: fol. (in sixes), π^2, A–Z^6, Aa–Dd^6 Ee^6 (Ee4+'Ee5') Ff–Rr^6, Sſ^6 (Sſ1+'SſII') Tt–Zz^6, Aaa–Bbb^6. Pp. [4], 1–192, 219, 231, 195–332 [2], 333–38, 341, 340, 341–82, 303, 384–482 [2], 483–4, 435, 486–511, ς12, 513–76. First three leaves signed. (−π1, 2, +A4, +B4, +Bb4, +Cc4, +Hh4, +Sſ4, +Aaa4, +Bbb4; inserts signed 'Ee5' and SſII' respectively. Rr1 missigned 'Kr'.)

Later issue, with Alexander's Supplement inserted:
Collation: fol. (in sixes), π^2, A–Z^6, Aa–Dd^6, Ee^6 (Ee4+¶^{4}, ✳^{6}), Ff–Rr^6, Sſ^6 (Sſ1+'SſII'), Tt–Zz^6, Aaa–Bbb^6. Pagination as above, but with pp. [20] instead of pp. [2] after p. 332. Of these, ¶1^r is numbered 335, ¶2^r 334, ¶3^r 335, the rest are unnumbered in state i (see below), the pages are unnumbered in state ii of the insert. Signatures as above, except for the insert, for which see below.

Contents: π1^r, title; π1^v, blank; π2^{rv}, Sidney's dedication to the Countess of Pembroke; A1^r–Rr2^r, *Arcadia*; Rr2^v–Sſ5^v, *Sonnets*; Sſ6^r–Xx1^v, *Defence of Poesie*; Xx2^r–Bbb3^r, *Astrophel and Stella*; Bbb3^v–Bbb6^v, *The May Lady*.

This is a page-for-page reprint of the 1605 edition, omitting Sanford's preface to the Reader. One extra poem is added by the insertion of a single leaf 'SſII' between Sſ1 and Sſ2. In an earlier issue a single leaf 'Ee5' is inserted between Ee4 and Ee5: '*Thus far the worthy Author* . . .', eighteen lines of explanation of the break between the 'New' and the 'Old' *Arcadia*. The inserts are not found in some copies, but the catchwords clearly show that they are necessary, and that they must have come adrift in the course of time. They were probably printed on one sheet, for the Beverley Chew copy in the Hunting-ton Library (69479) has both leaves bound between Ee4 and Ee5; they were probably never separated for binding. As the 1613 editor seems to have gone back to the 'Old' *Arcadia* for some corrections to the text, this edition has some authority, and it is likely that the Countess of Pembroke gave her blessing to the *Supplement* by Sir William Alexander which is found in a later issue of this edition. The singleton 'Ee5' is now replaced by ten leaves with which Alexander attempted to bridge the gap in the text.

Alexander's Supplement

The supplement was entered in the Stationers' Register to W. Barrett on 31 August 1616, and the rights for the 'five shettes' were transferred to M. Lownes on 22 March 1619, which suggests that it was being printed about three years after publication of the earlier copies of the 1613 edition. This may offer an explanation of why so comparatively few copies of the 1613 folio have the *Supplement*. Three distinct settings of type of the *Supplement* exist, of which two (i and ii) are found bound in the 1613 volume. All three states are found in copies of the various issues of the next (1621) edition.

An unsophisticated copy of 6*b* in the original calf binding in the writer's collection has insert ii between Ee4 and Ee5. It is of particular interest for dating the supplement, for it has an inscription by the first owner at the foot of the title: 'Addictus Bibliotheca Jacobus Fetzerij Lond. 1618'. The same Fetzer gave a copy of Drummond's *Poems* 4°, 1616 to the Bodleian Library (Arch. Bodl 200). This copy remained in England for some years, for a friend, Joachim Morsius, wrote Latin epigrams on Sidney on the first blank leaf in London in January 1620. I acquired the volume from Holland.

i. *Collation:* fol., ¶⁴, ✱⁶ = 10 ll.; 1, 2, 3 numbered on rectos '335', '334', '335', respectively. ¶1, 2 and ✱1, 2, 3 signed.

No drop-title. Text begins: 'Thus the fire of rage . . .'. Shoulder-note: 'Here this | Story, left | vnperfect | by the Au- | thour, is | continued | by Sʳ. *W.A.*', on ¶1ʳ. Running headlines, recto; '*Lib.* III.', verso: '*Arcadia.*'. Text ends on ✱6ʳ, signed 'S. W. A.', and has a large triangular tailpiece.

The insert was printed by W. Stansby for W. Barrett? (new *STC*).

ii. *Collation:* fol., ¶⁴, ✱⁶ = 10 ll.; no pagination. π1, 2 and ✱2, 3 signed. No drop-title. Text begins: 'The fire of rage . . .'. No shoulder-note. Running headlines, recto: '*Lib.* III.,' verso: '*Arcadia.*'. Text ends on ✱6ʳ . . . 'their prosperous returne.', after which follows a 9-line explanatory note: 'If this little Essay . . .', signed 'S. W. A.' Triangular tailpiece as in i.

Printed by W. Stansby for W. Barrett? Certainly before 1618 (see above).

iii. *Collation:* fol., π⁸, ee² = 10 ll.; pagination 327–31, 328, 333–46. First four leaves of sheet π signed 'Ee2' 'Ee3' 'Ee4' 'Ee5', ee1 signed.

Drop title: '*A ſupplement of the ſaid defect by* | *Sir* W.A.'. Text begins: 'The fire of rage . . .'. No shoulder-note. Running headline, recto and verso, between rules: LIB.III. ARCADIA. [*and numeral*], except on π1ʳ, where *ARCADIA* has been omitted. Text ends on ee2ᵛ; '. . . their prosperous returne.' The note 'If this little Essay . . .' takes up eight lines and is signed '*S.W.A.*'. There is no tailpiece.

Printed in Dublin, 1621.

i was clearly intended for the 1613 edition as the text follows on the catchword 'Thus' on Ee4ᵛ. ii could fit either the 1613 or the 1621 edition. Copies with Waterson's imprint appear to have state i, those with Lownes's imprint have state ii, although the use in the London issues of the 1621 edition is indiscriminate. iii was printed to fit harmoniously into the 1621 volume. The misleading signature 'Ee2' indicated to the binder that the insert should follow immediately after Ee1 (of Ee²). The pagination fits the pagination of the 1621 edition.

The Mason–Grafton–Heber–Edwards–Bemis–Widener copy of the 1613 edition is bound in red morocco powdered with small gilt hearts and flames with a central ⋈ surrounded by four smaller *S*s. There is something fishy about the volume. First comes a very clean title-page of 6*a*, followed by a tattered, frail, and brittle title of 6*b*. A large ink stain in the middle has made a hole. At the foot of the title is the inscription: 'This was the Countess of Pembrokes owne Booke given me by the Countess of Montgomery her daughter 1625. Ancram.' The second title is shorter than the body of the book. The next few leaves are also brittle. Dr William A. Jackson pointed out that the binding is about thirty years older than the book, and of continental origin. He thought the inscription might be a fabrication. In the Duke of Grafton's sale catalogue (lot 363, 8 June 1815) attention is drawn to the '*beautiful ancient binding*', and the inscription on the second title. The first title is not mentioned. There is no mention of it either in Heber's sale, pt. IV, lot 3047, in a catalogue that had been provided with ample notes by the (notorious) bibliographer John Payne Collier. Though Collier had been known to forge Elizabethan and Jacobean literary hands (e.g. Drayton's), he must have been very precocious to have had a chance to practise on this book. The volume may be an early example of *remboîtage*, and the inscription genuine, though whose the initials were we may never know. Who was M A W? Alan G. Thomas in his catalogue 17, 1966, had a Venetian *Toscanelli*, 1574, bound in Paris *c.*1600 with a semé of identical stamps of flames and S fermés (item 241, illustrated).

Sixth edition. *STC* 22544 and 22544a.

COPIES: 6*a*. *with single insert 'Ee5'*
    L. (682.d.11.). L³⁸. C.G.⁴. LEIC²; HN. F (2). N. HD. Y. CAL. PN. WASH². COR; ARTHUR A.
    HOUGHTON (sold, Christie's, 12 June 1980, lot 430, £700 to Salisbury).
    RINGLER. JJ.
    with Alexander's Supplement.
    HD (14457.23.8.7 F✳, state i). BUXTON (lacks SΠ; state i).
   6*b*. *with single insert 'Ee5'*
    O.L³⁰. BIRM.; MADRID (National Library); HN. HD (Heber–Bemis, see above).
    Y (R. Burton). F. PH.; BUXTON. JJ.
    with Alexander's Supplement.
    O³² (state ii); SHR (state ii); KRAUS (Cat. 90, item 31, state ii) JJ
    (Fetzer's copy). *State of inserts not known:* HURD EPISCOPAL LIBRARY, KIDDER-
    MINSTER (lacks insert). UNIVERSITY COLLEGE, SWANSEA.; ILL. CU. BRYN MAWR.

7*a*. [*Within an architectural compartment of four pieces forming a portico with twisted baroque pillars at the sides, and with the initials 'I.R.' at the top. McK. &F.* 274] THE | COVNTESSE | OF PEMBROKES | ARCADIA. | WRITTEN BY SIR | PHILIP SIDNEY | KNIGHT. | [*rule*] | Now the fift time publiſhed, | with ſome new Additions. | [*rule*] | Alſo a ſupplement of a defect in | the third part of this | HISTORY. | By Sir W. ALEXANDER. | [*Within a slot in the pediment*] DVBLIN, | Printed by the Societie of | STATIONERS. 1621. | *Cum Privilegio.*

Collation: fol. (in sixes; π², ¶², A–Z⁶, Aa–Dd⁶, Ee¹⁰ (Ee⁹+ee²), Ff–Zz⁶, Aaa–Bbb⁶. Pp. [8], 1–37, 48, 39–41, 43, 42, 44–6, 37–87, 90–156, 357–66, 377, 368, 169–92, 293, 194–219, 222, 221–4, 215, 226–314, 351, 316–24, 352, 326–31, 328, 333–51, 357, 353–5, 256, 352, 358–74, 381, 376–97, 498, 399–400, 413, 402–588. First three leaves signed (−π1, 2−¶2+Ee4, +Ee5 +ee1; Hh3 missigned 'Gg3').

Contents: π1 blank; π2ʳ, title; π2ᵛ blank; ¶1ʳᵛ, Sidney's dedication to the Countess of Pembroke; ¶2ʳᵛ, H. S[anford].'s dedication to the Reader; A1ʳ–Rr1ᵛ, *Arcadia*; Rr2ʳ–Sf5ᵛ, *Sonnets*; Sf6ʳ–Xx1ᵛ, *Defence of Poesie*; Xx2ʳ–Bbb3ʳ, *Astrophel and Stella*; Bbb3ᵛ–Bbb6ᵛ, *The May Lady.*

This edition is a reprint of the 1613 folio, but Sanford's preface, omitted in the latter, has again been included. The Stationers' Register records (20 December 1619): 'Agreed that the book called the Arcadia, that is begun to be ymprinted in Ireland be finished, and that as many be kept there as thought fit and the residue brought over; Waterson and M. Lowndes to have them at the rate they paid for those they last printed in England [i.e. the 1613 edition]'. This explains the London reissues of the Dublin edition with Lownes's or Waterson's imprint during the next few years. Not only has the title been cancelled, but in some copies at least, Alexander's *Supplement* has been bound up from the earlier printings. Although this is not invariable, Waterson's imprint appears to go with setting i, Lownes's with setting ii of the *Supplement.*

The first three lines of the comment on Ee1ᵛ: 'Thus far the worthy Author . . .' exists in two forms which may be distinguished:

a: THus far the worthy Author . . . Arcadia of | his, which only paſſed . . .: hauing a pur-|poſe, likewiſe to haue new ordred . . . had he not been |

b: Thus far the worthy Author . . . Arcadia of | his, which onely . . . hauing a purpoſe | likewiſe to haue new ordered . . . had hee not beene |

Examples of setting *a* are found in JJ 7*a* (insert iii), JJ 7*c*, 7*d*, and 7*e* (all with insert ii), of *b* in JJ 7*e* (insert i).

Seventh edition, first issue. *STC* 22545.

COPIES: L (C.40.1.6., state iii). O. O⁵. C(2). LEEDS. M. D⁶ (2); HN (iii). HD (iii). F (2, one imp.). ILL. CH. TEX; BUXTON (iii). JJ (2, both iii).

7*b*. (Another issue.) [*Within the pig-and-marjoram compartment, McK. &F.* 212]
THE | COVNTESSE | OF | PEMBROKES | ARCADIA. | WRITTEN BY SIR | PHILIP SIDNEY | Knight. | NOW THE SIXT TIME PVB- | LISHED. | LONDON, | Imprinted by *H.L.* for *Simon Waterſon*, | and *Mathew Lownes*. 1622.

Collation: fol. (in sixes), π², ¶², A–Z⁶, Aa–Dd⁶, Ee² (Ee1 + π⁴ ✱⁶) Ff–Zz⁶ Aaa–Bbb⁶. The Dublin title and its conjugate blank have been replaced by a cancel title and a conjugate blank. The *Supplement* of the Dublin printing has in this and the following issues usually been replaced by one of the former printings (i and ii).

Seventh edition, second issue. *STC* 22545.5.

COPIES: Y (i) BO² (imp. lacks supplement). TEXAS TECH, Lubbock, Texas; JJ (iii).

7*c*. (Another issue.) [*Within the pig-and-marjoram compartment, McK. &F.* 212]
THE | COVNTESSE | OF | PEMBROKES | ARCADIA. | WRITTEN BY SIR | PHILIP SIDNEY | Knight. | NOW THE SIXT TIME PVB- | LISHED. | LONDON, | Imprinted by *H.L.* for *Simon*, | *Waterſon*. 1622.

Collation: as 7*b*.

Seventh edition, third issue, *STC* 22545.7

COPIES: O (ii). O¹² (iii, *a*) (this copy has Hh2, 3 missigned 'Gg2' and 'Gg3'). SHEF. M⁴ (imp.). BRISTOL; Y (i). ILL, TEX, MCG; JJ (ii, *a*; Hh3 missigned 'Gg3').

7*d*. (Another issue.) [*Within the pig-and-marjoram compartment, McK. &F.* 212]
THE | COVNTESSE | OF | PEMBROKES | ARCADIA. | WRITTEN BY SIR | PHILIP SIDNEY | Knight. | NOW THE SIXT TIME PVB- | LISHED, WITH NEW | ADDITIONS. | LONDON, | Imprinted by *H.L.* for *Mathew* | *Lownes*. 1622.

Collation: as 7*b*.

Seventh edition, fourth issue. *STC* 22546.

COPIES: L (C.21.d.22. (ii)). O⁷; F (i). N (ii). BO². DAR; JJ (ii).

7*e*. (Another issue.) [*Within the pig-and-marjoram compartment, McK. &F.* 212]
THE | COVNTESSE | OF | PEMBROKES | ARCADIA. | WRITTEN BY SIR | PHILIP SIDNEY, | Knight. | NOW THE SIXT TIME PVB- | LISHED. | *LONDON* | Imprinted by *H.L.* for *Matthew* | *Lownes*. 1623.

Collation: as 7*b*.

Seventh edition, fifth issue. *STC* 22546a.

COPIES: L (12403.g.8. (i)). L^{30}. O (i). C^3. D^6. E. LIV^3. LEEDS PL; HD (i). F (ii); BUXTON (ii). JJ (2, one i, one ii).

8*a*. [*Within an elaborate decorative compartment, McK. & F.* 224] THE | COVNTESSE | OF | PEMBROKES | *Arcadia.* | Written by Sir *Philip Sidney* | KNIGHT. | Now the fixt time publiſhed, | *with ſome new Additions.* | [*rule*] | Alſo a ſupplement of a defect in | *the third part of this Hiſtorie*, | By Sir W. ALEX-ANDER. | LONDON, | Printed by *W.S.* for *Simon* | *Waterſon.* | 1627.

Collation: fol. (in sixes), π^4, A–Z^6, Aa–Zz^6, Aaa–Bbb^6, 'Yy'^{6}, 'Zz'^{6}, Eee–Fff^6. Pp. [8] 1–37, 48 ('38' correct in some copies), 39–46, 37, 48–93, 96, 95–152, 253, 154–6, 357, 358, 159–66, 377, 368, 169–482, [483], [484], 485–575, 676, 541–64, 601–24. First three leaves signed (−π1, 2, 3−Sf2; Ccc and Ddd are missigned 'Yy' and 'Zz' because the printer followed the signatures in the Dublin edition from which this edition was set.

Contents: π1, blank: π2^r, title; π2^v, blank; π3^{rv}, Sidney's preface to the Countess of Pembroke; π4^{rv}, Sanford's preface to the Reader; A1^r–Sf1^v, *Arcadia*; Sf2^r, title: *A* | SIXTH BOOKE, | TO | THE COVNTESSE | OF PEMBROKES | ARCADIA: | Written by *R.B.* of Lincolnes | Inne Eſquire. | [*rule*] | *Sat, ſi bene; ſi male, nimium.* | [*rule*] | [*device, McK.* 149] | [*rule*] | LONDON, | Printed by *H.L.* and *R.Y.* | 1628.; Sf2^v, blank; Sf3^r, Beling's preface to the Reader; Sf3^v–Xx2^v, text; Xx2^v–Yy6^r, *Sonnets*; Yy6^v–Bbb1^v, *Defence of Poesie*; Bbb2^r–Fff3^r, *Astrophel and Stella*; Fff3^v–Fff6^v, *The May Lady*.

The bulk of the book was printed by William Stansby, the *Sixth Book* by Lownes and Young. This is a reprint of the former editions, with the addition of Sir Richard Beling's additional chapter. This had previously appeared separately in quarto, in Dublin 1624 (*STC* 1805). H. Lownes's part was assigned to G. Cole and G. Latham 6 November 1628; to R. Young 6 December 1630.

Eighth edition, first issue. *STC* 22547.

COPIES: L. L^2. L^{38} (imp.). O. O^9. O^{21}. C. C^2. C^4. C^5. D^2. M (?). BRADFORD PUBLIC LIBRARY. SHEF.; HN. HD. Y. F (3). CH. N. CHI. BO. ILL. COR. WIS. CU.; NW. WEL. ROYAL LIBRARY, COPENHAGEN; BUXTON.JJ. (2). PENSHURST. QUARITCH, cat. 1027, item 195, 1983.

8*b*. (Another issue.) i. [*Within the pig-and-marjoram compartment, McK. & F.* 212] THE | COVNTESSE | OF PEMBROKES | ARCADIA. | Written by Sir PHILIP SIDNEY | KNIGHT. | Now the ſeuenth time publiſhed, | *with ſome new Additions.* | With the ſupplement of a Defect in the third | *part of this Hiſtory*, *by Sir* W. A. *Knight.* | Whereunto is now added a fixth BOOKE, | *By* R.B. *of Lincolnes Inne, Eſq.* | [*rule*] | LONDON printed by H.L. and R.Y. and are | fold by S. WATERSON in S. Pauls Church- | yard, 1629.

ii. [*as* i, *but with variant imprint*] . . . LONDON printed by H.L. and R.Y. and are | fold by R. MOORE in S. Dunftons Church- | yard, 1629.

Collation: fol. (in sixes), π^4 (−π2), A–Z^6, Aa–Zz^6, Aaa–Bbb^6, 'Yy'^{6}, 'Zz'^{6}, Eee–Fff^6.
Contents: π1^r, cancel title; π1^v, blank; original π2 excised; π3^r–Fff3^v as A.
A copy of 8*b*ii in my possession still has π1 and π2 *in situ.* π1.4 and π2.3 are conjugate, and from examination of the watermark in other copies, it appears that the cancel title is printed on the blank, the conjugate of π4.

Eighth edition, second issue. i. *STC* 22548; *b STC* 22548a.

COPIES: i. L.O.C. E; TOKYO; Y; BUXTON. 2, i and ii. O.C.RGU.; HN. Y. N.; JJ (3, ii).

9. [*Within the pig-and-marjoram compartment, McK. & F.* 212] THE | COUNTESSE | OF PEMBROKES | ARCADIA. | Written by Sir PHILIP

SIDNEY | KNIGHT. | Now the eighth time publiſhed, | *with ſome new Addi-tions.* | With the ſupplement of a Defect in the third | *part of this Hiſtory, by Sir* W. A. *Knight.* | [*rule*] | Whereunto is now added a ſixth BOOKE, | *By* R.B. *of Lincolnes Inne, Eſq.* | [*rule*] | LONDON, | Printed for SIMON WATERSON and | R. YOUNG, Anno 1633.

Collation: fol. (in sixes), ¶⁴, A–Z⁶, Aa–Zz⁶, Aaa–Fff⁶. Pp. [8] 1–156, 357–8, 159–66, 377, 368, 169–92, 293, 194–259, 250, 261–482 [483] [484] 485–604, 607, 606–7, 606, 609–24. First three leaves signed (−¶1, 2; ¶3 signed ¶).

Contents: π1, blank; π2ʳ, title; π2ᵛ, blank; ¶3ʳᵛ, Sidney's dedication to the Countess of Pembroke; ¶4ʳᵛ, Sanford's preface to the Reader; A1ʳ–Sf1ᵛ, *Arcadia*; Sf2ʳ, title to the sixth book by Beling, as in 8, but with new imprint: LONDON, | Printed for *T.D.* and *R.Y.* | 1633.; Sf2ᵛ, blank; Sf3ʳ, Beling's preface; Sf3ᵛ–Xx2ʳ, the *Sixth Book*; Xx2ᵛ–Yy6ʳ, the *Sonnets*; Yy6ᵛ–Bbb1ᵛ, *Defence of Poesie*; Bbb2ʳ–Fff3ʳ, *Astrophel and Stella*; Fff3ᵛ–Fff6ᵛ, *The May Lady.*

T.D. presumably stands for Thomas Downes. This is a page-for-page reprint of 8, with no new material. The four preliminary leaves form one quire; watermarks clearly show this, despite the odd position (on the third leaf) of the signature ¶.

Ninth edition. *STC* 22549.

COPIES: L. O. O¹⁷. O²¹. L³⁰. L⁴³. C⁵ (imp.). M. M². ETON. NEK; HN. HD. Y (2, one imp.). F (3). CH. NY. WASH². ILL. MICH. GRO. KAN. V. CHI. PN. PEN. TEX; BUXTON. WILLIAM M. BOND. JJ.

10a. [*Within the pig-and-marjoram compartment, McK. & F.* 212] THE | COUNTESSE | OF PEMBROKES | ARCADIA, | Written by Sir PHILIP SIDNEY | KNIGHT. | Now the ninth time publiſhed, with a | twofold ſupple-ment of a defect in the third | Book: the one by Sʳ W. A. Knight; the | other, by Mʳ *Ja. Johnſtoun* Scoto-Brit. | dedilcated to K. *James,* and now | annexed to this work, for | the Readers be- | nefit [*rule*] | Whhreunto is alſo added a ſixth Book, | By R.B. of Lincolnes Inne, Eſq. | [*rule*] | *LONDON* [last 'N' turned], | printed for *J. Waterſon* and *Roung,* 1638.

Collation: fol. known only from preliminaries π⁴, unsigned.

Contents: π1 absent, presumably blank; π2ʳ, title, π2ᵛ, blank; π3ʳᵛ, Sidney's dedication to the Countess of Pembroke; π4ʳᵛ, Sanford's preface to the Reader.

Tenth edition, first issue. *STC* 22550, footnote.

The layout of Sidney's dedication to his sister and Sanford's to the Reader does not follow that of the 1633 folio (no. 9), whereas the final version, 10d, reprints 9 line for line and page for page. The present has several misprints. It is not obvious why the layout for the preliminaries was abandoned, but the table below enumerates the transition to 10d, via 10b and 10c. There is a watermark (a heraldic shield) in π2, but none in π3 or π4, supporting the view that the first quire consisted of four leaves. There is a double impression of the type on π3ʳ in blind, suggesting that this is an early trial setting, as do also the turned type (see table below). See also *The Library*, 5th Series, No. 22, 1 (March 1967), 67–9.

COPY: JJ (π2–4).

10b. (Another issue.) [*Title as* 10a, *except that* 'dedilcated' *has been corrected to* 'dedicated'. *The other misprints persist.*]

Collation: fol. (in sixes), π⁴, rest as 10d.

Contents: title and contents as 10a, the rest as 10d..

Tenth edition, second issue. Not in *STC*.

This issue has the mentioned correction on the title. The preliminaries no longer show turned type; see table below.

COPY: MARSHALL W. RISSMAN.

10c. (Another issue.) [*Title as* 10*b.*]

Collation: fol. (in sixes), π², ❧², rest as 10*d*.

Contents: π1, blank; π2ʳ, title, π2ᵛ, blank; ❧² and the rest as 10*d*, except that Johnstoun's supplement (aa1ʳ–bb4ʳ) is bound between ❧2 and A1. ❧2 unsigned.

Tenth edition, third issue. Not in *STC*.

The copy in my collection is in contemporary black morocco, gilt. The blank π1 is present and conjugate with π2, the title, which has a watermark of a large heraldic shield (similar to that in 10*a*). ❧1 is conjugate with ❧2, which has a watermark of a jug.

COPY: JJ (Graham Pollard, Sotheby's 4 July 1978, lot 458–Maggs, cat. 994, item 2855, 1979).

10*d*. (Another issue.) [*Within the pig-and-marjoram compartment, McK. & F.* 212] THE | COUNTESSE | OF PEMBROKES | ARCADIA, | Written by Sir PHILIP SIDNEY | KNIGHT. | Now the ninth time publiſhed, with a | twofold ſupplement of a defect in the third | Book: the one by Sʳ *W. A.* Knight; the | other, by Mʳ *Ja. Johnſtoun* Scoto-Brit. | dedicated to K. *James*, and now | annexed to this work, for | the Readers be- | nefit. | [*rule*] | Whereunto is alſo added a sixth Booke, | By *R.B.* of Lincolnes Inne, Eſq. | [*rule*] | *LONDON,* | Printed for *J. Waterſon* and *R. Young*, 1638.

Collation: fol. (in sixes), π⁴, A–Z⁶, Aa–Zz⁶, Aaa–Fff⁶, aa⁶, bb⁴. Pp. [8] 1–97, 9, 99–156, 357, 158–66, 177, 368, 169–259, 250, 261–434, 437, 436–78, 467, 468, 481–2, [483], [484], 485–535, 530, 537–624, [20]. First three leaves signed (−π1, 2; π3 signed ❧; −Y2; Zz3 missigned 'Zz2.').

Contents: π1, blank; π2ʳ, title; π2ᵛ, blank; π3ʳᵛ, Sidney's dedication to the Countess of Pembroke; π4ʳᵛ, Sanford's preface; A1ʳ–Sf1ᵛ, *Arcadia*; Sf2ʳ, title to Beling's *Sixth Book*, imprint now reads: LONDON, | Printed for *T.D.* and *R.Y.* 1638. | Sf2; Sf2ᵛ, blank; Sf3ʳ, Beling's preface; Sf3ᵛ–Xx2ʳ, the *Sixth Book*; Xx2ᵛ–Yy6ʳ, the *Sonnets*, Yy6ᵛ–Bbb1ᵛ, *Defence of Poesie*; Bbb2ʳ–Fff3ʳ, *Astrophel and Stella*; Fff3ᵛ–Fff6ᵛ, *The May Lady*; aa1ʳᵛ, James Johnstoun's preface to 'James Sixt'; aa2ʳ–bb4ʳ, *A Supplement to the third booke of Arcadia.*; bb4ᵛ, blank.

Tenth edition, fourth issue. *STC* 22550.

The layout of the title, with corrections, was retained, but the preliminaries, as in 10*c*, have been reset from the 1633 edition. It is the commonest of the early *Arcadia* s. The first four leaves now form one sheet, for both BUXTON and JJ have watermarks in π3 and π4. Harper printed quires A–O, Young the rest.

COPIES: L. L⁴³. O. O¹¹. O³⁹. C. C⁹. C¹⁷. E. E² (imp.). NMU. SOUTHAMPTON PUBLIC LIBRARY. CREDITON. INN; HN. HD. Y. F (5, 2 imp.). LC. N. CHI. ILL. CAL². PH. VERMONT UNIVERSITY. HAMILTON COLLEGE, CLINTON, NY. CLAREMONT, CAL. BO². WELLESLEY. MICH. PML. DAR. PN. LEHIGH. TEX.; BUXTON. JJ. PENSHURST.

The table on pp. 302–3 sets out the main differences between the four issues of the 1638 *Arcadia*.

11. THE | COUNTESS | OF | PEMBROKE'S | ARCADIA | WRITTEN BY | Sʳ PHILIP SIDNEY | *KNIGHT.* | [*rule*] | *The tenth Edition.* | With his Life and Death; a brief Table of the principal | heads, and ſom other new Addi-tions. | [*rule*] | [*printer's device, McK.* 404, *with initials altered to I. Y.*] | [*rule*] | *LON-DON,* | Printed by *William Du-Gard*: and are to bee ſold by | *George Calvert,*

10a

π3ʳ [*Two rules above a rectangular headpiece with a central seated Bacchus, satyrs with bow and arrow, rabbits, etc. (The same ornament is found on aa1ʳ, at the head of Johnstoun's dedication to King James).*]
TO MY | DEARE LADY | AND | SISTER, THE COUNTESSE | *of* PEMBROKE. |

Then follow 19 lines of text, opening with a large ornamental initial 'H', indenting five lines. This initial also occurs on aa1ʳ.

last line: 'in loose sheets of paper, most of it in your presence, the'
catchword: 'reft'
line 13: 'such frinds'
line 14: 'theballance' [no space]
There is no signature.

π3ᵛ [*headline between double rules:*] *The Epistle Dedicatory.* | [ordinary italic 'E', 'st' tied.] 20 lines of text.
last line: '*Sidneis.*', signed: '*Your loving brother,* | PHILIP SIDNEY. |'
line 5: [■]would have growne a monster[■] [two

10b

as 10a.

no 'turned letters'

10c and 10d

π3ʳ [*Two rules above a narrow rectangular headpiece composed of three rows of small ornaments, acorns, vases, and fleur-de-lys.*]
TO MY DEARE LADY | AND SISTER, THE COUN- | TESSE OF PEMBROKE. |

Then follow 23 lines of text, opening with the same large initial found in the early setting.

last line: 'it, if it had not beene in some way delivered, would have |'
catchword: 'growne'
line 13: 'such friends' 'the ballance'
signature: ❧ [under 'way' of last line]

π3ᵛ [*headline between double rules:*] *The Epistle Dedicatory.* | [upper case epsilon and long italic s] 14 lines of text.
last line: 'principall ornament to the family of the *Sidneis.*', signed as the earlier state.

'turned letters' in Moxon's sense (*Mechanick exercises* (1958), p. 353)]

   line 7: 'But his chief safety shal be ▮ the' ['turned letter']

   line 10: 'geater offender'

   line 18: 'Prayes'

π4^r [*Two rules above a large rectangular headpiece, with a central half-length female figure, holding a vase from which emerge branches with flowers, butterflies, birds, etc.* (41 × 145 mm.).]

TO THE READER.|

   Then follow 22 lines of text set in italic with a large ornamental initial 'T' indenting four lines. this initial also occurs on 2L4^v.

   last line: 'he either sees, or from wiser judgements than his own may heare'|

   catchword: 'that'

   line 11: 'Which part wth what'

π4^v [*Running title between double rules*] To the Reader.|

   29 lines of text set in italic signed 'H.S.'

   line 12: 'Lips. *If it be true that likenesse*'

as 10a

as 10a

line 1: 'growne a monster,'

line 2: 'But his chiefe safety shall

line 3: 'be, the'

line 6: 'greater offender'

line 13: 'prayes'

π4^r [*Two rules above a narrow rectangular headpiece composed of small ornaments, three rows as on π3^r*].

TO THE READER.|

   Then follow 26 lines of text set in italic with a bigger initial 'T' indenting five lines, found also on V2^r.

   last line: 'der: Never was Arcadia free from the cumber of such Cattel.|'

   catchword: 'To'

   line 11: 'Which part with what'

π4^v ditto

   24 lines set in italic signed 'H.S.'

   line 7: 'Lippes'

   line 8: 'that likenesse'

at the half Moon in the new buildings in *Paul's* | Church-yard; and *Thomas Pierrepont*, at the Sun in | *Paul's* Church-Yard, M.DC.LV.

Collation: fol. (in sixes), frontispiece, A⁴, b⁴, c⁴, d⁴, B–Z⁶, Aa–Zz⁶, Aaa–Iii⁶, Kkk². Pp. [34], 1–624, [28]. First three leaves signed (–A1–A3–b3–c3–d3–Tt2–Kkk2, A2 mis-signed 'A3', Dd2 missigned 'D2').

Contents: frontispiece-portrait of Sidney, reversed copy of Elstrack's engraving (*Hind* II, 189, 55) in the *Baziliωlogia* series; in a panel below the Sidney arms; A1ʳ, title; A1ᵛ, blank; A2ʳᵛ, Sidney's dedication to the Countess of Pembroke; A3ʳᵛ, Sanford's preface to the Reader; A4ʳ–c1ʳ, *The Life and Death of Sʳ Philip Sidney*, signed φιλοφιλιπωος; c1ᵛ, extract from Camden's *Annales* recording Sidney's death; c2ʳ–d4ʳ, commendatory verses from Owen's *Epigrams*, John Foot, the New College verses *Peplus*, the Oxford *Exequiae*, the Cambridge *Lachrymae*, and the verses in St Paul's; d4ᵛ, extract from Heylin's *Cosmography*; B1ʳ–Tt1ᵛ, *Arcadia*; Tt2ʳ, title to Beling's sixth book, with imprint: *LONDON,* | Printed by *William Du-Gard*, 1654; Tt2ᵛ, blank; Tt3ʳ, Beling's preface; Tt3ᵛ–Yy2ʳ, the *Sixth Book*; Yy2ᵛ–Zz6ʳ, *Sonnets*; Zz6ᵛ–Ccc1ᵛ, *Defence of Poesie*; Ccc2ʳ–Ggg3ʳ, *Astrophel and Stella*; Ggg3ᵛ–Ggg6ᵛ, *The May Lady*; Hhh1ʳᵛ, Johnstoun's preface to James VI; Hhh2ʳ–Iii4ʳ, *A Supplement to the third book of Arcadia*; Iii4ᵛ–Iii5ᵛ, *A Remedie for Love*; Iii6ʳ–Kkk1ᵛ, an *Alphabetical Table*; Kkk2, blank.

This edition reprints 10, but adds poems on Sidney, an anonymous *Life*, and the *Remedie for Love.*

Eleventh edition, *Wing* S3768.

COPIES: L. O.; HN. F. HD. BR. CHI.; RINGLER. BUXTON. JJ (2). PENSHURST, etc.

12. THE | COUNTESS | OF | PEMBROKE'S | ARCADIA | WRITTEN BY | Sir Philip Sidney | *KNIGHT.* | [*rule*] | *The eleventh Edition.* | With his Life and Death; a brief Table of the principal | Heads, and ſom other new Addi-tions. | [*rule*] | [*printer's device, McK. 404, initials altered to I.Y.*] | [*rule*] | *LONDON,* | Printed by *Henry Lloyd*, for *William Du-Gard*: and | are to bee ſold by *George Calvert*, at the half Moon in the new | buildings; and *Thomas Pierre-pont*, at the Sun in St. *Paul's* | Church-yard, MDCLXII.

Collation: fol. (in sixes), A⁴, b⁴, c⁴, d⁴, B–Z⁶, Aa–Zz⁶, Aaa–Iii⁴, Kkk². Pp. [32], 1–624, [28]. First three leaves signed (–A1–A3–b3–c3–d3–Tt2–Kkk2).

Contents: as 11, except that the title to Beling's *Sixth Book* (Tt2ʳ) has the imprint: *LONDON,* | Printed by *Henry Lloyd*, MDCLXII.

This is a page-for-page reprint of 11. It has no portrait. Mr John Sparrow gave me a copy of this edition (formerly in the possession of James Stewart Geikie, MD) which is bound in a resplendent contemporary red morocco binding, gilt in the same manner and with the same tools as the Third Folio from the Ham House Collection (Sotheby sale, 21 June 1938, illustrated) for the mysterious 'S.P', whose initials also here appear on the spine. This collector must have had very high standards and one wishes that his identity could be established.

Twelfth edition. *Wing* S3769.

COPIES: L. O; HD. F; BUXTON JJ (2) etc.

13. THE | COUNTESS | OF | PEMBROKE'S | ARCADIA | WRITTEN BY | Sir Philip Sidney | *KNIGHT.* | [*rule*] | *The Thirteenth Edition.* | [*rule*] | With his Life and Death; a brief Table of the principal | Heads, and ſome other new Additions. | [*double rule*] | *LONDON,* | Printed for *George Calvert*, at the *Golden-Ball* in | *Little-Britain*, MDCLXXIV.

Collation: fol. (in sixes), frontispiece, A⁴, b⁴, c⁴, d⁴, B–Z⁶, Aa–Zz⁶, Aaa–Iii⁶, Kkk². Pp. [34], 1–624, [28]. First three leaves signed (–A1–A3–b3–c3–d3–Tt2–Kkk2).

Contents: as 12, except that a portrait again has been added as frontispiece. This is either a drastic reworking or a copy of the portrait in 11. The shaded background of the former is now white, and the space below the portrait no longer carries the Sidney arms, but a legend: 'The true Portraicture . . .' (four lines). The subtitle at Tt2 has the imprint: *LONDON* | Printed for *George Calvert*, at the *Golden-Ball* in | *Little Britain*, MDCLXXIV.

A page-for-page reprint of 12. Although no edition is called the twelfth on the title, there is no doubt that none has disappeared. The edition numbering was erratic (the 1599 piracy did not help) and it appears to be a coincidence that the 'Thirteenth' really is the thirteenth edition.

Court Book D, Stationers' Company for 1 March 1674/5 reads: 'Ordered that the Assignm^t of part of Sr Phi. Sidneys Arcadia be forthwth Entered to Mr. Jonathan Edwin wth a Salvo Jure' and: 'Ordered that the Assignm^t of one Moyety of Sr Willm Alexanders Additions to the Arcadia be forthwth entered to Mr George Calvert a Member now sitting at the Table wth a Salvo Jure'. These entries are matched by transfers in the Stationers' Register on 13 March 1674/5. Calvert transfers to Edwin his rights in *Arcadia* 'wth addicons'. Edwin transfers to Calvert his rights in Alexander's Additions.

Thirteenth edition. *Wing* S3770.

COPIES: L. O. C. (2, one lacks portrait). M; HN. F. HD. Y.; BUXTON. JJ. PENSHURST, etc.

14*a*. THE | WORKS | OF | The HONOURABLE | Sr *Philip Sidney*, Kt. | In PROSE and VERSE. | [*rule*] | In THREE VOLUMES. | [*rule*] | CONTAIN-ING, | I. The COUNTESS of *Pembroke's* ARCADIA. | II. The DEFENSE of POESY. | III. ASTROPHEL and STELLA. | IV. The REMEDY of LOVE; SONNETS, &c. | V. The LADY of *May*. A MASQUE. | VI. The LIFE of the AUTHOR. | [*rule*] | [*quotation from Spenser's Astrophel*] | [*rule*] | The FOUR-TEENTH EDITION. | [*rule*] | *LONDON*: | Printed for E. TAYLOR, A. BETTESWORTH, | E. CURLL, W. MEARS, and R. GOSLING. | MDCCXXV. PRICE 15s.

Collation: 8°, Vol. I: A^6, A^8 B^8, B–Z^8, Aa–Dd^8, Ee^2 + 3 plates.
    Vol. II: π^1, B–Z^8, Aa–Hh^8, [Ii]^1 [=π2] + 3 plates.
    Vol. III: π^2, A–D^8, B–N^8 + 1 plate.
Vol. I: pp. [12] 1–419. Vol. II: pp. [2] 401–881. Vol. III [4] 1–64, 1–184 [8].
First four leaves signed (Vol. I—^{1}A1—^{1}A4—Ee2. Vol. II—π1—[Ii]1. Vol. III—π1.2—A1—^{2}B1. Vol. I ^{1}A3 missigned 'A4'.).

Contents: Vol. I: Engraved portrait of Sidney by Vertue; A1^r, collective title as above; A1^v, blank; A2^r–A3^v, dedication to the Earl of Leicester by the editor (John Henley); A4^r, sub-title: THE WORKS . . . VOL. I . . . Printed in the Year MDCCXXV; A4^v, blank; A5^r–A6^v, Sidney's dedication to the Countess of Pembroke; ^{2}A1^r–B2^v The *Life of Sidney*; B3^r–B5^r, *Testimonies* by Camden, Carew, Heylin, Lloyd, Temple, Lee, and Philips; B5^v–B8^v, *Criticisms on Pastoral Writing*; ^{2}B1^r–Ee2^r, Books I and II of the *Arcadia*. An engraving by G. van der Gucht after L. Cheron precedes each book.
Vol. II: π1^r, subtitle: THE WORKS . . . VOL. II . . . Printed in the Year MDCCXXIV; π1^v, blank; B1^r–Ii1^r, Books III–V; an engraved plate by I. Pine after L. Cheron precedes each book.
Vol. III: π1^r, subtitle: THE WORKS . . . VOL. III . . . Printed in the Year MDCCXXIV; π1^v, blank; π2^r, *Explanation* of some Characters . . .; π2^v, blank; A1^r–D8^v, A SIXTH BOOK . . . Printed in the Year M.DCC.XXIV; ^{2}B1^r, sub-title: THE POETICAL WORKS . . . Printed in the Year M.DCC.XXIV; ^{2}B1^v, blank; ^{2}B2^r–E2^v, the *Defence of Poesie*; E3^r–K1^v, *Astrophel and Stella*; K2^r–K3^v, A *Remedy for Love*; K4^r–M4^v,

Sonnets and Translations; M5ʳ–N4ᵛ, *The Lady of May*; N5ʳ–N6ʳ, Postscript; N7ʳ–N8ᵛ, The Table. An engraving by G. van der Gucht before Book VI.

This is a reprint of 13 in a handier format. The poems are printed so that they could appear separately, with separate signatures and pagination, although I have never come across this section bound separately in an 18th-century binding. This is the first illustrated edition.

Fourteenth edition, first issue.

COPIES: L. O. JJ, etc.

14*b*. (Another issue.) THE | WORKS | of the HONOURABLE | *Sir* Philip Sidney, *Knt.* | In PROSE and VERSE. | [*rule*] | In THREE VOLUMES. | [*rule*] | CONTAINING, | I. The Countefs of PEMBROKE'S ARCADIA. | II. The DEFENCE of POESY. | III. ASTROPHEL and STELLA. | IV. The REMEDY of LOVE; SONNETS, *&c.* | V. The LADY of MAY. A MASQUE. | VI. The LIFE of the AUTHOR. | [*rule*] | [quotation from Spenser's *Astrophel*] | [*rule*] *The* FOURTEENTH EDITION. | [*rule*] | LONDON: | Printed for W. INNYS in *Pater-nofter-Row.*

Collation: 8°. Vol. I: π², 2π⁴, A⁸, B⁸, B–Z⁸, Aa–Dd⁸, Ee²+ 3 plates.
       Vols. II and III as 14*a*.
In Vol. I π2 is signed A2, 2π1 is correctly signed A3—correctly, that is, had the first six leaves formed one sheet. Only the title has been reset, as above.

Fourteenth edition, second issue.

COPY: BUXTON.

15. THE | WORKS | OF | THE HONOURABLE | Sir *Philip Sidney*, Kt. | In PROSE and VERSE. | [*rule*] | IN THREE VOLUMES. | [*rule*] | . . . THE FIFTEENTH EDITION. | [*rule*] | *DUBLIN:* | Printed by S. POWELL, | For T. MOORE, at *Erafmus's Head* in | *Dame-ftreet*, Bookfeller, MDCCXXXIX.

Collation: 12°, Vol. I: A⁴, B–S¹², T⁸. Vol. II: A⁴, B–P¹², Q⁶. Vol. III: A–N¹², O⁶. First five leaves signed.

Contents: as 14. Vol. I: A1ʳ collective title; A2ʳ, sub-title to Vol. I. Vol. II: A1ʳ, sub-title to Vol. II; Vol. III: A1ʳ, sub-title to Vol. III; D2ʳ, sub-title to Beling's *Sixth Book*; F11ʳ, sub-title to the Poetical Works; Q6ʳᵛ, *Books Printed for, and Sold by T. Moore* . . .

This edition is a close reprint of the 1725 London edition, without any portrait or other engravings. It is the last of the old editions of *Arcadia*, which was not reprinted till the following century.

Fifteenth edition.

COPIES: L. BUXTON. JJ, etc.

TRANSLATIONS

It is for some future writer to compile a complete list of translations of the *Arcadia*. M. Wilson (*Sir Philip Sidney* (1950), p. 142) quotes without giving the source the detail that a German admirer was able to reckon over thirty foreign editions. Marie de' Medici in 1622 sent Jean Baudoin to England to learn English and to translate the *Arcadia* (John Buxton, *Sir Philip Sidney and the English Renaissance* (1954), pp. 134–5). I have been able to find records and have examined some of the following translations. Few are represented in the British Library and the Bodleian.

French

15.11. L'ARCADIE DE LA COMTESSE DE PEMBROK ... Mise en nostre langue par I. Baudoin. A Paris. Chez Toussaint du Bray. 1624–5.

8°. Three volumes, each with an additional engraved title, and at the end of the preliminary matter in each of the three volumes the same engraved portrait of Sidney by L. de Courbes.

COPIES: L (imp.). An immaculate copy in the original reversed calf is 8°.S.137 Art in the Bodleian Library.

15.12. Another edition. Translated by Mlle Geneviève Chappelain. Paris. 1625.

8°. I–III. Each part with an additional engraved title.

COPY: L.

15.14. Unpublished translation by Jean Loiseau de Tourval, c.1605–11. Bodleian Library (MS Rawl. D.920).

Dutch

15.21. D'Engelsche Arcadia ... voor Adrian Gerritsz en Felix van Sambix de Jonghe. Delft. 1639.

12°. Three volumes. Engraved title to each part.

15.22. Another edition: ... de tweeden Druck ... Delft. 1641/1642.

12°. Three volumes. Engraved title to each part.

COPY: L.

15.23. Another edition: ... den derden Druck. Gerrit Willemsz Doornick. Amsterdam. 1659.

12°. Three volumes. Engraved title to each part.

COPY: Bodleian Library (Vet. B3 f. 229).

Italian

15.31. L'Arcadia della Contessa di Pembrok. Portata dal Francese dal Signor Livio Alessandri. Venice. 1659.

German

15.41. ARCADIA Der Gräffin von Pembrock. ... Nachmalen von unterschiedlichen vornehmen Personen in Frantzösische; Nun aber aus beyden in unser Hochteutsche Sprach fleissig und treulich übersetzt Durch VALENTINUM THEOCRITVM von Hirschberg [*i.e. Martin Opitz*]. Mit schönen neuen Kupfferstücken gezieret. Gedruckt zu Franckfurt am Mayn bey Caspar Rötell In Verlegung Matthäi Merian. 1629.

4°. π¹,):(⁴, A–Ddddd⁴. Three leaves signed (−):(1).

Contents: π1ʳ, engraved title, dated 1630; π1ᵛ, blank;):(1ʳ, letterpress title;):(1ᵛ, engraved coat of arms of the Landgräfin zu Hessen;):(2ʳ–):(3ʳ, Merian's dedication to the Landgräfin;):(3ᵛ–):(4ᵛ, Opitz's preface to the Reader, signed V.T.; A1ʳ–Ddddd3ᵛ, the text (paginated 1–766); Ddddd4ʳ, postscript:

L.S.

Habes hic, LECTOR, quoad verba, flores & elegantias totius Antiquitatis Graecae & Latinae; quoad res, characterismos omnium virtutum & vitiorum: ut authorem hunc viri & authores nostri temporis celeberrimi jure vocârint *INCOMPARABILEM, INIMITA-BILEM* SIDNEIVM.

Ddddd4ᵛ, blank.

This, the first German translation, is perhaps the most remarkable of all, for it has a series of twenty full-page engravings by Merian illustrating episodes in the book printed in the text. They were used again in the following edition, but are really too large to fit comfortably into an octavo page. They merit republication; they are little known, probably because the book is rare.

COPIES: L. Royal Library, Copenhagen. A presentation copy, bound in red velvet, with gilt gauffred edges, given to Landgraf Georg II of Hessen, the husband of the dedicatee, is in the writer's collection.

15.42. Another edition. . . . übersetz von M[artin] O[pitz] V[on] B[reslau] . . . Frankfurt am Mayn in Wolffgang Hoffmans Buchtruckerey . . . 1638.

8°. A–Rrr⁸, Sss². The last leaf has a brief life of Sidney. This edition reprints Merian's twenty engravings in the text, really too large for the smaller page.

COPIES: L. Bodleian Library, Antiq.e.G. $\dfrac{1638}{3}$.

15.43. Another edition. Leiden. 1642.

Peter Juel, in the list of books he bought on his way back to Denmark after his sojourn in Oxford (*Nordisk Tidsskrift for Bok-och Biblioteksvaesen*, vol. XXXV, 1948, p. 149) during 1646/7, notes: 'Arcadia Herrn Philippsen von Sidney: zu Leiden. anno 1642.' This must be this edition, but I have been unable to trace that copy.

15.44. Another edition. Frankfurt. 1643.

8°.

COPY: L.

15.45. Another edition. Leiden. 1646.

12°. Two volumes.

COPY: L.

MRS STANLEY'S ADAPTATION OF THE *ARCADIA*

15.61. Sir *PHILIP SIDNEY'S* | ARCADIA, | MODERNIZ'D | [*double rule*] | By Mrs. *STANLEY.* | [*double rule*] | [*vignette of Britannia*] | [*double rule*] | *LONDON*: | Printed in the Year MDCCXXV.

Collation: fol. π² a² b² B–Z² Aa–Zz² Aaa–Zzz² Aaaa–Zzzz² 5A–5Z² 6A–6O². 11 [*12*] [1]–511 [512]. First leaf signed [–π¹]

Contents: π1ʳ, title; π1ᵛ, blank; π2ʳᵛ, A List of Subscribers' Names; a1ʳ–a2ᵛ, *To Her Royal Highness the Princess of Wales*, dedication signed D. Stanley; b1ʳ–b2ᵛ, Preface, unsigned; B1ʳ–6 O2ʳ, text; 6 O2ᵛ, blank.

[*Another state of the title:*] [*within double rules*] Sir *PHILIP SIDNEY'S* . . .

First Edition. Apart from the presence or absence of double rules, the two states are otherwise identical, from the same setting of type. Though copies are often described as being on 'large paper', all copies I have seen appear to be on the same fine and thick paper, and it is possible there were no 'small-paper copies'.

ASTROPHEL AND STELLA

16. Syr P.S. | *His Aftrophel and Stella.* | Wherein the excellence of fweete | Poefie is concluded | (∴) | *To the end of which are added, fundry| other rare Sonnets of diuers Noble| men* and Gentlemen. | (★) | [*type ornament*] | At London, | Printed [*by J. Charlewood*] for Thomas Newman. | *Anno. Domini.* 1591.

Collation: 4°, A–L⁴, pp. [8] 1–80.

Contents: A1ʳ, title; A1ᵛ, blank; A2ʳᵛ, dedication to 'Ma. Frauncis Flower, Esquire', signed Tho: Newman; A3ʳ–A4ᵛ, 'Somewhat to reade for them that list,' signed Tho: Nashe.; B1ʳ–I3ʳ, 'Sir P.S. His Astrophel And Stella', 107 unnumbered sonnets + ten songs 'Other Sonnets of variable verse'; I3ᵛ–L4ᵛ, 'Poems and Sonets of Sundrie other Noble men and Gentlemen.', i.e. twenty-eight sonnets signed 'Daniell', five sonnets by Campion, a poem by Greville (signed E.O.) and an anonymous poem 'If flouds of teares'.

In spite of Newman's claim (in the preface) to accuracy, this, the first quarto, is printed from a corrupt text. There are several printer's errors. The publication was unauthorized, and in the following February Daniel published a corrected text of twenty-four of his sonnets. The book was not entered in the Stationers' Register, and from the Wardens' accounts for 18 September 1591 it appears that the book was called in.

First edition. *STC* 22536.

COPIES: BRITISH LIBRARY. G.11543. (Grenville); TRINITY COLLEGE, CAMBRIDGE. VL.,7.51. (Beaupré Bell, 1730.) Lacks A2–4. PENSHURST. Lacks A1–4.

17. ❧ SIR P.S. HIS | ASTROPHEL AND | *STELLA*. | Wherein the excellence of fweete | Poefie is concluded. | [*type ornament*] | At London, | Printed [*by J. Danter*] for Thomas Newman. | *Anno Domini.* 1591.

Collation: 4°, A–H⁴, pp. [2] 1–61 (62).

Contents: A1ʳ, title; A1ᵛ, blank; A2ʳ–H4ᵛ, 'Sir P.S. His Astrophel and Stella', 107 unnumbered sonnets + ten other poems.

A corrected second edition of 16, omitting Newman's dedication and Nashe's preface. The corrections, made by collating a copy of 16 with the manuscript, were pretty haphazard, and Newman cannot have taken the rebuff over the first quarto very seriously. The poems by other authors were omitted.

Second edition. *STC* 22537.

COPIES: BRITISH LIBRARY. G. 11544. (Grenville); BRITISH LIBRARY. f.39.c.34. (Ant. à Wood); a copy was formerly in REPRESENTATIVE CHURCH BODY, DUBLIN. Cashel x.7. Lacks H1 and H4; HUNTINGTON LIBRARY 69457. (B. H. Bright–(8 Apr. 1845, lot 5242, £28 to Rodd). Corser-Huth (8 July 1918, lot 6863, £580 to G. D. Smith).) Rough edges, crimson mor. by Rivière. ⟩⟩ a fragment, leaves B2 and C2 used as endleaves in Edward Livelie's *The True Chronologie of the Times of the Persian Empire* 1597 in contemporary limp vellum (Sotheby's, 28 Nov. 1961, lot 381, A. Gifford–Baptist College Library, Bristol).

18. Syr P.S. | *His Astrophel and Stella.* | Wherein the excellence of fweete | Poefie is concluded. | (∴) | *To the end of which are added, fundry| other rare Sonnets of diuers Noble| men and Gentlemen.* | (★★★) | [*publisher's device, McK.* 167β] | At London | Printed [*by F. Kingston*] for *Matthew Lownes.*

Collation: 4°, A–K⁴. No pagination. First three leaves signed (−A1.).

Contents: A1ʳ, title; A1ᵛ, blank; A2ʳ–F3ᵛ, Astrophel and Stella; F4ʳ–H3ʳ, 'Other sonnets of variable verse.'; H3ᵛ–K4ᵛ, 'Poems and Sonnets of sundrie other Noblemen and Gentlemen.'

The device is in the second state, after 'T.M.' were removed. The earliest use of this form in a dated book by Lownes is in 1598, from which year this reprint of Newman's first quarto probably dates. The printer was probably Felix Kyngston (see also John Buxton, 'On the Date of *Sir P.S. His Astrophel and Stella . . . Printed for Matthew Lownes.*', *Bodleian Library Record*, vol. VI, no. 5, 1960, p. 614).

Third edition. *STC* 22538.

COPIES: BODLEIAN LIBRARY. Malone 617 (6). Bound in early 18th-century calf with Spenser's *Complaints*, 1591; *Colin Clout*, 1595; *Foure Hymnes*, 1596; *Prothalamion*, 1596; *Shepheardes Calender*, 1597; and *Defence of Poesie*, n.d.; HUNTINGTON LIBRARY. Title in facsimile, top corners throughout restored, also some lower corners; some leaves defective. Crimson straight-grain mor. (Britwell, 16 Dec. 1919, lot 94, £270 to G. D. Smith); ARTHUR J. HOUGHTON, JR. Purple levant mor. (Sotheby's 6 May 1901, £200–W. A. White, Cat. 1926, p. 181–Rosenbach, Blue Poetry Cat. 1941, no. 677, $9750.), sold Christie's, Pt. II, 12 June 1980, lot 431, £24,000 to Fleming.

THE PSALMS OF DAVID

To Sidney the Psalms were poetry of the sublimest kind and it was natural that he should attempt to turn them into verse, using a different stanza for each. The Book of Common Prayer and the Geneva Bible were his sources, Marot's and Beza's French Psalter his model. He completed forty-three Psalms before his death, and the Countess of Pembroke paraphrased the rest. Sir William Drummond refers to an edition of 'some psalms of Dauid to the french Tunes, in Meter. S. Philip Sidney | Iosua Syluester | Francis Dauison | . . . 40.41.42S. Phil. Sydney. . . . All the other psalmes by Io. Standish. | The Booke is printed for Iohn Standish | dwelling in St. Bartholomews neer Christ Church | in the Long Walk' (Nat. Library of Scotland, MS 2060, f. 150). Such an edition does not appear to have survived, and apart from a single psalm printed in the *Guardian* no. 18 (1713) and seven in Henry Harrington's *Nugæ Antiquæ* in 1775 and 1779, the complete text did not appear until 1823. At least fifteen MSS are, however, still extant, and the book must have been circulated widely in that form during the earlier part of the 17th century.

19. THE | PSALMES OF DAVID | TRANSLATED INTO | DIVERS AND SUNDRY KINDES OF VERSE, | MORE RARE AND EXCELLENT | FOR THE | *Method and Varietie* | THAN EVER YET HATH BEEN DONE IN ENGLISH. | BEGUN BY | THE NOBLE AND LEARNED GENT. | SIR PHILIP SIDNEY, KNT. | AND FINISHED BY | THE RIGHT HONORABLE | THE COUNTESS OF PEMBROKE, | HIS SISTER. | [*rule*] | NOW FIRST PRINTED FROM | *A Copy of the Original Manuscript,* | TRANSCRIBED BY JOHN DAVIES, OF HEREFORD, | IN THE REIGN OF JAMES THE FIRST.

Collation: 12°, a⁶ B–M¹² N¹², pp. [i]–xii [1]–285 [286]. First two leaves signed (−a1−a2, a3 missigned 'a2'). The fifth leaf of signatures B–N missigned 'B3', 'C3', etc.

Engraved frontispiece by C. Wilkin after J. Oliver of Sidney, and engraving by B. Redding after Simon Passe's portrait of the Countess of Pembroke.

Contents: a1^r, half-title; a1^v, blank; a2^r, title; a2^v, imprint; a3^r-a6^r, 'Advertisement', unsigned, but by the editor, Samuel Weller Singer; B1^r-N11^r, text; N11^v, blank; N12^r, colophon; N12^v, blank. Published in brown boards, printed label on the back.

This volume formed part of a series of 'Early English Poets'. 250 copies were printed. The imprint on a2^v reads: 𝕱𝖗𝖔𝖒 𝖙𝖍𝖊 𝕮𝖍𝖎𝖘𝖜𝖎𝖈𝖐 𝕻𝖗𝖊𝖘𝖘, | BY | C. WHITTINGHAM, | FOR | ROBERT TRIPHOOK, | OLD BOND STREET. | 1823. The Penshurst MS was used as printer's copy, supplemented by Bodleian MS Rawl. poet. 25.
First edition.

MISCELLANEOUS WORKS

20. THE | MISCELLANEOUS WORKS | OF | [*in red:*] 𝕾𝖎𝖗 𝕻𝖍𝖎𝖑𝖎𝖕 𝕾𝖎𝖉𝖓𝖊𝖞, 𝕶𝖓𝖙. | WITH A LIFE OF THE AUTHOR AND ILLUSTRATIVE NOTES | BY WILLIAM GRAY, ESQ. | OF MAGDALEN COLLEGE, AND THE INNER TEMPLE. | [*Talboys's printer's device*] | [*in red:*] 𝕺𝖝𝖋𝖔𝖗𝖉 | PRINTED AND PUBLISHED BY D. A. TALBOYS | MDCCCXXIX.

Collation: 8°, [π]^2 [A]^2 [χ]^1 a–d^8 e^4 (−e4 (= 'Y3')) B–X^8 Y^4 (Y2+'Y3'). Pp. [i]–[viii] [2] [1]–329 [330]. First two leaves signed (−[π]1.2–[χ]1; e4 signed 'Y3').

Contents: [π]1^r, half-title; [π]1^v, quotation from Cowper's *Task*; [π]2^r, title; [π]2^v, blank; [A]1^r–[A]2^r, Editor's Preface; [A]2^v, blank; [χ]1^r, Contents; [χ]1^v, blank; a1^r–e3^r *Life of Sir Philip Sidney*; e3^v, blank; B1^r–F1^v, the *Defence of Poesy*; F2^r–L7^r, *Astrophel and Stella*; L7^v, blank; L8^r–P2^r, *Miscellaneous Poems*; P2^v, blank; P3^r–Q3^v, *The Lady of May*; Q4^r–Q6^v, *Valour Anatomized*; Q7^r–R7^r, *Letter to Queen Elizabeth, Anno 1580*; R7^v, blank; R8^r–T1^r, *Defence of Leicester*; T1^v, blank; T2^r–Y4^r, (16) *Letters*; Y4^v, blank.

Some of the *Miscellaneous Poems* are spurious, but six were printed from MSS for the first time.[1] Ordinary copies are printed on paper with vertical chainlines, watermarked 'Batsford & Co 1829)'. Sheet [π] is, however, printed on paper without chainlines. Some copies are printed on large and thick paper without chainlines, watermarked 'Whatman 1827' (or 1828). Ordinary copies were published in grey boards, with printed label on the back.

THE DEFENCE OF POESIE

21. THE | DEFENCE OF | Poefie. | By Sir Phillip Sidney, | Knight. | [*printer's device, McK. 299.*] | LONDON | Printed [*by T. Creede*] for *William Ponſonby.* | 1595.

Collation: 4°, [A]^2 B–I^4 K^2 ([A]1 lacking in copies traced). All four leaves signed (−[A]1 (?), −K2).

Contents: [A]1 absent in copies seen, ? blank; [A]2^r, title; [A]2^v, blank; B1^r–K2^v, text.

Ponsonby's quarto was entered in the Stationers' Register on 29 November 1594. There can be little doubt that it antedates the Olney quarto of the same year. It was entered on 12 April 1595, but the entry is erased and a note added: 'This belongeth to Master Ponsonby by a former Entrance and an agreement is made between them wherby Master Ponsonby is to enjoy the copie according to the former Entrance.' The printer was Thomas Creede, whose initials are found in the device.

First edition. *STC* 22535.

[1] 'Two Pastoralls, made by Sir Philip Sidney, neuer yet published' were first printed in Davison's *A Poetical Rapsody*, 1602 (reprinted 1608, 1611, 1621). It is generally agreed that this, the only source for these poems, is a careful printing of an authentic MS.

COPIES: BRITISH LIBRARY. Russia. (Locker–Van Antwerp (23 Mar. 1907, lot 210, £110 to Quaritch)); BODLEIAN LIBRARY. Lacks A1.2. Early 18th-cent. calf, bound with *Astrophel and Stella*, etc. (see 18); HARVARD. Title in facsimile. Green mor. (W. A. White, bought from Rodd, 31 May 1912, for $450); ROBERT H. TAYLOR. Title in facsimile. Red mor. (Chatsworth, formerly bound with four pieces by Spenser, see *Hayward* no. 23. Christie's, 30 June 1958, lot 96); ROSENBACH FOUNDATION. (Presumably the copy sold at Sotheby's 6 May 1901, lot 110, £120.) JJ. Fragment, consisting of B1–4 and E2–3. Probably printer's waste, as sheet B has not been cut.

22. *AN* | APOLOGIE | for Poetrie. | Written by the right noble, vertu- | *ous, and learned, Sir* Phillip | Sidney, *Knight.* | *Odi profanum vulgus, et arceo.* | [*rule*] | [*type ornament*, 38 × 26 *mm*] | | [*rule*] | AT LONDON, | Printed [*by J. Roberts*] for *Henry Olney*, and are to be fold at | his fhop in Paules Church-yard, at the figne | of the George, neere to Cheap-gate. | *Anno.* 1595.

Collation: 4°, A–L⁴. First three leaves signed (−A2 −A3).

Contents: A1, blank except for 'A'; A2ʳ, title; A2ᵛ, blank; A3ʳᵛ, 'To The Reader', signed Henry Olney.; A3ᵛ, Faults escaped; seven lines; A4ʳᵛ, 'Foure Sonnets written by Henrie Constable to Sir Phillip Sidneys soule.'; B1ʳ–L3ᵛ, text; Lʳ, blank. Some copies of Olney's edition undoubtedly were taken over by Ponsonby. Olney's title was cancelled, and Ponsonby added his own, but not the preface. The All Souls Copy is unsophisticated, and was bought in the 17th century by the donor, Thomas Lee, for 3*d.* The last word 'at' in the second line of the imprint has dropped out in the Pierpont Morgan copy.

Second edition. STC 22534 & 22534.5.

COPIES: L. L³⁰. O (2 copies). C²(imp.). E². LINC. (lacks A3); HN (Britwell). HD (White). Y. PML. PFOR (Huth). F. NY. WEL.; LONGLEAT. JJ. Lacks A1 and A3–A4. Cont. limp vellum (Roger Senhouse, Sotheby's, 18 Oct. 1971, lot 283).

COPIES WITH SHEET A CANCELLED, AND PONSONBY'S TITLE (21) SUBSTITUTED: ALL SOULS COLLEGE, OXFORD. 17th-cent. binding. THOMAS LEE, HUNTINGTON. Modern mor. (Hoe.) Mrs GRANT H. WEBB.

23. THE | DEFENSE | OF | POESY. | BY | Sir *PHILIP SIDNEY,* Kt. | *GLASGOW:* | Printed by R. URIE, MDCCLII.

Collation: 8° (in fours), A–N⁴ O². Pp. [1]–106 [107–108]. First two leaves signed. (−A1 −O2).

Contents: A1ʳ, title; A1ᵛ, blank; A2ʳ–O1ᵛ, text; O2ʳ, *From Sir William Temple's Miscellanies*; O2ᵛ, *Books printed by Robert Urie.*

Some copies, at least, were issued uncut in blue boards with grey paper back.

Third separate edition.

24. SIR PHILIP SYDNEY'S | DEFENCE OF POETRY. | AND, | OBSERVATIONS ON POETRY | AND ELOQUENCE, | FROM THE DISCOVERIES | OF | BEN JONSON. | [*rule*] | LONDON: | PRINTED FOR G.G.J. AND J. ROBINSON, PATER-NOSTER ROW; | AND J. WALTER, CHARING-CROSS. | MDCCLXXXVII.

Collation: 8°, a² B–K⁸. Pp. [4] 1–144. First four leaves signed.

Contents: a1ʳ, title; a1ᵛ, blank; a2ʳᵛ, *Advertisement*, unsigned; B1ʳ–G1ʳ, *Defence of Poesy*; G1ᵛ, blank; G2ʳ, subtitle to Ben Jonson's *Observations*; G2ᵛ, blank; G3ʳ–K8ᵛ, *Observations from Ben Jonson's Discoveries.*

This edition was edited by Joseph Warton, who clearly shared Horace Walpole's lack of appreciation and petty opinion of the *Arcadia.*

Fourth separate edition.

A LETTER TO ROBERT SIDNEY

25. [*Within double rules*] PROFITABLE | *Inftructions;* | Defcribing what fpeciall | Obferuations are to be taken by | *Trauellers in all Nations,* | States and Countries; | Pleafant and Pro- | fitable. | *By the three much admired,* | ROBERT, late Earle of *Effex*. | Sir PHILIP SIDNEY. | *And,* | Secretary DAVISON. | [*rule*] | LONDON; | Printed for *Beniamin Fifher*, at the | Signe of the *Talbot*, without | Alderfgate. 1633.

Collation: 16° (in eights), [π]¹A–G⁸H⁶ [−H⁴=[π]1]. Pp. [18] 1–103 [104–106]. First four leaves signed (−[π]1−H4, B3 missigned B5).

Contents: [π]1ʳ, title; [π]1ᵛ, blank; A1ʳ–A8ᵛ, To the Reader, unsigned; B1ʳ–C4ᵛ, Most Notable and Excellent Instructions for Trauellers (by Davison); C5ʳ, subtitle: [*within double rules*] TWO | EXCELLENT | LETTERS CON- | cerning Travell: | One written by the | late Earle of ESSEX, | the other by Sir *Philip* | SIDNEY. | [*type ornament*] | LONDON, | Printed for *Beniamin Fifher*, at the | Signe of the *Talbot*, without | Alderfgate. 1633.; C5ᵛ, blank; C6ʳ–F5ʳ. Essex's letter; F5ᵛ–H4ʳ, Sidney's letter; H4ᵛ, blank; H5, blank.

The title, a singleton in the copies seen, presumably equals H6. It is of course possible that [π]1 had a blank conjugate, and that H6 was blank. I have alone of Sidney's many letters included this, which appears to have been circulated at the time, and found its way into print. There are at least thirteen MS copies of Sidney's letter extant.

COPIES: L. L³⁸. O. C⁵. CARLISLE. CARTMEL; HN. HD. Y. F. IC. ILL. N.; PENROSE. JJ.

First edition. *STC* 6789.

MORNAY'S *TREWNESSE OF CHRISTIAN RELIGION*

26. [*Within compartment, McK. & F.* 117] A | Woorke | concerning the trew- | *neffe of the Christian* | Religion, written | *in French*: | Againft Atheifts, Epicures, Paynims, Iewes, | Mahumetifts, and other Infidels. | *By Philip of Mornay Lord of* | *Pleffie Marlie.* | Begunne to be tranflated into Englifh by Sir | *Philip Sidney* Knight, and at his requeft | finifhed by *Arthur Golding*. | ¶Imprinted at London for *Thomas* | *Cadman*. 1587.

Collation: 4° (in eights), ❋⁴ ❋❋⁸ ❋❋❋² A–Z⁸ Aa–Qq⁸ Rr⁴. Pp. [28]1–[642]. First four leaves signed (−❋1 −❋4 −❋❋❋ij, Ee4 missigned 'E4'.).

Contents: ❋1ʳ, title: ❋1ᵛ, blank; ❋2ʳ–❋4ᵛ, dedication to Robert, Earl of Leycester, signed Arthur Golding; ❋❋iʳ–❋❋iiijᵛ, dedication to Henrie, king of Nauarre, signed Du. Plessis; ❋❋iiijʳ–❋❋❋ijʳ, The Preface to the Reader; ❋❋❋ijᵛ, The Summes of the Chapters; A1ʳ–Rr4ʳ, the text; Rr4ᵛ, colophon: Imprinted at London by George Robinson for Thomas Cadman . . . 1587.

First edition. *STC* 18149. Reprinted 1592, 1604 (with a new preface to Henry, Prince of Wales, which is also in the 1617 edition, although the Prince died in 1612), 1617. The 1604 edition is a piracy, and not, as Lowndes has it, the best edition.

There is dispute about how large a portion can be assigned to Sidney's hand. This was his first printed work.

27. VALOUR | ANATOMIZED | IN A | FANCIE. | [*rule*] | By Sir PHILIP SIDNEY. | 1581. | [*rule*] | [*device, with fleur-de-lys and inscription IN DOMINO CONFIDO*] | [*rule*] | LONDON, | Printed in the year 1651.

On Y1r–Y4r of *Cottoni Posthuma:* . . . *LONDON*, Printed by *Francis Leach*, for *Henry Seile* . . . 1651, 8°. Edited by James Howells. This tract is followed by a poem *Wooingstuffe* (on Y4v), signed Philip Sidney, certainly also spurious. The work was reprinted in the subsequent editions of 1672 and 1679. (*Wing* C6485, 6, 7.)

28. *ALMANZOR,* | AND | *ALMANZAIDA.* | A | NOVEL. | [*rule*] | Written by | *Sir PHILIP SIDNEY*, | And found fince his Death amongft his PAPERS. | [*double rule*] | *LONDON*, | Printed for *J. Magnes* and *R. Bentley*, | in *Ruffel-ftreet*, near the *Piazza*, in | *Covent-garden:* 1678. | A3.

Collation: 12°, A⁶ B–E¹² F⁶.
First edition. Wing L446.
Really by Mlle de la Roche-Guilhem. Sidney's name was used by the booksellers to make the book more readily saleable.

BIBLIOGRAPHY

What follows is necessarily a selective list. Other bibliographical guides are noted in section 3 below. Unless otherwise specified, place of publication is London.

1. EDITIONS

Feuillerat, A., ed., *The Complete Works of Sir Philip Sidney* (4 vols.; Cambridge, 1912–26; reissued, minus most of the verse, as *The Prose Works of Sir Philip Sidney* (Cambridge, 1962 *et seq.*)).

Ringler, W. A., Jr, ed., *The Poems of Sir Philip Sidney* (Oxford, 1962).

Duncan-Jones, K., and van Dorsten, J. A., eds, *Miscellaneous Prose of Sir Philip Sidney* (Oxford, 1973).

Robertson, J., ed., *The Countess of Pembroke's Arcadia (The Old Arcadia)* (Oxford, 1973).

Duncan-Jones, K., ed., *The Countess of Pembroke's Arcadia (The Old Arcadia)*. The World's Classics (Oxford, 1985).

Shepherd, G., ed., *An Apology for Poetry or The Defence of Poesy* (London and New York, 1965; repr. Manchester, 1973).

Rathmell, J. C. A., ed., *The Psalms of Sir Philip Sidney and The Countess of Pembroke* (New York, 1963).

Evans, M., ed., *The Countess of Pembroke's Arcadia* (Harmondsworth, 1977; modernized text of the *New Arcadia*).

Selections

K. Duncan-Jones has edited *Selected Poems* (Oxford, 1973). There are selections of poetry and prose by D. Kalstone (New York, 1970) and by R. Kimbrough (2nd edn; Madison, Wisc., 1983).

Facsimiles

The Scolar Press has published facsimiles of *Astrophil and Stella* and of the *Defence*, Kent State University Press of the 1590 *Arcadia*, and Scholars' Facsimiles and Reprints (Delmar) of the 1598 *Arcadia*.

2. LIFE AND LETTERS

(*a*) *Life*

Buxton, J., *Sir Philip Sidney and the English Renaissance* (1954; 2nd edn, 1964, repr. 1965).

Gouws, J., ed., *The Prose Works of Fulke Greville Lord Brooke* (Oxford, 1986).

Howell, R., *Sir Philip Sidney: The Shepherd Knight* (1968).

Lanham, R. A., 'Sidney: the Ornament of his Age', *Southern Review* (Adelaide) 2 (1967), 319–40.

Levy, F. J., 'Sir Philip Sidney Reconsidered', *ELR* 2 (1972), 5–18.
Osborn, J. M., *Young Philip Sidney, 1572–1577* (New Haven and London, 1972).
van Dorsten, J. A., *Poets, Patrons and Professors: Sir Philip Sidney, Daniel Rogers and the Leiden Humanists* (Leiden, 1962).
—— 'Literary Patronage in England: The Early Phase', in G. F. Lytle and S. Orgel, eds., *Patronage in the Renaissance* (Princeton, 1981), pp. 191–206.
Wallace, M. W., *The Life of Sir Philip Sidney* (Cambridge, 1915).
Wilson, M., *Sir Philip Sidney* (New York, 1932).

Books dedicated to Sidney are listed in Ringler's entry in the *NCBEL*.

(*b*) Letters

All known letters to and from Sidney are currently being edited for Oxford University Press by C. S. Levy and R. Kuin.

Beal, P., ed., *The Index of English Literary Manuscripts*, i. (1450–1625), pt. 2 (1980), pp. 465–88.
Feuillerat, A., *Works* iii (prints 115 of Sidney's letters).
Languet, H., *H. Langueti epistolae ad P. Sydnaeum* (Frankfurt, 1633; Leiden, 1646).
Levy, C. S., 'A Supplementary Inventory of Sir Philip Sidney's Correspondence', *MP* 67 (1969–70), 177–81.
Osborn, J. M., *Young Philip Sidney, 1572–1577* (New Haven, 1972; based on 76 additional letters).
Pears, S. A., ed., *The Correspondence of Sir Philip Sidney and Hubert Languet* (1845; repr. 1971).

3. BIBLIOGRAPHIES, ETC.

Publications on Sidney are listed annually in the *MLA Annual Bibliography* and in the *Sidney Newsletter*.

Colaianne, A. J., and Godshalk, W. L., 'Recent Studies in Sidney', *ELR* 8 (1978), 212–33.
Donow, H. S., *A Concordance to the Poems of Sir Philip Sidney* (Ithaca, 1975).
—— *The Sonnet in England and America: A Bibliography of Criticism* (Westport, Conn., 1982).
Godshalk, W. L., 'Recent Studies in Sidney', *ELR* 2 (1972), 148–64.
Harner, J. L., *English Renaissance Prose Fiction, 1500–1660: An Annotated Bibliography of Criticism* (Boston, 1978; a second volume, covering the years 1976–83, was published in 1985).
Rees, J., '400 Years On: Sidney Today', *Cahiers Élisabéthains* 15 (1979), 87–95.
Ringler, W. A., Jr., Sidney entry in Vol. i of *The New Cambridge Bibliography of English Literature* (Cambridge, 1974).

Washington, M. A., *Sir Philip Sidney: An Annotated Bibliography of Modern Criticism, 1941–70* (Columbia, Missouri, 1972).

4. MAJOR GENERAL STUDIES

Connell, D., *Sir Philip Sidney: The Maker's Mind* (Oxford, 1977).

Davis, W. R., and Lanham, R. A., *Sidney's Arcadia* (New Haven, 1965): contains Davis, *A Map of Arcadia: Sidney's Romance in its Tradition*, and Lanham, *The Old Arcadia.*

Hamilton, A. C., *Sir Philip Sidney: A Study of his Life and Works* (Cambridge, 1977).

Kalstone, D., *Sidney's Poetry: Contexts and Interpretations* (Cambridge, Mass., 1965).

Kimbrough, R., *Sir Philip Sidney* (New York, 1971).

Montgomery, R. L., *Symmetry and Sense: The Poetry of Sir Philip Sidney* (Austin, 1961).

Myrick, K., *Sir Philip Sidney as a Literary Craftsman* (Cambridge, Mass., 1935; 2nd edn, with a revised bibliography by W. L. Godshalk, Lincoln, Neb., 1965).

Nichols, J. G., *The Poetry of Sir Philip Sidney: An Interpretation in the Context of his Life and Times* (Liverpool, 1974).

Raitière, M. N., *'Faire bitts': Sir Philip Sidney and Renaissance Political Theory* (Pittsburgh, 1984).

Rudenstein, N. L., *Sidney's Poetic Development* (Cambridge, Mass., 1967).

van Dorsten, J., Baker Smith, D., and Kinney, A. F., eds, *Sir Philip Sidney: 1586 and the Creation of a Legend* (Leiden, 1986).

Waller, G. F., and Moore, M. D., eds, *Sir Philip Sidney and the Interpretation of Renaissance Culture* (1984).

5. STUDIES OF INDIVIDUAL TEXTS

(a) *The Lady of May*

Axton, M., 'Robert Dudley and the Inner Temple Revels'. *Historical Journal* 13 (1970), 365–78.

—— 'The Tudor Mask and Elizabethan Court Drama', in Axton and B. Williams, eds, *English Drama: Forms and Development* (Cambridge, 1977), pp. 24–47.

—— *The Queen's Two Bodies: Drama and the Elizabethan Succession* (1977).

Jones, M., 'The Court and the Dramatists', in J. R. Brown and B. Harris, eds, *Elizabethan Poetry* (Stratford-upon-Avon Studies 9, 1966), pp. 169–95.

Montrose, L. A., 'Celebration and Insinuation: Sir Philip Sidney and the Motives of Elizabethan Courtship', *RD* ns 8 (1977), 3–35.

—— '"Eliza. Queene of Shepheardes", and the Pastoral of Power', *ELR* 10 (1980), 153–82.

Montrose, L. A., 'Of Gentlemen and Shepherds: The Politics of Eliza-
bethan Pastoral Form', *ELH* 50 (1983), 415–59.
Orgel, S., *The Jonsonian Masque* (Cambridge, Mass., 1965).
Smith, B. R., 'Landscape with Figures: The Three Realms of Queen
Elizabeth's Country-House Revels', *RD* ns 8 (1977), 57–115.
Stillman, R., 'Justice and the "Good Word" in Sidney's *The Lady of May*',
SEL 24 (1984), 23–38.

(*b*) The *Old Arcadia*

Altman, J. B., *The Tudor Play of Mind: Rhetorical Inquiry and the Development
of English Drama* (Berkeley, 1978).
Astell, A. W., 'Sidney's Didactic Method in the *Old Arcadia*', *SEL* 24
(1984), 39–52.
Chalifour, C. L., 'Sir Philip Sidney's *Old Arcadia* as Terentian Comedy',
SEL 16 (1976), 51–63.
Challis, L., 'The Use of Oratory in Sidney's *Arcadia*', *SP* 62 (1965),
561–76.
Davidson, C., 'Nature and Judgment in the *Old Arcadia*', *PLL* 6 (1970),
348–65.
Dipple, E., ' "Unjust Justice" in the *Old Arcadia*', *SEL* 10 (1970), 83–101.
Ford, P. J., 'Philosophy, History, and Sidney's *Old Arcadia*', *CL* 26 (1974),
32–50.
Fowler, A., 'Sestina Structure in *Ye goatherd gods*', in his *Conceitful
Thought: The Interpretation of English Renaissance Poems* (Edinburgh,
1975), pp. 38–58.
Hamilton, A. C., 'Sidney's *Arcadia* as Prose Fiction: Its Relation to its
Sources', *ELR* 2 (1972), 29–60.
Lanham, R. A., '*The Old Arcadia*' in Davis and Lanham, *Sidney's Arcadia*
(New Haven, 1965).
Marenco, F., *Arcadia Puritana* (Bari, 1968).
—— 'Double Plot in Sidney's *Old Arcadia*', *MLR* 64 (1969), 248–63.
McCoy, R. C., *Sir Philip Sidney: Rebellion in Arcadia* (New Brunswick,
1979).
Moore, D., 'Philisides and Mira: Autobiographical Allegory in the *Old
Arcadia*', *Spenser Studies* 3 (1982), 125–37.
Parker, R. W., 'Terentian Structure and Sidney's Original *Arcadia*',
ELR 2 (1972), 61–78.
Stillman, R. E., 'The Perils of Fancy: Poetry and Self-Love in *The Old
Arcadia*', *TSLL* 26 (1984), 1–17.
—— 'The Politics of Sidney's Pastoral: Mystification and Mythology in
The Old Arcadia', *ELH* 52 (1985), 795–814.
—— *Sidney's Poetic Justice* (Lewisburg, 1986).

Weiner, A. D., *Sir Philip Sidney and the Poetics of Protestantism: A Study of Contexts* (Minneapolis, 1978).

(c) A Defence of Poetry

Barnes, C., 'The Hidden Persuader: The Complex Speaking Voice of Sidney's *Defence of Poetry*', *PMLA* 86 (1971), 422–7.

Coogan, R. M., 'The Triumph of Reason: Sidney's *Defense* and Aristotle's *Rhetoric*', *PLL* 17 (1982), 255–70.

—— 'More Dais than Dock: Greek Rhetoric and Sidney's Encomium on Poetry', *SLI* 15 (1982), 99–113.

Craig, D. H., 'A Hybrid Growth: Sidney's Theory of Poetry in *An Apology for Poetry*', *ELR* 10 (1980), 183–201.

Ferguson, M., *Trials of Desire: Renaissance Defences of Poetry* (New Haven, 1983).

Hardison, O. B., Jr., 'The Two Voices of Sidney's *Apology for Poetry*', *ELR* 2 (1972), 83–99.

Heninger, S. K., Jr., *'Touches of Sweet Harmony': Pythagorean Cosmology and Renaissance Poetics* (San Marino, 1974).

—— '"Metaphor" and Sidney's *Defence of Poesie*', *John Donne Journal* 1 (1982), 117–49.

—— 'Sidney and Serranus' Plato', *ELR* 13 (1983), 146–61.

—— 'Sidney and Boethian Music', *SEL* 23 (1983), 37–46.

—— 'Speaking Pictures: Sidney's Rapprochement between Poetry and Painting', in Waller and Moore, eds (see section 4), pp. 3–16.

Kinney, A. F., 'Parody and its Implications in Sidney's *Defence of Poesie*, *SEL* 12 (1972), 1–19.

Levao, R. A., *Renaissance Minds and Their Fictions* (Berkeley, 1985).

Pigman, G. W., III, 'Versions of Imitation in the Renaissance', *RQ* 33 (1980), 1–32.

Raitière, M. N., 'The Unity of Sidney's *Apology for Poetry*', *SEL* 21 (1981), 37–57.

Robinson, F. G., *The Shape of Things Known* (Cambridge, Mass., 1972).

Sinfield, A., 'The Cultural Politics of the *Defence of Poetry*', in Waller and Moore, eds (see section 4), pp. 129–43.

Stump, D. V., 'Sidney's Concept of Tragedy in the *Apology* and in the *Arcadia*', *SP* 79 (1982), 41–61.

Ulreich, J. C. Jr., '"The Poets only Deliver": Sidney's Conception of Mimesis', *SLI* 15 (1982), 67–84.

Webster, J., 'Oration and Method in Sidney's *Apology*: A Contemporary Account', *MP* 79 (1981), 1–15.

—— ed. and trans., *William Temple's 'Analysis' of Sir Philip Sidney's 'Apology for Poetry'* (New York, 1984).

Weiner, A. D., 'Moving and Teaching: Sidney's *Defence of Poesie* as a Protestant Poetic', *JMRS* 2 (1972), 259–78.

(*d*) *Astrophil and Stella*

De Grazia, M., 'Lost Potential in Grammar and Nature: Sidney's *Astrophil and Stella*', *SEL* 21 (1981), 21–35.

Duncan-Jones, K., 'Sidney, Stella and Lady Rich', in van Dorsten, Baker Smith, and Kinney, eds.

Ewbank, I.-S., 'Sincerity and the Sonnet', *E&S* (1981), 19–44.

Ferry, A., *The 'Inward' Language: Sonnets of Wyatt, Sidney, Shakespeare and Donne* (Chicago, 1983).

Fienberg, N., 'The Emergence of Stella in *Astrophil and Stella*', *SEL* 25 (1985), 5–19.

Hulse, C., 'Stella's Wit: Penelope Rich as Reader of Sidney's Sonnets', in *Rewriting the Renaissance. The Discourses of Sexual Difference in Early Modern Europe*, ed. M. W. Ferguson, M. Quilligan and N. J. Vickers (Chicago, 1986), pp. 272–86.

Jones, A. R., and Stallybrass, P., 'The Politics of *Astrophil and Stella*', *SEL* 24 (1984), 53–68.

Marotti, A. F., ' "Love is not love": Elizabethan Sonnet Sequences and the Social Order', *ELH* 49 (1982), 396–428.

Miller, J. T., ' "Love doth hold my hand": Writing and Wooing in the Sonnets of Sidney and Spenser', *ELH* 46 (1979), 541–58.

—— ' "What may words say": The Limits of Language in *Astrophil and Stella*', in Waller and Moore, eds (see section 4), pp. 95–109.

Neely, C. T., 'The Structure of the English Renaissance Sonnet Sequence', *ELH* 45 (1978), 359–89.

Sinfield, A., 'Astrophil's Self-Deception', *EIC* 28 (1978), 1–18.

—— 'Sidney and Astrophil', *SEL* 20 (1980), 25–41.

Traister, D., ' "To Portrait That Which In This World Is Best": Stella in Perspective', *SP* 81 (1984), 419–37.

Warkentin, G., ' "Love's sweetest part, variety": Petrarch and the Curious Frame of the Renaissance Sonnet Sequence', *Renaissance and Reformation* 11 (1975), 14–23.

—— 'The Meeting of the Muses: Sidney and the Mid-Tudor Poets', in Waller and Moore, eds (see section 4), pp. 17–33.

Webster, J., ' "The Methode of a Poete": An Inquiry into Tudor Conceptions of Poetic Sequence', *ELR* 11 (1981), 22–43.

(*e*) *The* New Arcadia

Adler, D. R., 'Imaginary Toads in Real Gardens', *ELR* 11 (1981), 235–60.

Amos, A., *Time, Space and Value: The Narrative Structure of the 'New Arcadia'* (Lewisburg, 1976).

Chaudhuri, S., 'The Eclogues in Sidney's *New Arcadia*', *RES* ns 35 (1984), 185–202.

Craft, W., 'The Shaping Picture of Love in Sidney's *New Arcadia*', *SP* 81 (1984), 395–418.

—— 'Remaking the Heroic Self in the *New Arcadia*', *SEL* 25 (1985), 45–67.

Davis, W. R., *A Map of Arcadia. Sidney's Romance in its Tradition*, in Davis and Lanham, *Sidney's Arcadia* (New Haven, 1965).

—— *Idea and Act in Elizabethan Fiction* (Princeton, 1969).

Duncan-Jones, K., 'Sidney and Titian', in J. Carey, ed., *English Renaissance Studies* (Oxford, 1980), pp. 1–11.

Farmer, N. K., Jr., *Poets and the Visual Arts in Renaissance England* (Austin, 1984).

Greenblatt, S. J., 'Sidney's *Arcadia* and the Mixed Mode', *SP* 70 (1973), 269–78.

—— 'Murdering Peasants: Status, Genre, and the Representation of Rebellion', *Representation*, 1 (1983), 1–29.

Greenfield, T., *The Eye of Judgement: Reading the 'New Arcadia'* (Lewisburg, 1982).

Hamilton, A. C., 'Elizabethan Romance: The Example of Prose Fiction', *ELH* 49 (1982), 287–99.

—— 'Elizabethan Prose Fiction and some Trends in Recent Criticism', *RQ* 37 (1984), 21–33.

Helgerson, R., *The Elizabethan Prodigals* (Berkeley, 1976).

Lee, J., 'The English Ariosto: The Elizabethan Poet and the Marvelous', *SP* 80 (1983), 277–99.

Margolies, D., *Novel and Society in Elizabethan England* (1984).

McCanles, M., 'The Rhetoric of Character Portrayal in Sidney's *New Arcadia*', *Criticism* 25 (1983), 123–39.

—— 'Oracular Prediction and the Fore-Conceit of Sidney's *Arcadia*', *ELH* 50 (1983), 233–44.

—— 'Reading Description in Sidney's *New Arcadia*: A Differential Analysis', *UTQ* 53 (1983), 36–52.

McCoy, R. C., *Sir Philip Sidney: Rebellion in Arcadia* (New Brunswick, 1979).

Norbrook, D., *Poetry and Politics in the English Renaissance* (1984).

Patterson, A. M., *Censorship and Interpretation* (Madison, Wisconsin, 1984).

Raitière, M. N., 'Amphialus' Rebellion: Sidney's use of History in the *New Arcadia*', *JMRS* 12 (1982), 113–31.

Roberts, J. A., *Architectonic Knowledge in the 'New Arcadia'* (Salzburg, 1978).

Salzman, P., *English Prose Fiction, 1558–1700: A Critical History* (Oxford, 1985).

Sinfield, A., 'Power and Ideology: An Outline Theory and Sidney's *Arcadia*', *ELH* 52 (1985), 259–77.

Skretcowicz, V., Jr., 'Sidney and Amyot: Heliodorus in the Structure and Ethos of the *New Arcadia*', *RES* ns 27 (1976), 170–4.

—— 'Symbolic Architecture in Sidney's *New Arcadia*', *RES* ns 33 (1982), 175–80.

Thuente, D. R., 'Pastoral Narratives: A Review of Criticism', *Genre* 14 (1981), 247–67.

Vos, A., '"Good Matter and Good Utterance": The Character of English Ciceronianism', *SEL* 19 (1979), 3–18.

INDEX